{ art of the everyday }

I0795985

art of the everyday

Dutch Painting and the Realist Novel

RUTH BERNARD YEAZELL

PRINCETON UNIVERSITY PRESS
Princeton & Oxford

Copyright © 2008 by Princeton University Press

Published by Princeton University Press, 41 William Street,
Princeton, New Jersey 08540

In the United Kingdom: Princeton University Press, 99 Banbury Road,
Oxford OX2 6JX

press.princeton.edu

All Rights Reserved

First paperback printing, 2009
Paperback ISBN 9780691143231
Ebook ISBN: 9781400832750

The Library of Congress has cataloged the cloth edition of this book as follows:

LIBRARY OF CONGRESS CATALOGING-IN-PUBLICATION DATA
Yeazell, Ruth Bernard.
Art of the everyday : Dutch painting and the realist novel / Ruth Bernard Yeazell.
p. cm.
Includes bibliographical references and index.
ISBN 978-0-691-12726-2 (hardcover : alk. paper) 1. English fiction—
19th century—History and criticism. 2 Art and literature—Great Britain—
History—19th century. 3. French fiction—19th century—History and criticism.
4. Art and literature—France—History—19th century. 5. Realism in literature.
6. Painting, Dutch—17th century—Influence. I. Title.
PR878.A74Y43 2008
823'.809357—dc22 2007017263

British Library Cataloging-in-Publication Data is available

Publication of this book has been aided by the Frederick W. Hilles
Publication Fund of Yale University.

This book has been composed in Adobe Caslon

Printed on acid-free paper. ∞

Printed in The United States of America
3 5 7 9 10 8 6 4 2

For Annabelle Bernard

{ contents }

illustrations

Color Plates (following page 136)

Figures

{ acknowledgments }

Working with pictures as well as with books happily multiplies one's debts. For early leads in the literature, I am particularly grateful to Peter Brooks and Leah Price. At different stages of the project, Colin Gillis, Aaron Matz, and Juliette Wells energetically tracked down sources; Wayne Franits, Emilie Gordenker, Richard Helgerson, and Peter Sutton kindly assisted with the location of particular images; and Erica Sayers saved me from many a technological crisis. An invitation from Keith Wilson to contribute to a volume in honor of Michael Millgate helped to stimulate my thinking about Hardy; and I am grateful to the University of Toronto Press for permission to include a longer version of that essay here. Tim Barringer generously commented on my discussion of Ruskin and Thoré-Bürger; and Leah Price responded with her characteristic acuity both to the chapter on George Eliot and to the conception of the book as a whole. Conversations with Leah about the nineteenth-century novel were among the great pleasures that attended the writing throughout. Graduate students in a recent seminar on Dutch painting and the novel kept me mindful about how much we still don't understand about realism. For vital encouragement and support over the years, I would also like to thank Emily Bakemeier, Richard Brodhead, David Bromwich, Ann Gaylin, Myra Jehlen, Maria Menocal, Amy Meyers, Jack Meyers, Linda Peterson, David Quint, and Katie Trumpener.

A fellowship from the Rockefeller Foundation for a residency at the Bellagio Study Center provided a magnificent setting in which to think more about Hardy and Proust, as well as an inspiring group of people with whom to share ideas about Dutch pictures. Reproduction of such pictures here would not have been possible without the continuing support of the Provost's Office at Yale University and a generous grant from the Frederick W. Hilles Publication Fund, which enabled some of them to appear in color. I owe a particular debt to Aaron Matz, who took time out at an especially demanding period of his life to help me with some of the more opaque passages of French. Responsibility for any errors remaining is of course my own. I couldn't ask for a more responsive editor than Hanne Winarsky at Princeton University Press: her enthusiasm and efficiency made all the difference to the final production of this book. As always, my greatest debt is to Alexander Welsh. It is difficult to imagine completing this or any book without Sandy's criticism, his impatience, and his love. This book is dedicated to my mother, Annabelle Bernard, whose working life has always been an example and whose own love for Dutch painting has also kept me going.

{ preface }

How is a novel written in nineteenth-century Britain or France like a picture painted in seventeenth-century Holland? To pose this question is not to engage in a modern parlor game but to address a problem in the history of taste: what did the art of the Dutch Golden Age mean to the nineteenth century, and what was at stake when critics invoked its precedent—as they often did—to justify or attack the realistic fiction of their day? Why should the novelists themselves have been drawn to seventeenth-century Dutch art, and why nonetheless did "Dutch painting" in fiction remain a source of deep ambivalence even for those who most obviously looked to such painting for a model? This book sets out to answer such questions by taking seriously the practice of comparing realist novels to Dutch pictures.

Realism that self-consciously names itself as such is a nineteenth-century phenomenon. But before "realism" in its aesthetic sense migrated from France to England, critics on both sides of the Channel spoke of "Dutch painting"; and the phrase became a kind of shorthand for many of the characteristics we now associate with the bourgeois novel. The representation of ordinary people and acts rather than heroic and mythical ones; the attention to everyday customs and habits, especially those that change with relative slowness over the centuries; the detailed rendering of material objects and settings, particularly the domestic interiors of the lower and middle classes: these were among the features that were regularly summoned up when nineteenth-century writers invoked Dutch painting as a precedent for their own art of fiction. Whether they used the analogy to denigrate the novel, as many did, or openly allied themselves with the Dutch, like the early George Eliot, they were also aware that the popularity of both forms posed a continuing challenge to established hierarchies of value.

Both the novelists' imaginative responses to Dutch painting and their anxiety about the model can only be understood in the context of aesthetic debates that go back at least to the Renaissance. The tension between high theory and low genre, as I characterize it, can be readily documented on both sides of the Channel, beginning with Roger de Piles and other Continental theorists, and continuing in a line of British pronouncements that descends from Jonathan Richardson and Joshua Reynolds to John Ruskin. The novel, too, was generally looked down upon as an art form at least until the time of Walter Scott, whose death in 1832 was marked not only by eulogies of his own work but by increasing celebration of other writers for their fictional depictions of familiar life, social and domestic, indoors and out. Yet well after Scott's death, the analogy to Dutch painting continued to serve commentators who associated the very popularity of the novel with its equivocal merits as art. Only when the photographic reproduction of the visible world began to take the place once occupied by the faithful mimesis of the painters did the idiom of "Dutch painting" gradually disappear from nineteenth-century rhetoric about the novel. The rediscovery of Vermeer in those same decades simultaneously encouraged viewers to see the artfulness that had always been present in the painting of his countrymen. By the early twentieth century, both the received idea of Dutch painting and its relation to fiction had been radically altered.

Precisely which pictures writers had been looking at is not always easy to determine. Inexpensive prints of Dutch paintings had been circulating in France and Britain since at least the early decades of the eighteenth century; and from the opening of the Louvre in 1793 until well after the National Gallery in London acquired Sir Robert Peel's important collection of Dutch and Flemish art in 1871, museums on both sides of the Channel increasingly made such art available to local viewers. It was at the Louvre that Balzac presumably saw a picture by Gerrit Dou of which he made playful use in a tale of 1840; and it was at the National Gallery that Thomas Hardy could admire a landscape by Meindert Hobbema whose emotional effect he specifically recorded in his notebook. From Reynolds's journey to Holland and Flanders in 1781 until Marcel Proust's visit to the Netherlands in 1902, travel made possible other resonant encounters with Dutch painting. George Eliot's defense of Dutch art in her first published novel clearly owes something to the sight of a particular Gerrit Dou at Munich, while Proust's encounter with Vermeer's *View of Delft* in The Hague was still a cherished memory when he composed the fifth volume of his masterwork nearly two decades later. By the middle of the nineteenth century, photographs could also begin to supplement or replace a writer's access to the originals: so Proust, for example, bought a photographically illustrated study of Vermeer after seeing some of the paintings again at a Paris exhibit of 1921. Yet with the partial exception of Proust himself, specific responses to individual pictures or artists figure less in this story than a set of associations that circulated even in the absence of the images that had originally inspired them.

The "Dutch painting" of my title is as much a nineteenth-century idea as a seventeenth-century phenomenon. While I could not have written this book without modern scholarship on Dutch and Flemish art, I am more concerned with how the nineteenth century understood such images than I am with the contexts for which they were originally intended. Contemporary historians, in fact, are often quite critical of the nineteenth century's reception of Dutch art—arguing, for example, that the iconological significance of many images failed to register on an increasingly secular age, or that the image of daily life in Dutch genre painting is far more selective and formulaic than those who first celebrated its realism were prepared to recognize. The frequent conflation of Dutch and Flemish art in the period understandably troubles modern scholars, as does the anomaly that many works produced in the Dutch Republic do not seem to have been included under the rubric of "Dutch painting." When nineteenth-century writers conjured with the phrase, they primarily had in mind genre, landscape, still life, and portraiture—the types of picture at which Northern artists were thought to excel—rather than the historical and mythological subjects that were also produced by artists in seventeenth-century Holland. Like most critical terms, notoriously including "realism" itself, "Dutch painting" named a set of overlapping and related characteristics rather than a single clearly defined phenomenon, but its very versatility made it all the more useful for those who associated it with the new art of the novel.

At different stages of their careers, each of the principal writers I examine—Balzac, George Eliot, Hardy and Proust—strove to create illusions of the real by reproducing in words some version of Dutch painting. While national traditions of scholarship often treat these writers separately, they shared an attraction to a form of realism that had no need of linguistic translation; and that common inheritance makes itself felt even when they are not directly in dialogue with one another. Although these novelistic versions of Dutch art most often resemble what we now call "genre" painting, that term did not really settle into its present meaning until the latter half of the nineteenth century, after many of the novels in question were written. Indeed, the modern understanding of genre as the representation of everyday life and the novel's affinity with such representation grew up together; and it is one of the central aims of this book to help us understand why this should be so. While the etymological history of the term "genre" is frequently rehearsed in scholarly treatments of Dutch painting, the implications of the category still invite theoretical speculation. Like the realist novel, the very idea of genre painting depends on our capacity to recognize anonymous persons as somehow like ourselves. The simple act of identification by which we look at such a painting and see a woman sewing or a group of peasants fighting, rather than the specific subject of a portrait or a history painting, requires us to assimilate what we are seeing to a familiar category of human life. The line between genre, on the one hand, and still life or landscape, on the other, is by no means absolute; and the major novelists of my study clearly drew on them all, as they conjured up the man-made and natural worlds their ordinary people inhabited. While Balzac's fame as a "Dutch painter in prose" seems principally to have rested upon his descriptions of material objects and household interiors, George Eliot appears to have thought first of the unidealized human figure when she associated her own art with that of the Dutch. But even a Balzac still life is always a detail within a larger genre painting, and George Eliot's commonplace figures are never without their defining particulars of habitation and dress. As for Hardy, he characteristically fused landscape and genre in composing what he called—in the subtitle of his second novel, *Under the Greenwood Tree*—his "Rural Painting of the Dutch School." Though Proust owed much to each of these predecessors, he finally cared less for the subject of a picture than for the distinctive style of the artist. Yet the descriptive method of *À la recherche du temps perdu* has its own affinities with Dutch genre; and the greatest exemplar of the artist's style, in Proust's eyes, was a painter of everyday life named Johannes Vermeer.

For each of these novelists, I argue, Dutch painting is especially identified with beginnings—both in the sense that it is often a method of scene-setting, as in so many volumes of Balzac's *Comédie humaine*, and in the sense that its representation of everyday life forms the ground against which the desires that drive the narrative are plotted. Particularly in the case of George Eliot, turning to the model of Dutch art was also a method of embarking on a career as a novelist—a way of forestalling her own impulses toward idealization and abstraction by first training her attention on the commonplace and the local. Her vehement defense of Dutch painting against those "lofty-minded people" who had hitherto kept it in its place partly originated in a quarrel with herself. At the same time, what might be characterized as the ambiguous or incomplete secularization of Golden Age art—whereby so many faithful imitations of mundane appearances carry traces of emblematic and scriptural meanings—particularly appealed to a writer who sought to naturalize religion rather than abandon it. Though her own work increasingly turned away from the model of the Dutch, the relative warmth that greeted Hardy's early pictures of rustic life clearly owes much to the precedent she had created. Like George Eliot, too, Hardy clearly associated Dutch pictures with his own rural past; and what Proust would later call, in an evocative phrase, "the Dutch painting of our memory" is impossible to separate from the indebtedness of all these novelists to the example of the painters.

Yet the very identification of Dutch painting with material detail and the rituals of everyday life meant that even the novelists most drawn to its mode of realism inevitably plotted against it. Though Lessing famously argued that all painting is essentially static (and thus opposed to the temporal art of "poetry"), there is a good reason why Hardy identified his least plotted novel with a Dutch painting, just as Scott associated Jane Austen's "Flemish" art with a novel that had, as he saw it, "even less story" than usual. Unlike the history painting of the Italians, which told a story, or at least alluded to one, and thereby appealed to the more intellectual capacities of the spectator, the "low" genres of the North had long been identified with the absence of narrative. For classical theorists, who sought to dignify painting as a labor of the mind rather than the hands, the highest art was that which approximated to the status of language: while the Italians sought to abstract and generalize, according to this paradigm, the Dutch attended too closely to the visible surface of things—producing an art of "mere" images and nothing more.

When Elizabeth Barrett Browning said of Balzac that he had "a Dutch hand and an Italian soul," she thus drew on a centuries-old opposition to identify another conflict that in one form or another characterizes each of the novelists I study. In *La recherche de l'absolu*, Balzac himself allegorized the conflict somewhat differently, by setting the endlessly ungratified desire of his protagonist, an obsessive dreamer who self-destructively seeks in alchemy a key to the Absolute, against the "quiet happiness" of his Flemish household—a household suggestively filled with Dutch and Flemish paintings, whose maintenance repeatedly depends on the practical realism of its women. Though Balzac clearly sympathizes with both parties to the conflict, it is the madness of his dreamer that drives his plot, even as related forms of obsessive desire—whether for love, wealth, or power—fuel so many of his narratives in the *Comédie humaine*. Unlike Balzac, who repeatedly oscillates between "Dutch" and "Italian" impulses, George Eliot and Hardy begin with Dutch painting only to turn away from its example in their later work. While George Eliot's idealizing and abstracting impulses increasingly drew her back to the history painting of the Italian Renaissance and Hardy's taste would increasingly incline toward Turner and the impressionists, neither novelist ever completely abandoned the idea of the real associated with Dutch painting. Proust's taste is closer to Hardy's: his fictional painter owes much to Turner and Monet, among others, and his own art has often been compared to that of the impressionists. But just as description and narrative are virtually inseparable in *À la recherche du temps perdu*, so Proust seems less restive with Dutch painting than his predecessors. By refusing to separate the mind and matter of Dutch painting, he also helps to make clear what they too had known all along.

art of the everyday

one

The Novel as Dutch Painting

In a memorable review of Jane Austen's *Emma* (1816), Walter Scott celebrated the novelist for her faithful representation of the familiar and the commonplace. Austen had, according to Scott, helped to perfect what was fundamentally a new kind of fiction: "the art of copying from nature as she really exists in the common walks of life." Rather than "the splendid scenes of an imaginary world," her novels presented the reader with "a correct and striking representation of that which [was] daily taking place around him." Scott's warm welcome of *Emma* has long been known to literary historians and fans of Austen alike. But what is less often remarked is the analogy to visual art with which he drove home the argument. In vividly conjuring up the "common incidents" of daily life, Austen's novels also recalled for him "something of the merits of the Flemish school of painting. The subjects are not often elegant and certainly never grand; but they are finished up to nature, and with a precision which delights the reader."[1]

Just what Flemish paintings did Scott have in mind? If it is hard to see much resemblance between an Austen novel and a van Eyck altarpiece or a mythological image by Rubens, it is not much easier to recognize the world of *Emma* in the tavern scenes and village festivals that constitute the typical subjects of an artist like David Teniers the Younger (figs. 1-1 and 1-2). Scott's repeated insistence on the "ordinary" and the "common" in Austen's art—as when he welcomes her scrupulous adherence to "common incidents, and to such characters as occupy the ordinary walks of life," or describes her narratives as "composed of such common occurrences as may have fallen under the observation of most folks"—strongly suggests that it is seventeenth-century genre painting of which he was thinking; and Teniers was by far the best known Flemish painter of such images.[2] (He had in fact figured prominently in the first Old Master exhibit of Dutch and

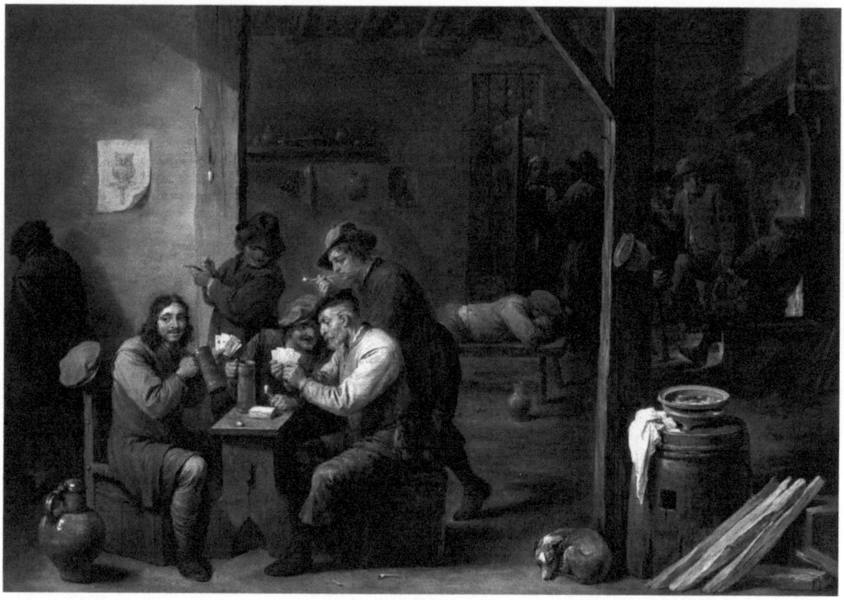

Figure 1-1. David Teniers the Younger: *Tavern Scene*, 1658. National Gallery of Art, Washington, D.C. Gift of Robert H. and Clarice Smith. Image © 2006 Board of Trustees, National Gallery of Art, Washington, D.C.

Flemish painting sponsored by the British Institution in London the previous year.)[3] But nineteenth-century writers did not often distinguish closely between the Dutch and the Flemish in this connection; and Scott's allusion to "the Flemish school" serves less to evoke individual pictures or even artists than to conjure up Netherlandish genre as a whole. Like "Dutch painting" or "the Dutch school"—phrases that recur with even more frequency in the criticism of the period—it is shorthand for a type of painting that itself, as we shall see, is a painting of types. That such phrases simultaneously evoke ideas of the generic or the typical and of the meticulously detailed and particular (what Scott here calls "precision") is a seeming contradiction that goes to the very heart of the ambivalence that Dutch painting, whether on canvas or in words, could inspire.[4]

Scott's comparison of Austen's art to that of Flanders was not the first analogy between the novel and Netherlandish painting; and it was certainly not the last.[5] At least as early as 1804, Anna Barbauld had already used the analogy to characterize the painstaking detail of Samuel Richardson: the author of *Pamela* and *Clarissa*, in her words, had "the accuracy and finish of a Dutch painter . . . content to produce effects by the patient labour of

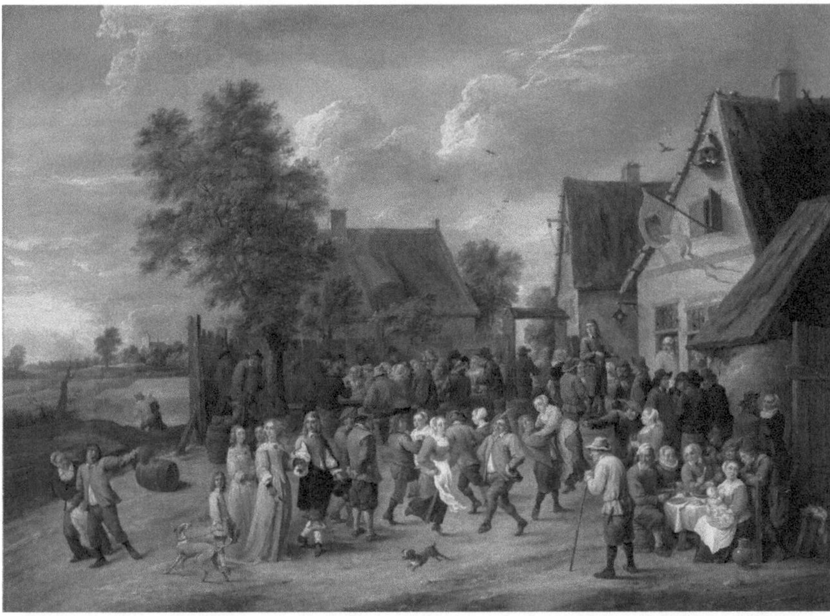

Figure 1-2. David Teniers the Younger: *Village Festival with Aristocratic Couple*, 1652. Musée du Louvre, Paris. Photo Credit: Erich Lessing/Art Resource, N.Y.

minuteness"—a phrase that Leslie Stephen echoed almost exactly when he in turn evoked the novelist's "Dutch painting of extraordinary minuteness" in an essay in the *Cornhill* more than half a century later.[6] Reviewing *Northanger Abbey* and *Persuasion* in 1821, Richard Whately repeated Scott's comparison of Austen's fiction to Flemish painting and added an allusion to the "Dutch school" as well.[7] In 1859, George Henry Lewes returned to the Flemish analogy in an essay that sought to defend Austen's art from the strictures of Charlotte Brontë—an essay that also seized the occasion, not coincidentally, to contend that Austen's "sympathy with ordinary life" had much in common with that of the recently published *Scenes of Clerical Life* by George Eliot.[8] As we shall see, the latter's own defense of her art by analogy to Dutch painting in *Adam Bede* that same year predictably encouraged many of her critics to pursue the comparison in the decades that followed. Yet Anthony Trollope was also compared to a Dutch painter, and so too were Harriet Martineau, Elizabeth Gaskell, and Margaret Oliphant—whose *Chronicles of Carlingford* were implicitly chided for their affinity with that "apostle of the Dutch school, Mr. Thackeray."[9] Even Thackeray's most celebrated rival was assimilated to the "school": while one reviewer confined himself to a single scene, calling the banquet at Todgers' in *Martin Chuzzlewit* (1844) a "notable . . . piece of Dutch painting," Charles Kingsley's impatient allusion in *Alton Locke* (1850) to "these days of Dutch painting and Boz" managed to make Dickens and the Dutch virtually synonymous, before he in turn grudgingly set out to satisfy the presumed appetite for such art with a detailed description of an "old eccentric's abode."[10]

Having evoked "the merits of the Flemish school" rather warmly in his review of *Emma*, Scott himself returned to the analogy more than a decade later—only now it was Daniel Defoe whose fictions were more equivocally praised for the resemblance:

> The air of writing with all the plausibility of truth must, in almost every case, have its own peculiar value; as we admire the paintings of some Flemish artists, where, though the subjects drawn are mean and disagreeable, and such as in nature we would not wish to study or look close upon, yet the skill with which they are represented by the painter gives an interest to the imitation upon canvass which the original entirely wants. But, on the other hand, when the power of exact and circumstantial delineation is applied to objects which we are anxiously desirous to see in their proper shape and colours, we have a double source of pleasure, both in the art of the painter, and in the interest which we take in the subject represented. Thus the style of probability with which De Foe invested his narratives, was perhaps ill bestowed, or rather wasted, upon some of the works which he thought proper to produce.[11]

There is no ambiguity here about the kind of low genre painting Scott has in mind. Defoe's rogues and criminals would certainly seem more at home in a tavern by Teniers than would an Emma or a Mr. Knightley (see fig. 1-1). The allusion to "mean and disagreeable" subjects nonetheless helps to illuminate the faint condescension with which Scott had earlier praised Austen's "Flemish" art for confining itself to "the middling classes of society"—while "those which are sketched with most originality and precision, belong to a class rather below that standard."[12] His class discriminations are carefully calibrated, but in both cases Flemish painting evokes the representation of the lower orders as well as the circumstantial details of the novelists' style.

Despite Scott's well-known distinction between his own "Big Bow wow strain" and "the exquisite touch" with which Austen rendered "ordinary common-place things and characters,"[13] one French authority identified the author of *Waverley* too with the tradition of Netherlandish painting in fiction. According to Hippolyte Taine in his *Histoire de la littérature anglaise* (1863), Scott was "like a painter who, having finished with great ceremonial paintings, finds an interest and a beauty in the bourgeois houses of some provincial dump, or in a farm framed by beds of beetroots and turnips"—a painter of "interior and genre pictures, so local and minute, and which, like those of the Flemish, indicate the rise of a bourgeoisie." For Taine, Scott's true contribution was not the imaginative reconstruction of history but the representation of "the real and modern world," a representation that had profoundly influenced—and by no means all to the good—a "whole literature" that followed:

> Miss Austen, Miss Brontë, Mrs. Gaskell, George Eliot, Bulwer, Thackeray, Dickens, and so many others paint especially or entirely, as he does, contemporary life as it is, without embellishment, at all ranks, often amongst the people, even more often amongst the middle class. And the same causes which made the historical novel by him and others come to nothing made the novel of manners by these authors succeed. They were too minute copyists and too decided moralists, incapable of the great divinations and the wide sympathies which open up history; their imagination was too literal, and their judgment too fixed. It is precisely with these faculties that they created a new species of novel, which proliferates today in thousands of offshoots, with such abundance that talents in this branch of literature may be counted by hundreds, and that one can only compare for original and national vigor to the great age of Dutch painting.[14]

Great as it may be, the "great age of Dutch painting" is clearly a doubtful precursor for the new age of the novel.

I shall return to the implications of Taine's mixed assessment throughout this book. But it is worth noting here that the very numbers in which this "new species" proliferates is one source of the critic's unease—as well as a reason for the analogy to a visual tradition famous for the very abundance of the images it produced. If Dutch painting constituted the "first mass consumers' art market" in Europe, as Simon Schama contends, then the nineteenth-century novel was surely the second; and the popularity of both forms raised continual questions about canons of taste and hierarchies of value.[15] Indeed, Taine may be writing at the moment only about English literature, but he is quite clear that Dutch painting in fiction is not confined to England. "Ask a cook which picture she prefers in the museum," he observes caustically, "and she will show you a kitchen, in which the saucepans are so well done that one is tempted to dip into the soup." Such cooks—or rather, the readers for whom they stand—are now apparently everywhere in Europe: "this inclination . . . is now European," and the novel which responds to such taste is a European phenomenon. (Where the English differ, Taine suggests, is their impulse to moralize the picture.)[16]

Though I shall argue that there were in fact particular reasons to connect English fiction to Dutch painting, Taine was not alone in finding such painting everywhere in the novel. He does not add any Continental names to the litany of "Miss Austen, Miss Brontë," and the rest, but many readers thought that Balzac especially belonged in their company. In a study of Netherlandish art published six years later, Taine himself would compare Rembrandt to Balzac; but by the time that he thus reversed the direction of the analogy (Rembrandt was "comme notre Balzac"), the comparison of the French novelist to Dutch and Flemish painters had become commonplace on both sides of the Channel.[17] In fact Balzac's realist novels had scarcely begun to appear in the 1830s before critics drew on the analogy to note the extraordinary detail with which his people and places were evoked. At least as early as 1833, the *Revue des deux mondes* suggested that an old woman in *Le médecin de campagne* might have had "her wrinkles counted by the brush of Gerrit Dou," and allusions to Dou, Teniers, Rembrandt, and others regularly recurred in the decades that followed. In France one reviewer characterized *Père Goriot* (1834) as a "tableau flamand," and another invoked the "pinceau flamand" of *César Birotteau* (1837);[18] in England *Eugénie Grandet* (1833) was "*a Dutch picture of an interior*"—this in a review that otherwise excoriated the novelist—while Balzac himself was "a painter of the Flemish school" or a "Dutch painter in prose."[19] As the number of volumes in the *Comédie humaine* multiplied, Balzac's fiction became a whole gallery of Netherlandish art:

> We have all passed entire hours in the galleries of the Louvre in contemplating some of those marvelous interiors by van Ostade, Metsu, or Gerrit Dou, into which our imagination enters, takes up residence, and amuses itself; M. de Balzac sometimes knows how to give to his novels the kind of mysterious attraction these pictures present. . . . The world that M. de Balzac has the gift of understanding and reproducing is the same as that of these bourgeois painters.[20]

Balzac was not the only Continental writer to be identified—whether for good or ill—with such pictures. In 1861, for example, Flaubert was attacked for creating a world that resembled "a Flemish or Dutch museum," and the analogy was used for other realists, some German as well as French, throughout the century.[21] But the sheer fecundity of Balzac's art—both the astonishing rate at which the novels appeared and the descriptive abundance of his style—made him an especially salient figure for a kind of art that was itself strongly associated with the proliferation of detail. "Where another writer makes an allusion," as Henry James memorably put it, "Balzac gives you a Dutch picture." That so much of Balzac's descriptive energy was directed toward the representation of houses and their interiors—what James called his "passion for bric-à-brac"—intensified his association with the domestic realism of so much Netherlandish painting.[22] Indeed, it is very much to the point that the use of the word "réalisme" in an aesthetic sense seems to have first come into circulation with an 1846 study of Dutch and Flemish art,[23] and that its earliest migration into English seems to have been an anonymous essay on Balzac in the *Westminster Review* of 1853—an essay that partly sought to counter "the well-known comparison of Balzac to the Dutch painters." (The comparison was fair enough, the critic conceded, "as regards the truthfulness with which he has depicted interiors, and the habits of some homely characters," but it failed to do justice to other aspects of his art—including "his exquisite female characters.")[24]

That the nineteenth century saw Dutch painting virtually everywhere in the novel may suggest that the analogy was used rather loosely, but it also testifies, as I shall argue, that fundamental characteristics of the genre itself were at stake: in associating narrative fiction with the visual art of the seventeenth-century Netherlands, nineteenth-century commentators were both registering and uneasily displacing many of those elements that we have come to identify, after Ian Watt, with the "formal realism" of the novel.[25] Although literary historians sometimes write as if the novel were the first genre in which such realism dominates an entire work (as opposed to figuring in the margins, like servants in Greek tragedy or peasants scrupulously depicted on the borders of a medieval manuscript),[26] many of the images produced by seventeenth-century Netherlandish painters clearly provided an important precedent; and however vaguely they conjured with the analogy, nineteenth-century writers were well aware of the fact. The detailed rendering of material particulars, the representation of "ordinary" people and events rather than heroic and mythical ones, the close attention to the rituals and habits of daily life, especially the domestic life of the middle classes: all these familiar characteristics of novelistic realism had their visual analogues in the so-called Golden Age of Dutch painting—the approximately hundred years, from 1580 to 1680, in which artists had produced the numerous images that continued to circulate through Europe in the centuries that followed.

The productivity of those years was truly extraordinary: by some recent estimates, over five million works were painted in seventeenth-century Holland.[27] While many of these did not survive, others not only survived but multiplied. Both in eighteenth-century France, where the vogue for Dutch and Flemish painting first established itself among the great aristocratic collectors as well as the heterogeneous crowds who frequented the Parisian city fairs, and in late eighteenth- and early nineteenth-century Britain, where many of the works from the French collections migrated in the aftermath of the Revolution and the Napoleonic Wars, the taste for Netherlandish art had been further popularized by influential collections of engravings like Jean Baptiste Pierre Lebrun's three-volume *Galerie des peintres flamands, hollandais et allemands* (1792–96), or John Smith's nine-volume *Catalogue Raisonnée of the Works of the Most Eminent Dutch, Flemish and French Painters* (1829–42)—not to mention the less costly reproduction of individual prints.[28] The very abundance of images that would prompt anxious analogies to the contemporary proliferation of the novel also meant that nineteenth-century writers could expect their readers to have some sense of what allusions to such art signified. Before there was "realism" in a literary sense there was Dutch painting, both as a phenomenon and as a paradigm for criticism.[29]

This is not to say that "Dutch painting" (or Flemish, for that matter) always signified the same thing. Like most critical terms, including such notoriously vexed examples as "realism" or "the novel," it named a set of family resemblances rather than a clearly defined essence—a set of overlapping and related characteristics, not all of which were necessarily invoked in any single use of the phrase. At the risk of overschematizing, let me spell out the range of lexical definitions that could be in play whenever a nineteenth-century writer compared a novel or an excerpt from a novel to Dutch painting:

> *Dutch painting*. 1) the precise transcription of detail, especially of material surfaces, such as those of furniture or dress; more generally, the copying of such appearances. 2) an abundance of such detail, sometimes at the expense of a governing intellectual or spiritual order; by extension, an excess of the trivial. 3) an attention to transient matters of costume or custom; the recording of the historically specific and local rather than the general or universal. 4a) the representation of ordinary or common subjects, both in the class of the

> persons depicted and in the familiarity of their activities; typical rather than exceptional persons or events; b) more specifically, the representation of the home, especially of domestic interiors and of women engaged in household activities. 5) the representation of low or vulgar subjects both as to the class of persons depicted and as to the nature of their activities: smoking, eating, drinking, etc. 6) in connection with landscape, the representation of the cultivated, tamed or domesticated; or of the literally or metaphorically flat. *See also* Dutch art, the Dutch school, Flemish painting, etc.

Yet even as this brief taxonomy may help to clarify some of what was meant when nineteenth-century writers reached for the analogy, it threatens to obscure the way in which such definitions overlap and entail one another, so that to make the allusion was to call up a whole set of connotations at once. Thus whether or not "mean and disagreeable" subjects, in Scott's phrase, were overtly at issue, to compare a novel to Dutch painting was almost invariably to associate it with the comparatively low and humble—a long intellectual tradition, as we shall see, having identified the "lowness" of such painting not just with the order of people depicted but with its very attention to matter itself. So too the feminized subjects of many Dutch and Flemish paintings meant that an aura of domesticity and femininity (and their implied limitations) often hovered around the paradigm in nineteenth-century criticism—as in Elizabeth Barrett Browning's dismissive allusion to Jane Austen as a "Dutch painter" of English "middle life," whose "*ladyhood*" was "stronger in her than her humanity."[30] As if to think of Dutch painting were automatically to conjure up images of women in the kitchen, the same critic who associated the *Chronicles of Carlingford* with the "Dutch school" also scolded Oliphant for attending too much to the housekeeping side of novel writing: "the artist's concern is like Mary's, with the spiritual guest, not like Martha's, with the platters and household serving."[31] The small scale of so many Dutch paintings, whose size was determined by the fact that they were designed for private households rather than public spaces, and the meticulous detail for which Northern art was famous, especially that of the so-called *fijnschilders* (literally, fine painters) like Gerrit Dou and Frans van Mieris the Elder (figs. 1-3 and 1-4), could easily reinforce nineteenth-century associations of the feminine with the detailed and the trivial—and of all three with certain tendencies in the novel.[32] Writing of the early George Eliot, for example, the youthful Henry James characterized her "observation" as "decidedly of the feminine kind: it deals, in preference, with small things"—this in a review that began by

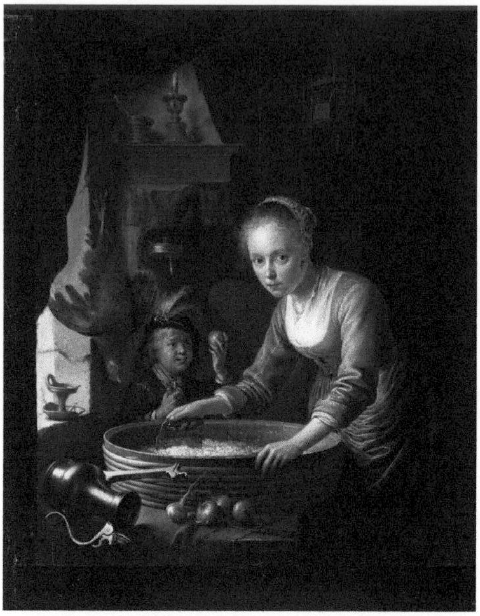

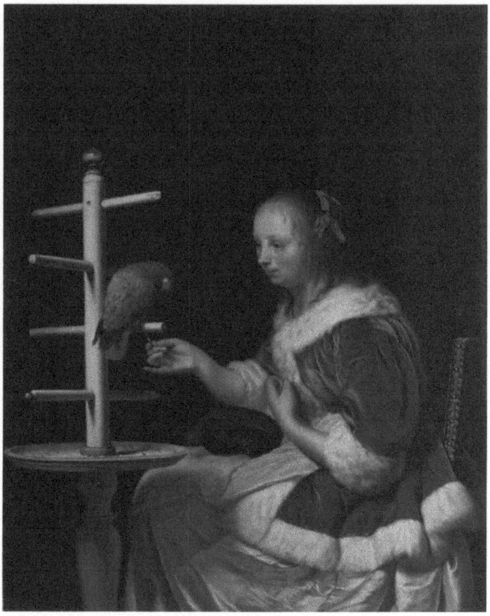

Left: Figure 1-3. Gerrit Dou: *Girl Chopping Onions*, 1646. Royal Collection, London. The Royal Collection © 2006 Her Majesty Queen Elizabeth II
Right: Figure 1-4. Frans van Mieris the Elder: *A Woman in a Red Jacket Feeding a Parrot*, c. 1663. National Gallery, London. © The National Gallery, London

quoting the novelist's own defense of her art on the model of Dutch painting and that followed with praise for her scenes of "low life" after "the Dutch masters whom she emulates."[33] In a related vein, Leslie Stephen elaborated at length on how "the feminine element in Richardson's character" manifested itself in that "interest in small details, which only women exhibit in perfection," before announcing that "the result of all this is a sort of Dutch painting of extraordinary minuteness."[34]

Of course, novels are not paintings, though they may aspire to evoke visual images; and while paintings may incorporate words and imply narratives, they have at most a limited capacity for storytelling. But the perceived limitations of painting—especially painting of a certain kind—are very much to the point: to the degree to which nineteenth-century viewers saw Dutch painting as the "mere" recording of material detail, the apparent stasis and meaninglessness of that detail could be at once attractive and disquieting. What Roland Barthes has called the appearance of "an entirely self-sufficient nominalism" in Dutch painting—"an art of the catalogue . . . of the concrete itself"—continually haunts nineteenth-century appropriations of the analogy.[35] The ambivalence with which critics approached Balzac's descriptive set pieces is a case in point, as they hovered between admiration for his painterly skill and the sense that an excess of matter threatened not merely to impede the narrative but to drain it of meaning altogether. "Often when in a story the action is running thin," as Henry James wittily remarked, "he stops up your mouth against complaint, as it were, by a choking dose of brick and mortar."[36] While Balzac's defenders praised the verisimilitude of his detail or argued that it served to characterize his people and explain their actions, less sympathetic readers concluded that "he painted to paint," in the words of one French critic—that "the mise en scène" had "invaded the idea; the material preoccupation killed the intellectual synthesis."[37]

Balzac's "mighty passion for *things*," as James summed it up, made him an easy target for such criticism.[38] But the association with Netherlandish painting, I would argue, often carries something of this charge—even when a novelist's detail is far less obviously material than is Balzac's. Austen, for example, is hardly a visual artist at all: so little does she indulge in physical description of any kind that Scott's comparison of her to a Flemish painter can initially seem rather puzzling. Despite the fact that Emma, like Eugénie Grandet after her, begins and ends her narrative in the paternal household, there is nothing in Austen's novel that resembles the "Dutch" interior in which Balzac sets the history of his provincial heiress. While the opening pages of Balzac's novel appear to give the reader an exhaustive account of the Grandet house in Saumur, from the stone of which it is built ("tufa—a white stone peculiar to the shores of the Loire" and "so soft" that it is now marked by "numberless irregular holes, whimsically shaped by the inclemency of the climate") and the precise configuration, materials, and state of decay of its archway and door, to a thorough inventory of the articles of furniture that occupy the large hall where much of the action takes place—not to mention the appearance of the room's walls (gray panels with ancient moldings) and ceiling (gray beams, whose interstices are filled by a mortar which has yellowed with age) or the number of its windows (two)—the reader of *Emma* knows only that Hartfield is "a comfortable home," which "in spite of its separate lawn and shrubberies and name," really belongs to the "large and populous village almost amounting to a town" that constitutes Highbury.[39] Since "there was scarcely an evening in the week in which Emma could not make up a card-table" for her father (*E*, 17), the Woodhouses apparently possess such an object, but it has nothing like the substance or location in space of the equivalent piece of furniture at the Grandets': "An old cardtable in marquetry, whose upper part formed a chess board, was placed in the area between the two windows. Above this table was an oval barometer with a black border, ornamented by bands of gilt wood, on which the flies had frolicked so licentiously that the gilding was in question" (*CH* 3: 1040). Of course *Emma* does have its share of homely details, such as the "minced chicken and scalloped oysters" with which the company at the first card party are fed, or the "eight cows, two of them Alderneys" that Harriet Smith enthusiastically recalls from her recent visit to the Abbey-Mill Farm (*E*, 20, 23). But the "Flemish" precision that Scott registered is primarily a question of manners and customs, habits of speech, and nuances of character. (Tellingly, in fact, the immediate example he offers in support of his claim is an extended dialogue—a slightly irritable conversation between Mr. Woodhouse and Isabella on matters ranging from the benefits of gruel to the comparative merits of their physicians.) Like Richardson's "Dutch" minuteness, which for Stephen was exemplified in the protracted account of the preparations for the hero's wedding in *Grandison*, Austen's "minuteness of detail"—the phrase is Whately's—has relatively little to do with objects as such.[40]

Yet for a long tradition of aesthetic theorizing, the very specificity of the realistic detail identified it with the historically local and the transient—and these in turn with the perishability of matter itself. When Edward Bulwer-Lytton announced in 1838, "There would be, indeed, something inane and trifling, or mean and vulgar, in Dutch copies of the modern still life," the "Dutch copies" he had in mind were contemporary novels of manners. "The young author will be surprised to find, that exact and unexaggerated fidelity has never been the characteristic of the greatest novelists of their own time," Bulwer-Lytton declared—adding for good measure that such "exact portraiture . . . revolts our taste as an effeminate attention to trifles." After all, "in a few years the mere portraiture of manners is obsolete. It is the knowledge of what is durable in human nature that alone preserves the work from decay."[41] Some thirty years later, R. H. Hutton echoed this verdict, as he prematurely attributed the imminent death of the novel to the prevailing taste for "realism": "Nothing is true in most novels except their descriptions of manners, and the instant those descriptions cease, from social changes, to be true, the novels themselves disappear."[42] Though Hutton did not specifically evoke the analogy to painting, a similar judgment was often in the air when critics remarked the Netherlandish detail of the novel.

When writers addressed themselves to the temporal character of the novel itself rather than the judgment of posterity, however, they were more likely to associate such detail with stasis than with transience. It is no accident that Scott identified Austen's "Flemish" art with a novel that had, by his account, "even less story" than usual—as if the evocation of such images were naturally opposed to the movement of plot.[43] From one perspective, of course, all painting is essentially static: at least since Lessing's celebrated essay on the *Laocoon* (1766), it has been commonplace to distinguish the temporal art of "poetry" from the spatial art of images—from which generic logic it follows that any attempt to imitate the effects of painting in words will necessarily disrupt the temporal flow of narrative.[44] Yet for classical art theory, as we shall see, the great prestige accorded history painting derived in large part from its closer approximation to the status of language: unlike still life, landscape, and genre painting—the visual categories in which Northern artists were principally thought to excel—history painting evoked a narrative and thereby appealed to the more intellectual capacities of the spectator. There was painting and painting, in other words; and what "Dutch painting" signified in this connection was an art that attended only to the visible surface of things, an art of "mere" images and nothing more. Coleridge was referring to description in poetry rather than the novel when he complained that "the work was so dutchified by minute touches that the reader naturally asked why words & not painting were used"; but his deliberately awkward neologism makes all too clear the lofty contempt this "dutchified" art could inspire.[45]

I shall return to such theorizing and its implications in the chapter that follows; but for now I simply want to suggest how it could be adapted for criticism of domestic realism in fiction. In an essay that appeared in *Blackwood's* in 1845, Archibald Alison explicitly invoked the authority of Joshua Reynolds, as he set out to attack the vogue for realism by mapping the generic hierarchy of neoclassical art theory onto literary distinctions between the romance and the novel. In Alison's telling formulation, "descriptions of still life—pictures of scenery, manners, buildings, and dresses—are the body, as it were, of romance; they are not its soul." While they have their place in a narrative, "the skilful artist" is to "regard them as an inferior part only of his art," duly subordinated to the grand passions that move the plot. Elsewhere in the essay Alison makes quite clear that such descriptions are the verbal equivalent of Dutch and Flemish painting—the novels associated with them bearing "the same relation to the lofty romances of which our literature can boast," in his phrase, "that the Boors of Ostade, or the Village Wakes of Teniers, do to the Madonnas of Guido, or the Holy Families of Raphael."[46] Ten years later R. H. Hutton would advance a similar argument against what he chose to call, among various other labels, "the realistic," "the statical," and the "quiet, chatty school of novelists"—a school of which Austen, significantly, was "by far the most distinguished representative." Contending that "a plot of some rapid movement is of the very essence of art," Hutton also managed to suggest that only such rapid movement could reveal the "deeper" aspects of human nature. The "more faithfully" the novelist "delineates the ordinary tone and manners of cultivated society," on the other hand, the less likely he is to sound those depths. "As Dutch paintings of the highest imitative perfection soon weary because the mind cannot rest long on a mere lesson in accurate details," so Austen and her school "soon weary us, because what we naturally seek after is wanting."[47]

The paradigm of Dutch painting did not always signify so negatively, however. Despite the faint whiff of condescension, Scott's enthusiasm for Austen was genuine, as was Whately's; and their analogies to Netherlandish art were intended as praise. In France especially, critics could evoke the comparison simply to commend the descriptive powers of a novelist, and the radical Théophile Thoré—who became perhaps the century's most ardent champion of Dutch painting—hardly meant to denigrate Balzac when he repeatedly associated his work with that of Jan Steen. For novelists themselves, as subsequent chapters of this book will show, Dutch painting could figure the necessary grounds of their art as well as its possible limits. But I do want to suggest that a long history of theorizing about the visual arts made such painting a convenient trope for some recurrent anxieties about the status of domestic realism in fiction. What might be called the discontents of such realism were never far away when nineteenth-century critics invoked the precedent of Dutch painting, even when the overt aim was to defend the novelists in question—as in this backhanded compliment from an English reviewer in 1883:

> I by no means wish to decry the commonplace, or to hint that the novel which confines itself to this sphere is a degraded type. There is room, let Mr. Ruskin say what he will, for Dutch art as well as Italian art. Miss Burney, Miss Austen, Mrs. Gaskell, Anthony Trollope, these and others have given abiding pleasure to too large a number of their fellow-creatures, for their exquisite, if low-soaring, art to be treated with contempt.

What room there was for Dutch art, in this case, was to be carved out at the expense of the "new school of fiction"—the label that W. D. Howells had defiantly adopted for the novels of Henry James, and that the reviewer turned against both Americans, who were condemned, in effect, for taking their material too seriously. Unlike Austen, who once again figured as the "consummate master" of her art, the authors of *A Modern Instance* and *The Portrait of a Lady* had failed to learn that "the commonplace must be treated both lightly and cheerfully." In such an art, "transcendentalism and tragedy are alike out of place. Her novels end, instead of beginning, with a wedding."[48]

This may seem a defense of realism only when it manages not to be realistic at all. But it is more useful as a reminder that there are many realisms, even if they necessarily share certain family resemblances, and that the domestic kind that the early nineteenth century associated with Netherlandish painting differed significantly, for example, from the kinds later identified with the novels of Flaubert and Zola. Indeed, by the time of this attack on the "new school of fiction" (which also included a passing swipe at Zola), British critics were more concerned to fend off the influence of the French than they were about the precedent of the Dutch; while the French themselves were as much engaged in debating their own forms of realism, both visual and verbal, as in drawing analogies to the achievement of the Netherlandish painters. From the viewpoint of the Victorians in particular, perhaps the most conspicuous difference between the fiction of their French contemporaries and the art of the seventeenth-century Netherlands concerned the representation of sexuality: unlike the French novel, Dutch painting—to put it simply for the moment—was realism with its clothes on.[49] Its verbal equivalent might constitute the "body . . . of romance," to adopt Alison's phrase, but that body, as most nineteenth-century viewers saw it, was not an obviously eroticized one. Whatever ambivalence the apparent materialism and even sensuality of Dutch art could inspire in the Victorians, both the domestic setting of so many images and the relative absence of the nude made its realism seem far removed from the carnal license of a *Madame Bovary* or a *Nana.* In this respect, at least, the paintings of the Dutch Golden Age seemed to have more affinities with the mainstream tradition of the novel as it had developed in Britain—affinities that can in turn be traced to their common origins in a Protestant and bourgeois culture. When Hippolyte Taine wished to set the art of the Netherlands in context, he pointedly contrasted the adulterous fictions of "Latin" countries like France with the conjugal virtues of the English novel—its "painting of chaste love and praise of marriage" serving as a synecdoche for the domestic values of Holland and Britain alike.[50]

"The household," as Martha Hollander has recently observed, was "the central metaphorical focus through which Dutch culture represent[ed] itself";[51] and while the borders that divided that feminized household from the world outside may have remained more fluid in seventeenth-century

Holland than in nineteenth-century Britain, in this connection too the Victorians might well have thought of their novels as peculiarly "dutchified." Broadly understood, of course, the domesticity of Dutch painting was one of the principal reasons why it became a paradigm for novels on both sides of the Channel—their common subject matter perhaps owing something to the fact that seventeenth-century Dutch artists, unlike their Italian counterparts, characteristically worked, as novelists did, at home.[52] But like British novels after them, Dutch paintings were particularly influenced by the ideals of household virtue and marital companionship that began to circulate in the domestic conduct books of seventeenth-century Europe—many of which, as it happened, first traveled to Holland from England.[53] When Dutch paintings traveled the other way, as large numbers did in the late eighteenth and early nineteenth centuries, it is hardly surprising that the British associated them with the novels they knew so well, even if the reasons for their affinities were more often sensed than articulated explicitly. So Anna Jameson, for example, looked at Nicolaes Maes's picture of a young woman at her needle (plate 1) and thought of the domestic virtues of a beloved Scott heroine. "The sentiment of home-felt tranquillity and feminine occupation was never more beautifully rendered," she wrote of Maes's *Girl Sewing* in 1844; "the same kind of feeling, produced, in another form, Jeannie Deans."[54] It was considerably more of a stretch to associate Dutch painting with English novels that always end in a wedding, but something of the same kind of feeling, in Jameson's phrase, apparently connected both arts with vague ideas of domesticity and contentment.

"Dutch painting," of course, had long signified more—and other—than a tranquil domesticity. But by the time that this rather idyllic version of novelistic realism was being deployed to chastise the newer versions of the Americans and the French, such painting was also being supplanted by another paradigm for the faithful mimesis of the visible world. Where once "Rembrandt" might have served as shorthand for a certain kind of realism, more and more critics had recourse to the photograph instead—"Rembrandt perfected," as Samuel Morse had called it in 1839.[55] Even the art of Balzac, that preeminent "Dutch painter in prose," was increasingly compared to that of the daguerreotype.[56] For better or for worse, both mimetic accuracy, on the one hand, and "mere copying," on the other, would become predominantly the province of the photographer—as in Charlotte Brontë's notorious (and relatively early) comparison of *Pride and Prejudice* to "an accurate daguerreotyped portrait of a common-place face."[57] And even as the photographic reproduction of the visible world began to occupy the rhetorical place once reserved for the virtuoso imitations of the Northern painters, so the photographer's self-evidently mechanical apparatus absorbed much of the animus that had long been directed, as we shall see, at the merely "mechanical" skills those painters supposedly exhibited.[58] The analogy to Dutch painting did not disappear; but both the reception of that painting and the form of the novel itself changed markedly in the course of the century. When George Moore praised Flaubert's *L'éducation sentimentale* in an essay of 1897 by comparing it to the "finest work by Peter de Hooch or Van der Meer [Vermeer]," it was not the minuteness of the novel's details to which he called attention but their artful selection: "Nothing has been omitted that could be included, nothing has been included that could be omitted; every detail contributes to enforce the unity of the picture. . . . For beauty of selection, for beauty of drawing, for beauty of colour, the Dutchmen have not done better."[59] This is still the novel as Dutch painting; but we have come rather far from Taine's cook and her instinctive preference for pictures of saucepans.

The "beauty of selection" that Moore identified with Dutch painting had always been there, of course, though the recovery of the hitherto neglected Vermeer in Théophile Thoré's influential study of 1866 would have made it easier to see. Of all the major Dutch painters, Vermeer was the most gifted at the art of leaving out; and what Harry Berger has called the "conspicuous exclusions" in his work presumably taught Moore, as they have taught us, to recognize related choices and omissions in the work of Vermeer's contemporaries as well.[60] Indeed, Moore's yoking of him with de Hooch in this regard seems notably modern, even as we are likely to share his implicit ranking of both painters over eighteenth- and early nineteenth-century favorites like Teniers or Gerrit Dou. But that should not tempt us to forget that theirs too was necessarily an art of selection—as is all art, for that matter, including that of the photographer. However meticulous the details, or familiar the resulting image, the "exact copying" with which Dutch painting was often associated was an illusion.[61] To the degree that Dutch art became a paradigm for unmediated transcription in words as well as pictures, it was premised, in other words, on a fundamental misconception—or at least a willful misreading—of what that art entailed.[62]

So too with the subject matter of Dutch painting, whose reflection of daily life was far more selective than many nineteenth-century commentators were prepared to recognize. As recent art historians have made clear, many common aspects of life in seventeenth-century Holland were never pictured or pictured only rarely, while others became standard motifs, elegantly varied from one image to another. Sailors and dockworkers, for example, rarely figure in genre scenes, despite the fact that they comprised a significant proportion of the population. For much of the Golden Age, Holland was at war, but although soldiers often appear in guardrooms, brothels, and domestic settings, comparatively little of the violence made it directly into painting. (Flemish artists, by contrast, did produce battle scenes in some numbers.)[63] Even when it came to the ordinary landscape-with-windmill, Lawrence Goedde has argued, "certain aspects of real mills were expected to appear in pictures and certain others were not."[64] In domestic scenes themselves, perhaps the most conspicuous absence was typically the man of the house, whose presence was often signified only by a portrait on a wall or a cloak thrown over a chair.[65] Among the activities of the women, certain homely tasks acquired particular prominence: spinning, for example, figures frequently in genre paintings of the period, though the evidence suggests that by and large women of that time had ceased to spin for the use of their own households.[66] To note such facts is not to contend that the nineteenth century was wrong to see such pictures as vivid representations of the daily and the ordinary, only to emphasize that such representations were constructions, like any other, and that to evoke them—especially in collective phrases like "the Dutch school" or "Dutch painting"—was inevitably to conjure with a particular set of formulae and conventions. It was also, inevitably, to take a part for the whole—not just by conflating Dutch art with Flemish, but by identifying all of it with the low genres in which Northern artists were particularly thought to excel. As recent scholars have emphasized, there were also painters of historical and mythological subjects in the seventeenth-century Netherlands, as well as those strongly influenced by Italianate and French traditions.[67] Though this book will continue to use the idiom that nineteenth-century critics and theorists adopted, it should be clear that "Dutch painting" signifies what it did for them, rather than our current understanding of the historical phenomenon.

When nineteenth-century writers thought of the novel as Dutch painting, they appear to have meant above all those images we know as genre: though both still life and landscape had their roles to play, as we shall see, it was the novel's affinity with "scenes of common and domestic life"—the phrase is Diderot's—that most obviously prompted the analogy.[68] In truth the modern definition of genre painting and its association with the novel grew up together. When Diderot wrote his *Essai sur la peinture* in 1765, he himself did not distinguish between such common and domestic scenes and all the other types then known as *peinture de genre*—a category that had come to include everything other than the pictures of historical or religious subjects traditionally classified as *peinture d'histoire*. Though the process by which a word that originally meant "kind" or "manner" came to mean one kind in particular remains somewhat obscure, the first attempt to stipulate a definition has been credited to the French theorist Quatremère de Quincy, who announced in 1791 that "le genre proprement dit" (genre properly so called) meant "des scènes bourgeoises."[69] (How precisely de Quincy intended his class distinction is not clear; but rather than conclude, as does one modern scholar, that the phrase should probably be translated as "scenes of everyday life,"[70] I take the ambiguity as instructive—a similar ambiguity as between "bourgeois" and "everyday" having considerable relevance for novels of the period.) Incidental uses of "genre" in the modern sense have been traced to England in the 1820s and to Germany in the early 1830s, but even after Franz Kugler's influential *Handbuch* of 1837 defined it as "the representation of everyday life," the term remained in flux on both sides of the Channel for several decades, before more or less settling into its present meaning in the 1860s and 1870s.[71] The same years in which the paradigm of Dutch painting most dominated criticism of the novel, in other words, were the years in which the everydayness of that painting was being progressively articulated.

This history is of more than etymological significance, because it bears on the question of just how much the everyday in this sense was a nineteenth-century discovery. Noting that some paintings we now classify as genre in fact contain elements that can hardly have been true to life—impossible architectural details, for example, or Arcadian landscapes that look more Italian than Dutch—one modern scholar has argued that it is the anonymity of the human figures in such images rather than their quotidian character that should define the category.[72] And surely anonymity is a necessary condition of genre, distinguishing it, on the one hand, from portraiture and, on the other, from history painting—both of which depend on the viewer's knowledge that a specific person, whether real or fictional, is intentionally represented. In an eloquent meditation on Dutch painting, Tzvetan Todorov has drawn attention to this distinction by remarking the alternative titles traditionally assigned to a picture in the Louvre by Rembrandt or his school: whether the image should be called *La sainte famille* (*The Holy Family*) or *Le ménage du menuisier* (*The Carpenter's Household*) (fig. 1-5) is clearly a question of whether it is to be understood as history or genre. That Rembrandt rarely produced what we now call genre as such, and that the picture apparently acquired its secular title when it arrived in France in the eighteenth century, would appear to settle the question,

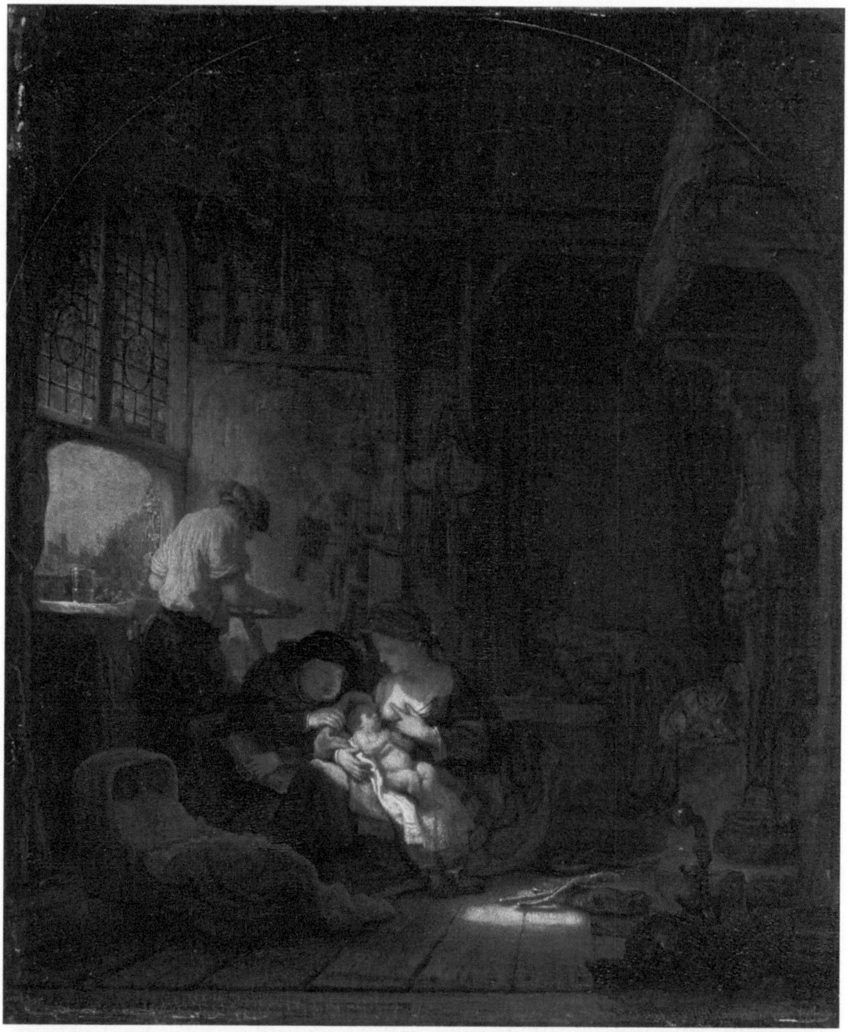

Figure 1-5. Rembrandt van Rijn (and pupil?): *The Holy Family* (also called *The Carpenter's Household*), 1640. Musée du Louvre, Paris. Photo Credit: Réunion des Musées Nationaux/Art Resource, N.Y.

even as it succinctly demonstrates how an idea of the everyday could be retrospectively imposed on an image with very different intentions.[73] Yet matters are not so simple, if only because Rembrandt's holy family has been so thoroughly incarnated in the humble forms of a seventeenth-century Dutch carpenter and his *ménage*. Unlike a Raphael painting of the same subject (fig. 1-6)—to invoke a comparison made repeatedly by

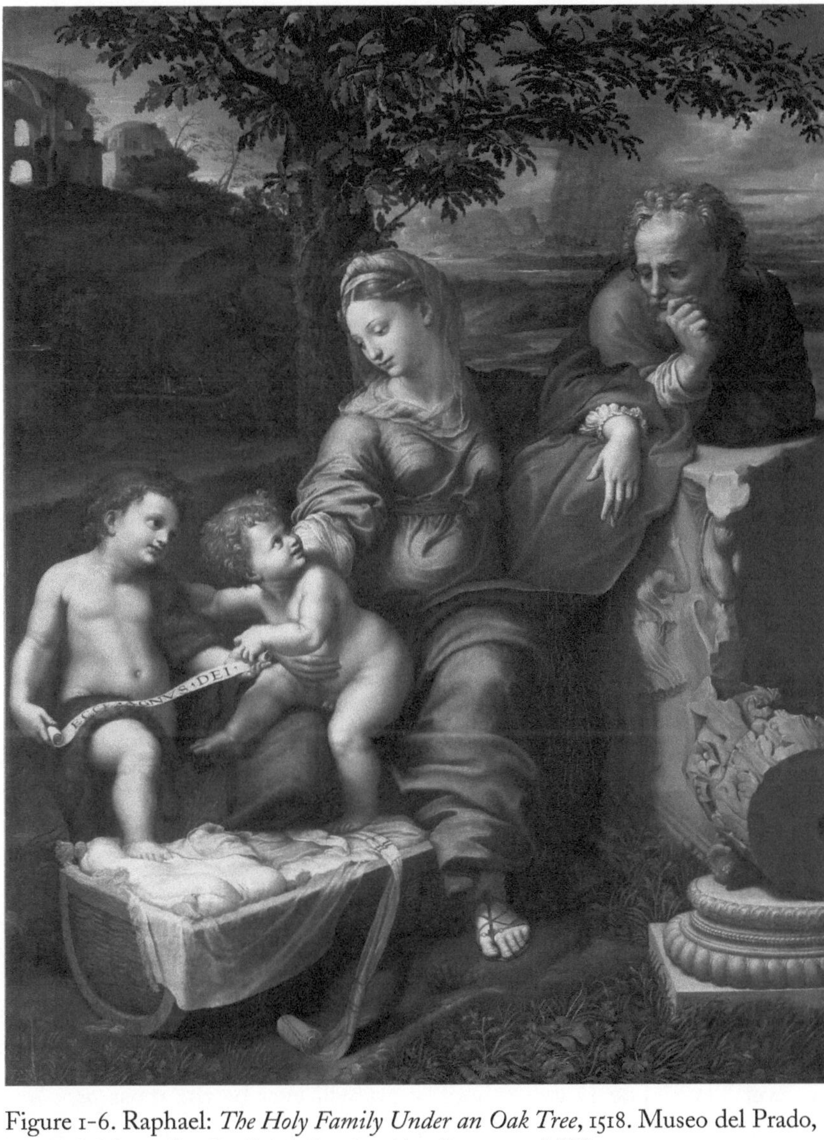

Figure 1-6. Raphael: *The Holy Family Under an Oak Tree*, 1518. Museo del Prado, Madrid. Photo Credit: Erich Lessing/Art Resource, N.Y.

nineteenth-century commentators—the Rembrandt deliberately elicits the sort of confusion reflected in the double titles. His evocation of scripture is also, and simultaneously, a representation of everyday life in seventeenth-century Holland.

The possibility that a holy family might appear to be nothing but a carpenter's household goes to the heart of a controversy that long raged over the intentions and effects of Dutch painting. Sometimes framed as a debate between iconologists and anti-iconologists, it was fundamentally an argument about the legacy of nineteenth-century realism and its appropriation (or misappropriation) of Dutch art.[74] I shall return to that debate and its origins in the following chapters. But wherever one draws the line for an individual artist or image, it is clear that to see Dutch painting as only a faithful imitation of mundane reality, devoid of any moral or spiritual meaning, was to see partially at best. As historians have been demonstrating for the last several decades, the impulse to emblem making and allegorizing—let alone simple moralizing—had hardly disappeared from seventeenth-century Netherlandish culture. Under the iconological scrutiny of modern scholars, the merry company around the dinner table is revealed as a feast for the prodigal son, or the innocent-seeming still life is decoded as a warning against vanity; viewed in the light of economic history, on the one hand, and seventeenth-century conduct books, on the other, the spinning housewife proves to be a domestic ideal rather than the representation of a daily reality. Yet if it is relatively easy to conclude that Rembrandt's carpenter is meant to be identified as Joseph, or that Jan Steen's *Easy Come, Easy Go* (fig. 1-7) illustrates a proverb, many a Dutch painting makes it far harder to decide just where symbolizing or moralizing ends and "mere" picturing begins. And even when the holy family is recognized amidst the prosaic details of a seventeenth-century household, those details still retain their "reality effect," to adopt Roland Barthes' phrase.[75] For nineteenth-century novelists as well as their critics, it was an effect their own art of the everyday had to reckon with.

Rembrandt's Joseph is not anonymous; but many of the figures in Netherlandish painting clearly were, and others became so over the course of the centuries that separated them from their original contexts. And it was in part that very anonymity—an anonymity nonetheless rendered with detailed attention to the individual and the particular—that enabled Dutch genre paintings to be readily assimilated to nineteenth-century visions of the "everyday." "The Dutch school of art will ever be the most *popular*," Anna Jameson remarked rather equivocally in 1844, "because it appeals to the popular sources of sympathy and wonder. Everybody has sympathy for the concerns of every-day existence—for the elegant repose of the lady at her toilet—for the joyous revelry of peasant life. Every one has wonder for the excellence addressed to the eye."[76] It is far from clear that "sympathy" with the figures depicted was the primary aim of seventeenth-century genre paintings, especially when the figures in question were peasants.[77] But Jameson's response does suggest another reason why so many nineteenth-century writers were tempted to see in such painting a visual analogue for

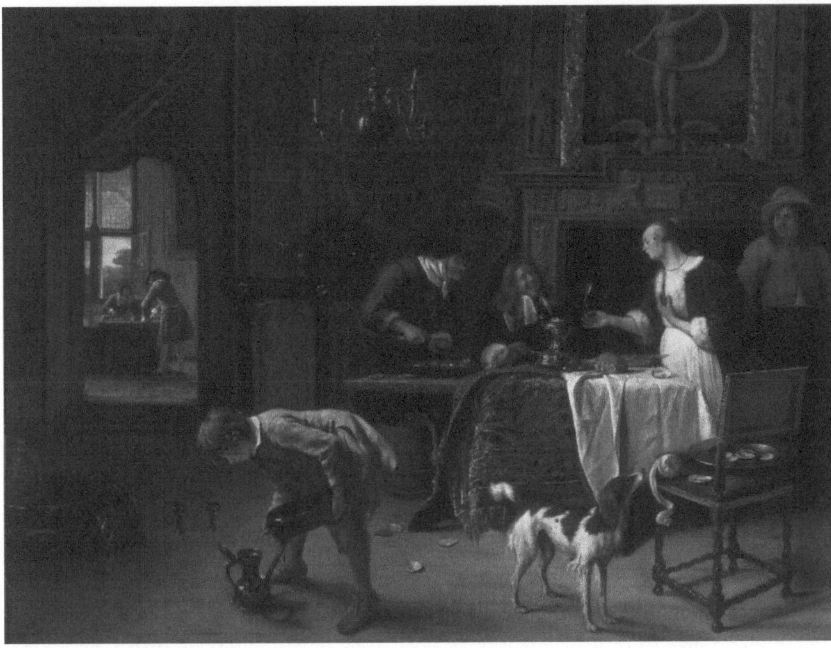

Figure 1-7. Jan Steen: *Easy Come, Easy Go.* Museum Boijmans Van Beuningen, Rotterdam

the novel. Just as the novel differentiated itself from earlier forms of narrative, as Catherine Gallagher has argued, by substituting fictional "nobodies" for the extratextual referents of personal satire and scandalous allegory, so genre distinguishes itself from history painting by representing "nobody *in particular*"—Gallagher's apt phrase for figures who refer to no recognizable persons outside the artwork itself and whose highly circumstantial realization drives home their nonallegorical status. And just as the novel encouraged the sympathetic identification of its readers precisely because its protagonists were fictional "nobodies"—and thus "potential objects of universal identification"[78]—so the anonymous figures of genre could prompt a viewer like Jameson to imagine that "everybody" would have sympathy for their "every-day existence." Fifteen years later, George Eliot would make the story of her first novel "pause a little," while she turned a similar intuition about the effects of Dutch painting into a manifesto for her own mode of realism. Professing to find "a source of delicious sympathy" in a type of painting that "lofty-minded people despise," the narrator of *Adam Bede* (1859) deliberately set herself against a long tradition of theoretical responses to Dutch painting.[79] It is to some of those "lofty-minded people" that I now turn.

{ two }

Low Genre and High Theory

When John Ruskin contemplated the work of "the various Van somethings and Back somethings," as he put it with chauvinist contempt in the first volume of *Modern Painters* (1843), he was evidently not inclined to half measures. "Their effect on the public mind is so totally for evil," he wrote of the Dutch landscapists later in the same volume, "that . . . I conceive the best patronage that any monarch could possibly bestow upon the arts, would be to collect the whole body of them into one gallery and burn it to the ground." Though he was willing to concede that "an artist of real judgment" might have something to learn from such paintings, any instructive value they might offer the discriminating practitioner was clearly outweighed by their disastrous influence on the taste of the public at large; and as the self-appointed reformer of that taste, Ruskin was more than ready—rhetorically at least—to consign them to the flames.[1]

Ruskin, of course, is a special case; and his animus toward Dutch painting is in some respects more idiosyncratic than representative. Despite repeated journeys to the Continent, he never visited Holland;[2] and his prejudices about the people as well as their art had evidently been encouraged by his teachers—one of whom he would later characterize as "a violent hater of the old Dutch school, and . . . the first who told me that they were 'sots, gamblers, and debauchees, delighting in the reality of the alehouse more than in its pictures'" (35:309). Especially in the early volumes of *Modern Painters*, the Dutch primarily served as whipping boys for his impassioned defense of J. M. W. Turner; and Ruskin's readiness to spend "so many pages in vituperating" them—as he himself retrospectively put it (33:289)—may be partly explained by the comparatively weak examples of their work he had seen. His knowledge of Dutch painting had been originally formed at the Dulwich Gallery—the only public venue in Britain at the time for studying the Dutch school, according to Anna Jameson, but one whose collection typically excited "disappointment" in knowledgeable viewers. (In Jameson's judgment, Dulwich lacked a "single picture which [could] be esteemed first-rate, either absolutely as a work of art, or relatively with regard to the style and master.")[3] By the time that Ruskin did see what he termed "a vast mass of Dutch pictures of good quality (as Dutch)" in Dresden and Munich, he was not prepared to alter his judgment: "I . . . dislike them—the landscapes I mean—more than ever."[4]

Ruskin's aversion to the Dutch is the more striking because *Modern Painters* in many ways set itself against the very paradigm that had previously kept them in their place. Though the generic hierarchies of neoclassical theory had already substantially broken down when he began to publish in the 1830s, there is no question that his vigorous defense of the hitherto lowly art of landscape helped to further their collapse.[5] Unlike many of the theorists who preceded him, Ruskin was not interested in celebrating history painting, or in explaining why Italian artists were superior to Northerners. It was not because they were landscape painters that he attacked the Dutch but because they were, by his account, such poor ones: they had "libelled the sea" (3:85), or covered "acres of canvas" with skies so ordinary and dull that they were "beyond the reach of criticism, for he who tells you nothing cannot tell you a falsehood" (3:371). Nor was it because Dutch artists attended to the local and the particular that Ruskin castigated them: though he could be scathing about "the calculable bricks of the Dutch house-painters" (3:32), the future champion of the Pre-Raphaelites was hardly opposed to detail as such. "It is *impossible*," he announced with characteristic emphasis, "to go too finely, or think too much about details in landscape, so that they be rightly arranged and rightly massed" (3:341). Specifically countering the neoclassical doctrine that a common Nature must be abstracted from particulars, Ruskin insisted that "the lowest details" deserved the painter's scrupulous attention, provided only that they contributed to the "final purpose" of the whole (3:33, 32). "The more a painter accepts nature as he finds it," he declared in the third volume of *Modern Painters* (1856), "the more unexpected beauty he discovers in what he at first despised" (5:58)—a rule that Mary Ann Evans would quote when she reviewed the volume in an anonymous piece that same year, and one that could easily have served as a key to the very painting he so consistently reviled. As the future George Eliot read him only a few months before she began her first work of fiction, "the truth of infinite value that he teaches is *realism*—the doctrine that all truth and beauty are to be attained by a humble and faithful study of nature."[6] That he nonetheless should be classed

Dutch School of Painting (including often, in Ruskin's usage, the Flemish school): barren technique of (except Rubens, Rembrandt, and Vandyck), **3**, 90; battle-pieces, **7**, 368; cattle-pieces, **7**, 333, 342, **18**, 309, **22**, 312; chiaroscurist, **22**, 311, 313, **20**, 127–8; clouds in, **3**, 370; contemplative of lemon pips, **23**, 326; deceptive imitation of, **5**, 37, **10**, 219, trickeries of, **20**, 173; degraded art into toys for boudoirs, **14**, 179, **16**, 320; details of, excessive, **3**, 341 *n.*, every brick painted, **3**, 32, 330; distance from the eye in, **15**, 360; dogs in, **7**, 337; a D. picture like a Florentine table, **7**, 364; effects of light, **23**, 348; English faith in, **35**, 401, vogue, **12**, 161; excelled in laying on paint, **12**, 506; finish of, **24**, 156, polished, **5**, 156; first irreligious art, **7**, 331–2; flower-pieces, dew-drops and insects, **14**, 377, 379–80; influence of, **24**, 40, evil, **3**, 188, on modern English art, **7**, 369; insensitive conception, **7**, 364, 369, **10**, 219; lacks imagination, **22**, 313; landscape, **9**, 448:—flat country, **5**, 238, **6**, 435, hybrid, **7**, 255, merits and defects, **3**, 188, natural but vulgar, **5**, 408, R.'s dislike of, **7**, liii., **14**, 179, shared by Harding, **35**, 309; typical landscape described, **7**, 365 *seq.*, unromantic, **33**, 290, 375; leaf-painting, **7**, 55, 57; libellers of the sea, **3**, 85; limitation of view, saw only grayness and shininess, **7**, 364; literal and brutal, **22**, 41, 42; mean and minute, **7**, 54; miniature methods and crowded incidents, **14**, 387; no infinity in, **7**, 55; notion of a swan, **22**, 45; patience, **5**, 23, **7**, 364; polish of, **27**, 646; respect for rural life, **7**, 332; Reynolds on, **5**, 21–4; ruined by browns, **15**, 138 *n.*, 415 *n.*; R. could be just, even to the, **4**, 335 *n.*; R. no power of sympathy with, **1**, xxxi., **7**, 363; sea-painting, **3**, 85, 516, 566–7 (*see* Backhuysen, Vandevelde); shadows in, **3**, 305; sight-point, **15**, 303; skies (early school), **3**, 351, 356; still life and dead game, **25**, 27; street views, **7**, 255; subjects of, **7**, 331–2, trivial, **5**, 64; tavern fumes of, **20**, 79; technical connexion with Greek school of shade, **22**, 313; temper of, quiet and cold, **13**, 545; the more skilful masters of the, **28**, 391; tree-drawing, **7**, 91, 92, 94; vituperation of, in *Mod. P.*, **33**, 289; vulgarity, **7**, 364, **19**, 50; vulgar vermilion of, **15**, 421; workmanlike, **7**, 363

Figure 2-1. Index entry for Dutch painting in *The Works of John Ruskin*, ed. E. T. Cook and Alexander Wedderburn, 39 vols. (London: George Allen, 1903–12)

among those "lofty-minded people" who despised Dutch pictures is a paradox that says much about Ruskin, but even more about the extraordinary persistence of some deep-seated associations those pictures carried with them. For all the anomalousness of his position, the sheer intensity of his response—not to mention the power of his rhetoric—makes him an unusually revealing guide to what had long been at stake in the resistance to Dutch painting (fig. 2-1).

As his disgusted allusion to "the reality of the alehouse" suggests, Ruskin's contempt for Dutch art is impossible to separate from his disapproval of its subject matter. "It is not by the mode of representing and saying, but by what is represented and said," he announced in the first volume of *Modern Painters*, "that the respective greatness either of the painter or the writer is to be finally determined" (3:88). Though this seems to say that subject matter alone determines the value of art, it would be truer to the spirit of Ruskin's criticism as a whole to say that he refuses to distinguish between aesthetic concerns, on the one hand, and moral and spiritual ones, on the other—and that it is precisely because he insists on identifying them that he can provide such an illuminating commentary on assumptions that many of his predecessors leave implicit. Not that all previous critics of Dutch art shared his vehement revulsion from the "pleasures of the alehouse and the card-table" (his shorthand for the painting of Teniers—7:369). Even after he abandoned the strict Evangelicalism in which he was raised, Ruskin retained many of its values and prejudices;[7] and the disgust with which he could write of "the wholly carnal work of Wouvermans" (7:370) or dismiss "the petty skill that was bred in the fumes of the taverns of the North" (20:79) is peculiarly his own. Indeed, the fact that most of the paintings he actually examines are landscapes rather than pictures of taverns or brothels can make his allusions to "the renderings of besotted, vicious and vulgar human life perpetrated by Dutch painters" (19:50) seem all the more gratuitous.

Yet such objections to the carnal and the crude in Dutch painting are almost as old as that painting itself—not just in scurrilous attacks like an anonymous British satire of 1674, whose Dutch artist would "undertake to draw a Fart / With all delineaments of Art,"[8] but in the sober commentary of the Flemish-born theorist, Gerard de Lairesse, whose *Groot schilderboek* of 1707 brought neoclassical standards to bear on native tradition by issuing its own strictures on "Tobacco-smoakers . . . nasty Children easing Nature, and other Things more filthy."[9] From the comparatively restrained observation of the seventeenth-century French theorist Roger de Piles that most Flemish painters "know how to imitate Nature, at least as well as the Painters of other Countries, but they make a bad choice in Nature it self,"[10] to Horace Walpole's characterization of the Dutch as "those drudging Mimics of Nature's most uncomely coarsenesses" or the pronouncement of the nineteenth-century British painter William Collins (as quoted by his novelist son) that "most of the Dutch pictures are composed of subjects gross, vulgar, and filthy,"[11] Ruskin's objections to the matter of Dutch painting had ample precedent—and so, more tellingly, did his habit of confounding the subjects represented in some images with the character of the art as a whole. It is as if the lowest matter in Dutch painting, by which commentators generally meant the most appetitive and animal-like, exerted a gravitational pull on all the rest—as in Humphrey Repton's complaint that the Dutch school "degrad[ed] nature, by selecting low, vulgar, and gross subjects, representing men when they are losing their reason, and brutifying into mere animals,"[12] or, more subtly, in the epitome of Dutch painting with which William Hazlitt chose to attack the poetry of Crabbe: "the adept in Dutch interiors, hovels, and pig-styes must find in Mr. Crabbe a man after his own heart." Though elsewhere Hazlitt was willing to concede Dutch painters a limited excellence—observing, for example, that "their pictures at least show, that there is nothing in nature, however mean or trivial, that has not its beauty and some interest belonging to it, if truly represented"—the aggressive reduction of his descending appositives, from interior to pig-sty, succinctly illustrates a pervasive tendency in hostile commentary on Dutch art.[13]

Some of the obsession with scenes of drunkenness and debauchery in Dutch painting is peculiar to the nineteenth century: as Harry Mount has shown, a new insistence on decorum, in Britain especially, prompted reevaluations of particular seventeenth-century artists, even as it inspired contemporary genre painters to clean up and sentimentalize the models of their predecessors.[14] But already in eighteenth-century France a similar process was underway, as the abbé Raynal testified when he associated the appeal of Chardin's images with their success in avoiding the more disagreeable subjects of the Flemish: "Indeed, smoking rooms, fist fights, the needs of the body—in short, Nature captured at its most abject—are the subjects most commonly treated by the Browers, Ostades, and Teniers, etc. M. Chardin has always avoided these images so humiliating to humanity." Like many other commentators, Raynal writes here of "the Flemish painters in general," as if all Northern art could be reduced to images of "Nature . . . at its most abject."[15] On the other side of the Channel, even Hogarth sought to distance himself from the purported vulgarity of "the true Dutch taste," as he put it in an advertisement of 1751 for a parody of Rembrandt that he managed to pass off as a hoax on several subscribers.[16] Several years before this incident, he had attacked that taste more obliquely, by designing a series of pseudo-Dutch pictures for the walls of the ambitious merchant who has married off his daughter to the dissolute earl in *Marriage à la Mode* (1745). In addition to a kitchen still life, Hogarth's merchant owns two genre scenes: one of a smoker lighting his pipe from the inflamed nose of his companion, and the other of a man urinating against a

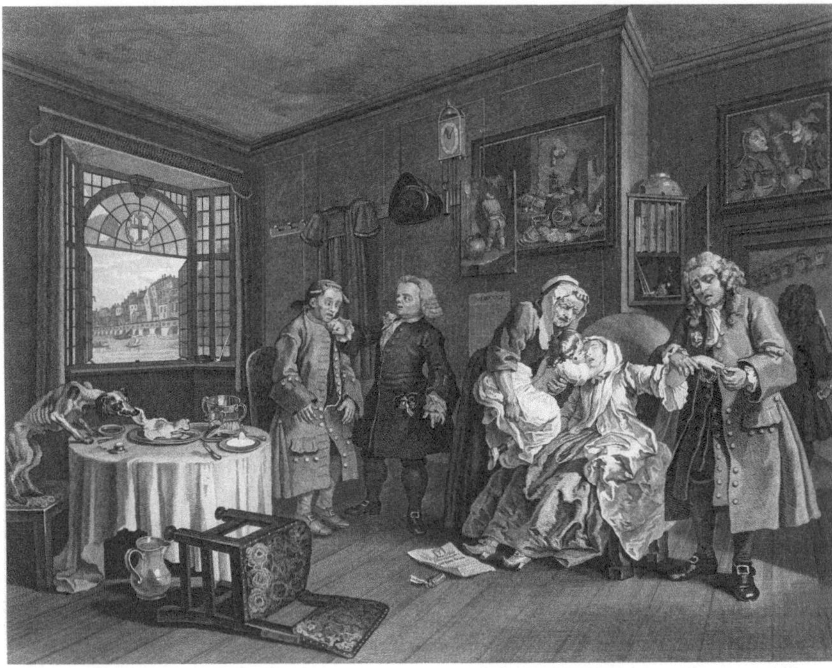

Figure 2-2. William Hogarth: *Marriage à la Mode* (plate 6), 1745. Lewis Walpole Library, Yale University

wall (fig. 2-2). Despite his considerable debt to Northern art—or because of it—both Hogarth and his supporters were determined to distinguish his work from what Walpole termed the "indelicacies of Flemish and Dutch painters."[17] A century later, the painter Richard Redgrave was only engaged in a more extreme version of the same exercise when his description of Hogarth's print inadvertently managed to turn the functions of the body itself into an unfortunate legacy from Holland: "the pictures on the walls are here of the Dutch school, representing Dutch wit and Dutch filth—eating, smoking, drinking, and their Dutch consequences."[18]

No doubt the gradual refinement of manners partly explains this growing distaste for such "abject" images. What Norbert Elias has termed the "civilizing process" makes the relative coarseness of an earlier era at once more offensive to the later one and more noticeable. But as Ruskin's case suggests, national and ethnic prejudices also had their role to play in such judgments, especially when British or French commentators were tempted to displace onto the Dutch those aspects of life, in Raynal's phrase, "so humiliating to humanity." There was ample precedent for Hazlitt's casual reference to pig-sties, or the malicious wit with which Ruskin attributed an awkward study of a swan—pointedly contrasted with one of Turner's—to the "essentially piggish nature" of the Dutch artist: "and so he has ended in making . . . this sleeping swan's neck as nearly as possible like a leg of pork" (22:46.) The Anglo-Dutch wars of the seventeenth century had already produced a considerable polemical literature that delighted in finding the "hog" in the Dutch word for high (*hoog*), for example, or in punning on the lowness of Dutch geography: "An Hollander is not an High-Lander, but a low-lander for he loves to be down in the dirt and wallow therein."[19] Just as Ruskin scarcely troubled to distinguish between "the renderings of besotted, vicious and vulgar human life perpetrated by Dutch painters" and the "sots, gamblers, and debauchees" who ostensibly constituted the Dutch nation, so many commentators willfully confused the peasants who appear in some images with the people as a whole—"coarse boors" being one of the most common of the derogatory epithets applied to the Dutch over the centuries. Less crude, but no less pervasive, stereotypes identified them as materialistic traders, or as dull plodders, phlegmatic and cold.[20] Precisely because the Dutch painted themselves rather than historical or mythical figures, the tendency to confound judgments about the pictures and the people may have been particularly pronounced. Of course, every group attracts stereotypes, and those associated with the Dutch could also be viewed in a very different light: as we shall see, generalizations about national character were still very much in play when some nineteenth-century writers sought to defend Dutch art as the reflection of an industrious and freedom-loving people. It is not the stereotyping itself that signifies in the present context, but how overdetermined was the tendency to associate "low" matter of various kinds—matter understood *as* low—with the paradigm of Dutch painting.

Dutch art was not all drunkenness and debauchery, needless to say, even for Ruskin; nor were hovels and pig-sties the sort of images that critics of the novel usually had in mind when they compared its realism to that of Dutch pictures. Taine's association of Scott with a Flemish painter who "finds an interest and a beauty . . . in a farm framed by beds of beetroots and turnips" was more nearly anticipated by Benjamin Haydon's impatient allusion in a diary entry of 1808 to the "mindless imitation of carrots," while the Frenchman's comparison of the novel-reader to a cook admiring well-painted "saucepans" in a museum had its analogue in the same diarist's complaints about contemporary viewers' preference for the trivial details of a painting: "What do they admire in it? The character or the mind? No, the dutch part, the touching, the knifes, the pewter plates, and tin saucepans."

Haydon's anger is ostensibly directed at the inappropriate closeness from which these viewers choose to examine a picture, but his remarks make clear that the disparity between far and near in such a case really measures the distance between high and low, mind and matter:

> instead of standing at an awful distance, and surveying with dread great works . . . instead of being ambitious of having their Souls elevated, and their minds expanded, instead of this, to see them rush, with their heads jammed as if in a wedge, clap up their glasses before a Picture, "three feet long, and two feet wide," and uttering exclamations of ravishment and rapture at a smutty crock, or a brass candlestick . . . [21]

To view "great works" from an awed distance is to elevate the soul and expand the mind; to admire crockery up-close is "the dutch part"—"mindless," and presumably soulless as well. A similar hierarchy governs Ruskin's pointed comparison between "great" schools and "small" according to the subjects they represent: "a Dutchman can be just as solemnly and entirely contemplative of a lemon pip and a cheese paring, as an Italian of the Virgin in Glory" (23:326). Not just lemon and cheese but a pip and a paring: Ruskin's version of Dutch still life deliberately reduces it to matter at its most trivial, even as he pointedly opposes that matter to the Madonna at her most elevated. Though pips and parings might appear to be just the sort of details he elsewhere characterized as deserving the artist's utmost attention, in Ruskin's eyes they signified the unredeemed "vulgarity" of Dutch painting—a vulgarity very little different, finally, from that he associated with pictures of drunkenness and debauchery.

Ruskin was hardly doing anything very unusual in calling Dutch painting vulgar, but what he meant by "vulgarity" is worth examining, since his definition is both idiosyncratic and illuminating. He himself devoted an entire chapter of *Modern Painters* to elaborating his sense of the term—an exercise he explicitly undertook in order to place his account of the Dutch school in context—and I shall return to that discussion shortly. What he did not mean, or did not mean simply, however, was that Dutch painters devoted themselves to representing the lower orders. Yet the status of the persons represented—what we would anachronistically call their "class"—obviously had its own role to play in the long-standing denigration of Dutch painting. Indeed, to the extent to which the hierarchy of status was presumed to correlate with a hierarchy of mind over matter, it is often impossible to distinguish between them: "coarse boors" are coarse because they are boors, and lofty-minded disdain for "the needs of the body," to adopt Raynal's phrase, necessarily looks down on those presumed to manifest such needs most unrestrainedly. When Ruskin contemptuously dismissed the typical sky in Dutch landscape as "quite good enough for cattle to graze, or boors to play at nine-pins under" (3:371), he meant that boors and cows alike are too insensitive to deserve anything better.

Of course, not all Dutch painting depicted peasants, although the evidence suggests that inexpensive prints of such subjects—known as "Drolls" or "Drolleries"—were the first to travel in large numbers outside the Netherlands, and that the taste for more refined images of domestic life only developed gradually over the course of the eighteenth century.[22] When Dryden prefaced his translation of *De Arte Graphica* with an essay on the "Parallel betwixt Painting and Poetry" (1695), he took for granted that "inferiour persons, and low Subjects" were more or less identical, and that what comedy was to the literary hierarchy, Dutch genre was to the visual—"a kind of Picture, which belongs to Nature, but of the lowest form." Dryden's allusion to "the painting of Clowns, the representation of a *Dutch* Kermis, the brutal sport of Snick or Snee, and a thousand other things of this mean invention" makes clear that he was not thinking of bourgeois interiors.[23] Yet even when images of well-scrubbed kitchens and comfortable parlors were as familiar as taverns and hovels, many commentators on the "Dutch school" did not trouble to distinguish between them. In Martin Shee's versified *Elements of Art* (1809), for example, "the humbler beauties of Batavian skies" apparently cover boors and bourgeoisie alike:

> . . . Painting there, no epic wreath requires,
> Nor feels, nor feigns to feel poetic fires;
> Content on boors and burgomasters still,
> At wakes and weddings, to display her skill.[24]

Not until the middle of the nineteenth century, in fact, did theorists explicitly formulate the distinction we now recognize between low genre and high—a distinction that is itself fundamentally one of class. (Though the German credited with first defining these terms in 1842 referred to "low genre . . . with its tendency toward the comic," and "high genre . . . where moral order prevails," his immediate predecessor had written more frankly of "coarse, comical motives," on the one hand, and representations of "the well-to-do," on the other.)[25] From such a perspective, Gerard ter Borch's ladies in satin evidently inhabit a different sphere from the peasants of Adriaen Brouwer, for example (figs. 2-3 and 2-4). But for most of the period

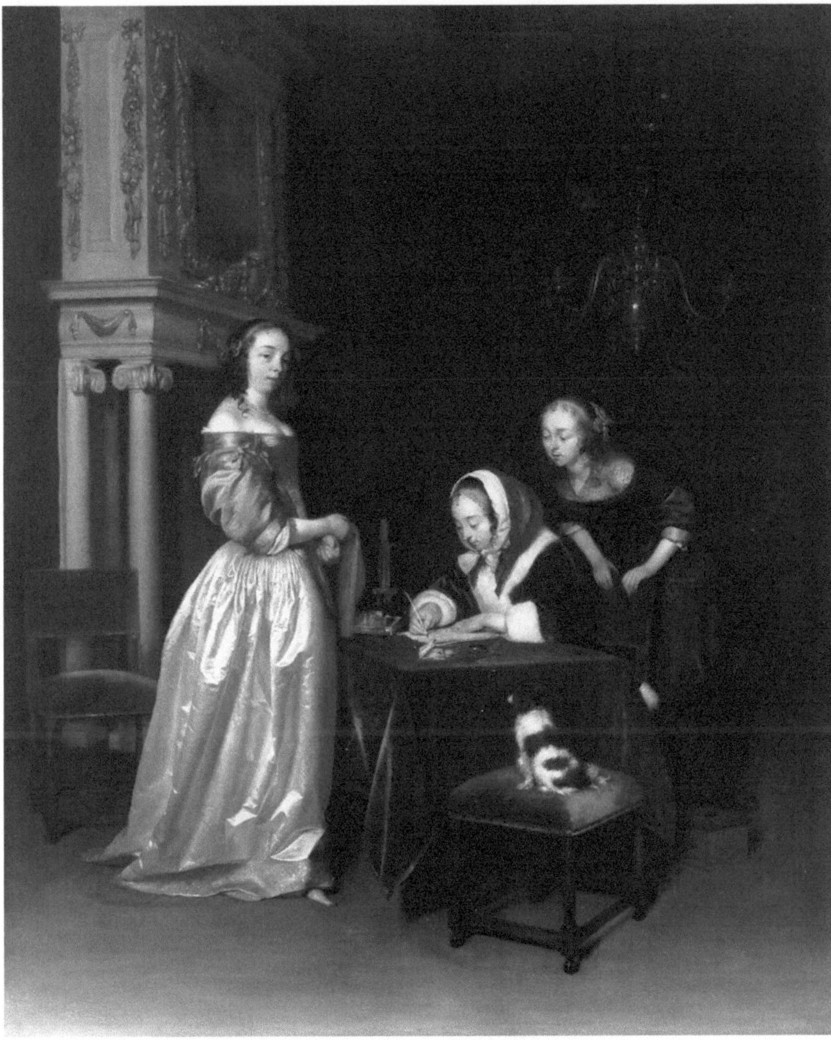

Figure 2-3. Gerard ter Borch: *Curiosity*, c. 1660. The Metropolitan Museum of Art, New York. The Jules Bache Collection, 1949 (49.7.38). Image © The Metropolitan Museum of Art

in question, they would both have been classed as figures of common and domestic life, and even ter Borch's elegant ladies could not quite escape the low associations of the company in which they found themselves. Writing of the Dutch school in 1844, Anna Jameson could still allude indiscriminately to "the revels of drinking boors . . . ladies and gentlemen eating oysters, girls 'chopping onions,' and so forth"—all of which, she confessed, she

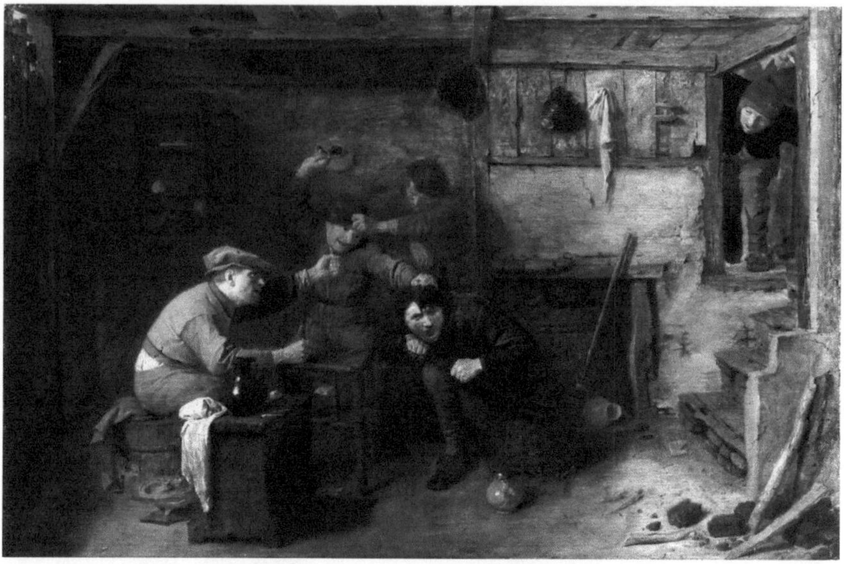

Figure 2-4. Adriaen Brouwer: *Peasants Fighting*, 1625–38. Bayerische Staatsgemäldesammlungen, Alte Pinakothek, Munich

had once thought "unredeemed common-place and vulgarity."[26] Though she was now inclined to accord such pictures a limited value, others were not persuaded. In the following year, Archibald Alison confidently drew on the paradigm of Dutch painting in order to attack "the doctrine now so prevalent . . . that the manners of the middle or lowest class," as he revealingly put it, "are the fit object of the novelist." With a little rhetorical push from "the Boors of Ostade" and "the Village Wakes of Teniers," the representative protagonists of such novels in Alison's telling undergo a rapid downward mobility, from "cheesemongers and grocers"—his first example of how "the lofty art of romance" has descended—to "murderers and burglars" and "the refuse of the common-sewers."[27]

"If everything that is natural, and we see around us, is the fit object of imitation, and perpetuating in literature," Alison announced, then "it can no longer be called one of the *Fine* Arts. It is degraded to a mere copying of nature in her coarsest and most disgusting, equally as her noblest and most elevating, aspects."[28] Though this might appear to be just another way of saying that the vulgarity of the novel's subjects degrades the novel itself, the allusion to the "*Fine* Arts" and the language of "mere copying" betray the influence of another line of argument—one that Alison inherited most immediately from Joshua Reynolds, but whose origins long antedate

Reynolds's *Discourses*. From this perspective, it is not only the matter of Dutch painting that is the sign of vulgarity but the manner—the "mere copying" that proves the painter himself, to oversimplify for a moment, no gentleman.[29] Indeed, if the Dutch had not existed, one is tempted to say, they would have had to be invented—so happily did they serve to absorb certain anxieties that had long haunted the profession. At least since the fifteenth century, theorists had sought to elevate the status of painting—and of painters—by countering the perception that it was a mere craft or trade. Contending that it should properly be classed among the liberal arts instead, Alberti and others emphasized that the painter worked with his mind as well as his hands, that he dealt in "ideas" every bit as intellectually demanding as those of mathematics and poetry. Whether these ideas were understood as Neoplatonic forms that existed a priori, or as derived, in Aristotelian fashion, from studying and combining the imperfect beauties found in nature—and both arguments were advanced in one of the most influential treatises on the subject, Giovanni Pietro Bellori's *Le vite de' pittori, scultori et architetti moderni* (1672)—the important point is that in forming such conceptions, the artist proved himself the master of the natural world and not its subject.[30] As Bellori put it in a passage Dryden chose to translate in his introduction to *De Arte Graphica*, the artist's function is to form "a Model of the Superiour Beauties; and reflecting on them endeavour to correct and amend the common Nature."[31]

Bellori himself was more concerned with the decline of Italian painting since the days of Raphael and Reni than in chastising the Dutch. But for a host of subsequent commentators, the opposition between Italy and the North, history painting and the lesser genres, turned on the difference between those who corrected Nature and those who merely followed her. So Jonathan Richardson, for example, closely echoed Bellori—"A Painter must Raise his Ideas beyond what he sees, and form a Model of Perfection in his Own Mind which is not to be found in Reality"—even as he set out a typical ranking of pictures at the beginning of the eighteenth century:

> There is Some Degree of Merit in a Picture where Nature is Exactly copy'd, though in a Low Subject; Such as Drolls, Countrey Wakes, Flowers, Landscapes, *&c.* and More in proportion as the Subject rises, or the End of the Picture is this Exact Representation. Herein the *Dutch*, and *Flemish* Masters have been Equal to the *Italians*, if not Superior to them in general. What gives the *Italians*, and Their Masters the Ancients the Preference, is, that they have not Servilely follow'd Common Nature, but Rais'd, and Improv'd, or at least have

> always made the Best Choice of it. This gives a Dignity to a Low Subject . . . and This, when the Subject it self is Noble, is the Perfection of Painting.

At the very top of this hierarchy, not surprisingly, are "the Histories of the best *Italian* Masters; chiefly those of *Rafaëlle*; He is the great Model of Perfection!"[32] In such histories, a noble subject is nobly executed—which is to say that the painter has not servilely followed nature but raised and improved it.

Few epithets more consistently accompany the denigration of the Dutch painter than "servile" and "mechanical"; and while they do not necessarily mean the same thing, both accuse him of lacking the qualities of mind and spirit that enable nobler artists to free themselves from a debasing subjection to the material. The evidence suggests that the idiom of "servile" copying or imitation may owe its currency to a much-quoted line from Horace's *Epistles* (I. xix. 19)—*O imitatores servum pecus!* (Oh servile herd of imitators!)—though the objects of Horace's scorn were poets who copied other poets, not those who imitated nature too closely. When Roger de Piles quoted the line in his commentary on *De Arte Graphica*, the servility in question still entailed copying other painters, but it is not difficult to imagine how the sense was extended to cover other kinds of imitation as well. To "copy and purloyn the works of others," Piles says in Dryden's translation, is "to creep and grovel on the ground."[33] It might seem that following "Common Nature," as in Richardson's version of the phrase, could hardly be more abject than this; but the commonness of what is imitated obviously adds its own weight to the charge. The effect was much the same in French when Richardson's aristocratic contemporary, the Marquis d'Argens, referred disgustedly to "little Dutch pictures" whose "only merit . . . is a servile imitation of the lowest form of nature."[34] (Compare Ruskin's scornful allusion to "small squares of Dutch canvas, containing only servile imitations of the coarsest nature" [12:161], or Henry James's characterization of a painting by Isack van Ostade as "so servile to base fact.")[35] If those who master nature by improving her are painting's aristocrats, noble and free, those who merely follow her are little more than slaves—their ignobility confirmed by the baseness of that to which they enslave themselves.

Both "servile" and "noble" in such contexts are, of course, metaphors; but the distinctions they register are nonetheless not merely verbal. In eighteenth-century England especially, the question of where the painter ranked in the status hierarchy was a question of some urgency. "'Tis not every *Picture-Maker* that ought to be called a *Painter*, as every *Rhymer*, or

Grubstreet Tale-Writer is not a *Poet*, or *Historian*," Richardson anxiously declared in 1715: "A *Painter* ought to be a Title of Dignity."[36] Yet until the end of the seventeenth century a single craft guild, the Painters-Stainers' Company, had included everyone from artists to house-painters, without distinction.[37] Unlike Italy and France, England lacked a well-established tradition of history painting and the dignities that attended it—a circumstance of which men like Richardson and Reynolds were all too aware. Though a number of explanations were offered for England's deficiency in this regard—including the influence of the climate—the combined effects of Protestant iconoclasm and the comparative weakness of the monarchy were undoubtedly the most prominent.[38] Without the requisite patronage and the large public buildings in which to exhibit his work, a would-be history painter was at a distinct disadvantage. In these respects, the English were uncomfortably close to the Dutch; and the need to distinguish themselves from that nation of craftsmen made English theorists even more sensitive to the negative paradigm of Dutch painting than their Continental counterparts. Even after the founding of the Royal Academy in 1768—an act deliberately aimed at remedying the situation by encouraging the production of history painting on a large scale—it was far from evident that "the final triumph of the intellectual component of the painter's art over the technical aspect" that one recent historian has located in this moment was assured.[39] Indeed from Richardson's *Essay on the Theory of Painting* (1715) through James Barry's *Inquiry into the Real and Imaginary Obstructions to the Acquisition of the Arts in England* (1775) and Reynolds's *Discourses* (1769–90; pub. 1797), English theorists continued to worry the question, as they self-consciously set out to elevate the ambitions of the nation's painters by clearly subordinating the "mechanical" elements of their activity to the intellectual. Though there were notable differences among them, and Reynolds's own attitudes shifted subtly over the course of his career,[40] they broadly shared in a common enterprise—an enterprise that necessarily entailed keeping Dutch pictures in their place.

To show that painting conveyed "Ideas," according to Richardson, was to show that it qualified as a "Language"—"one of those particulars which raises the Dignity of Human Nature so much above the Brutes"—while "those Employments are Servile, and Mechanical, in which Bodily Strength, or Ability, is only, or chiefly required," because "in such cases the Man approaches more to the Brute, or has fewer of those Qualities that exalt Mankind above other Animals."[41] It is easy to see how the "low" subjects of Dutch painting—especially those that appeared to reduce people themselves to the animal-like—could serve to reinforce this hierarchy.

Certainly Ruskin was not afraid of driving home the analogy: "No effort of fancy will enable me to lay hold of the temper of Teniers, or Wouvermans, any more than I can enter into the feelings of one of the lower animals. . . . All their life and work is the same sort of mystery to me as the mind of my dog when he rolls on carrion" (7:363).[42] Yet even characteristics that might seem anything but brutish, such as the meticulous detail of Dutch pictures, had their place in the argument. If pictorial "ideas" required a process of generalizing and abstracting, as neoclassicists like Reynolds contended, then an abundance of detail potentially signified an absence of mental work: rather than engage in what Reynolds termed the "real labour,—the labour of thinking," the painter who attends too closely to the local and the particular settles for the "mere mechanical labour of copying."[43] While the great artist seeks to uncover the "universal Nature" that all men have in common, the lesser one contents himself with mindlessly imitating what is immediately around him. After making clear that "Painting must lose its rank, and be no longer considered as a liberal art" if its excellence depended only on the imitation of nature, Reynolds set out in an early letter to the *Idler* (1759) to classify the Italians and the Dutch in these terms:

> The Italian attends only to the invariable, the great, and general ideas which are fixed and inherent in universal Nature; the Dutch, on the contrary, to literal truth and a minute exactness in the detail, as I may say, of Nature modified by accident. The attention to these petty particularities is the very cause of this naturalness so much admired in the Dutch pictures, which, if we suppose it to be a beauty, is certainly of a lower order, that ought to give place to a beauty of a superior kind, since one cannot be obtained but by departing from the other.[44]

Though he would soften the starkness of this contrast in his later writing, especially after his journey to Holland and Flanders in 1781, he never really abandoned its fundamental logic. Just as the third Discourse (1770) begins by announcing that "a mere copier of nature can never produce any thing great" and instructs the student to "permit the lower painter . . . to exhibit the minute discriminations, which distinguish one object of the same species from another [,] while he, like the philosopher, will consider nature in the abstract," so the thirteenth (1786) contends, even more drastically, that painting "is, and ought to be . . . strictly speaking, no imitation at all of external nature." Indeed, "so far therefore is servile imitation from being necessary," the same Discourse remarks apropos of a painting by Jan Steen, "that whatever is familiar, or in any way reminds us of what we see and hear every day, perhaps does not belong to the higher provinces of art, either in poetry or painting."[45]

For Reynolds and other neoclassicists, even the mastery of color for which the Dutch and Flemish were famous paradoxically confirmed their inferior status. The principle that "it is not the eye, it is the mind, which the painter of genius desires to address" meant that color was classed among the "merely ornamental" aspects of painting, its sensuous appeal duly subordinated to the intellectual pleasures of design.[46] As Dryden had already put it when he translated *De Arte Graphica* into "plain *English*": "Colouring" is "*The Bawd of her Sister*, the Design or Drawing."[47] In this respect, the Netherlandish painters were often grouped with the Venetians (as opposed to the Tuscans and the Romans), while the reputation of both peoples as traders intensified their association with a debasing and potentially feminizing luxury.

Though Ruskin, too, had no use for Dutch colors, this was one judgment he emphatically did not share. For the great champion of Turner—and the ardent admirer of Titian—color was no seductive accessory but "the purifying or sanctifying element of material beauty" (7:417n); and despite a passing swipe at "the vulgar vermilion of the Dutch" (so different, in his eyes, from "*Venetian* red"—15:421), he was more likely to deplore the "grayness and shininess" of their canvases or the brown tones he attributed to excessive application of varnish (7:364; 15:138n). (In fact, it was the discoloration of the varnish over time that produced the effect he deplored.)[48] Yet for all his quarrels with Reynolds, the terms in which Ruskin denigrated the Dutch were remarkably similar to those he had inherited. He may have insisted on educating the eye to look closely rather than to abstract and generalize, but he "never . . . ceased to rate the Dutch painters for their meanness or minuteness," as he himself noted (7:54). Just as Reynolds had contended that "some inferior dexterity, some extraordinary mechanical power is apparently that from which they seek distinction,"[49] so Ruskin complained that "the object of the great body of them is merely to display manual dexterities of one kind or another" (3:188); and even more than Reynolds, he persisted in identifying the Dutch with "mechanics" and "mechanism" rather than thought (3:90, 7:54, 57, 364). The first volume of *Modern Painters* dismissed Ruisdael on the grounds "that there appears no exertion of mind in any of his works" (3:517), while the fifth generically summed up "a Dutch painter" as "a respectable tradesman furnishing well-made articles in oil paint" (7:364).

A tradesman is not usually a man who works at a trade: Ruskin's slur characteristically confounds the former identification of the painter as craftsman with the stereotype of the Dutch as traders, as if to remove even the dignity of manual labor from those "well-made articles in oil paint." Indeed, to the degree to which he wished not to denigrate manual work but to encourage it, Ruskin's contempt for the "manual dexterities" of the Dutch may seem self-contradictory. If Dutch painters are "vulgar" in his view—as they unquestionably are—it cannot simply be because they work with their hands. Like many nineteenth-century writers, Ruskin retained the old status terms while attempting to redefine them; and neither his account of "vulgarity" nor of its predictable opposite, "gentlemanliness," is wholly consistent. According to the chapter on the subject that precedes his final treatment of the Dutch in *Modern Painters*, "a true gentleman" is one who "feels rightly on all occasions," while "vulgarity resolves itself into want of sensibility" (7:349)—a distinction that may seem to have relatively little to do with the aesthetic judgments that follow. But by insisting that vulgarity in "its essential, pure, and most fatal form" is the "inability to feel or conceive noble character or emotion" (7:359–60), and by repeatedly associating the insensible with matter divorced from spirit, Ruskin is able to arrive at his most sweeping claim: the "vulgarity" of Dutch painting is that of a world from which God has been utterly banished. While a faint recollection of "spiritual thought" still lingers in some pictures by Rembrandt and Rubens, in the "pastoral landscape" of the Dutch—which here seems to mean both landscape and genre—"not only all faith in religion, but all remembrance of it" has disappeared. Even by Ruskin's standards, the prophetic vehemence of his rhetoric is stunning:

> Absolutely now at last we find ourselves without sight of God in all the world.
>
> So far as I can hear or read, this is an entirely new and wonderful state of things achieved by the Hollanders. The human being never got wholly quit of the terror of spiritual being before. Persian, Egyptian, Assyrian, Hindoo, Chinese, all kept some dim, appalling record of what they called "gods." Farthest savages had—and still have—their Great Spirit, or, in extremity, their feather-idols, large-eyed; but here in Holland we have at last got utterly done with it all. Our only idol glitters dimly, in tangible shape of a pint pot, and all the incense offered thereto, comes out of a small censer or bowl at the end of a pipe. "Of deities or virtues, angels, principalities, or powers, in the name of our ditches, no more. Let us have cattle and market vegetables." (7:331–32)

As an account of religious belief in seventeenth-century Holland, this is clearly a travesty; but as a reductio ad absurdum of the theoretical resistance to Dutch painting it is nonetheless revealing. Though neoclassical theorists were more apt to speak of the artist's ideas than of his spiritual terrors, they too identified "high" art with an effort to transcend the material world. So Winckelmann had characterized the artist's general ideas as "raised above the reach of mortality" and "exalted above the pitch of material models," while Reynolds had described the arts in their "highest province" as addressed not "to the gross senses, but to the desires of the mind"—what he tellingly termed "that spark of divinity which we have within, impatient of being circumscribed and pent up by the world which is about us."[50] To the extent that the "low" genres of Dutch painting were thought to lack such evidence of divinity, they were necessarily associated, by contrast, with the material and the mortal.[51] Neither Reynolds nor Winckelmann specifically identified that painting with death, yet there is a sense in which Ruskin was only following out their logic when he called Dutch artists "unspiritual or deathful" and condemned the "whole school" as "inherently mortal to all its admirers" (7:369)—a phrase that characteristically refuses to distinguish between a loss of visual discrimination and the death of the soul. Ruskin surely knew that there was more to Dutch painting than "cattle and market vegetables," but the phrase devastatingly sums ups his account of a pictorial tradition in which the only life that remains is the domesticated stuff of consumption and trade.

The sheer extravagance of Ruskin's rhetoric helps to clarify what had long been at stake in the contempt for Dutch art. But it also testifies to his sense of embattlement—his keen awareness that popular taste at midcentury was largely against him. From the landscapes of Thomas Gainsborough to the genre paintings of David Wilkie—hailed by his contemporaries as "the British Teniers"—the Netherlandish influence on nineteenth-century British artists and viewers alike was inescapable. In the last volume of *Modern Painters* (1860), Ruskin dated the beginning of that influence to a period some seventy years earlier (7:369); and although he did not specify what he had in mind, he was presumably thinking of the great flood of Netherlandish painting that had begun to enter the country from French collections in the wake of the Revolution and the Napoleonic Wars. Those years were in fact a high-point for British acquisition of Dutch art, as wealthy purchasers like Sir Robert Peel and the Prince Regent—"whose exclusive predilection for pictures of the Dutch and Flemish schools," in Anna Jameson's phrase, "is well known"—amassed the great collections that still form the core of the nation's public holdings in the area.[52] (Peel's son sold his father's collection to the National Gallery in 1871.) But as Hogarth's attack on

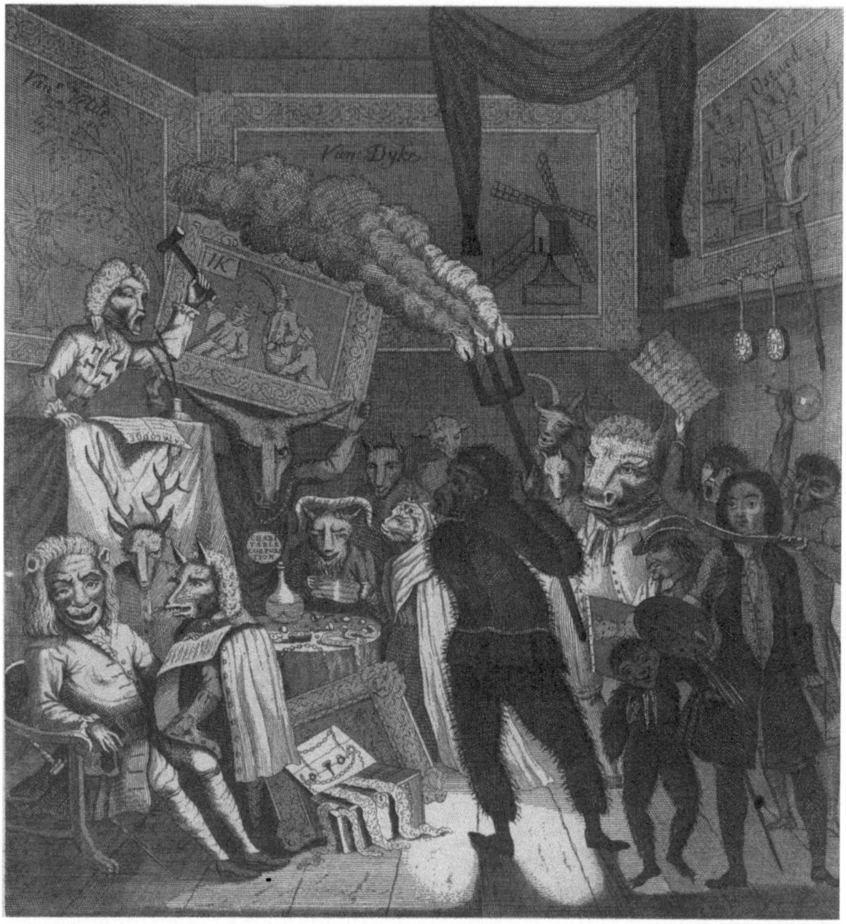

Figure 2-5. Anon.: *Satire on Picture Auctions*, c. 1766. Lewis Walpole Library, Yale University

"the true Dutch taste" in 1751 would suggest, the popular appeal of Dutch pictures in Britain significantly antedated the nineteenth century.[53] A pair of anonymous prints from 1758 and 1766, both of them satires of contemporary art auctions, make clear that "the various Van somethings," in Ruskin's contemptuous phrase, were already being eagerly bought and sold in mid-eighteenth-century England (figs. 2-5 and 2-6).[54] (Note how the partly legible signatures on the image above visibly anticipate Ruskin's anathema.) And despite the efforts of the satirists—not to mention the arguments of Reynolds and others—the appetite for such art showed no signs of abating. A year before the first volume of *Modern Painters* appeared in 1843, the art dealer John Smith had issued the last of his massive nine-volume *Catalogue*

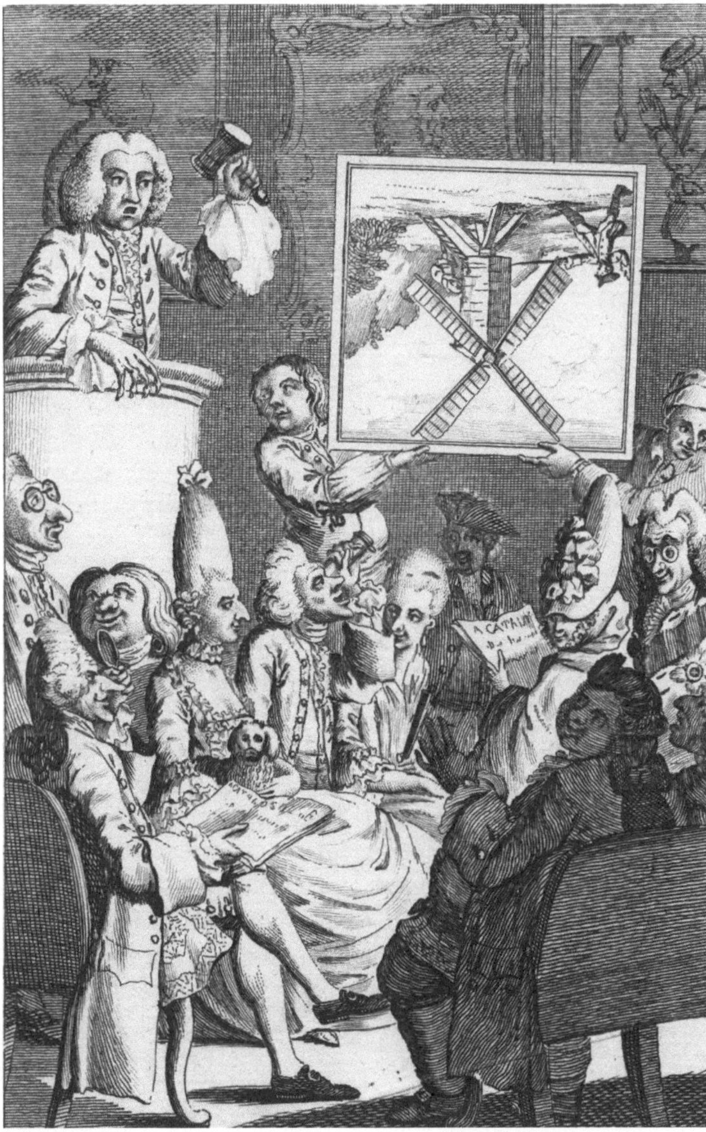

Figure 2-6. Anon.: *The Auction, or Modern Connoisseurs*, from *Oxford Magazine*, 1758. Lewis Walpole Library, Yale University

Raisonnée of the Works of the Most Eminent Dutch, Flemish, and French Painters (1829–42)—a work that simultaneously reflected contemporary taste and served to consolidate it. Smith's own first volume had begun in 1829 by pointedly noting how "Pictures of the first class of the DUTCH AND FLEMISH SCHOOLS have constantly increased in value."[55] Ruskin was not the only dissenter: Hazlitt scathingly attributed George IV's "exclusive predilection" for Northern art to its lack of any ideas that would challenge his complacency.[56] But such objections do not seem to have significantly affected the popular appeal of Dutch pictures. In a late lecture of 1883, Ruskin himself was forced to conclude that all the energy he had devoted to "vituperating" them had been "vain." The "brown daubs" of the Dutch were still "hung in the best rooms of the National Gallery," he reported sadly, while "the loveliest Turner drawings" were confined to the cellar (33:289–90).

What Harry Mount has aptly termed "the conflicting estimations of Netherlandish art offered by theory and the market" were similarly evident in France,[57] though the vogue for Dutch and Flemish art seems to have gotten under way there even earlier than in Britain, and to have conquered the theoretical resistance more thoroughly. Unlike the English, who came late to history painting and to the theory that justified it—and were all the more defensive about low genres as a consequence—the French elite seem to have partly tired of the neoclassical hierarchy by the beginning of the eighteenth century, without explicitly formulating a system to replace it.[58] Most modern commentators agree that the hegemony of the French Academy had seriously weakened by the time that soldiers returning from the wars in Flanders in the first decades of the century helped to stimulate a new interest in Northern painting.[59] Rapidly disseminated through engravings,[60] the popularity of Dutch and Flemish painting was widely acknowledged to have surpassed that of the Italians by midcentury, even by those who continued to deplore the phenomenon.[61] The appearance of Jean-Baptiste Descamps' influential guide to Northern art, *La vie des peintres flamands, allemands et hollandois* (1753–64), testified to the demand, as did the increasing prices for Dutch genre, which rose steadily on both sides of the Channel. By the later decades of the eighteenth century, works by favorites like Dou and Teniers were among the most expensive on the market.[62] (At one French sale in 1777, for example, a small grocer's scene by Dou went for more than double the price of a half-length St. Peter by Guido Reni.)[63] And collectors were hardly the only ones to respond to the appeal of Dutch painting. In a *pensée* published after his death, Diderot famously remarked that he "would give ten Watteaus for one Teniers"—a preference for "rusticity" over "delicacy" that nonetheless obscures the degree to which the Flemish-born Watteau had himself helped transport Northern styles to France.[64] Then as now, the debt of Chardin and Greuze to Netherlandish genre painters was still more obvious, even if commentators like Raynal chose to emphasize the Frenchmen's alleged refinement of their predecessors.[65] Well before Wilkie became known as the British

Teniers, the French were already bestowing their version of the honorific on all three artists—not to mention several painters less familiar to modern viewers.[66]

Where Dutch painting was concerned, in other words, the practice of admiring, collecting, and imitating was long at odds with theory—even, in some cases, for the theorists themselves.[67] Walpole may have fulminated against "those drudging Mimics of Nature's most uncomely coarsenesses," but the family collection he was describing included a substantial number of Netherlandish pictures.[68] More tellingly, almost a third of the works in Reynolds's own collection were by Dutch and Flemish artists.[69] Responding with comparative sympathy to such pictures on his journey to Flanders and Holland in 1781, Reynolds himself suggested that their attraction was especially difficult to put into words, as if the very medium of theory militated against them. "One would wish to be able to convey to the reader some idea of that excellence, the sight of which has afforded so much pleasure," he wrote in his record of that journey; "but as their merit often consists in the truth of representation alone, whatever praise they deserve, whatever pleasure they give when under the eye, they make but a poor figure in description." The examples he offers are "A MARKET-WOMAN with a hare in her hand, a man blowing a trumpet, or a boy blowing bubbles, a view of the inside or outside of a church"; and the implicit contrast, as always, is with history painting and with Italy. "Painters should go to the Dutch school to learn the art of painting," Reynolds concludes, but "they must go to Italy to learn the higher branches of knowledge."[70]

"It is to the eye only that the works of this school are addressed," Reynolds wrote; and even as neoclassical theory proved increasingly obsolete in the century that followed, something very like this equivocal praise would continue to echo in partial defense of Dutch art.[71] For some commentators, the technical virtuosity of Dutch painters partly redeemed their unacceptable subjects: the same William Collins who characterized those subjects as "gross, vulgar, and filthy" conceded that "notwithstanding these objections," the Dutch were "most profoundly skilled in the great technical beauties and difficulties" of their art—a contradiction he resolved by contending that only painters like himself had "legitimate" grounds for admiring them.[72] Though Anna Jameson understood Reynolds to have similarly intended his remarks for "the eye of a *painter*," she was willing to extend such visual pleasure to the "cultivated . . . amateur" as well. Her 1844 *Companion* to the private galleries of London directly quotes from Reynolds's *Journey* before going on to note "the contrast between the burlesque, low comedy, and sometimes utter vulgarity" of a Teniers, and "the *spirituel* elegance of the treatment," or to observe of Nicolaes Maes's *Young Girl Peeling Apples* (plate 2) that "the beauty of the treatment redeems the triviality of the subject."[73]

Others went further, and attempted to argue that the visual appeal of Dutch art virtually made its subject matter irrelevant. Early in the century, Richard Payne Knight sought to explain how we can be delighted with a painted "copy" when "we should, perhaps, turn away with disgust and abhorrence from the original" by suggesting that the Netherlandish painters had managed to separate qualities "pleasing to the eye" from the "otherwise offensive" aspects of what they painted. Taking for granted that the pictures of Rembrandt, Ostade, Teniers, and Fyt (the seventeenth-century Flemish painter, Jan Fyt) were "unquestionably beautiful and pleasing to all mankind," despite their faithful imitation of unpleasant things, Payne Knight concluded that "in these copies, the mind perceives only the visible qualities; whereas, in the originals, it perceived others less agreeable united with them."[74] While the popularity of narrative painting among the Victorians meant that most British critics would continue to talk about a picture's subject as much—or more—than its "visible qualities,"[75] some notable voices on the Continent began to celebrate Dutch art for its pictorial virtues alone. The influential lectures on art that Hegel delivered in the 1820s are often credited with helping to advance this purely aesthetic view of Dutch painting; and though Hegel himself is hardly consistent in this regard—at some moments, for example, he defends the subjects of Dutch pictures as expressions of the "freedom and joyfulness" of the citizens who painted them—he is certainly capable of seeming to value the school for its technique alone. "And in fact if we want to know what painting is," he says of the Dutch at one point, "we must examine these little pictures in order to say of this or that master: *He* can paint." The same lecture brushes aside a catalogue of subjects that extends from grapes and flowers to smoking, teeth-extraction, and "domestic scenes of the most varied kind" on the grounds that "the world provides us with plenty of things like this. What should enchant us is not the subject of the painting and its lifelikeness, but the pure appearance which is wholly without the sort of interest that the subject has."[76] Whether or not Eugène Fromentin knew these lectures—they had been translated into French by the middle of the century—a similar attention to "pure appearance" governed the well-known account of Dutch and Flemish art that he published in 1876. According to *Les maîtres d'autrefois*, one of the first things that strikes a student of Dutch art is "the total absence of what we now call *a subject*"—by which he means, Fromentin makes clear, not "this vast company of genre scenes" but a major event in ancient or modern history. In his much-quoted formula, "the great Dutch School appeared to think of nothing but painting well. It was content to look around it and to dispense with imagination."[77]

It is hardly surprising that such equivocal praise still remains controversial among scholars of seventeenth-century painting.[78] Hegel may have been prepared to celebrate "appearance for its own sake" in Dutch art, but he also presumed that "there are higher, more ideal, materials than the representation of such joy and bourgeois excellence in what are always inherently insignificant details," as he put it; and he never clearly abandoned the view that "the higher art will be that which has as its task the representation of this higher content."[79] Fromentin's sympathetic attention to the Dutch painters was more sustained, but for all the words he spent on them, "to think of nothing but painting well" comes perilously close in his account to not thinking at all. Very little separates his claim that "Holland has imagined nothing, but she has painted miraculously well,"[80] from Reynolds's belief that "it is to the eye only that the works of this school are addressed"; and both verdicts scarcely alter the old hierarchy whereby the mental heights belong to Italy, while the Dutch remain content with the sensory lowlands.

But perhaps the most enthusiastic advocate of Dutch painting in the nineteenth century was determined on a more radical reversal of the traditions he had inherited. For Théophile Thoré, writing under the resonant pseudonym of William Bürger, the art of seventeenth-century Holland was, "quite simply, ART FOR MAN," as he triumphantly closed the first of his two volumes on the Dutch school in 1858; and it was in every way the equal of those Italian masterworks that had long set the standard by which works of painting were judged.[81] Thoré, who began his career as a left-wing journalist and art critic, had adopted his pseudonym after his exile from France for political activity in 1849—Bürger of course means "citizen" or "freeman" in German—and throughout his writing on Dutch art, this self-proclaimed freeman identified that art with the liberation of mankind from the rule of court and church alike.[82] (The "William" probably testifies to the same Anglophilia that elsewhere prompted a tribute to the "genius" of the "Anglo-Saxon race.")[83] Best known today for his recovery of a hitherto obscure Johannes Vermeer in a pair of pioneering articles that appeared in 1866, Thoré-Bürger preceded his work on the "sphinx" of Delft with two volumes on the museums of Holland, published in 1858 and 1860, that meticulously catalogued and commented on their collections. Yet even as he discriminated individual paintings and painters from one another—an act that itself, as we shall see, significantly countered the old practice of treating them all as one—he left no doubt that he sought to rescue the school as a whole from the "traditional orthodoxy" that had condemned it. The true subject of *Musées de la Hollande* is the "singular" achievement of the Dutch—an achievement Thoré-Bürger consistently associated with the political and religious liberty of the people (1:xi).

Like so many before him, Thoré-Bürger often turned to the art of Renaissance Italy for comparison; but unlike his predecessors, he strenuously opposed the generic hierarchy that had kept Dutch painting in its place, even as he opposed the political and economic hierarchies the aesthetic ranking reflected. "Catholic Italy made its gods and heroes," he characteristically remarked in defense of Ostade. "Let us permit Holland to make for us a few men and tramps [bohémians]" (1:92). Instead of representing "popes and princes," he contended, the Dutch had for their models "rough sailors, brave musketeers, unpretentious burgomasters, honest and cheerful workers, the crowd, everyone, in a land of equality. And no doubt their persons are as alive as any painted prince whatsoever" (2:xiv). Even when he was looking at what a twentieth-century scholar would describe as "one of the most vivid images of dissipation and indulgence ever painted,"[84] Thoré-Bürger refused to concede that the old distinctions of high and low were at issue. "I grant that its subject is a little improper," he says of the picture by Jan Steen that he calls the *Orgy* (2:115), and which is now generally known as the *Drunken Couple* (plate 3). (As he dryly notes, John Smith, with "sa décence anglaise," called it simply *The Toast*—2:114.) But rather than suggest that technique alone redeems an otherwise scabrous subject, he offers an ironic analogy to the images of "sensual love" that constitute a "favorite theme of the whole Latin Renaissance":

> Leonardo, Raphael, Titian, Carracci and the others, while they were all creating Madonnas, Holy Families and Martyrs, continued the cult of Aphrodite, Danaë, Leda, Omphale, Europa—and Ganymede also! there's an orthodox one! Would it be the complete nudity of the figures that saves the virtue of these noble artists? To glorify Venus, is it necessary to remove her veils? Did Jan Steen do wrong to leave his courtesan a red stocking and not remove her petticoat? Yes, that's doubtless what betrays the immorality.
>
> Seriously, since all is permitted to the *ideal* and to allegory, let's leave them alone, on the moral issue, these good Hollanders who

> care little for the hieroglyphics of pagan or Catholic mythology, and who paint, quite simply, human life. (2:115–16)

Though modern scholars often complain that the discovery of Dutch "realism" in the nineteenth century meant the loss of its moral significance, Thoré-Bürger has no trouble recognizing the didactic character of Steen's picture—which is summed up, as he notes, by the emblem-like inscription being unveiled by the female musician to the right. ("Of what use are a candle and glasses / Since the owl doesn't want to see?"). He even mischievously terms Steen "more severe" than Poussin (2:116). But there is no question that what he values in this and other Dutch paintings is less the moral instruction they provide than their vivid representation of what he calls—again "quite simply"—"human life."

In an historicist move typical of nineteenth-century progressives, Thoré-Bürger dealt with the conflict between classical theory and Dutch practice by substituting the horizon of time for the vertical ranking of genres: rather than discriminate between high and low, he chose to speak of past and future, or—a distinction he often treats as synonymous—of death and life. From this perspective, the art of the Italian Renaissance, however magnificent, belonged to the past. "Life was blazing out in Holland; why set out for the home of the dead?" he characteristically writes of the Italianate painting of the Utrecht-born Cornelis Poelenburgh: "Poor great Italy had accomplished its work" (1:145–46). An extended comparison of Raphael's *School of Athens* with Rembrandt's *Anatomy Lesson* concludes by relegating the former to the realm of myth and death, while the painting of a corpse proves, paradoxically, an image of life itself: "The object of painting is natural life, not the abstract idea, hypothetical and illusory, but the idea incarnated in a pulsing form, the idea incorporated, *imbodied* [*sic*], as the English say" (1:204). Recounting how he had been continually haunted by the artistic conflict between North and South until he happened upon a pair of opposite-facing pictures in an illustrated magazine, the second volume of *Musées de la Hollande* offers a visual emblem for the historicist solution he proposes: a Janus-like double *R*, signifying Raphael and Rembrandt, respectively—their monograms forever back-to-back as their magazine portraits have placed them (fig. 2-7).

> As for those two, are they not, in effect, the Janus of art? Raphael looks back; Rembrandt looks ahead. The one saw an abstract humanity, under the symbols of Venus and the Virgin, of Apollo and

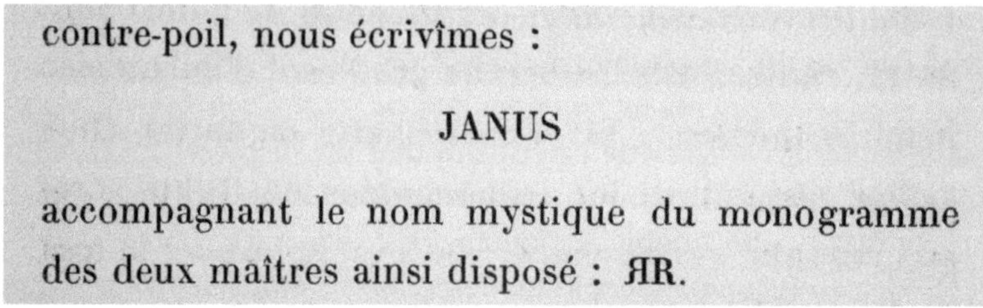

contre-poil, nous écrivîmes :

JANUS

accompagnant le nom mystique du monogramme des deux maîtres ainsi disposé : ЯR.

Figure 2-7. Janus figure for Raphael and Rembrandt, from W. Bürger [Théophile Thoré], *Musées de la Hollande*, vol. 2 (Paris: Jules Renouard, 1860)

> Christ; the other looked directly, and with his own eyes, at a real and living humanity. One is the past, the other, the future. (2:x)

While other schools were dominated by a few masters and their followers, the particular merit of the Dutch school, in Thoré-Bürger's eyes, was precisely its absence of hierarchy. Seventeenth-century Holland had "the unique privilege," as he put it, of having produced "more than a dozen artists," each "perfect" in his own way, and none in any sense subordinate to the others (1:79)—a situation that could only have developed in "a land of free thought, where imaginations, like minds and consciences, have an absolute independence" (1:80). "Each has his original character and personal style" (1:79); and rather than rank them, Thoré-Bürger prefers to identify and celebrate that distinctiveness. When he occasionally lapses—confessing, for example, that he finds Wouwerman, "for all his qualities, not absolutely at the same height" as the principal figures—he immediately catches himself: "Bah! all these hierarchies in painting signify nothing" (1:126).[85] Later, in his study of Vermeer, he would reach for a neologism to express the same vision:

> In other schools, there is a hierarchy. The Dutch school is a *panarchy*, if one may be permitted to speak thus. In Holland, each painter is a *master*, in whatever genre he demonstrates his distinctiveness. Brower and the Ostades, Both, Berchem and du Jardin, Paul Potter, Gerrit Dou, Albert Cuyp and van der Neer, van Goyen and Wynants, de Heem and Hondecoeter, van der Heyden, Wouwerman, the van de Veldes, Ruisdael and Hobbema, ter Borch and Metsu, Pieter de Hooch, Jan Steen, and how many others, are perfectly masters, each according to his own species, just as much as Rembrandt and Frans Hals. Lion, eagle, butterfly, oak, violet, ruby, emerald—all have equal title in creation.

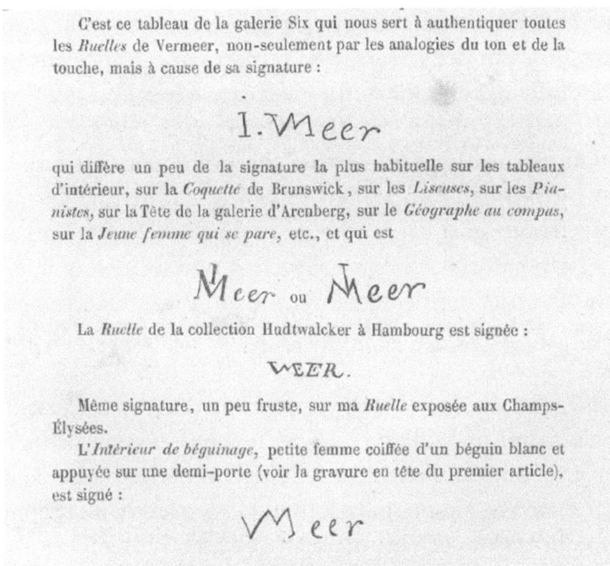
C'est ce tableau de la galerie Six qui nous sert à authentiquer toutes les *Ruelles* de Vermeer, non-seulement par les analogies du ton et de la touche, mais à cause de sa signature :

I. Meer

qui diffère un peu de la signature la plus habituelle sur les tableaux d'intérieur, sur la *Coquette* de Brunswick, sur les *Liseuses*, sur les *Pianistes*, sur la Tête de la galerie d'Arenberg, sur le *Géographe au compas*, sur la *Jeune femme qui se pare*, etc., et qui est

Meer ou Meer

La *Ruelle* de la collection Hudtwalcker à Hambourg est signée :

MEER.

Même signature, un peu fruste, sur ma *Ruelle* exposée aux Champs-Élysées.

L'*Intérieur de béguinage*, petite femme coiffée d'un béguin blanc et appuyée sur une demi-porte (voir la gravure en tête du premier article), est signé :

Meer

Figure 2-8. Vermeer signatures, from W. Bürger [Théophile Thoré], "Van Meer de Delft," *Gazette des beaux-arts* (1866)

For Thoré-Bürger, to recover Vermeer from obscurity is simultaneously to distinguish his hand from that of others and to admit him into this egalitarian company: "It is necessary, if you please, that we accept Vermeer of Delft into this pléiade of the Dutch 'little masters,' and as their equal. Like them, he is naturally original, and that which he has made is perfect."[86]

Though the study of Vermeer is particularly obsessed with identifying that hand as it signed itself on a painting—going so far as to reproduce the various marks of the autograph directly on the page (fig. 2-8)—nothing more consistently characterizes Thoré-Bürger's method throughout his work on Dutch art than his attentiveness to the individual signature, both in the sense of personal style and in that of the proper name the painter has actually inscribed on the canvas. While Ruskin deliberately refuses to distinguish between one "Van something" and another, Thoré-Bürger is perpetually in search of the individualizing mark. And his zeal is all the greater, it seems, because the names of so many Dutch painters do at first look alike, whether because the profession of artist has descended, as it often did, in the family (as in the brothers Ostade, Adriaen and Isack, or the four van der Weldes, including two Willems, father and son); or because the surname of one turns out to be the first name of the other, like two of the "Victors" he distinguishes in *Musées de la Hollande* (2:40); or simply because several different painters happen to share the same name, as in the four "distinct" Jan van der Meers, two of them also father and son, among whom he carefully differentiates the "Van der Meer de Delft" we know as Vermeer.[87] In defense of this practice, *Musées de la Hollande* even manages to suggest that it is really Italian rather than Dutch art that all looks alike: so much do the works of an Italian school resemble one another, Thoré-Bürger implies, that most cannot be given a proper name, and attributions even to the best-known artists nonetheless remain disputable. Once the hand of a Dutch artist has been recognized, on the contrary, it can never be misconstrued: "the *Dropsical Woman* is entirely Gerrit Dou's, and not at all someone else's" (1:80).

Thoré-Bürger was not the only nineteenth-century commentator to associate the character of Holland's art with the liberation of its people. He himself may have been influenced by Hegel's remarks on the "spiritual freedom" that the newly emancipated Dutch registered in their painting,[88] though his conception of seventeenth-century Holland probably owed more to the recent appearance of John Lothrop Motley's *Rise of the Dutch Republic* (1855), with its celebratory narrative of the nation's revolt from Spanish rule.[89] Peter Demetz has suggested that in the wake of the July Revolution, French writers in particular looked to the Dutch as "heralds of a republican and realist age";[90] and both Taine and Fromentin would soon follow Thoré-Bürger in identifying Holland's achievement in art with its successful resistance to despotism. An important corollary of such political accounts was a new attentiveness to the differences between Dutch art and Flemish: unlike earlier commentators, who tended to treat the schools as identical, those who believed they saw in Dutch painting the visible results of Holland's liberation from Spain were more inclined to distinguish its free and Protestant art from one that still reflected the influence of monarchy and Catholicism. Despite a title that evokes the Netherlands as a whole, Taine's *Philosophie de l'art dans les Pays-Bas* (1869) would suggest that the wars of independence ended by cutting both nation and art "in two,"[91] while Fromentin would devote separate sections of *Les maîtres d'autrefois* to the painters of Belgium and Holland. But no one was more insistent on this distinction than Thoré-Bürger, who concluded the first volume of *Musées de la Hollande* by characterizing the "abyss" that opened between the two peoples after the separation of 1579: "Rubens was among the conquered and the slaves; Rembrandt, among the conquerors and the free men. There is above all the difference in their geniuses" (1:320, 321). The long-standing association of Dutch painting with "servile" imitation may have originated in a very different idea of slavery, but Thoré-Bürger's radical inversion of the old topos is nonetheless striking. From this perspective, the truly "free" artist is not one who aristocratically improves upon nature but one who is himself free from the rule of aristocrats.

Thoré-Bürger's defense of Dutch art, needless to say, is hardly impartial. The tendentious arithmetic by which Holland outproduces "even the most fecund" of other schools when it comes to masters, for example, depends on counting not the Italian school as a whole but Florentines and Venetians separately—a tactic that keeps Leonardo and Michelangelo in one group, Titian and Tintoretto in another, and makes no mention of Raphael (1:79). Despite Thoré-Bürger's insistence on the utter distinctiveness of Dutch hands, subsequent scholarship would inevitably correct a number of his own attributions, including, most famously, some enthusiastic—but erroneous—identifications of Vermeer. Nor was he above exploiting the market to drive home his argument. His paean to the artistic individuality "inherent in a land of free thought" concludes by announcing that it is this very distinctiveness of Dutch paintings that has helped to account for their rise in price—the relevant comparison, of course, being with those doubtfully attributed Italian pictures, which could easily prove a poor investment: "One does not willingly give a hundred thousand francs for a picture which could be an imitation of a school, or a copy" (1:80).[92] Indeed that "land of free thought" itself constitutes an oversimplification almost as sweeping as "the faithless and materialized mind of modern Europe" with which Ruskin (7:327), writing at the same moment, associated his dramatically different account of Dutch art. Like Ruskin's vulgarly secularized Holland, Thoré-Bürger's gloriously liberated one represents a partial truth at best, even if it virtually mirrors the other's version of the historical record.

Though Thoré-Bürger seems to have known Ruskin's work, there is no evidence that he had the English critic in mind when he set out to counter those who chose to "anathematize" the "originality" of the Dutch in 1858 (1:xi).[93] (The second volume of *Musées de la Hollande* appeared in 1860, the same year as the last of *Modern Painters*.) But it would be hard to think of a more thoroughgoing reversal of all that was implied in Ruskin's hypothetical consignment of "the various Van somethings and Back somethings" to the flames than the argument and practice of this French contemporary. Even on a rare occasion when they happened to see with the same eyes, their conflicting ideas of Dutch art yielded radically different verdicts. Though both recorded their revulsion at the composition and coloring of Rubens's *Juno and Argus* (especially the sprawling of the decapitated corpse across the right foreground of the picture; fig. 2-9), Thoré-Bürger predictably attributed its weaknesses to the "bad influence" of Italy, while

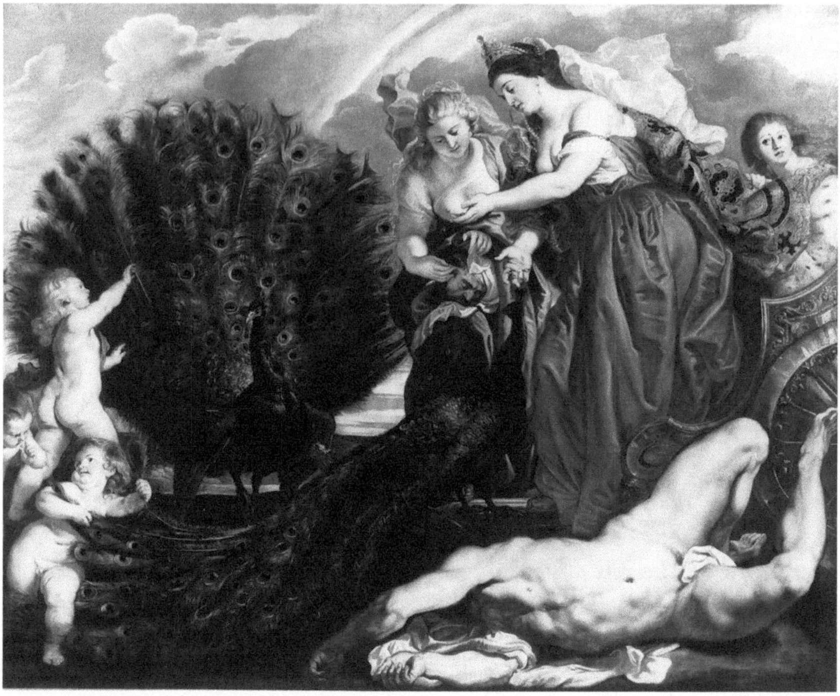

Figure 2-9. Peter Paul Rubens: *Juno and Argus*, c. 1611. Wallraf-Richartz Museum, Cologne. Photo Credit: Rheinisches Bildarchiv

Ruskin—just as predictably—decreed the opposite: "In the fleshly baseness, brutality and stupidity of its main conception, is the Dutch part of it; that is Rubens' own."[94] Between his Flemish birth and his Italian training, Rubens is especially vulnerable to this sort of nationalist stylistics; and while both critics grudgingly admired his achievement, neither was in any case particularly drawn to his work. Nor was a history painting on the grand scale of *Juno and Argus* what either usually meant by Dutch art. It is on the low genres—on the very idea of the low, in fact—that they sound both more characteristic and more revealing. When Ruskin wrote that "a Dutchman can be just as solemnly and entirely contemplative of a lemon pip and a cheese paring, as an Italian of the Virgin in Glory" (23:326), he took the ontological gap between pips and Virgins pretty much for granted, but Thoré-Bürger delighted in upending such assumptions. If *Musées de la Hollande* says nothing of Virgins and lemons, it more than once compares an Italian Madonna to a Dutch chicken—contending that the celebrated bird-painter, Melchior d'Hondecoeter, for example, "has expressed the maternity of hens as well as Raphael that of virgins": "We have there, by Hondecoeter, a mother hen who would brave the *Madonna in Her Chair* for tenderness." Elsewhere it declares a hen and chicks by Jacomo Victor preferable to a Bolognese *Mater dolorosa*—the bird in question being at once "more simple and less deceptive" (1:161; 2:316).

For Thoré-Bürger, such comparisons were not merely mischievous. Nor were they simply the result of cheerful anthropomorphizing, though he evidently liked to recognize human emotions in the various animals and birds his beloved artists had depicted on canvas. "Life" and its variants are nearly as central to Thoré-Bürger's lexicon as "man"—and "life" as he sees it is evident everywhere in Dutch painting, even when no living creature, strictly speaking, appears in the picture. The discussion of Victor's bird paintings in the second volume of *Musées de la Hollande* is immediately followed by a treatment of what the French call *nature morte*, but here as throughout his writing on the Dutch school, Thoré-Bürger insists that his countrymen's term for the genre is badly mistaken: "*Nature morte* est absurde" (2:317). His report on the Manchester Exhibition of 1857 had already declared a preference for the English term "still life," and though he did not explicitly say so, he was well aware that this was much closer to the Dutch original—*stilleven* also being a term he would sometimes employ instead of, or in addition to, the French.[95] But it is not so much linguistic accuracy that seems to have moved him as the conviction, to quote the Manchester book, that "il n'y a rien de mort dans la nature": "there is no death in nature."[96] The second volume of *Musées de la Hollande* elaborates this claim in a lengthy passage that begins, reasonably enough, by defending the life of flowers, only to end with Ovidian metamorphosis and something very like pantheism:

> Do flowers not live? They have their respiration and their health; they are cheerful and brilliant, or sad and dull; they move ceaselessly, if almost imperceptibly, turning themselves toward the light, turning aside to permit treacherous branches to pass, they sag under the influence of dryness, swell and bloom under the caress of a ray. Flowers are not *nature morte*! There is no dead nature.
>
> Everything lives and everything moves, everything aspires or expires, everything transforms itself at each instant. Everything takes or gives something around itself, modifying its environment, with an irresistible perseverance, at the same time as its own life. Everything communicates with everything and participates in the collective life [*la vie solidaire*]. There is no dead nature!

> The wine in this crystal glass evaporates in the sun and disappears into the invisible.—This casket of gold is worn out by contact with the oriental carpet on which it is placed.—This Damascus blade attracts atoms of moisture and grows from them a rusty envelope, and, with time, this fur of rust will devour the blade of steel.—If these two vases collided too heavily, the hard stone would shoot forth sparks.
>
> Everything acts and reacts in the ceaseless vortex of the universe. Everything is at the same time a thing and a live being, a work and a worker. There is no dead nature!
>
> —*Omnia mutantur, nil interit.* (2:317–18)

It is not clear that Thoré-Bürger is thinking of a particular painting when he thus evokes these representative objects of Dutch still life—though the emphasis on motion, intensified by the reflexive verbs of the French ("s'agitent . . . se tournent . . . s'écartent . . . s'infléchissent . . . se gonflent . . . s'épanouissent . . . se métamorphose . . . s'évapore . . . s'en va . . . s'use . . . s'en fait . . . se heurtaient"), risks the implication that such a picture should no more be called "still" than it should be called "dead." By the time he reaches for the citation from Ovid—"All things change, nothing perishes"—everything, from flowers to vases, has been equally animated.[97]

As if responding directly to Ruskin's dismissal of "the whole school" as "inherently mortal to all its admirers" (7:369), Thoré-Bürger thus banishes even the possibility of death from the lowest of Dutch genres. Of course, the mortality of which Ruskin accused Dutch art had more to do with the insensitivity of its creators, as he saw it, than with the literal lifelessness of their subjects; while Thoré-Bürger himself could sometimes suggest, Ruskin-like, that the vitality of a painting derived from "the poetic faculty" of the painter (1:38)—a power to "incarnate" or "embody" an idea that he particularly associated with Rembrandt (1:204). At other times, he appears simply to have reveled in the variety of human life Dutch painters represented on canvas—an outpouring of energy he in turn identified with a newly liberated Holland. Yet the very intensity with which he sought to animate *nature morte* suggests that even for Thoré-Bürger something in the low matter of Dutch art still remained to be exorcised. Indeed, his strenuous insistence on the life of things may have had less to do with any commitment to pantheism than with the strength of his desire to counter the lingering association of that art with the sheer inertia—the mere dead weight, one might say—of the material.[98] If nothing really dies, and everything is equally animated, then all distinctions of high and low, spirit and matter, simply disappear.

Even Balzac's passionate engagement with things did not go so far as this. Yet the novelist also sought to make Dutch pictures move; and he too delighted in the sheer abundance of ordinary life those pictures represented. Thoré-Bürger himself compared *La comédie humaine* to the art of Jan Steen and Pieter de Hooch; and like George Eliot and Hardy after him, Balzac clearly invited such comparisons. While none of these novelists shared Thoré-Bürger's politics, the spirit in which each of them gave narrative life to Dutch painting had much in common with that of the radical Frenchman. But Ruskin too spoke for the nineteenth century, however extravagant his rhetoric; and something of the resistance he articulated can also be felt even—or especially—in the novelists who looked most directly to the Dutch for a model. It was not only the critics, as we shall see, who remained deeply ambivalent about "Dutch painting" in fiction.

{ three }

Balzac's Bourgeois Interiors and the Quest for the Absolute

Confronted with a particularly attractive painting by Pieter de Hooch in the Musée van der Hoop in Amsterdam, Thoré-Bürger momentarily appeared to share Reynolds's view that the merits of Dutch art did not lend themselves to verbal translation. Identifying the unnamed image as "the most beautiful" of the four de Hoochs in the collection, Thoré-Bürger pronounced it "a marvel!"—only to add immediately, "very difficult to describe, since the superlative value of this painting is in the effects of light." But no sooner did he seem to confess himself at a loss for words than he managed to find them again by invoking the example of Balzac. The great champion of Dutch art would in fact devote several more paragraphs to the picture in question, but not before offering up this brief excursus on the novelist:

> Balzac has the habit of beginning his novels with a detailed topography of the localities in which the drama must take place. He first creates his *milieu*, after the manner of the Eternal Father planting his earthly paradise with trees and flowers, before putting in man and woman. Tell me where you are, I will tell you what you will do there. If Eve picked the apple, it is because there were apple trees in fruit there.—Having once entered into the house of father Grandet of Saumur, one knows the miser and foresees that his daughter Eugénie will soon fall in love with the first comer, to divert herself [se désennuyer] in this sad cage.
>
> Balzac's topographic procedure is often useful for giving an idea of Pieter de Hooch's paintings, in which the domestic interior, the *home* of the English, with all its charms, has so much importance.

> It's not that the people are accessories there, but that they are inseparable from the place. It's all created for them, especially the light that animates and enlivens them. It's all a harmonious milieu, in which one goes to live as if at home [comme chez soi]—a place to do something, nothing much, perhaps nothing at all.[1]

As we have seen, Thoré-Bürger was not doing anything new in drawing an analogy between Balzac and Dutch painting. By the time that this appeared in 1860, the association had become a critical commonplace—so familiar that the critic could now reverse the direction of the comparison and invoke the method of the nineteenth-century novelist to help convey the art of his seventeenth-century predecessors. One of the most popular of Balzac's works, in his day as in ours, *Eugénie Grandet* (1833) in particular had often been compared to Dutch painting—and for good reason, as I shall argue below. But it is perhaps less obvious why the picture at which Thoré-Bürger was looking should have conjured up analogies with the famous novel about a miser and his daughter in the provincial town of Saumur. A late de Hooch (1670) that now hangs in the Rijksmuseum in Amsterdam (plate 4), the painting dates from a period in the artist's career when the representation of upper-class luxury had largely replaced the more modest settings of his earlier domestic images;[2] and neither the fashionable woman with her lapdog, nor the elegant room she inhabits, with its marble floor and large windows opening on an Amsterdam canal, bears any immediate resemblance to Balzac's provincial heiress in her dark and gloomy house—a house famously introduced in the novel's first line as inspiring in the viewer "a melancholy equal to that provoked by the most somber cloisters, the most lifeless moors, or the saddest ruins."[3] Nor, for that matter, does the novel include anyone like the elaborately dressed child in the doorway. Despite the shadowy foreground of the painting, both the luminous effects to which Thoré-Bürger calls attention and the domestic harmony he evokes would seem very far indeed from that "sad cage," as he himself puts it, of the Grandet household—a domestic environment whose oppressive atmosphere, at once physical and psychological, is further intensified by the miser's penury with candles.

In Balzac's novel, the women of the house make their tacit compromise with that oppression by spending all their time in the warmer months of each year by the window closest to the doorway; and it may be that the position of the woman in de Hooch's painting, her chair elevated on the little platform known as a *soldertje*,[4] prompted vague recollections of the customary place occupied by Mme Grandet and her daughter in the parlor at Saumur. "In a window nearest the door," we are told at the beginning of the novel, "there was a straw chair whose feet were mounted on blocks in order to raise Mme Grandet to a height that would permit her to view passers-by. A work-table in faded cherry wood filled the embrasure, and the small armchair of Eugénie Grandet was placed close by. For fifteen years, all the days of the mother and the daughter had peacefully passed away in this place, in constant work, from the month of April until the month of November" (*CH* 3:1041). A study of Balzac published two years after his death had in fact cited this very description of the Grandet women's seating arrangements in order to argue that the novelist's "tableaux d'intérieur" should be grouped with the best of the Dutch and Flemish masters. (In this case, the description called to mind the memory of a little canvas by Gerrit Dou.)[5] But whatever details may have prompted the allusion to *Eugénie Grandet*, Thoré-Bürger's enthusiastic identification of the de Hooch with the method of Balzac, and that in turn with the charms of a deliberately anglicized "*home*," is both instructive and misleading.[6] Like Balzac himself, whom he once tried to interest in some art dealing,[7] Thoré-Bürger strongly associated Dutch painting with scenes of domestic life; and like Balzac, he insisted that the human figure in such scenes is somehow inseparable from the material environment in which it is embedded. One might even argue that in thus idealizing the image of home and managing to glide over its darker aspects, the critic was only engaged in the sort of whitewashing that the novelist, too, indulged in whenever he professed his work's unqualified allegiance to the social virtues of the family.[8] Yet this "wild [farouche] republican Thoré," as a letter of Balzac's had once impatiently termed him,[9] also looked at Dutch painting through eyes quite different from those of the novelist—not least because he managed to see in its bourgeois interiors the freedom-loving spirit which he identified with its creators. For all the painstaking detail with which Balzac built up his representations of domestic life, and for all that he evidently owed to the Netherlandish masters, the "Dutch painter in prose" was always deeply divided about Dutch pictures.[10]

Nineteenth-century commentators compared Balzac's novels to Dutch painting at least in part because he had invited them to do so. As early as 1830, in a brief preface to the first of the tales he chose to gather under the title *Scènes de la vie privée*, he laid down the gauntlet. The final paragraph of the preface reads in full:

> The author will permit himself only one personal observation. He knows that certain minds will be able to reproach him with having often weighed himself down with apparently superfluous details.

> He knows that it will be easy to accuse him of a sort of puerile *garrulousness.* Often his pictures will appear to have all the faults of the compositions of the Dutch school, without offering their merits. But the author can excuse himself in saying that he has destined his book only to intelligences more candid and less jaundiced [blasées], less educated and more indulgent than those of these critics whose competence he declines to recognize. (*CH* 1:1174)

Here Balzac manages both to identify with the Dutch and keep his distance—leaving his "more indulgent" readers to decide whether he possesses the merits of the school rather than its faults, or whether he is actually engaged in another kind of art altogether. What is clear is that he associates those "apparently superfluous details" with the work of the Dutch and that he knows full well how they can likewise seem the mark of his own. A postscript to the same edition returns to the question of details—this time to claim them, more aggressively, as the principal merit of his art. Forestalling yet another potential criticism of his *Scènes*—that he has borrowed the subject of one tale from another novelist—he simultaneously denies the charge and dismisses it as irrelevant, since inventing new plots, he insists, is no longer possible in any case. "But today, when all possible combinations seem exhausted, when all situations have been worn out . . . the author firmly believes that details alone will henceforth constitute the merit of works improperly called *Novels* [*Romans*]" (*CH* 1:1175).[11]

The *Scènes de la vie privée* were not Balzac's first works of fiction, but their uneasy identification with Dutch pictures marks a self-conscious turn in his art. Unlike the pot-boilers that he had written under several different pseudonyms in the 1820s, these "scenes"—explicitly labeled as such and signed with his own name—would apparently count less on their twists of plot than on the abundant details with which they were composed. Together with *Le dernier Chouan* (1829)—the historical novel modeled on Scott that he had published the previous year—they were also the first of his works to be eventually incorporated into his collective monument, *La comédie humaine*. Even in advertising his historical fiction, Balzac had already begun to compare it to *tableaux de genre*: "genre paintings in which national history would be depicted in the little-known facts of our manners and our customs" (*CH* 8:1680).[12] But it was the scenes of private life, by his own account, that most obviously risked comparison to Dutch pictures; and it was the preface to those scenes that most nearly anticipated—or provoked—the terms in which his fiction would so often be judged. Balzac could hardly have been surprised when two months later a reviewer for the

Globe chose to quote his words back at him, in order to conclude that the novelist had been only too right in suggesting that his scenes had all the faults of Dutch painting. Those vaunted details, by this account, yielded only a static and lifeless tableau:

> Here is his procedure: he sees a house, examines it before and behind, and describes it from top to bottom until the last nail; then he enters, finds one, two, three individuals whom he describes in their turn—their clothes, faces, gestures and habits. Next he explores with a magnifying glass the relations that exist among them—a third description that soon leads to a fourth. Nothing is more provoking than these figures who pose immobile, waiting to be painted.[13]

Others, as we have seen, would adopt the analogy in a warmer spirit, as when Balzac's friend and fellow-writer Samuel-Henry Berthoud cheerfully enlisted him in the "Flemish school" of literature—Berthoud himself was of Flemish origin—and argued that the "perfection" and "finish" of his details most recalled the art of that "celebrated painter" ter Borch. "What would become, under a less skilled brush, insignificant trivialities" were somehow redeemed, Berthoud implied, by the novelist's touch: "He knows how to give the most vulgar objects a very great value. The meanest copper cauldron that he deigns to paint shines like gold."[14] Yet if Balzac presumably preferred such praise to the contempt of the *Globe*, his own identification with Dutch art was both more complicated and more ambivalent than critics like Berthoud suggested. From the beginning, the fiction itself tells another story.

The *Comédie humaine* opens, in fact, with the tale of an artist who falls in love with a Dutch picture. Though Balzac would later speak of *Le dernier Chouan* as his "first" work (*CH* 8:903), it was the *Scènes de la vie privée* that he would place at the head of the monument when he decided to issue his works under their collective title in 1842; and it was the tale then called *La maison du chat-qui-pelote* (literally, *The House of the Cat Who Plays Ball*) that he would chose to introduce them.[15] The *maison* in question, we are told in the first line, was "one of those valuable houses that enable historians to reconstruct old Paris by analogy"; and the tale begins, as so many of Balzac's narratives will begin, with a detailed description of its structure.[16] In this case, however, it quickly becomes clear that we are looking at the tumbledown house through the eyes of a fictional observer, a young man whose "archeological enthusiasm" for the old building (including its ancient sign of a tennis-playing cat) reveals its true object when the figure of a young girl is briefly framed in a window (*CH* 1:39). With a notable reservation, to which I shall return, this first portrait of the heroine might itself be a Dutch picture. Clothed in brown and surrounded by the massive casement, whose "rough contours" and "blackened sill" make a "charming contrast" with her youthful form (*CH* 1:43), Balzac's character could almost be taken for the meditative young woman in Nicolaes Maes's *Daydreamer*, for example (plate 5)—even as her placement more generally recalls numerous images in which seventeenth-century painters, inspired by the example of Gerrit Dou, similarly exploited the frame of a window or doorway to set off the female figure.[17]

But it is another Dutch picture, we soon learn, that had originally captured the attention of the hero. The girl at the window is Augustine Guillaume, the younger daughter of an old merchant clothier who conducts his venerable business at the sign of the cat and ball; and when Théodore de Sommervieux first caught sight of her one evening, she formed part of "a picture that would have arrested every painter in the world":

> The shop, not being yet lit, formed a dark ground in the depths of which could be seen the merchant's dining room. A hanging lamp shed that yellow light which gives so much charm to the pictures of the Dutch school. The white linen, the silverware and the cut glass formed bright accessories which further embellished the lively contrasts of light and shade. The figure of the father of the family and that of his wife, the faces of the clerks and the pure figure of Augustine, at two steps from whom stood a large chubby-cheeked girl, composed such a curious group; these heads were so original, and each character had such a candid [franche] expression; one understood so well the peace, the silence and the humble life of this family, that to an artist accustomed to express nature, there was something hopeless in wishing to render this fortuitous scene.

The artist who chances on this scene is all too prepared to fall in love with Dutch painting. Having just returned from a long sojourn in Rome, "his eyes surfeited with Raphael and Michelangelo," Sommervieux is on the rebound, in effect, from the high art of the Italians. In this domestic tableau he sees the very antithesis of the "grandiose" and the "pompous"; and "from the enthusiasm aroused in his impassioned soul by the natural picture he contemplated, he passed naturally to a profound admiration for its principal figure." The same light that "gives so much charm to the pictures of the Dutch school" sheds its glow particularly on Augustine's face; and she appears to him—the words are telling—"an exiled angel recalling heaven" (*CH* 1:52–53).[18]

Sommervieux marries Augustine, but not before he has translated his vision to canvas. The two pictures inspired by this encounter—one the domestic tableau itself and the other a portrait of the heroine—win universal acclaim when they are exhibited at the Salon. Indeed, "the interior scene created a revolution in painting"—a revolution whose equivocal result, according to the narrator, is that "all our expositions" are now crowded with genre painting. *Tableaux de genre* appear these days in such "prodigious quantity," he dryly reports, "that one could believe they were produced by purely mechanical means" (*CH* 1:54). But if the art inspired by Dutch painting is a popular success, the marriage itself proves a failure. The bourgeois scene from which Sommervieux lifted his bride, the tale implies, represents a way of life whose rhythms are fundamentally opposed to those of the artist. The very fact that it composes itself as a genre painting argues against it: the typicality and anonymity of the scene, signs of an action at once familiar and repeatable, testify to a world that stolidly resists the restless imagination of the painter. As Monsieur Guillaume exclaims when he hears of the sensation that Sommervieux's paintings have caused in the Salon: "Is it so very amusing then to see in a picture what one encounters every day in our street?" (*CH* 1:57).

From the beginning, Balzac makes clear, everyone who belongs to the *Chat-qui-pelote*, both shop and household, operates according to time-honored laws of custom and habit. The narrative itself is set in an unspecified past,[19] when "one saw less rarely than today these old families in which were preserved, like precious traditions, the customs [moeurs] and costumes characteristic of their professions, and which remained in the midst of a new civilization like the antediluvian remains recovered by Cuvier in the quarries." One of "the notable guardians" of these "venerable customs [usages]," the honest clothier is now carefully cultivating them in his apprentices (*CH* 1:45). Even disruptions to routine are themselves familiar and recurrent—the "annual tumult" of stock-taking being "one of those tempests that could be called equinoctial on account of their periodic return" (*CH* 1:60, 59). As for the daughters of the establishment: "they knew perfectly how to keep house . . . were economical . . . had great respect for the qualities of a merchant"; and "seeing how the exemplary life of their parents rolled on, they cast their eyes only very rarely beyond the circumference of this old hereditary home, which, for their mother, was the universe" (*CH* 1:49–50). Though Balzac takes care to distinguish them—the older of the two is "the very picture of her mother," while the lovely younger one bears no resemblance to either of her parents (*CH* 1:48)—Augustine's difference from her background proves insufficient in the end. When the brief happiness of their first married year has passed, Sommervieux begins to crave both the diversions of *le grand monde* and the "poetry" to which his wife is insensible. "Poetry, painting, and the refined pleasures [jouissances] of the imagination have inalienable rights over lofty spirits," the narrator announces; and though the faithful Augustine sincerely loves her husband and struggles to meet his aspirations, she cannot escape the bourgeois limits of her upbringing. "She took her pedestrian way in the real world," the narrator revealingly remarks, "while he had his head in the skies" (*CH* 1:74). Her pitiful attempt to restore their original happiness by reproducing the conditions of the portrait ends in disaster: the furious artist destroys his painting, and the death of its subject soon follows.

The "inalienable rights" of the imagination notwithstanding, Balzac's sympathies are clearly divided in this tale, whose later pages turn primarily to the viewpoint of the wife. Augustine Sommervieux is the first in a long line of virtuous and patient heroines in his fiction; and her anguished efforts to measure up to her husband—"if I am not a poet," she thinks, "at least I will understand poetry"—are genuinely moving, even if her long-suffering devotion becomes rather unbelievable by the end (*CH* 1:77). Indeed, the principal evidence that Balzac finally identifies more with the painter than his wife may be their shared impulse to idealize her. Sommervieux might have felt weary of the Italians when he first chanced upon his Dutch picture, but he was still apparently looking for the womanly ideal their painting had immortalized: "Abandoned for a long time to the fire [fougue] of Italian passions, his heart demanded one of those modest and reverent virgins that he had known how to find, unfortunately, only in painting at Rome" (*CH* 1:53). In the illuminated figure of Augustine he believes he sees just such an image; and his vision of the "exiled angel" in her bourgeois interior is confirmed (or anticipated) by the opening picture of her framed in the window—a picture that manages to combine the details and arrangement of a Dutch painting with a face that belongs, we are told, to "the sublime compositions" of Raphael. "It was the same grace, the same tranquility of those virgins that has become proverbial" (*CH* 1:43). The appearance of this Raphael virgin in the Dutch frame is, of course, the anomaly to which I alluded earlier; and the difficulty of deciding whether she is the narrator's vision or the painter's only emphasizes their shared point of view.[20] Like his young artist, as we shall see, Balzac never lost his attachment to the feminine ideal he associated with Raphael's work;[21] and like Sommervieux, too, the novelist would persist in imagining that he could locate her form even in the midst of Dutch pictures. Nearly fifteen years later, he was still consciously at work on the problem: "I believe I can make of it a fine painting of the Dutch School," he wrote to Madame Hanska of *Les petits bourgeois*—a novel that would begin by explicitly evoking this tale and that would remain unfinished at the time of his death—"but I want a Raphael head in the middle of it."[22]

Though no artist wanders by to see her, even Grandet's dark house briefly contains an Italian madonna. Describing the modest heroine on the brink of love, the narrator pauses to imagine how a painter searching for "a type of Mary's celestial purity" might have found in Eugénie a model worthy of Raphael (*CH* 3:1076). Later, when "the dignity of the beloved woman gave to her features that kind of radiance that painters figure by the aureole," he compares her to the virgin mother, rather than Mary before the Annunciation, and vaguely invokes "some Spanish painters" who have beautifully represented both (*CH* 3:1146–47). (In the first edition, these too were "Italians.")[23] Yet if *Eugénie Grandet* itself has more often prompted comparisons to Dutch pictures than to Italian or Spanish ones, that is in part because Balzac strenuously resists the impulse to detach its heroine—like Augustine Guillaume before her—from her setting. When the miser locks his daughter in her room for refusing to reveal what she has done with her gold, he merely narrows the domestic enclosure in which she otherwise lives. And when he then takes to observing her stealthily as she sits at her window, he helps to make that enclosure visible in a familiar genre picture—a picture that effectively reinforces the identification of woman and house by framing the one in the other. In both of these acts, of course, Grandet colludes with his creator.

Even for the provincial heroine of a nineteenth-century novel, Eugénie is extraordinarily housebound: though we hear of her attendance at church—a space never pictured—the only times we actually see her venture beyond the Grandet garden are a brief walk with her father in his meadow by the Loire and another with her parents and the faithful Nanon to bid farewell to her cousin as he departs from the quay. A single sentence that follows removes her from the house just long enough to acquire a token familiar from many Dutch genre paintings, where a woman similarly confined to domestic space is connected to the larger world (and sometimes implicitly to an absent lover) by the map that hangs on the wall behind her (figs. 3-1 and 3-2; cf. plate 1). "In returning from mass where she went the day after Charles's departure . . . she bought from the town bookseller a map of the world that she nailed near her mirror, in order to follow her cousin on his route to the Indies, to be able to put herself a little, evening

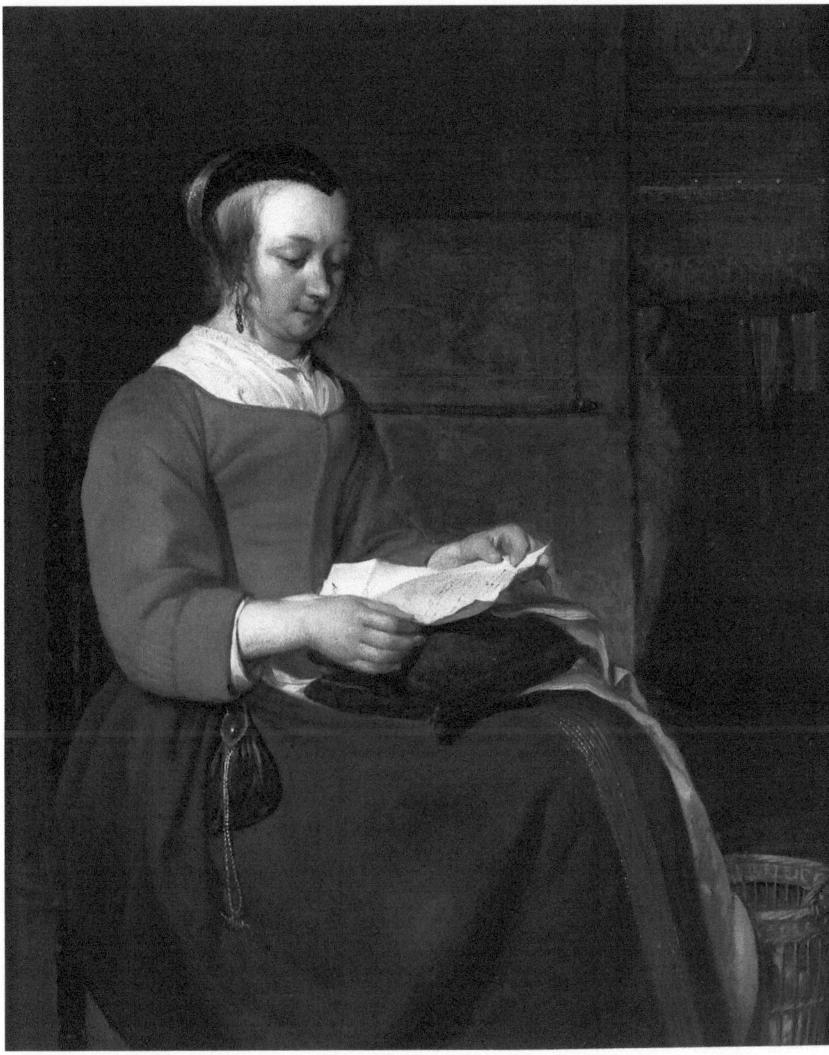

Figure 3-1. Gabriel Metsu: *A Young Woman Reading a Letter*, late 1650s. Private collection, New York

and morning, in the vessel that transported him there, to see him and to ask him a thousand questions" (*CH* 3:1147).[24] Eugénie expects the scene to be completed, as it is in Metsu's and ter Borch's paintings, by a letter; but by depriving her of that consolation for most of the novel, Balzac assures that she will be yet more thoroughly attached to the humble domestic objects that she has come to identify with her beloved cousin. The bit of wall that

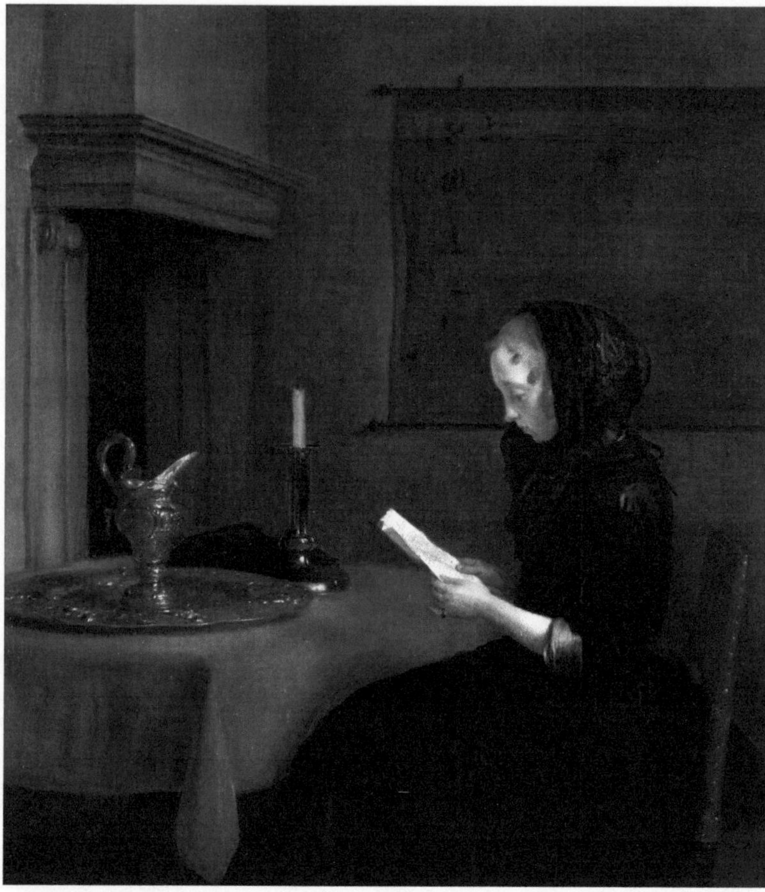

Figure 3-2. Gerard ter Borch: *Woman in Mourning Clothes Reading a Letter.* Private collection

she watched the sun illuminate the first morning after his arrival, the worm-eaten bench on which he declared his love, even the saucer that once held the sugar for his coffee and that she courageously returned to the table in defiance of her miserly father—all these, and of course the elegant dressing-case given her for safe-keeping when he departed for the Indies, become the fetishistic tokens in which she invests her emotional vitality. Both the fragility of her feelings and their humble reification are beautifully captured in a figure the narrator borrows from Bossuet: "Her happiness, gathered up one day like nails strewn on a wall, would not fill the hollow of her hand" (*CH* 3:1146). It is almost as if Eugénie herself were that wall—or as if the "*Dutch picture of an interior*" that one British contemporary saw in the novel were also a portrait of the heroine.[25] More than the entire scene of her history, the house at Saumur becomes, in the novel's own words, "the image of her life" (*CH* 3:1198).

Although Balzac himself does not explicitly invoke Dutch painting in this novel, the preface to the first edition leaves little doubt of the sort of picture he had in mind.[26] Insisting on the "modest intention of the author, who wishes here to be only the most humble of copyists," the preface evokes both the characteristic palette and the scale of Dutch pictures: it speaks of "figures, at first sight little colored, but whose details and half-tones solicit the most skillful touches of the brush," of "gray shadows" and "chiaroscuro," and of "the circle of minutiae" in which the painter of such a scene is obliged to move.[27] The preface also calls attention to the apparent tranquility of this picture—a tranquility at once deceptive, since beneath its surface "tumultuous passions secretly ravage" their possessors, and oddly genuine after all, since "the most passionate excitements [exaltations] end by abolishing themselves . . . in the constant monotony of habits [moeurs]" (*CH* 3:1026, 1025).

This, Balzac contends, is the truth of provincial life that his novel captures; and it is also, I would suggest, an account of how narrative in *Eugénie Grandet* ultimately resolves itself in genre painting. The story of Eugénie's awakening to love and her brief defiance of her father is a history of "first" times that temporarily unsettles an existence otherwise represented, as the novel says at one point, by "the same acts constantly performed with the chronometric regularity of the movements of an old clock" (*CH* 3:1173). Charles's unexpected knock disrupts the card-playing scene with which the novel opens; and "pour la première fois," in the novel's formula, Eugénie dreams of love or takes pleasure in her appearance, begins to conceal her thoughts or is tempted to commit a guilty act (*CH* 3:1073, 1077, 1122)—events defined as such by virtue of their difference from the static tableaux that the novel identifies with life in the provinces.[28] Like the mother and daughter "at their constant work" in the embrasure by the window (*CH* 3:1041), the card-players who routinely gather in the Grandet parlor constitute both a Dutch picture and an incitement to narrative; but in this novel, at least, Balzac chooses to keep that narrative largely internal. The card-playing scene is still repeating itself in the parlor toward the novel's close, seven years later; and after Eugénie's discovery of Charles's treachery, "she had nothing more to do," the narrator says, "except to spread her wings, aspire to heaven, and live in prayers until the day of her deliverance" (*CH* 3:1189). At the very end, the wealthy heiress has "the saintliness of a person who has not soiled her soul by contact with the world," but she still dresses as her mother did and stints the fire like her father (*CH* 3:1198). Only in the charitable acts by which Eugénie ends her days—and, of course, in those figurative wings—does Balzac represent his temptation to turn *tableau de genre* into sacred history.

More than the need to idealize women motivated Balzac's resistance to his own Dutch painting. Perhaps the novel that most clearly allegorizes the divided character of his art is the only one he actually set in Flanders—*La recherche de l'absolu* (*The Quest for the Absolute*) of 1834. To suggest that a novel can be read allegorically is already, of course, to suggest that something other than realism in the usual sense is at work in it; and in this case the author himself appears to have been of two minds as to how to characterize it. Originally classified among the *Scènes de la vie privée*, themselves appearing under the more general rubric of *Études des moeurs au XIXe siècle*, the novel finally took its place in the *Comédie humaine* eleven years later as an *Étude philosophique* (*CH* 10:1562–77)—its relative length making it something of an anomaly in a group that primarily consisted of short fantastic tales such as *Le chef d'oeuvre inconnu* (1831) or *Gambara* (1837).[29] Of course, this was hardly the only time Balzac shifted a work from one category to another—his system of classification is notoriously flexible and improvisatory—but in this case both the change itself and the direction of the change are instructive.[30] For the textual history of *La recherche de l'absolu* makes clear that the novel had its origins not in the metaphysical quest for which it is titled but in a scene of private life, and that it was only in the course of writing that the quest itself began to take over the narrative.[31] As readers of *La recherche* know, the novel as we have it reproduces this sequence, as the detailed description of a house and its inhabitants gives way to a narrative of scientific and spiritual obsession. Read one way, the novel dramatizes the conflict between the domestic peace of a bourgeois family and the obsessive quest that nearly destroys it. In what follows, I should like to suggest that there is also another way of putting this: more than any other Balzacian fiction, *La recherche* dramatizes—and implicitly comments on—the conflict between the Dutch painter and the visionary.[32]

The Dutch art with which this novel begins is not merely an analogy. *La recherche* opens with one of those painstaking descriptions of a bourgeois household that the author and his critics alike compared to Dutch pictures; but in this case the building itself is both a work of Flemish architecture and a virtual museum of Dutch and Flemish painting. "There exists in Douai," the first sentence reads in part, "a house whose physiognomy, interior arrangements and details have, more than those of any other building, preserved the character of those old Flemish structures, so naively appropriate to the patriarchal customs [moeurs] of that good country" (*CH* 10:657). As the description unfolds, we will learn (among much else) that this house has been known for more than two centuries as the Maison Claës, that it belongs to the wealthy descendant of "one of the most celebrated of those families of craftsmen to whom the Low Countries owed . . . [their] commercial supremacy" (*CH* 10:661), and that generations of collectors have gathered within its walls a rich assortment of art and furniture—the most valuable of all being the treasures in those apartments tradition has reserved for the private life of the family. Later still, we will learn that the house boasts more than a hundred and fifty pictures, including "choice bits by Rubens, Ruisdael, van Dyck, ter Borch, Gerrit Dou, Teniers, Mieris, Paul Potter, Wouwerman, Rembrandt, Hobbema, Cranach, and Holbein"—nearly all the period's favorite Dutch or Flemish painters, in other words, with a few Germans for good measure. ("Italian and French pictures were in the minority," the narrator adds, "but they were all authentic and of capital importance"—*CH* 10:683–84.) As it happens, this extraordinary gathering is also Balzac's first represented picture collection.[33]

Before he proceeds to elaborate, however, the novelist pauses to offer a characteristic defense of these preliminaries. "The events of human life, whether public or private, are so intimately tied to architecture," he announces, "that most observers can reconstruct nations or individuals in all the truth of their habits from the remains of their public monuments or by examining their domestic relics" (*CH* 10:657). This is more or less the same rule he had already invoked by calling the Maison du chat-qui-pelote "one of those valuable houses that enable historians to reconstruct old Paris by analogy" (*CH* 1:39); and variations of its formula—whereby places entail the persons who inhabit them and vice versa—would of course be reiterated again and again in defense of the descriptive detail for which the *Comédie humaine* is famous.[34] Here, however, the enunciation of the rule serves not only to justify the details that follow but to introduce something like a small essay on the character and customs of the Netherlands—an essay whose identification of the art with the people and the people with their art strikingly anticipates the method of Taine's *Philosophie de l'art dans les Pays-Bas.* Why is it "nearly impossible," the narrator asks, "not to be overcome with a kind of tender feeling by the painting of Flemish life, when the details are well rendered?" "Perhaps," he immediately answers himself, "it is, among different ways of living, that which best puts an end to human uncertainties." Note how the object in question appears to have shifted from a mode of painting to a way of life, even as the slippery pronouns in what follows continue to hover uncertainly between *la vie flamande* and its picturing. For the sake of clarity, I give both the French and the English:

> Aussi est-il presque impossible de ne pas être pris d'une espèce d'attendrissement à la peinture de la vie flamande, quand les accessoires en sont bien rendus. Pourquoi? Peut-être est-ce, parmi les différentes existences, celle qui finit le mieux les incertitudes de l'homme. Elle ne va pas sans toutes les fêtes, sans tous les liens de la famille, sans une grasse aisance qui atteste la continuité du bien-être, sans un repos qui ressemble à de la béatitude; mais elle exprime surtout le calme et la monotonie d'un bonheur naïvement sensuel où la jouissance étouffe le désir en le prévenant toujours.

> Thus it is nearly impossible not to be seized with a kind of tender feeling by the painting of Flemish life, when the details of it are well rendered. Why? Perhaps it is, among different ways of life, that which best puts an end to human uncertainties. It wouldn't exist without all the holidays, without all the family ties, without an abundant ease that attests to the continuity of well-being, without a repose that resembles beatitude; but it expresses above all the calm and monotony of a naively sensual happiness, in which satisfaction extinguishes desire by always anticipating it. (*CH* 10:658)

The remainder of this somewhat rambling excursus on art and life in the Netherlands will touch on a number of themes familiar to nineteenth-century commentators, from the "mellow" tones of Flemish interiors to the discovery of tobacco—by whose smoke, according to the novelist, the scattered traits of the nation's character were welded together. But whether he is evoking the "refined materialism" of their habits or describing a cast of mind so practical that it never "soars beyond the limits of the real world," as he revealingly phrases it, Balzac's account of Flemish life is saturated with images of bourgeois tranquility and satisfaction. Even the Fleming's "revolutionary force," in this telling, originates in nothing more than "the domestic desire to have elbow room at the table and complete ease" under his roof—as if the struggle for liberty itself could only be represented as one more scene of household comfort (*CH* 10:659, 660). That the novelist lovingly evokes this picture of Flemish life only to disrupt it should hardly be surprising: a state in which "satisfaction extinguishes desire by always anticipating it" may resemble "beatitude," but it hardly offers opportunity for

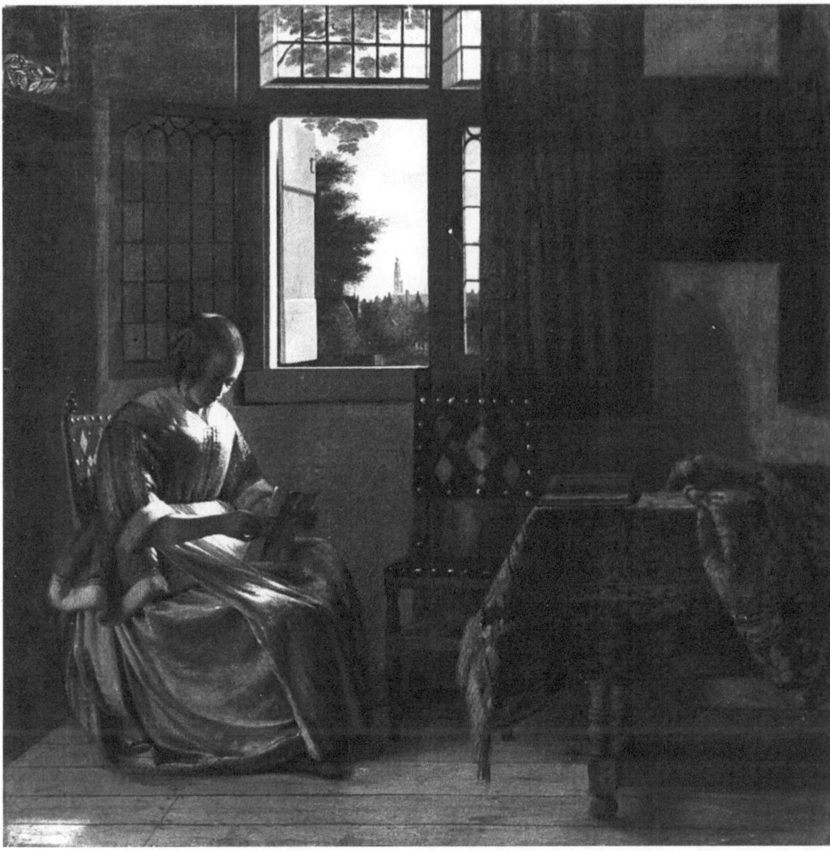

Figure 3-3. Pieter de Hooch: *A Woman Reading a Letter by a Window*, 1664. Museum of Fine Arts, Budapest

narrative (*CH* 10:658).[35] So much does his picture of Flemish life identify itself *as* picture, in other words, that Balzac's novel will inevitably plot against it.

The novel itself gets under way, as we might expect, by unsettling just such a picture—one of those bourgeois interiors that Balzac so often models on Dutch painting. Like the de Hooch that prompted Thoré-Bürger's associations with the novelist (plate 4)—or still more, perhaps, like another image from the same artist a few years earlier (fig. 3-3)—this depicts a woman seated at a window, her position calling attention to the fall of light and shadow in the room. Indeed, from his concentration on the effects of light to his careful noting of the figure's pose, Balzac makes his cues to the would-be painter quite explicit:

> The rays of the sun were then falling obliquely on the house, catching it at an angle, crossing the parlor, expiring in strange gleams on the woodwork that covered the walls beside the courtyard, and enveloping this woman in a purple zone projected by the damask curtain draped along the window. A mediocre painter who had copied this woman at this moment would certainly have produced a striking work with a head so full of sadness and melancholy. The pose of the body and that of the feet thrust out before her betrayed the listlessness [abattement] of a person who loses consciousness of her physical being in the concentration of forces absorbed by a fixed thought. (*CH* 10:667)

This is a picture of absorption, in Michael Fried's sense of the term—a picture whose realist effect is partly produced, as in much genre painting, by the pretense that the figure represented has no awareness of the observer's presence.[36] Even before Balzac tells us that she is crying, however, the lack of any companions or props to justify that absorption registers as an anomaly. Unlike either of de Hooch's paintings—or, for that matter, Balzac's pictures of the Grandet women at work or the Guillaumes at dinner—this is not an image of the everyday but a sign of its disruption. Though Balzac will not really explain the cause of his heroine's suffering until he has filled in the history of her marriage, the arrival of the man of the house—his gaze abstracted, his costume dirty and disordered—already makes clear that domestic routine is being sacrificed to "the neglect of genius" (*CH* 10:672).

The genius in question is Balthazar Claës; and it is his monomania, we gradually learn, that has disturbed the hitherto tranquil life of the household. Locked up all day and sometimes through the night in an expensively outfitted laboratory, he has been pursuing a secret quest that threatens to bankrupt the family—a quest whose very obscurity lends itself to a variety of interpretations. "To a priest he would have seemed full of the word of God; an artist would have saluted him as a great master; an enthusiast would have taken him for a Prophet of the Swedenborgian Church" (*CH* 10:673). Neighbors talk of a search for the philosopher's stone, and Balthazar himself speaks of a problem in chemistry; but not until his wife demands to know the nature of the "powerful" idea that has divided them does he finally reveal what he has been seeking (*CH* 10:713). This, of course, is the "Absolute" of the novel's title—an idea best defined, perhaps, as the single principle to which all matter can be reduced. (To his wife, Balthazar talks of "a substance common to all creation, modified by a unique force," and "the ultimate ground [raison suprême] of all the effects of nature"—*CH* 10:717.) If he can solve his problem, Balthazar believes, he will achieve both glory and riches. But while the evidence suggests that Balzac faithfully read up on his chemistry in preparation for the narrative,[37] it is the very abstraction and mystery of this quest that finally seems most notable. Though at one point Balthazar accidentally manages to transform a lump of carbon into a diamond, a quest for the Absolute, the novel implies, is by definition unrealizable. The triumphant "EUREKA!" with which he greets a newspaper report that the secret has been found is also the last word that he speaks, as the "veil" covering the "key to the enigma" is "belatedly rent by the bony fingers of Death" (*CH* 10:835).

Against this endless search for the unattainable, *La recherche de l'absolu* poses the generic repetition and domestic maintenance that it identifies with Dutch painting. Even as Balthazar keeps selling off the property to finance his experiments, the women of the house work to restore it, their dealings in finance and real estate serving in the context simply as more advanced forms of housekeeping. The novel begins, tellingly, with the Maison Claës in a perfect state of preservation, its cleanliness and stability appearing to have maintained themselves over the centuries by some Flemish law of homeostasis. "Ever since it was built," in Balzac's words, "this façade was carefully cleaned [se nettoyait] twice a year"; and "if some bit of mortar gave way in a joint, the hole closed up again [se rebouchait] immediately" (*CH* 10:664.) Balthazar has married for that "domestic life, so pleasant, so calm, called to his mind by the very name of Flanders" (*CH* 10:675); and though she herself is half-Spanish, Madame Claës proves an excellent housekeeper, who "took up with pride all the customs of the Flemish bourgeoisie and made it a point of self-respect . . . to maintain the smallest details of the house in their traditional neatness [propreté]" (*CH* 10:682). For a brief time, she even manages to woo her increasingly distracted husband away from his quest and back to the rounds of drinking, eating, and music-making that the novel explicitly figures as the perpetual scene of high genre: "It is always the pictures of Mieris or of ter Borch," the narrator says, "only without the red plumes on the pointed gray hats, the guitars and the beautiful costumes of the sixteenth [*sic*] century" (*CH* 10:728). When their own paintings must be sold to pay off Balthazar's debts, the prudent mother secretly reserves part of the purchase money to secure the welfare of her children—a plot device whereby the Dutch pictures within the novel eventually help to restore the picture that contains them.

Though there are sons in this family as well as daughters, the struggle between the preservation of the household and the quest for the Absolute is heavily gendered, with even the servants divided up accordingly. Unusually for Balzac, this novel reserves the impulse toward the sublime for its men, while aligning its women with the mundane world of domestic maintenance—what Norman Bryson, in an eloquent study of still life, has called the "rhopographic scale of values" (from *rhopos*: trivial objects, small wares, trifles) as opposed to the "megalographic" ambitions of history painting, both sacred and secular.[38] Some passing allusions notwithstanding,[39] women in *La recherche* are primarily identified with Dutch pictures rather than Italian ones. But it is the oldest daughter, Marguerite, whom Balzac particularly identifies with his homeostatic idea of Dutch painting. With a "physiognomy in accord with this house," and looks that are "the living image of a maternal grandmother . . . whose portrait, scrupulously preserved, testified to this resemblance," Marguerite is "truly the young Flemish girl as the painters of the country have represented her"—more thoroughly at home in such a picture, the novel suggests, than either of her parents (*CH* 10:726).[40] And it is Marguerite, of course, whose careful economy and hard work finally repair the family fortunes—though not before her scrupulous restoration of the ancestral household, even to the point of replacing some of the old pictures in their frames, has been once more utterly devastated by the "idea of the Absolute [which] had passed everywhere like a fire" (*CH* 10:829). At the close of the novel, we are assured that Marguerite again pays all her father's debts and restores the Maison Claës to a "modern splendor that must dispel any idea of its decline" (*CH* 10:834); but the only "tableau" of which we hear is "the touching picture that his beautiful family presented" to Balthazar as he lies dying (*CH* 10:833–34).

The author of the *Comédie humaine* was rarely of one mind about anything, but few Balzac novels are more divided in their sympathies than this Flemish fiction.[41] When Balthazar looks at his weeping wife and informs her of the elements into which he has "decomposed tears" (*CH* 10:719), or responds to her generous sale of the paintings by talking excitedly of his experiments, the narrator's irony seems unmistakable. "Madame Claës could not withstand the egoism of this answer," he remarks of the latter exchange, which leads directly to her death: "She expected passionate thanks for her sacrifices, and found a problem in chemistry" (*CH* 10:733). The domestic felicity accorded Marguerite—she marries a young man who falls in love with her in the picture gallery—also seems to weight the narrative toward what Balzac, writing of it to Madame Hanska, called "the hearth near its source." (The letter to his future wife alludes only to the domestic side of the novel.)[42] Throughout the novel, for that matter, our point of view remains for the most part with the women of the household, who rarely venture into the scientist's laboratory.[43] But it is hardly necessary to look for the authorial signature that has been teased out of Balthazar's name to recognize how much Balzac has invested in his visionary scientist—beginning, of course, with the very motor of his plot.[44] Monomania takes many guises in the *Comédie humaine*, from the artistic passion of Frenhofer or Gambara to the acquisitiveness of Grandet and the criminal grandiosity of Vautrin; but it always proves, as it does here, an excellent machine for narrative. Like Goriot's fanatic love for his daughters or the sexual appetite of Hulot, Balthazar's quest for the Absolute drives the action. Though the novelist characteristically enters with some zeal into the various financial arrangements by which Marguerite manages to recover the Claës estate, even that work would be unnecessary were it not for her father's obsession. The girl who resembles a picture of her ancestor acts to restore the status quo. Only death, on the other hand, can put an end to a desire that is by definition insatiable.

Yet even as the novel implies that a search for the Absolute must end in death, it also insists that Balthazar's quest is not merely futile. When his neighbors brand the dying man an "alchemist," the narrator denounces this as a calumny and bitterly condemns Douai for its failure to honor "the perseverance of the man of genius." Faced with "an indifference as brutal" as that which confronted "Dante, Cervantes, Tasso *e tutti quanti*"—the very precedents speak to Balzac's identification with his hero—the nineteenth-century scientist belongs to the ranks of those who will continue to die before their time, since "the people understand the creations of genius even more belatedly than do kings" (*CH* 10:830). A year after these words were published, their author was still engaged in the argument—the critics' reception of his hero having apparently offered further grounds for his concern about the benighted judgments of his contemporaries. In a preface to the *Études de moeurs* (1835) that was signed by Félix Davin but is generally understood to have been more or less dictated by Balzac himself, the author once again sought to correct those who associated his hero with the philosopher's stone: "Certainly, if the critics had read this book with some attention, which it much deserves, they would have seen that the sublime Fleming is as superior to the old or new alchemists as the naturalists of our era are to those of the middle ages" (*CH* 1: 1163).[45] The quest for the Absolute, in other words, looks forward, not back; while the novel's impressive grasp of modern science (according to the same preface) testifies to the genius of Balthazar and his creator alike.[46]

Of course, none of this confusion would have arisen had the novel not conjured with the figure of the alchemist in the first place; and it is tempting to suggest that in this respect, too, *La recherche de l'absolu* at once identifies with Dutch pictures and contends against them. Though the novel does not explicitly evoke any paintings of alchemists, Balzac surely knew that the subject had been a frequent one in Netherlandish art: four years earlier, *Gobseck* (1830) had already compared its eponymous usurer to "those alchemists and little old men painted by Rembrandt or Metsu" (*CH* 2:964). And if he had such paintings in mind when he wrote *La recherche de l'absolu*, he would also have known that the alchemist at work is typically represented as matter for ridicule. Indeed, it is precisely the domestic chaos that surrounds him that serves as the principal sign of his futility.

A popular engraving by Pieter Breughel the Elder in the sixteenth century established the motifs for many paintings that followed, from the littered quarters in which the alchemist labors to the misery he inflicts on his family—whose subsequent arrival at the almshouse appears in the frame on the right (fig. 3-4). The scholar at his desk drives home the moral, as he gestures to the confusion with one hand, while pointing with the other to a text whose inscription—"Alghe Mist"—puns on the term for the man before him and the words *al ghemist*, meaning everything is ruined or foul.[47] Though seventeenth-century painters like Ostade and Steen would no longer avail themselves of Breughel's narrative license, they would still retain some of the emblematic effects of the earlier image, while adapting their representations to the temporal conventions of realism (plates 6 and 7). In both paintings, the suffering caused by the alchemist's labors occupies the same space as the alchemist, even as his turned back marks the divide between them. (Note the small boy gnawing a bone in the dark recess of the Ostade, as well, of course, as the woman delousing a child in the same picture and the weeping mother with the child at her breast in the Steen.) While Ostade's *Alchemist* manages to turn a satirical emblem into one of his familiar scenes of peasant life, a Latin tag (rare for him) recalls the older tradition: an inscription on the paper below the alchemist's stool reads *oleum et operam perdis*—literally, "you lose your oil and labor."[48] Despite the realistic look of the Ostade, both his genre-like painting, whose alchemist clearly echoes Breughel's, and Steen's more obviously archaizing image, whose central figure sports the sort of antique costume that marks so many of his quacks and other charlatans, manage to suggest that there is something at once old fashioned and comic about the practice of alchemy.[49] Even a relatively dignified version by Teniers surrounds the alchemist with the customary disorder—the overturned vessels and discarded manuscripts

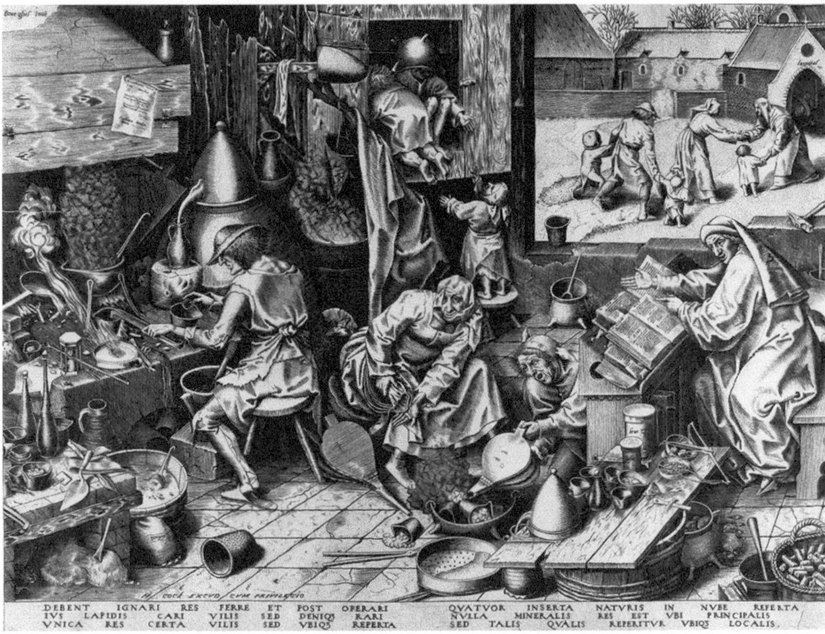

Figure 3-4. Pieter Breughel the Elder: *The Alchemist*, engraving after 1558. The Metropolitan Museum of Art, New York. Harris Brisbane Dick Fund, 1926 (26.72.29). Image © The Metropolitan Museum of Art

that evidently register the confusion and failure of his efforts (plate 8). Here, too, the principal figure pays no more attention to the viewer than he does to the others who inhabit his space: like his fellow-alchemists, he is an image of utter absorption.

For all the eagerness with which Balzac sought to defend his "sublime Fleming" (*CH* 1:1163), his only representation of Balthazar at work ingeniously exploits this tradition to draw a more critical picture. It is a picture seen, needless to say, through resolutely Flemish eyes—Marguerite, whose viewpoint now governs the narrative, having just received a bill for her father's experiments that threatens total bankruptcy. When Balthazar does not respond to her summons, she ventures up to his laboratory:

> Upon entering, she saw her father in the middle of an immense room, strongly lit, furnished with machines and dusty glass vessels; here and there were books, and tables cluttered with labeled and numbered products. On all sides, the disorder entailed by the preoccupation of the scientist was an offense [froissait] to Flemish practices

> [habitudes]. This mass of chemical flasks, retorts, metals, fantastically colored crystallizations, specimens hung on walls or thrown on furnaces, was dominated by the figure of Balthazar Claës, who, without his coat, his arms naked like those of a worker, showed a chest covered with hairs as white as his head. His horribly fixed eyes were trained on an air-pump. The container for this machine was capped by a lens formed by double convex glasses whose interior was filled with alcohol and which collected the rays of the sun then entering through one of the panes of the rose window in the garret. . . .
>
> The sight of her father, who, nearly on his knees before his machine, received directly the light of the sun, and whose scattered hairs resembled silver threads, his protuberant brow, his face contorted by a frightful attention, the singularity of the objects that surrounded him, the obscurity of the parts of this vast garret from which the strange machines sprang forth, all conduced to make an impression on Marguerite, who said to herself with terror: "My father is mad!" (*CH* 10:779–80)

Between the striking effects of light and shadow in the garret and the white-haired scientist in its midst, his gaze concentrated on a glass vessel, this scene most nearly resembles Teniers's *Alchemist*; and as in that painting, I would suggest, the jumble of objects strewn about conjures up their orderly opposite—those meticulous arrangements of domestic materials that Balthazar's wish to reduce matter to a unifying Idea necessarily violates.[50] From the standpoint of that "refined materialism" that the novel early identifies with Flemish art, the scientist's pursuit of the Absolute can only look like madness (*CH* 10:659). "On all sides," in Balzac's words here, "the disorder entailed by the scientist was an offense to Flemish practices." Not surprisingly, the representative of those practices will soon feel compelled to exile her father from the house.

Describing the cleanliness and "finish" of that house at the beginning of the novel, the narrator suggests that its appearance would have driven "a romantic" out of the apartment opposite, had one been lodging there (*CH* 10:664); and it is not too fanciful to suggest that this hypothetical restlessness finds its narrative outlet in Balzac's fictional scientist—a scientist, we recall, who might just as well pass for a mystic or an artist. In the eyes of this restless observer, the meticulous look of the Maison Claës would presumably have testified to the dullness and propriety of bourgeois life; but the fact that the manuscript of *La recherche* had originally identified that look with "the finish of the Dutch School" only serves to emphasize how much Balzac's representation of such a life owes to his idea of a certain kind of painting.[51] And in this novel especially, it is with an idea of the Dutch School (or the Flemish) rather than particular images that Balzac is conjuring. While legend has often attributed the realistic descriptions in the *Comédie humaine* to the local research on which they were based, all the evidence indicates that the novelist never set foot in Douai and that the Maison Claës corresponds to no actual structure: Balzac's typical old Flemish house is exactly that—an architectural type, created from memories of Flemish buildings in his native Tours and above all from books and pictures.[52] Even the novel's picture collection is a set of famous names rather than of individual images, as if the author were more interested in a generalized conception of Dutch and Flemish painting than in any particular instance of the category. This is not to say that Balzac never looked closely at such pictures; but it is to say that the author of *La recherche de l'absolu* focused less on the sensuous details of Netherlandish art than on the idea of the "real world" (*CH* 10:660) with which he associated them. Indeed, even when he appears to have had specific images in mind, he deliberately chooses to ignore their specificity, preferring instead to emphasize the generic recurrence they share: "It is *always* the pictures of Mieris or of ter Borch, *only without* the red plumes on the pointed gray hats, the guitars and the beautiful costumes of the sixteenth century" (*CH* 10:728; emphasis mine). Though the novel's modern editor has identified several works in the Louvre that probably inspired the comparison (figs. 3-5 and 3-6), the very signs by which she identifies them—the gray hats, the red plumes, the guitars (*CH* 10:1648)—are the details the novel itself cancels out. To look at van Mieris's women taking tea or ter Borch's music-makers in this way is to see a generalized image of everyday leisure among the *haut bourgeoisie*—an image constituted by all that does not change over the centuries. Against this vision of stasis, in which "satisfaction extinguishes desire by always anticipating it" (*CH* 10:658), *La recherche de l'absolu* plots its quest for the Absolute. If Balzac was finally right to classify the novel among the *Études philosophiques* rather than the *Études de moeurs*, that is because even his "Dutch" (or Flemish) painting is here subordinated to a relatively abstract account of the pleasurable inertia he associates with it—which is to say that his representation of domestic life in nineteenth-century Flanders keeps threatening to turn into an idea rather than a picture.[53]

The first full-length novels by Balzac would not be translated into English until 1859; but by the 1840s he already had an astute reader—and fervent

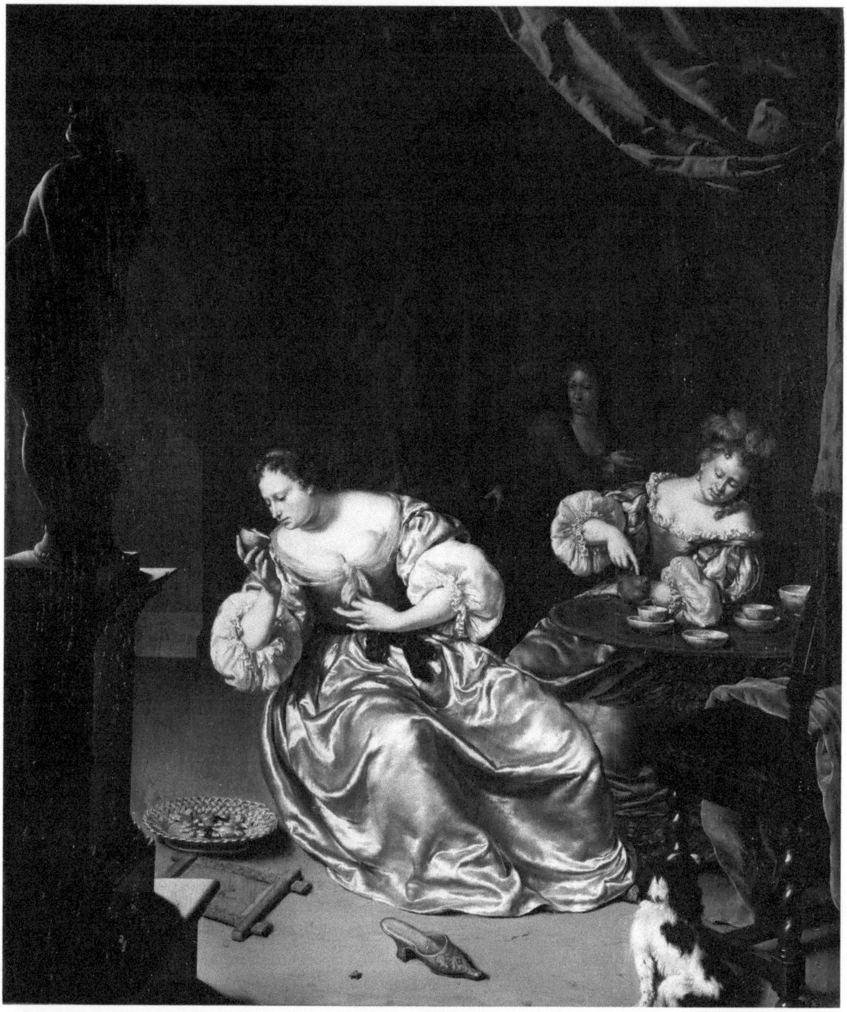

Figure 3-5. Willem van Mieris: *Teatime*, c. 1680–90. Musée du Louvre, Paris. Photo Credit: Erich Lessing/Art Resource, N.Y.

admirer—in Elizabeth Barrett Browning.[54] "To my apprehension, Balzac is a writer of extraordinary power," she wrote to her friend and fellow-poet Mary Russell Mitford in 1844: "& as a describer, . . take him from his descriptions of old houses, upwards, . . he is unrivalled. He has a Dutch hand, and an Italian soul—finishes, to the very down on the wing of a butterfly—yet comprehends wholeness & unity."[55] Though Balzac obviously could not have seen this particular analogy with painting, one imagines that

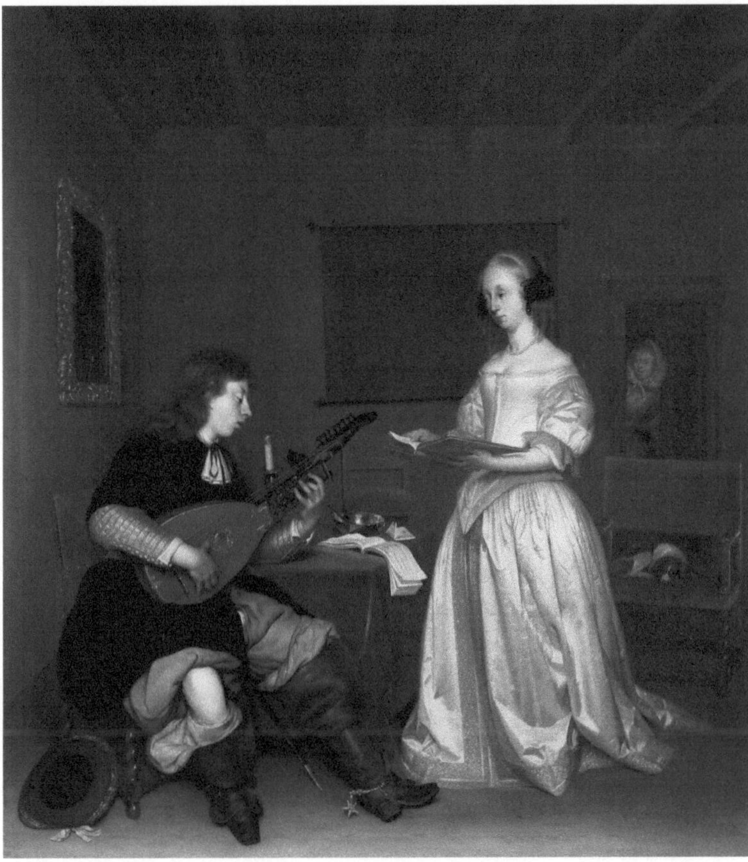

Figure 3-6. Gerard ter Borch: *The Duo: Singer and Theorbo-Player*, 1669. Musée du Louvre, Paris. Photo Credit: Erich Lessing/Art Resource, N.Y.

he would have been pleased by Barrett Browning's witty variation on the formula. Like the novelist himself, she begins with his descriptions of old houses, but the "Italian soul" with which she supplements his "Dutch hand" at once reinscribes a familiar hierarchy and testifies to a division in his art that had been evident from the first. To "take him from his descriptions of old houses, upwards" is to take him in a direction the novels often seem to invite—a subliming trajectory not very different, in the end, from the quest for the Absolute itself.[56] Yet the author of the *Comédie humaine* also needed his "Dutch hand," and not only, I would argue, for the famous scene-setting with which the novels begin. For a writer so inclined to the visionary as Balzac, the decision to "weigh . . . himself down with apparently superfluous details," to quote again from his early preface to the *Scènes de la vie privée* (*CH* 1:1174) was to make a crucial turn in the direction of realism. As he wrote of his quasi-autobiographical hero in *Louis Lambert* (1832), "a strong tendency drew him toward mystical works" (*CH* 11:594); and it is almost as if he sought the ballast of those potentially superfluous details to compensate for his more fantastic flights. "Facts are nothing," Lambert declares: "they do not exist; what survives of us is only ideas" (*CH* 11:687). "The real world" with which Balzac repeatedly identified Dutch pictures may have been highly mediated in its turn; but the attempt to imitate such pictures could still provide an important counterweight to Lambert-like visions.

Part Swedenborgian treatise, part history of a descent into madness, *Louis Lambert* itself is evidence of the kind of fiction Balzac was inclined to write without the model of Dutch pictures. But it may be more instructive to look briefly at another novel that appears to call very openly on such pictures, only to turn sharply away from their example. Though no less a reader than Henry James called it "nearly a masterpiece," *Le curé de village* (1841) is comparatively little read these days—and for good reason, I believe, despite a plot that includes secret adultery, murder, and a criminal who chooses to be executed without betraying his accomplice. ("So nearly a masterpiece yet so ultimately not one," was James's full verdict.)[57] Like so many Balzac fictions before it, *Le curé de village* opens with a detailed description of "one of those shops in which nothing seems to have changed since the Middle Ages"—the dusty walls, moss-covered window sills, and crumbling stairs here belonging to a miserly junk-dealer and his wife, who have settled down in Limoges after managing to squirrel away a considerable fortune (*CH* 9:641). Strongly reminiscent of the Guillaumes' shop, as well as the house of that other miser in Saumur, the Sauviats' house also frames, as theirs did, a Dutch picture of their daughter:

> On fine days those who looked up in passing . . . could see the daughter of the Sauviats seated at her window, sewing, embroidering, or drawing the needle above her canvas with a rather dreamy air. Her head stood out sharply among the flowers, which gave a touch of poetry to the brown and cracked sill of her window panes, set in their lead tracery. Sometimes the reflection of the red damask curtains added to the effect of this head, already so colored; like an empurpled flower, she rose above the aerial bed so carefully tended by her on her window sill. This simple [naïf] old house then held something simpler still: a portrait of a young girl, worthy of Mieris,

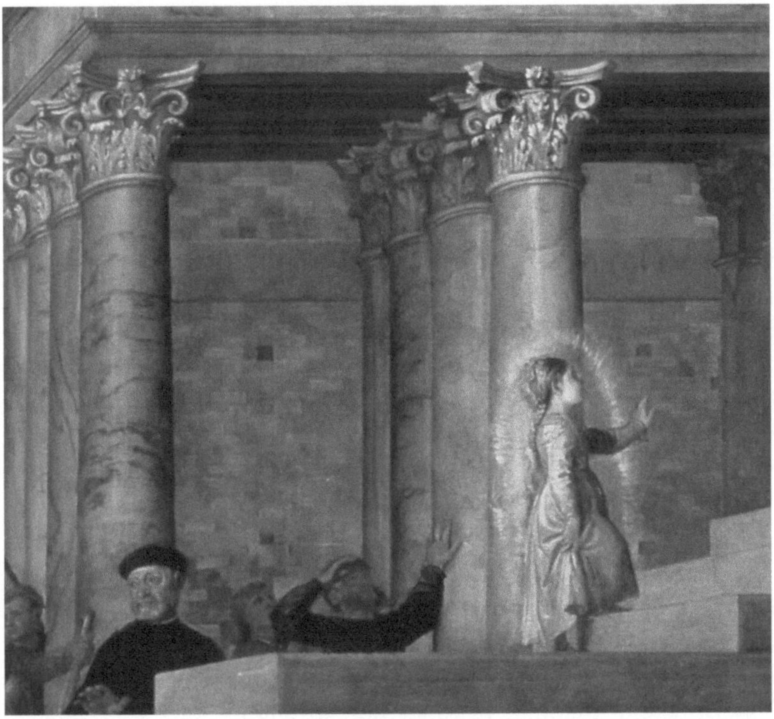

Figure 3-7. Titian: *Presentation of the Virgin in the Temple* (detail), 1539. Accademia, Venice. Photo Credit: Scala/Art Resource, N.Y.

> van Ostade, ter Borch and Gerrit Dou, framed in one of those old half-destroyed casements, worn and brown, of which their brushes were fond. (*CH* 9:653)

Balzac, too, has been fond of such pictures; but in this case his Dutch painting is terribly deceptive, and not only because he will once more imagine the young girl growing restless in her frame. While the image of a beautiful young woman in a bourgeois interior has always tempted him to violate the supposedly Balzacian law that attaches characters to their setting, *Le curé de village* dreams of doing away with material incarnation altogether. A saint's life briefly masquerading as a realist fiction, the novel aspires to a form of history that has no use for the homely details of Dutch art.[58]

By this point, the reader will not be surprised to learn that Véronique Sauviat also appears as a figure in Italian history painting—in this case, as "the sublime little Virgin of Titian in his great painting of the *Presentation at the Temple*" (fig. 3-7). This, of course, is Véronique as a child, and anyone who has seen Titian's picture, we are told, would know what she then was: "the same artless innocence, the same seraphic astonishment in her eyes, the same noble and simple attitude, the same childlike carriage." Unlike Augustine Guillaume and Eugénie Grandet, who are both on the brink of love when they resemble Raphael virgins, the heroine of *Le curé de village* begins life as a would-be Madonna; but in this intensely Catholic novel, the flesh must first be mortified before she can fulfill the promise of sainthood. What intervenes between the little Virgin—whose face "could one day be worth the brush of painters eagerly in search of ideal beauty" (*CH* 9:648)—and the girl in the Dutch picture is a case of small pox, which turns the once fair countenance into the roughened and rosy one that rises above the other blossoms like "an empurpled flower" (*CH* 9:653). Though she now more nearly resembles Eugénie, whose features were also slightly coarsened by the disease, the appearance of comparative ordinariness is an illusion—"a veil of flesh," in the novel's words, that temporarily serves to obscure the original beauty of a soul. Despite the ostensible loss of her looks, it is one of the novel's prevailing fictions that whenever Véronique is deeply moved—particularly by a religious emotion—the rays of "an internal light" efface the marks of the disease and the Little Virgin briefly shines through again (*CH* 9:652). For all its sensational plotting, the remainder of the novel merely works out the logic of this vision: arranging for the heroine's dramatic fall, her protracted repentance, and her final apotheosis, it treats the flesh as both inevitably corrupt and epiphenomenal. Long before we learn that she has spent the years since her criminal affair wearing a hair-shirt and eating nothing but dry bread and unsalted beans, the subliming trajectory of her narrative is clear. "To the Madonna of Raphael, shrouded for eleven years in the torn cloak of the smallpox, had succeeded the beautiful, noble, impassioned woman; and from this woman, stamped by secret suffering, there emerged a saint" (*CH* 9:744).

This vision of a female soul shining through its veil of flesh does not only appear in work explicitly dedicated, like *Le curé de village*, to Catholic themes.[59] Even Madame Grandet undergoes a similar "transfiguration" as she lies dying, while Eugénie herself, as we have seen, ends with nothing left to do "except to spread her wings" and "incline toward heaven" (*CH* 3:1161, 1189). But Eugénie is still alive in the present tense that closes her history—an achievement itself, as Naomi Schor has observed, for a nineteenth-century heroine—and homely details, however melancholy, continue to anchor her to this world.[60] In *Le curé de village*, by contrast, the particulars of the heroine's life disappear from the text well in advance of the heroine: though we gradually learn the general tenor of Véronique's guilty secret, no moment of that history—from her first meeting with the young man who becomes her lover to the crime in which she is vaguely implicated—is ever directly represented in the narrative. As if in complicity with the astute priests and doctors who repeatedly "pierc[e] the veil of flesh that cover[s] her soul" and discover her secret (CH 9:752),[61] the novel does its best to ignore that distracting intermediary, while devoting much space to lengthy excurses on Balzacian themes both political and religious: the unfortunate weakening of paternal authority, the abolition of primogeniture, the destructive effects of state education, and, above all, the superior wisdom of the Church in combating these evils. In *Louis Lambert*, Balzac's visionary protagonist dreams of a new scripture by which "FLESH WILL BE MADE WORD, IT WILL BECOME THE WORD OF GOD" (*CH* 11:689); and *Le curé de village* is clearly written in much the same spirit. Whether or not "the whole of Balzac's own enterprise," as Peter Brooks has written, "tends toward such a reverse incarnation, or disincarnation,"[62] the novelist who was tempted by such visions had all the more need of Dutch painting.

Not "man" but "God" is at the center of *Le curé de village*, Balzac explained to Madame Hanska;[63] and so rigorously does the novel follow through on its commitment to spiritual hierarchy that the crowds of ordinary folk who gather around their dying benefactress are finally prevented from hearing her public confession, which is reserved for the elite circle in the immediate vicinity of her deathbed. (Though Véronique intends otherwise, her friends succeed in thwarting her by choosing to stand at the right moment, and by weeping so loudly that they drown out her words.)[64] This is a long way, clearly, from the "ART FOR MAN" that Thoré-Bürger would later celebrate so enthusiastically.[65] Indeed, nothing could seem further from that cheerful vision of an art opposed to all hierarchy than Balzac's formal declaration in 1842 of his own allegiance to the "twin principles" of "Catholicism and Royalty" (*CH* 1:13). While the author of *Musées de la Hollande* would optimistically contemplate an unbroken line from the independent Hollanders to the *bürgerlische* revolutionaries of the nineteenth century, Balzac's scorn for the July Revolution and its culture could hardly have encouraged his identification with an art that put burghers in the place of saints and monarchs. Yet the *Comédie humaine*'s own art is deservedly famous for sustaining contradiction; and many of its most vividly realized characters are, of course, the very bourgeois its author officially detested.

Even as he was completing work on his novel of Catholic repentance, Balzac composed a satirical fiction about one such figure, a second-rate painter named Pierre Grassou, whose own attempts to imitate Dutch art will offer us a final look at the productive ambivalence of his creator.

A provincial bourgeois who originally arrived in Paris to work for a color merchant, the protagonist of *Pierre Grassou* (1840) makes his career by copying the work of his seventeenth-century predecessors—an exercise that simultaneously absorbs the novelist's genial contempt for the "servile imitation" so often charged against the painters of the Netherlands and manages to deflect that charge from those painters themselves (*CH* 6:1099). The premise that such a "mediocrity currently holds a place . . . in the sun" also affords Balzac the occasion for a satirical attack on contemporary taste—a failure of discrimination that he directly traces to the revolution of 1830 (*CH* 6:1096, 1092). Once the doors of the Salon were opened to every comer, according to the narrator, "all was lost" (*CH* 6:1092). *Pierre Grassou* still manages a covert defense of Dutch painting, but nothing like Thoré-Bürger's "panarchy."[66] Instead, we have Balzac's vision of the indiscriminate mass that now crowds the exhibitions and the "cruel maxim," at once political and aesthetic, by which "mediocrities" in all spheres now rise to prominence: "The principle of election, applied to all, is false" (*CH* 6:1101).

The agent of Grassou's career is the picture dealer, Élias Magus—here described, significantly, as "a kind of Dutch-Belgian-Fleming," though elsewhere in the *Comédie humaine* he appears alternately as a Sephardic Jew and a Pole (*CH* 6:1097).[67] After the painter's first attempt at a Salon piece is rejected, Magus not only manages to sell it but puts in an order for a number of others. Presumably taking his cue from the Salon effort—a village wedding "laboriously copied" from Greuze—the dealer issues his instructions: "Make me some Flemish interiors, an anatomy lesson, a landscape, and I will pay you" (*CH* 6:1096, 1098). From copying a sentimental descendant of the Dutch genre painters, Grassou thus proceeds to copying the Dutch themselves. Though his more gifted colleagues see in the results only "a servile imitation of Dutch landscapes, interiors by Metsu and . . . a copy of Rembrandt's *Anatomy Lesson*" (*CH* 6:1099), Magus is apparently satisfied; and Grassou manages to earn a sober living by continuing to supply him with their like. (Only later does the innocent artist learn that the dealer has been artificially aging his neatly polished pictures and passing them off as Old Masters.) But the work that makes the artist's reputation at the Salon of 1829 is a sentimental painting of a nineteenth-century subject whose principal components have also been substantially lifted from a seventeenth-century source. Entitled *La toilette d'un Chouan, condamné à mort en 1809*, the picture closely tracks Gerrit Dou's "masterpiece," *The Dropsical Woman* (plate 9):

> [H]e had turned the group in the *Dropsical Woman* toward the window, instead of presenting it full face. He had replaced the dying woman by the condemned man: same pallor, same look, same appeal to God. Instead of the Flemish doctor he had painted the cold and official figure of the clerk of the court, dressed in black; but he had added an old woman near the young girl of Gerrit Dou. Finally, the sadly meek figure of the executioner dominated this group.

"This plagiarism, very skillfully disguised, was not at all recognized," the narrator dryly remarks, though the crowds who flock to admire it could presumably have seen the original—Dou's best-known work at the time—hanging in the same Louvre that housed the exhibition (*CH* 6:1100).[68] We are not told what inspired Grassou's choice of subject; but the fact that his Salon entry also recalls Balzac's own work of that same year—*Le dernier Chouan* likewise made its appearance in 1829—suggests that this dogged imitator may have had more than one masterpiece in view.

For Balzac, the "huge success" of Grassou's "mediocre" picture points an obvious moral: "to invent in every field is . . . to die by inches; to copy is to live" (*CH* 6:1100, 1101). In this ironic fiction, the plagiarist even wins a cross of the Legion of Honor, while such recognition is still denied to that "great painter" Joseph Bridau (*CH* 6:1100)—and not coincidentally, one suspects, to Balzac himself. (The novelist would not be made a *chevalier* of the Legion of Honor until 1845.)[69] Indeed, here as elsewhere in the *Comédie humaine*, Balzac clearly delights in contrasting this second-rate artist with avatars of the real thing—particularly the quasi-autobiographical Bridau, whose large-scale canvases will still lack for buyers in *La rabouilleuse* (1842), while the bourgeois of that novel continue to decorate their homes with Grassou's small articles—but also historical figures like Ingres and Delacroix, whose names are briefly invoked at the beginning of this tale as signs of what has been lost ever since the Salon was democratized. Even Théodore Sommervieux makes a brief reappearance here in a vain attempt to teach the protagonist the secrets of composition. Grassou's servile imitation may also be read as ironically confirming Frenhofer's famous dicta to his fellow-painter in *Le chef d'oeuvre inconnu*: "The mission of art is not to copy nature but to express it! You are not a vile copyist, but a poet!" (*CH* 10:418).[70]

Though Grassou undoubtedly represents the antitype of the Balzacian artist, the role of Dutch painting in this satire is more complicated. For even as nearly everything about the diligent Grassou conjures up stereotypes of the Netherlands—from the "system of Dutch care" with which his studio is arranged to the bourgeois domesticity in which he ends, happily married to the daughter of a bottle merchant (*CH* 6:1093)—his very acts of imitation serve to assure that his models retain their status as originals. One of Grassou's more endearing characteristics, in fact, is that he himself knows the difference; and one of the tale's more amusing moments is his horrified discovery that his future father-in-law's vaunted picture collection actually contains nothing but his own copies: "He was Rubens, Paul Potter, Mieris, Metsu, Gerrit Dou! He was twenty great masters all by himself" (*CH* 6:1110). That his honest confession only increases the bottle merchant's admiration of his work—like other benighted viewers in the *Comédie humaine*, this bourgeois collector prefers the copy—just drives home Balzac's irony. "The *Dropsical Woman* is entirely Gerrit Dou's, and not at all someone else's," Thoré-Bürger would later insist by way of emphasizing the individuality of Dutch art;[71] and though Grassou's success might suggest otherwise, the satirist who imagined his career surely agrees with Thoré-Bürger. It is tempting to recall that Balzac had once advertised his own representation of the Chouan rebellion as a kind of genre painting—and that, too, he would certainly have affirmed, was not at all someone else's. *Pierre Grassou* does not say why Dou's picture should be regarded as a masterpiece; but it does suggest that Balzac, almost despite himself, could still identify with Dutch art.

{ four }

George Eliot's Defense of Dutch Painting

George Eliot began her career by defiantly identifying her art with Dutch painting. The well-known manifesto for which "the story pauses a little" in the seventeenth chapter of her first full-length novel, *Adam Bede* (1859), constitutes a defense of domestic realism in words and pictures alike. The chapter opens with the indignant protest of a "lady reader," who interrupts the narrative to deplore its portrait of an insufficiently zealous clergyman.[1] "This Rector of Broxton is little better than a pagan!" she exclaims; but the narrator refuses her hypothetical request to "improve the facts a little" and "touch . . . up" her picture "with a tasteful pencil" (17.175–76).[2] Characterizing herself, with heavy irony, as no "clever novelist," but one "obliged to creep servilely after nature and fact" (17.175), she justifies her practice by analogy to the faithful representation of ordinary life that she sees in Dutch painting:

> It is for this rare, precious quality of truthfulness that I delight in many Dutch paintings,[3] which lofty-minded people despise. I find a source of delicious sympathy in these faithful pictures of a monotonous homely existence, which has been the fate of so many more among my fellow-mortals than a life of pomp or of absolute indigence, of tragic suffering or of world-stirring actions. I turn without shrinking, from cloud-borne angels, from prophets, sibyls, and heroic warriors, to an old woman bending over her flower-pot, or eating her solitary dinner, while the noonday light, softened perhaps by a screen of leaves, falls on her mob-cap, and just touches the rim of her spinning-wheel, and her stone jug, and all those cheap common things which are the precious necessaries of life to her;—or I turn to that village wedding, kept between four brown walls, where an awkward bridegroom opens the dance with a high-shouldered,

> broad-faced bride, while elderly and middle-aged friends look on, with very irregular noses and lips, and probably with quart pots in their hands, but with an expression of unmistakable contentment and good-will. (17.177)

George Eliot wrote the volume of *Adam Bede* that opens with this chapter while traveling with George Henry Lewes in Germany; and it is quite possible that the rhetorical "turn" here records a literal turn as well, as she moved between history painting and genre in the Alte Pinakothek at Munich.[4] At least one of the images she evokes has, in fact, been persuasively identified with a picture in that museum—Gerrit Dou's *Das Tischgebet der Spinnerin* (*The Spinner's Grace*) (plate 10)—and I shall return to the implications of its presence shortly.[5] But first it is worth noting how the resisting reader—or is she now a viewer?—once again breaks into the text. This time it is the vulgarity of Dutch low life rather than the worldliness of English clergymen that inspires the protest. "Foh!" she says, "what vulgar details! What good is there in taking all these pains to give an exact likeness of old women and clowns? What a low phase of life!—what clumsy, ugly people!" The narrator's immediate response is to argue that love does not depend upon beauty. Then she turns back, by way of "beauty" itself, to the analogy with painting:

> All honour and reverence to the divine beauty of form! Let us cultivate it to the utmost in men, women, and children—in our gardens and in our houses. But let us love that other beauty too, which lies in no secret of proportion, but in the secret of deep human sympathy. Paint us an angel, if you can, with a floating violet robe, and a face paled by the celestial light; paint us yet oftener a Madonna, turning her mild face upward and opening her arms to welcome the divine glory; but do not impose on us any aesthetic rules which shall banish from the region of Art those old women scraping carrots with their work-worn hands, those heavy clowns taking holiday in a dingy pot-house, those rounded backs and stupid weather-beaten faces that have bent over the spade and done the rough work of the world—those homes with their tin pans, their brown pitchers, their rough curs, and their clusters of onions. In this world there are so many of these common, coarse people, who have no picturesque sentimental wretchedness! It is so needful we should remember their existence, else we may happen to leave them quite out of our religion and philosophy, and frame lofty theories which only fit a world of extremes. Therefore let Art always remind us of them; therefore

> let us always have men ready to give the loving pains of a life to the faithful representing of commonplace things. (17.177, 178)

George Eliot never names the "lofty-minded people" whose contempt for Dutch pictures ostensibly inspires her impassioned defense, but her own idiom clearly responds to the rhetoric that had long kept those pictures in their place. The aggressive irony with which she speaks of being "obliged to creep servilely after nature and fact" effectively claims as a badge of honor what had hitherto been one of the most conventional formulas for the denigration of Dutch painting. Rather than a slavish submission to nature, there is a note of noble commitment in "obliged," which gives a characteristically ethical charge to her realism. Throughout the chapter, the language of fidelity and truth-telling translates what had long been described as mere imitation into a moral imperative, as when she praises the "faithful" pictures of the Dutch, or compares her own practice to that of a witness in a court of law, "bound" to narrate her experience "on oath" (17.177, 175).[6] Reynolds had contended that what raised the artist above the mere copyist was "the real labour of thinking," a labor he consistently identified with the effort to improve on nature;[7] but George Eliot implicitly reverses that argument. While she shares his commitment to hard work—indeed the value of labor is one of the central themes of *Adam Bede*—the effort she has in mind is very different: "Falsehood," she says, "is so easy, truth so difficult." And by "falsehood," she makes clear, she means not just the lazy lie but the willful invention of a world better than this:

> The pencil is conscious of a delightful facility in drawing a griffin—the longer the claws, and the larger the wings, the better; but that marvellous facility which we mistook for genius, is apt to forsake us when we want to draw a real unexaggerated lion. Examine your words well, and you will find that even when you have no motive to be false, it is a very hard thing to say the exact truth, even about your own immediate feelings—much harder than to say something fine about them which is *not* the exact truth. (17.176–77)

In the third volume of *Modern Painters*, Ruskin had suggested that a griffin is "true" if the artist "did really see a griffin in his imagination," but the George Eliot of *Adam Bede*, at least, apparently adheres to a sterner standard.[8] Her evocation of the "rare, precious quality of truthfulness" in Dutch painting immediately follows.

Whether or not the novelist was consciously recalling Ruskin's griffin when she wrote this passage, there is no question that she knew the third volume of *Modern Painters*—having reviewed it for the *Westminster Review* only two years earlier—and no question, too, that she deeply admired it. Indeed, the review of Ruskin is among a handful of articles that have often been read as the future novelist's informal prolegomena to her art (the others are "The Natural History of German Life" and "Silly Novels by Lady Novelists," both also of 1856); and its ardent summary of Ruskinian doctrine would not be out of place in the seventeenth chapter of *Adam Bede*. "The truth of infinite value that he teaches is *realism*," to recall her words once again, "—the doctrine that all truth and beauty are to be attained by a humble and faithful study of nature, and not by substituting vague forms, bred by imagination on the mists of feeling, in place of definite, substantial reality."[9] But if George Eliot was prepared to extend this doctrine to the "vulgar details" of Dutch painting (17.177), it also seems clear that Ruskin would have strenuously resisted such an application of his teaching. While more than subject matter was at stake in his repudiation of the Dutch, the writer who repeatedly excoriated "the petty skill that was bred in the fumes of the taverns of the North" (20:79) could hardly have been expected to welcome those wedding guests "with quart pots in their hands"—let alone "those heavy clowns taking holiday in a dingy pot-house." Realism was one thing for Ruskin, and the careful depiction of "these common, coarse people" another. Though some have been tempted to argue that there is no essential difference between his aesthetics and those of the early George Eliot, on the matter of Dutch pictures, it seems clear, he belongs with the "lofty-minded people"—and "lady readers"—rather than with the narrator who urgently invites our sympathy.[10] And though George Eliot could not have known it, Ruskin's responses to her own fiction would in fact bear out her intuition that those who failed to sympathize with Dutch painting would likewise resist her "faithful pictures of a monotonous homely existence."[11] Of *The Mill on the Floss* (1860) he would write after her death: "There is not a single person in the book of the smallest importance to anybody but themselves, or whose qualities deserve so much as a line of printer's type in their description." While the novels of Scott were like "a picture of Angelico's," he could see in George Eliot only the consummation of "the English Cockney School"—its "personages . . . picked up from behind the counter and out of the gutter" (34:376, 378).

In truth, George Eliot carefully excludes "the gutter" from her conception of Dutch painting. The "monotonous homely existence" with which she identifies such painting is characterized by its very lack of extremes: "absolute indigence" is removed as firmly from the picture as "a life of pomp" (17.177). Great poverty and suffering, she repeatedly implies, are too unusual to count as the sort of ordinary life that the art of the Dutch—and by analogy, her own—seeks to represent. And one reason they are unusual, though she does not say so explicitly, is that everyone who does count in this world appears to work. "I would not, even if I had the choice, be the clever novelist who could create a world so much better than this, in which we get up in the morning to do our daily work," the narrator announces (17.176); and the signs of that work are repeatedly emphasized here, from the "work-worn hands" of the old women scraping carrots, to the "rounded backs" and "weather-beaten faces that have bent over the spade and done the rough work of the world" that belong to the holiday-makers in the pot-house. Even the light that illuminates the solitary diner pointedly touches the rim of her spinning wheel as well. Only the guests at the village wedding constitute an exception, and they are presumably "taking holiday" like the clowns. Though there is an important gap between these seventeenth-century peasants and the implicitly middle-class reader, who is urged to sympathize with vicars and shopkeepers as well as servants, it is striking how consistently the "commonplace" that unites them is identified with the exercise of honest labor. "Neither are picturesque lazzaroni or romantic criminals half so frequent as your common labourer," says the narrator, "who gets his own bread, and eats it vulgarly but creditably with his own pocket-knife." And "it is more needful that I should have a fibre of sympathy connecting me with that vulgar citizen who weighs out my sugar in a vilely assorted cravat and waistcoat, than with the handsomest rascal in red scarf and green feathers"—the latter presumably disqualifying himself by good looks and lack of employment alike (17.179). The "vulgar citizen" may not labor in the same sense as the man who "gets his own bread, and eats it vulgarly," but they share in the ordinariness—and the virtue—of "daily work."

As we have seen, the low status of Dutch painting itself had long been inseparable from its associations with manual craft; and in this sense, too, George Eliot's defense of narrative realism entails a tribute to labor. Rather than identify with the lofty theorists who had sought to elevate the art of painting by allying it with poetry, she aggressively reverses the comparison, claiming the dignity of those "faithful" Dutch pictures for her own art of writing. Though *Adam Bede* remains inescapably a work of the head rather than the hands, the novelist refuses to distance that work from the sort performed by her carpenter-hero.[12] Even her taste for the famously labor-intensive paintings of Gerrit Dou may not be irrelevant in this regard. Among the so-called *fijnschilders*—whose highly finished pictures the early nineteenth century generally preferred to the more open brushwork typically valued by modern viewers—Dou was particularly renowned for his patience and industry. As one British commentator had written only a few years before George Eliot's novel: "He cared not how he laboured or how protracted his labour was, so that he was enabled to attain to that degree of excellence to which he felt his genius was capable of leading him."[13] Legend reports that he devoted five days to the underpainting of a single hand, for example, and that he responded to praise for his meticulous painting of a tiny broom by replying that he had still three days' work to do on it.[14] *Adam Bede* itself opens with the question of whether or not a piece of work is finished—Adam's dreamy younger brother, Seth, having forgotten to complete the panels of a door on which he is working—and in the same chapter, Adam himself memorably scolds his fellow carpenters for the speed with which they fling away their tools when the clock strikes six. It is easy to imagine the sympathy with which both novelist and hero would have responded to the Dutch painter's legendary dedication to his labors.

Whether or not she knew such stories, George Eliot evidently took pleasure in contemplating Dou's work. A letter from Munich in 1858 records the "unspeakable relief" with which she sweeps from her mind a pretentious canvas by a contemporary history painter in order "to call up in . . . imagination a little Gerard Dow . . . seen hanging in a corner of one of the cabinets";[15] and *Adam Bede* clearly reenacts that process, as it turns from "cloud-borne angels" to "an old woman bending over her flower pot, or eating her solitary dinner"—both of them subjects frequently painted by Dou (figs. 4-1 and 4-2).[16] Yet if the details with which George Eliot evokes the old woman at dinner—"while the noonday light, softened perhaps by a screen of leaves, falls on her mob-cap, and just touches the rim of her spinning-wheel, and her stone jug"—confirm that she was recalling the particular picture she had seen at Munich (plate 10),[17] the main effect of the ekphrasis is to conjure up a kind of painting rather than an individual image. No original has yet been identified for the village wedding, with its "awkward bridegroom" and "high-shouldered, broad-faced bride," but while there may also be a specific picture behind this image as well, here, too, as throughout the chapter, George Eliot's language manages to suggest both close observation and typicality (17.177). "That" village wedding cannot be Pieter Breughel's *Wedding Dance* (fig. 4-3) at Vienna, since Breughel's famous painting is an outdoor scene, nor can it be Adriaen van Ostade's *Merrymakers in an Inn* (fig. 4-4), since there is no evidence that Ostade's dancers are a newly married couple; yet the very fact that the novelist's verbal picture partly corresponds to both these paintings—and to

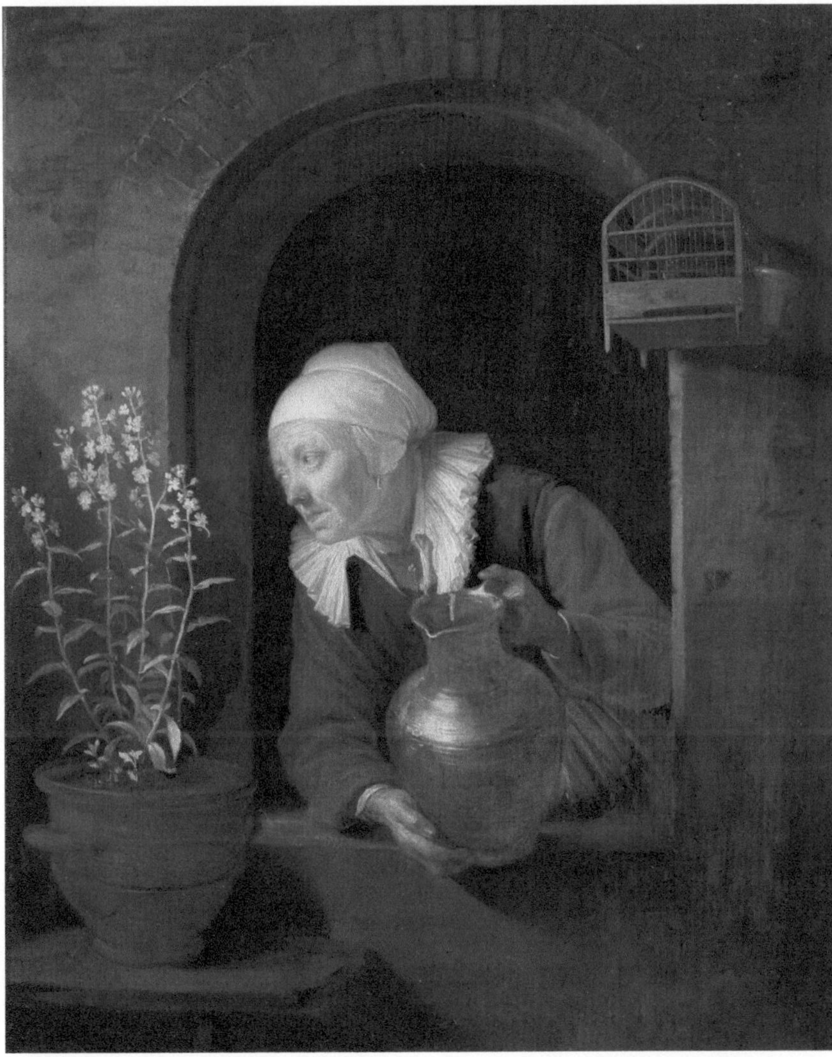

Figure 4-1. Gerrit Dou: *Old Woman at the Window, Watering Her Flowers*, c. 1660–65. Kunsthistorisches Museum, Vienna. Photo Credit: Erich Lessing/Art Resource, N.Y.

many others—is much to the point. Even before her plurals overtly generalize the paintings in question ("those old women scraping carrots with their work-worn hands, those heavy clowns taking holiday in a dingy pot-house . . . those homes with their tin pans . . . and their clusters of onions"—17.178), George Eliot's ekphrasis conveys the generic nature of

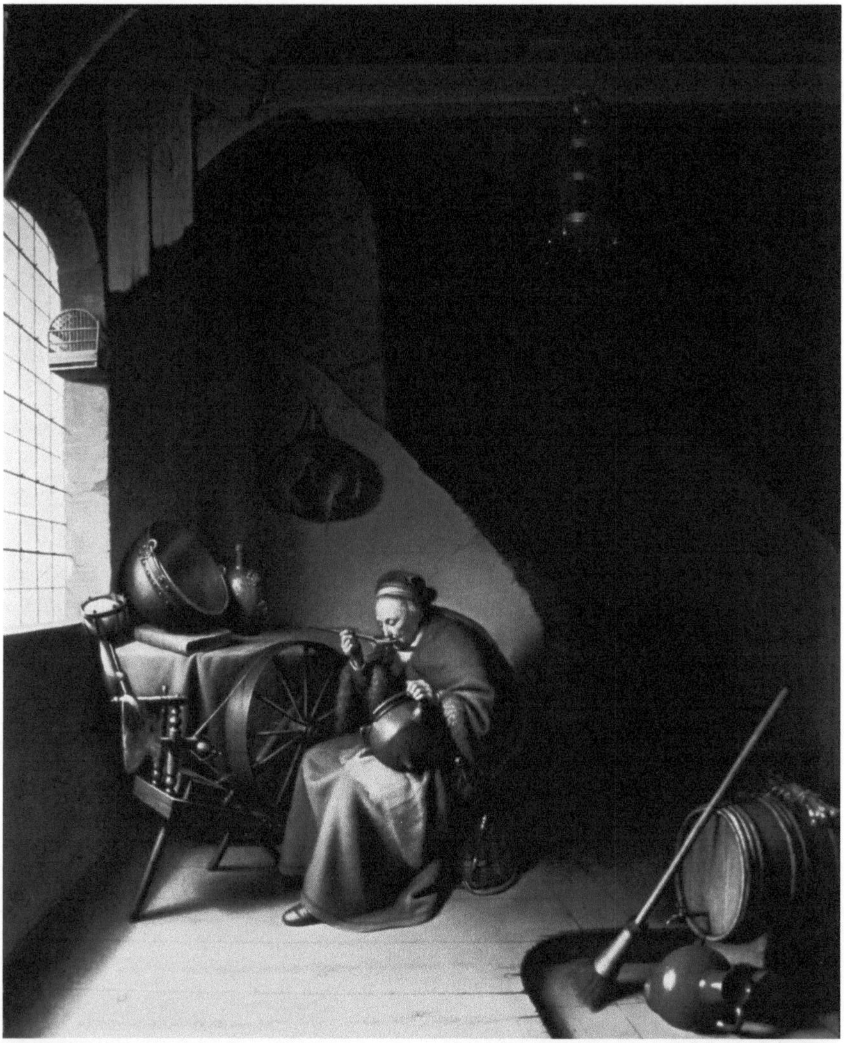

Figure 4-2. Gerrit Dou: *Woman Eating in an Interior*, c. 1632–37. Private collection. Photo credit: Kavaler/Art Resource, N.Y.

Dutch genre, its tendency to produce certain motifs over and over. And like the images it evokes, it produces an effect of the real by means of synecdoche, as certain representative details and scenes stand in for the places and events that make up daily life for most people.

"Monotonous homely existence," as the phrase implies, is not only a matter of work. It is the home in "homely," after all, that determines its sense of the commonplace, and the association of Dutch painting with

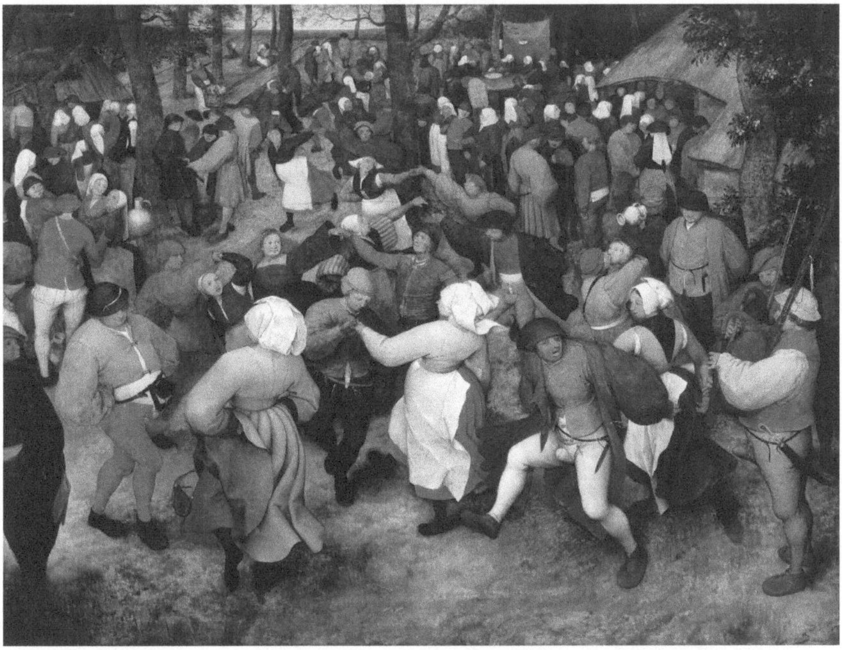

Figure 4-3. Pieter Breughel the Elder: *The Wedding Dance*, c. 1566. The Detroit Institute of Arts. City of Detroit Purchase. Photograph © 1984 The Detroit Institute of Arts

domestic life is even more prominent here than that with labor. Together with scenes of rural leisure and celebration (the pot-house, on the one hand, the village wedding, on the other), domestic interiors dominate this brief catalogue of images. Much of the work, in fact, is work done at home; and the monotony of homely existence derives as much from the repetitiveness of household tasks like scraping carrots or watering flowers as it does from the routine labor of the fields ("those rounded backs . . . that have bent over the spade"). If even holiday-making implicitly shares in this monotony, it does so by virtue of its identity as custom or ritual—an identity intensified here by its very representation as a genre painting, where anonymous figures take part in actions that are conventionally understood not as unique but repeatable. The couple dancing at their wedding are as nameless as the old women scraping carrots; and despite her broad face and high shoulders, the bride is not so much an individual as the representative of a type. "That" village wedding may signify a particular painting, but a village wedding, like a gathering at a pot-house, is the kind of event that recurs again and again.

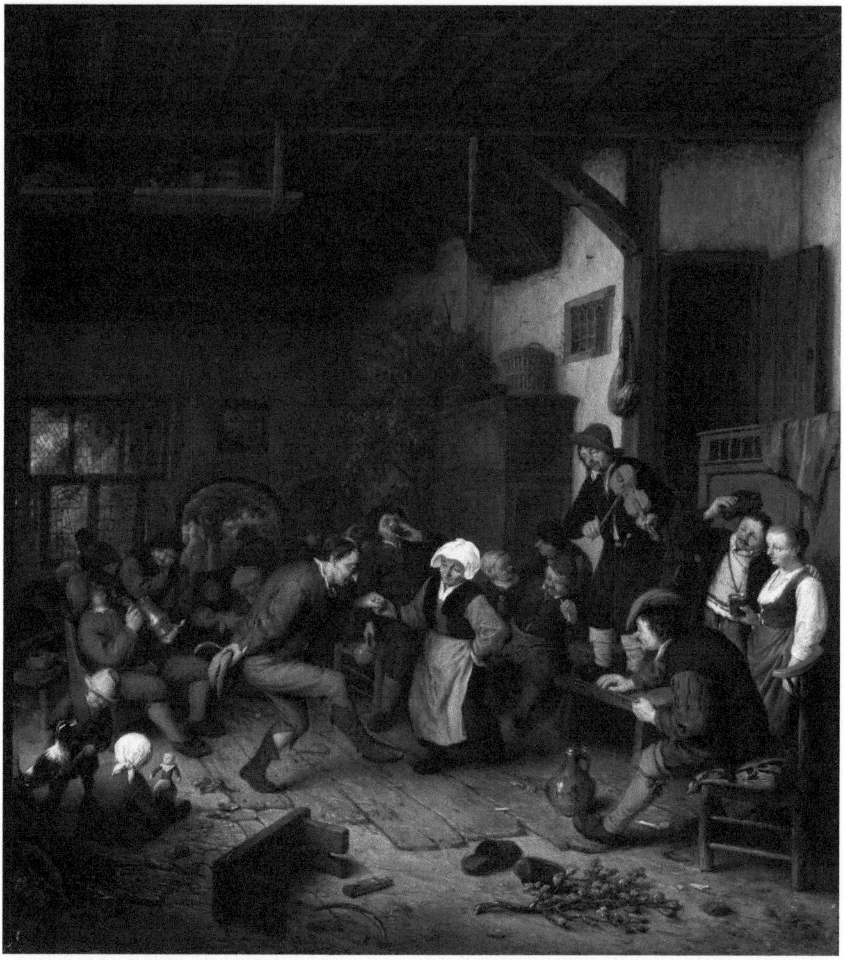

Figure 4-4. Adriaen van Ostade: *Merrymakers in an Inn*, 1674. The Art Institute of Chicago. George B. and Mary R. Harris Fund, 1894.1028. Reproduction: The Art Institute of Chicago

By this measure, of course, even George Eliot's early fiction rarely indulges in verbal genre painting for very long, since she aspires to represent all her figures, including the minor ones, as distinct individuals, whose possession of proper names is only the first sign of their particularized identities.[18] Nor is this the only sense, as we shall see, in which her novels inevitably depart from the model. Yet it is more than an accident of history that the writing of George Eliot's first novel coincided with travels that enabled her to look long and hard at Dutch painting—"I did not half satisfy my appetite for the rich collection of Flemish and Dutch pictures here," she wrote of her time in Dresden, "for Teniers, Ryckaert, Gerard Dow, Terburg, Mieris and the rest"—and the values with which she associated it would continue to shape all her work, even when she had apparently moved a considerable distance from the program articulated in *Adam Bede*.[19] The "faithful representing of commonplace things" is hardly a full account of George Eliot's realism, let alone of her fiction generally. But as I hope to show, the novelist had good reason for beginning her career by recalling her readers—and herself—to the merits of Dutch art.

George Eliot's early fiction is filled with scenes that prompt comparison to Dutch painting.[20] Especially in its first half, *Adam Bede* itself offers a rich catalogue of such pictures, from the repeated image of a woman posed in a doorway to detailed interiors like those of the Hall Farm and its dairy, or the scenes of communal ritual that mark Arthur Donnithorne's coming-of-age. Here, for example, is the first appearance of the woman in a doorway, as Adam carries the key of his workshop to a nearby house in the opening chapter:

> It was a low house, with smooth grey thatch and buff walls, looking pleasant and mellow in the evening light. The leaded windows were bright and speckless, and the door-stone was as clean as a white boulder at ebb tide. On the door-stone stood a clean old woman, in a dark-striped linen gown, a red kerchief, and a linen cap, talking to some speckled fowls which appeared to have been drawn towards her by an illusory expectation of cold potatoes or barley. (1.12)

One need not identify a particular model for this passage to recognize how much it has in common with Dutch painting: the predominantly neutral tones of the composition, set off by a touch of red, the attentiveness to the evening light, the registration of domestic cleanliness, and above all, perhaps, the implicit framing of the woman in relation to the architecture—not to mention the subject itself, at once rural, domesticated, and feminine—strongly call to mind the characteristics and motifs of countless Dutch pictures. The brief dialogue that follows gives the old woman a name (Dolly), makes clear that she is a servant, and identifies the house in question as that of Jonathan Burge, the carpenter and builder for whom Adam works; but the very fact that these identifications are temporarily delayed increases the genre-effect of the image.

The sequence of pictures by which the reader is gradually led from the exterior of the Hall Farm to Mrs. Poyser's kitchen lacks this sort of anonymity, yet the representation of Dinah at her household task, her face illuminated by the light reflected from other objects, is still more reminiscent of Dutch painting:

> Everything was looking at its brightest at this moment, for the sun shone right on the pewter dishes, and from their reflecting surfaces pleasant jets of light were thrown on mellow oak and bright brass;—and on a still pleasanter object than these; for some of the rays fell on Dinah's finely-moulded cheek, and lit up her pale red hair to auburn, as she bent over the heavy household linen which she was mending for her aunt. No scene could have been more peaceful. (6.73–74)

Though both the serenity of the scene and the precise notation of the light may prompt the modern reader to think of Vermeers like *The Milkmaid* or *The Lace-Maker* (plates 11 and 12), it would be historically more accurate to recall, for example, Anna Jameson's response to "the sentiment of home-felt tranquillity" in Maes's *Girl Sewing* (plate 1)—a picture whose handling of light she also characterized as "most exquisite."[21] Maes himself painted many variants of such subjects (plate 2), as did Pieter de Hooch, among others; and a number of these ended up, like the *Girl Sewing*, in British collections. The stasis of the novelist's picture, it should be said, is quickly interrupted by Dinah's aunt: "No scene could have been more peaceful," the passage continues, "if Mrs. Poyser, who was ironing a few things that still remained from the Monday's wash, had not been making a frequent clinking with her iron, and moving to and fro whenever she wanted it to cool" (6.74). But for as long as the action is suspended at least, "Dinah Mending Linen," like "Dolly in the Doorway," constitutes a verbal painting in the Dutch manner.

Though George Eliot's own picture represents a young woman mending linen and not an old one scraping carrots, it also anticipates, of course, those typical images of domestic labor that will be evoked in the seventeenth chapter. The glimpse of Hetty weighing butter in the Hall Farm dairy is another such picture (7.83); and so, still more obviously, is that of Lisbeth Bede knitting with "work-hardened hands," as she stands in her doorway awaiting Adam's return (4.39). Dinah, too, we soon learn, has the hands of a "workin' woman" (10.109); and while she apparently associates their roughness with her periods of employment in the Snowfield cotton-mill, we only see them, significantly, engaged in household labor. Like the Dutch painters, in other words, George Eliot renders certain kinds of scenes more visible than others; and the effect in this case is to make the world of her novel still more closely resemble that depicted by her seventeenth-century predecessors. (There are, needless to say, no images of cotton-mills in Golden Age painting, though there are numerous images of women working, as Dinah does, with the needle and the broom.)

Indeed, precisely because the preindustrial Midlands of the early fiction have so much in common with the Netherlands of Golden Age art, specifically pictorial influences are inevitably entangled with other affinities. Whether one thinks of material details—like the thatched roof and leaded windows of the Burges' house and the pewter plates at the Poysers'—or of domestic habits, like the obsessive cleanliness registered in both settings, the Dutch painting of *Adam Bede* is at once a matter of visual convention and of social fact; and it is not always possible to distinguish neatly between them. That Hayslope itself remains in many ways a peasant community, as George Eliot suggests more than once, means that its customs and rituals are not very far removed from those represented in countless low genre paintings two centuries earlier.[22] Even the densely cultivated landscape of dairies and farms contributes to the "Dutch" effect. The lowlands of Victorian realism are more than a function of geography, as George Levine has taught us,[23] but the gently rolling contours of the Warwickshire countryside could only have encouraged the early George Eliot to reimagine them as scenes from Dutch painting.

A glance at the table of contents will recall how much of *Adam Bede* is given over to picture—and how many of its pictures might be classified as genre. The chapter titles of the first half read like a catalogue of such images: "The Workshop," "The Preaching," "Home and Its Sorrows," "The Hall Farm," "The Dairy," "In the Cottage," "In the Wood," "The Two Bed-Chambers," "Church," "The Night-School and the Schoolmaster," "Going to the Birthday-Feast," "Dinner-Time," "The Health-Drinking," "The Games," "The Dance." Only the seventeenth chapter is entitled "In Which the Story Pauses a Little," but the story has been pausing in this sense ever since its opening paragraph, which undertakes not to tell what happened "on the eighteenth of June, in the year of our Lord 1799," but to "show . . . the roomy workshop of Mr. Jonathan Burge, carpenter and builder in the village of Hayslope," as it then "appeared" (1.5).[24]

Though the novel begins, conventionally enough, in the narrative past, its habit of shifting into the present tense—already evident in this opening scene—intensifies the impression that story is being suspended for picture. The fullest exercise in this mode is the sequence of views by which we are introduced to the Hall Farm in chapter 6, but there are briefer versions in the representation of Lisbeth in the doorway, our first glimpse of the rectory dining-room, the scene in the two bed-chambers, the description of the weather on Arthur's birthday, and elsewhere as well. While the predominant effect is simply to interrupt the action for scene-setting ("the room is a large and lofty one, with an ample mullioned oriel window at one end"—5.54), the on-goingness of the present also tends to make any human gestures in the picture seem not singular but typical and repeatable: "the door of the house is open, and an elderly woman is looking out" (4.39). In a related vein, note how the description of the weather on Arthur's birthday manages to associate the unique event of one man's coming-of-age with a recurrent "pause" in the cycle of the seasons:

> The thirtieth of July was come, and it was one of those half-dozen warm days which sometimes occur in the middle of a rainy English summer. No rain had fallen for the last three or four days, and the weather was perfect for that time of the year. . . . Perfect weather for an outdoor July merrymaking, yet surely not the best time of year to be born in. Nature seems to make a hot pause just then—all the loveliest flowers are gone; the sweet time of early growth and vague hopes is past; and yet the time of harvest and ingathering is not come, and we tremble at the possible storms that may ruin the precious fruit in the moment of its ripeness. The woods are all one dark monotonous green; the waggon-loads of hay no longer creep along the lanes, scattering their sweet-smelling fragments on the blackberry branches; the pastures are often a little tanned, yet the corn has not got its last splendour of red and gold; the lambs and calves have lost all traces of their innocent frisky prettiness, and have become stupid young sheep and cows. But it is a time of leisure on the farm—that pause between hay and corn-harvest, and so the farmers and labourers in Hayslope and Broxton thought the Captain did well to come of age just then. (22.247)

This is too generalized, perhaps, to count as landscape painting; but the "hot pause" it represents, at once static and repeatable, is a fitting introduction to the genre-like scenes of celebration that follow.

While it would be wrong to suggest that nothing happens in *Adam Bede* until "A Crisis" disrupts these peaceful pictures in chapter 27, the contrast between the relative stasis of the first three books and the rapid plot-making of the next two is nonetheless striking. Once again—and now quite literally—the table of contents tells the story: from the moment at which Adam precipitates that crisis by his accidental encounter with the lovers in the wood until "Another Meeting in the Wood" closes the fifth book some twenty chapters later, the titles virtually all refer to actions or events, on the one hand, or to units of time, on the other, as the swift-moving consequences of Hetty's seduction play themselves out. The fifth book is particularly relentless in its momentum, from Hetty's anguished flight, her arrest, and her trial for infanticide, through Arthur's melodramatic arrival at "The Last Moment" with her reprieve. Not until both these agents of plot have been expelled from Hayslope does the narrative come to rest again in genre painting, as the final book of the novel returns to the domestic and communal rituals—"At the Hall Farm," "In the Cottage," "The Harvest-Supper"—that the lovers' transgressions have disrupted.[25]

That this last book begins, as it ends, with a woman framed in a doorway not only twice recomposes the narrative as picture but confirms that picture itself as a sign of stability and recurrence.[26] Indeed, the iterative tense with which the narrator introduces the first instance makes it briefly unclear whether we are about to witness a particular scene or simply being told of a repeated one:

> The milking of the cows was a sight Mrs. Poyser loved, and at this hour on mild days she was usually standing at the house door, with her knitting in her hands, in quiet contemplation, only heightened to a keener interest when the vicious yellow cow, who once kicked over a pailful of precious milk, was about to undergo the preventive punishment of having her hinder-legs strapped.
>
> To-day, however, Mrs. Poyser gave but a divided attention to the arrival of the cows. (49.473–74)

Mrs. Poyser's habitual serenity on these occasions has been partly disrupted by the news of Dinah's intention to depart, but otherwise the picture is at once peaceful and familiar: apart from the Poyser child, Totty, who "is larger by more than two years' growth" than when we first saw her, and the black gowns that testify, we soon learn, to the death of the grandfather, "there is little outward change now discernable in our old friends, or in the pleasant house-place, bright with polished oak and pewter." (Note, too, the familiar recourse to the present tense.) Dinah is "patiently" sewing as Mrs. Poyser talks to her (49.473–74); and if this arrangement primarily resembles the earlier picture of Dinah mending linen while Mrs. Poyser irons, the latter's posture in the doorway also recalls both Dolly in the opening chapter and Lisbeth Bede, who likewise knits as she stands on her threshold looking outward. That these visual echoes suggest not merely the formal patterning of George Eliot's novel but the generic repetitions of daily life is confirmed by the last picture in the series—that of another woman in a doorway, who for a brief moment remains anonymous. "It is near the end of June, in 1807," the epilogue begins:

> The workshops have been shut up half an hour or more in Adam Bede's timber-yard, which used to be Jonathan Burge's, and the mellow evening light is falling on the pleasant house with the buff walls and the soft grey thatch, very much as it did when we saw Adam bringing in the keys on that June evening nine years ago.
>
> There is a figure we know well, just come out of the house and shading her eyes with her hands as she looks for something in the distance; for the rays that fall on her white borderless cap and her pale auburn hair are very dazzling. (537)

By the time the sun once again lights up her pale red hair, it is clear that the woman is Dinah; but the momentary confusion with Lisbeth is deliberate, as is the explicit return to the opening chapter of the novel. That generic repetition enables one figure to take the place of another is evident even before Seth remarks the resemblance and tacitly alludes to the death of her predecessor: "Thee't like poor mother used to be. She was always on the look-out for Adam" (538). As in the earlier scene at Hall Farm, the only signs of change are the death of the older generation and the growth of the younger: there is a "Lisbeth" here after all, but she proves to be "a small fair creature . . . little more than four years old" (537). The one thing that threatened the calm of that earlier scene was the possibility that Dinah might reject domestic life for the solitary vocation of the preacher. Now she, too, has been assimilated to the picture.

But what has any of this to do with that insufficiently zealous clergyman, the Rector of Broxton? For it is that handsome gentleman, after all, who provides the ostensible occasion for George Eliot's defense of Dutch painting—and not, as one might expect, that "aged peasant-woman" Lisbeth Bede (10.103), or even that excellent housewife, Mrs. Poyser. Though the novel does have its scenes of "heavy clowns taking holiday"—think, for example, of the farm laborers gathered at the Poyser table for the harvest supper—it is not these that prompt its eloquence on behalf of "commonplace things," but a conversation between two attractive and well-bred men that partly turns on an allusion to Aeschylus. (As readers will recall, this is the scene in which Mr. Irwine, from a mistaken sense of social delicacy, allows the opportunity of Arthur's confession to pass and thus indirectly contributes to the latter's eventual seduction of Hetty.) Indeed, with his aristocratic lineage, "plump white hand," and genial allusions to his own laziness (16.168), the Reverend Irwine would seem the least likely character in *Adam Bede* to inspire an aesthetic manifesto about pictures of old women scraping carrots. Yet this all-too-worldly clergyman is not the first of George Eliot's fictional clerics to occasion thoughts of such painting; and for all the seeming anomaly of the connection, there is good reason, I would suggest, why her wish to represent the clergy "solely in its *human* and *not at all* in its *theological* aspect"—to quote a letter from Lewes to her publisher, John Blackwood—should be associated in the novelist's mind with a defense of Dutch art.[27]

The immediate object of Lewes's remark was George Eliot's first work of fiction, *Scenes of Clerical Life* (1857), but the dialogue he thus initiated can still be heard in chapter 17 of *Adam Bede* as well. For if the "lady reader" whom the story pauses to address is of course an invention of the novelist's, she has one of her immediate sources in Blackwood himself.[28] Even as he agreed to publish the first of the *Scenes*, "The Sad Fortunes of the Reverend Amos Barton," in his magazine, Blackwood was already chafing a little at its anonymous author's clergymen, who "with one exception," as he wrote to Lewes, "are not very attractive specimens of the body."[29] When he later wrote to convey some divided responses to the story, the author herself chose to reply, in a letter notable both for her first use of the pseudonym "George Eliot," and for her first defense of that writer's art by analogy to the Dutch. "In reference to artistic presentation, much adverse opinion will of course arise from a dislike to the *order* of art rather than from a critical estimate of the execution. Any one who detests the Dutch school in general will hardly appreciate fairly the merits of a particular Dutch painting."[30] Blackwood never committed himself on the merits of "the Dutch school in general," but he was clearly uncomfortable with his new artist's approach to clerical portraiture. "When are you going to give us a really good active working clergyman, neither absurdly evangelical nor absurdly High Church?" he inquired after receiving an installment of the third story, "Janet's Repentance"; a later portion of the same work prompted him to observe rather plaintively, "Your Bishop is doubtless a true sketch, but I wish he had been a better sample of the cloth."[31] Once again George Eliot responded in terms that anticipate the seventeenth chapter of *Adam Bede*, as she defended her "particular Bishop" against any claim to represent "Bishops in general": "I undertake to exhibit nothing as it should be," she wrote in part, "only . . . to exhibit some things as they have been or are, seen through such a medium as my own nature gives me."[32]

Though George Eliot had once thought of extending her *Scenes* with the story of a Methodist woman preacher, as well as with a sketch she called the "Clerical Tutor," her decision to close the magazine serial and incorporate these into a novel instead seems to have been partly motivated by this running argument with her publisher.[33] Yet the argument did not end with the conclusion of "Janet's Repentance." Less than a week before the novelist set out for Germany with Lewes, she received a letter from Blackwood about the first volume of *Adam Bede*, which included, among other things, a characteristically wishful response to the portrait of Mr. Irwine: "The Vicar is a capital fellow and the visit to the sick room [of his sister] very touching, but I wish for the sake of my Church of England friends he had more of 'the root of the matter in him.' However I hope he is to sublime as the story goes on."[34] Rather than continue the correspondence, this time George Eliot chose to respond in the novel itself—the break between volumes affording an obvious place in which her story could "pause a little" for an aesthetic manifesto.[35]

In the end, of course, Blackwood was not the only resisting reader whom chapter 17 would address; and George Eliot's defense of her art was determined by far more than his persistent desire to touch up her portraits. Yet there is no doubt that his questioning of her clerical characters in particular touched a nerve—all the more because George Eliot's representation of the clergy "in its *human* . . . aspect" went to the very heart of her self-conception as a novelist. Though it is easier to see why she associated Dutch painting with the "homely details" of "Amos Barton" than with her portrait of Mr. Irwine,[36] all her representations of the clerisy are concerned to work out the relation between what Adam Bede calls religious "notions" and "feelings" (17.180)—a relation that the beginning novelist implicitly makes analogous to that between history painting, on the one hand, and Dutch genre, on the other. While the history painter, in this conception, reshapes his figures to accord with idealized abstractions, the genre painter teaches us to look sympathetically at people as they are; and in so doing, he teaches us the only form of religion that the early George Eliot was intent on preserving. Just as the narrator's "idealistic friend" would prefer "the sublimest abstract of all clerical graces . . . ever conceived by an able novelist" to that worldly holder of multiple livings, Mr. Irwine (17.177, 179), so she would presumably prefer pictures of the Madonna to images of old women scraping carrots. And just as she is nonetheless exhorted to look sympathetically at Dutch paintings and "to be in perfect charity" with the faulty Irwine, so Irwine himself approaches his parishioners with a sympathy and respect that finally count more as "real religion" than the purity of doctrine articulated by his zealous successor, Mr. Ryde (17.179, 182). Like the pronouncement that "religion's something else besides notions," this praise of Irwine purports to come from the elderly Adam Bede, with whom the narrator talked of these matters in later years (17.180); but in both cases, George Eliot makes clear, an older and wiser Adam speaks for the novelist.

There are many questions raised by this implicit argument—not least, as I shall suggest, whether Dutch genre paintings were ever really intended to induce "sympathy" in their viewers. And then there is the matter of the shifting relations between belief and feeling in George Eliot's own clerical portraits, whether in the characters themselves or in the responses they are meant to inspire in the reader. While Mr. Irwine's kindly treatment of his neighbors makes him both an exemplar and an object of those sympathies that for George Eliot signify more than any theological doctrine, Amos Barton finally arouses something like religious feeling in his parishioners—and, by extension, the reader—not by anything he says or does but only by suffering himself. Unlike Amos, who is "superlatively middling" in everything (40), including his theology,[37] or the comparatively latitudinarian Irwine, the Reverend Edgar Tryan in "Janet's Repentance" is a devout Evangelical; yet he manages to save the heroine from despair less by the words he speaks in confessing his own sin than by the feelings that accompany them. "It is possible, thank Heaven! to have very erroneous theories and very sublime feelings," the narrator of *Adam Bede* observes of the "old-fashioned" Methodism she attributes to Seth and Dinah (3.38); and if Tryan resembles Amos in being consecrated by suffering, he anticipates Dinah in his power to effect change in others. "The tale of the Divine Pity was never yet believed from lips that were not felt to be moved by human pity," George Eliot says, when Tryan decides to tell the story of his own past as a means of rescuing Janet Dempster (258); and for all the melodrama of "Janet's Repentance," it is this thoroughly human embodiment of sublime feeling that the novelist emphasizes both in his case and in Dinah's. What David Carroll has termed George Eliot's "own form of incarnationalism" is nowhere more explicit than in the passage that celebrates the effect of Tryan's confession on the wavering Janet:[38]

> Blessed influence of one true loving human soul on another! . . . Ideas are often poor ghosts; our sun-filled eyes cannot discern them; they pass athwart us in thin vapour, and cannot make themselves felt. But sometimes they are made flesh; they breathe upon us with warm breath, they touch us with soft responsive hands, they look at us with sad sincere eyes, and speak to us in appealing tones; they are clothed

> in a living human soul, with all its conflicts, its faith, and its love. Then their presence is a power, then they shake us like a passion, and we are drawn after them with gentle compulsion, as flame is drawn to flame. (263)

Readers of George Eliot know that such scenes and the concerns that animate them recur throughout the novelist's career, from Dinah's ministering to Hetty in the climactic prison scene of *Adam Bede* to the hero's reluctant reception of Gwendolen Harleth's confidences in *Daniel Deronda* (1876). "He was not a priest," Deronda thinks, when he is compelled to listen to Gwendolen's confession of her murderous wishes toward her late husband; but his very negation of a clerical role only calls attention to how thoroughly this secular scene has assimilated emotions that the novelist persists in terming "spiritual" and "sacred."[39] Deronda's own spiritual mentor is a Jewish visionary rather than an English clergyman; but when the novelist reports that "the first office Deronda had to perform for this Hebrew prophet . . . was to get him a healthy lodging," she is still attending to what she here calls "the irony of earthly mixtures" (43.466). Yet it was especially as a beginning novelist that George Eliot worried the question of how ideas may be made flesh, and that her self-conscious effort to embody spiritual abstractions in concrete particulars prompted her to look for a precedent to the visual art of the seventeenth-century Netherlands.

The very last essay that she wrote for the *Westminster Review* helps to make clear why thoughts of the clerisy should have been associated for George Eliot with the model of Dutch painting. Begun before "The Natural History of German Life" and "Silly Novels by Lady Novelists," and finished only after "The Sad Fortunes of the Reverend Amos Barton" had been submitted to Blackwood, "Worldliness and Other-Worldliness: The Poet Young" (1857) casts its satirical attack on the eighteenth-century poet as an exercise in "the natural history of the race"—the specimen at issue being "a remarkable individual of the species *divine*."[40] At once a prolegomenon to the fiction, like the better-known *Westminster* pieces that immediately preceded it, and a study in clerical life, like the early fiction itself, "Worldliness and Other-Worldliness" is also, by its author's own account, a determined repudiation of a writer she had once much admired. Rejecting her youthful enthusiasm for the "Night Thoughts" and other poems, she simultaneously indicts Young for his windy abstractions and for his egoism, even as she manages to suggest, characteristically, that the aesthetic and moral failures are one and the same. The trouble with Young, she argues, is that "his muse never stood face to face with a genuine, living human being" (349). His is a "telescopic view of human things" (359)—an "impiety towards the present and the visible" that she pointedly contrasts with "that genuine love which cherishes things in proportion to their nearness" (385). Though the essay identifies that love with the poetry of Cowper rather than the painting of the Dutch, the terms in which George Eliot praises the author of "The Task" clearly anticipate those in which she would soon defend Dutch pictures: "How Cowper's exquisite mind falls with the mild warmth of morning sunlight on the commonest objects, at once disclosing every detail and investing every detail with beauty!" (382).

More immediately to the point, the essay makes of such close attention to common things the only genuine measure of religious feeling. Rather than Young's personified abstractions, true religion, as George Eliot represents it, inheres in the ordinary details of a domestic scene:

> The adherence to abstractions, or to the personification of abstractions, is closely allied in Young to the *want of genuine emotion.* He sees Virtue sitting on a mount serene, far above the mists and storms of earth: he sees Religion coming down from the skies, with this world in her left hand and the other world in her right: but we never find him dwelling on virtue or religion as it really exists—in the emotions of a man dressed in an ordinary coat, and seated by his fire-side of an evening, with his hand resting on the head of his little daughter; in courageous effort for unselfish ends, in the internal triumph of justice and pity over personal resentment, in all the sublime self-renunciation and sweet charities which are found in the details of ordinary life.

"Emotion links itself with particulars," the passage continues; and even "the most untheoretic persons are aware of this relation between true emotion and particular facts" (371).

That George Eliot's prose here nonetheless betrays her own bent toward abstraction is more than an incidental irony. In attacking Young, the beginning novelist was not only repudiating her "youthful predilections and enthusiasm," but engaging in a continuing struggle with herself (358); and her insistence that art dwell on "ordinary" details, as I shall argue shortly, involved an effort of will as much as an instinctive preference. Yet first it is important to understand why the desire to represent "virtue or religion as it really exists" should have drawn her especially to the painting of the seventeenth-century Netherlands. What might be called the ambiguous or incomplete secularization of Golden Age art has been the source of much controversy in recent scholarship on the period, but the very fact that so many faithful imitations of mundane appearances also carry the traces of emblematic and scriptural meanings speaks directly to the aspirations of the early George Eliot.[41] Though she had long since rejected the fervent Evangelicalism of her youth, the beginning novelist sought to naturalize religion rather than to abandon it; and the influence of the Bible's iconography, as well as its language, would continue to make itself felt on her own scenes and metaphors throughout her career.[42] Only two years before turning to fiction, George Eliot had translated Ludwig Feuerbach's *Essence of Christianity* (1854), with its argument that "the essence of religion . . . is the *identity* of the divine being with the human" and its emphasis on the wholly human origins of the sacraments,[43] an emphasis that helped to shape the novelist's representation of her hero's "baptism" by suffering in the climactic episodes of *Adam Bede.* That process culminates in a thoroughly secular scene that nonetheless carries echoes of the Last Supper, as Adam consumes his bit of bread and wine in the "upper room" at Stoniton (42.425) while awaiting the outcome of Hetty's trial for infanticide.[44] Feuerbach says nothing about painting; but the writer who concludes his book, in George Eliot's translation, by speaking of the need "to vindicate to common things an uncommon significance"—to give "*life, as such, a religious import*"—could only have encouraged her own turn to the art of the seventeenth-century Netherlands.[45]

Adam Bede itself several times imagines how ordinary scenes might double as religious images—as when the narrator concludes her description of Mrs. Poyser and Dinah in the kitchen by suggesting that the women "might have served a painter as an excellent suggestion for a Martha and Mary" (6.74), or when Lisbeth twice responds to Dinah's silent manifestations by identifying her with the picture of an angel "a-sittin' on the grave" in Adam's new Bible (10.109; 14.140). In the latter case, the narrative characteristically distances itself from Lisbeth's simple faith, even as it uses her pictorial analogy to endow the human with a sacred aura. As for the narrator's hypothetical painting of Martha and Mary: a scene that already resembles a Dutch picture—this is the passage that begins by noting how the light is reflected from the pewter dishes onto Dinah's cheek—does not look any the less like such a picture for the shadowy presence of its biblical prototype.

Like many Dutch paintings, too, the juxtaposed portraits of Hetty at her mirror and Dinah at the window in the fifteenth chapter ("The Two Bedrooms") have been traced to originals in Protestant emblem books,[46] though in this case, ironically, the nineteenth-century novel may be still

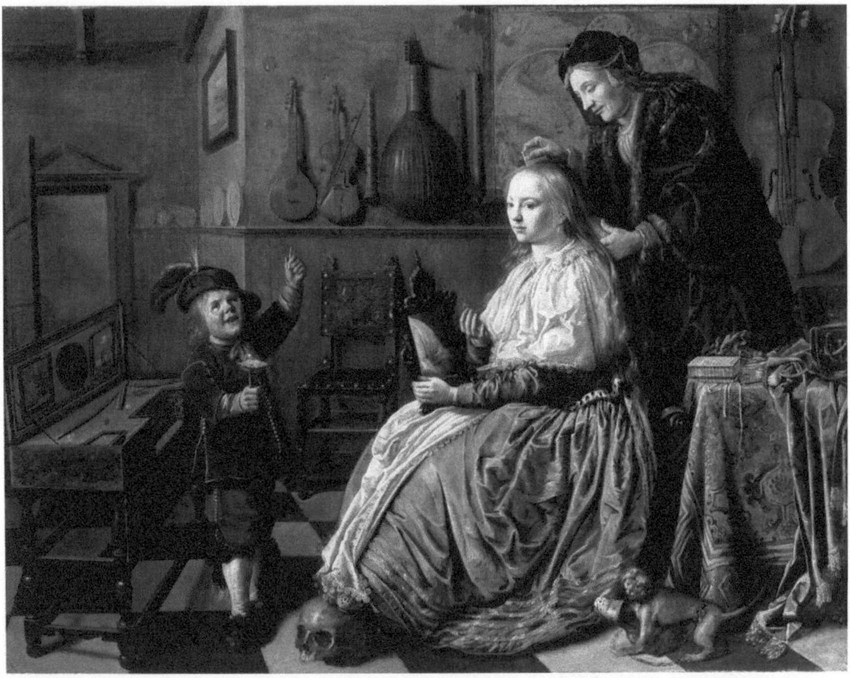

Figure 4-5. Jan Miense Molenaer: *Allegory of Vanity*, 1633. Toledo Museum of Art. Purchased with funds from the Libbey Endowment, Gift of Edward Drummond Libbey, 1975.21

closer to the spirit of the emblems than the seventeenth-century paintings that were their near-contemporaries. While Dutch genre offers many analogues for Hetty's *vanitas* figure (figs. 4-5 and 4-6), it is more apt to associate female virtue with a homely task like spinning than with a symbolic act like looking through a window.[47] (In the emblematic engraving with which Dinah's enlarged vision has been associated, the virtuous figure carries a telescope.) And unlike an image in an emblem book—or, of course, a novel—the very fact that most genre paintings lack an accompanying text necessarily attenuates any didactic intent.[48] Despite the labors of modern iconologists, it is easier for us to decide that we are being invited to condemn George Eliot's Hetty for her mirror-gazing than it is for us to arrive at a similar verdict about Gerrit Dou's anonymous woman at her toilet (fig. 4-6), for example. Some of that difference may have to do with our historical distance from a culture in which the conventional signs of a painting like Dou's could still be "read": hence the need for iconologists.[49] Still more of it has to do with the fact that scenes in novels, unlike most easel

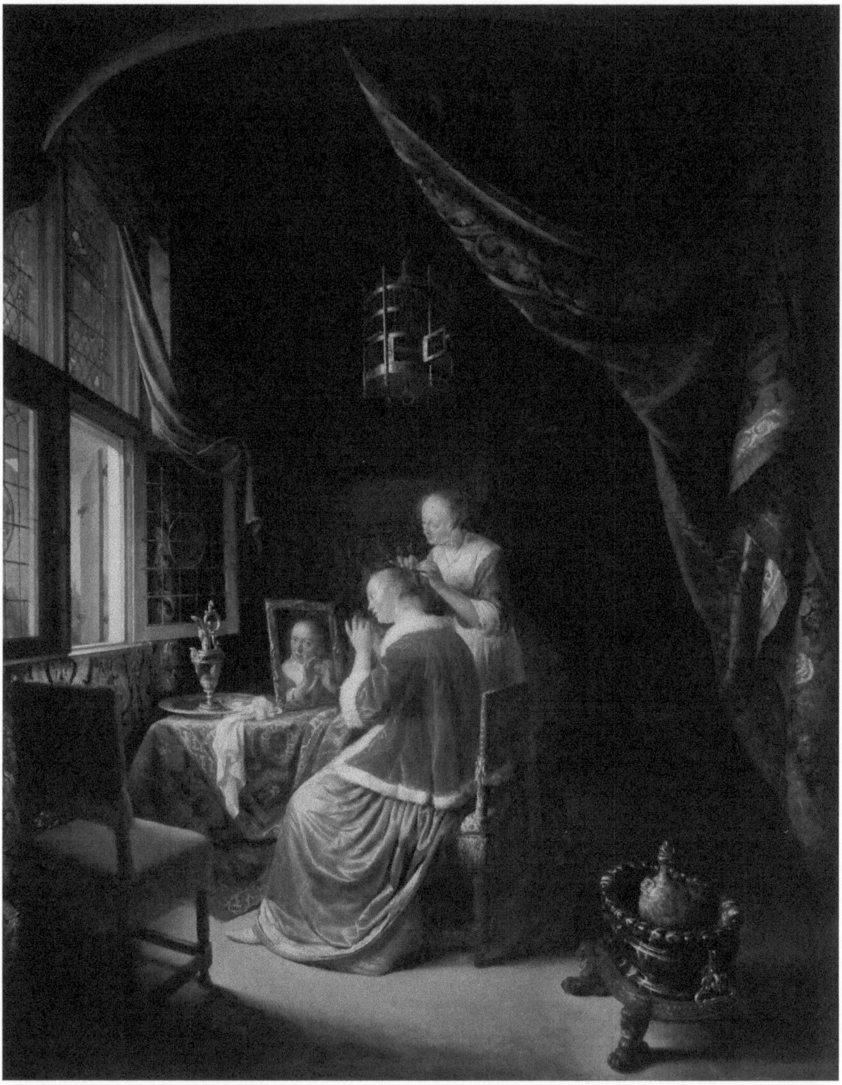

Figure 4-6. Gerrit Dou: *Young Woman at Her Toilet*, 1667. Museum Boijmans Van Beuningen, Rotterdam

paintings, always appear within a context. But even as such examples serve to remind us that novels are not pictures (and vice versa), it is still possible to recognize how much this novelist's moralized realism—or realistic incarnations of moralized prototypes—has in common with the visual art of the seventeenth-century Netherlands.

George Eliot was not the only English novelist to justify her clerical portraits by analogy to Dutch painting. A decade after the appearance of *Scenes of Clerical Life*, Anthony Trollope concluded his own chronicles of daily life among the clergy by defending himself against the charge that he had failed to depict a single "good" representative of the church. Like George Eliot, if less abstractly, the author of the Barsetshire novels characterized his project by emphasizing its human rather than its theological aspect: "I would plead," he wrote in the penultimate paragraph of *The Last Chronicle of Barset* (1867), "that my object has been to paint the social and not the professional lives of clergymen." And like George Eliot, he responded to his readers' criticism of those portraits by comparing his own art to that of the Dutch:

> There are those who have told me that I have made all my clergymen bad, and none good. I must venture to hint to such judges that they have taught their eyes to love a colouring higher than nature justifies. We are, most of us, apt to love Raphael's madonnas better than Rembrandt's matrons. But, though we do so, we know that Rembrandt's matrons existed; but we have a strong belief that no such woman as Raphael painted ever did exist. In that he painted, as he may be surmised to have done, for pious purposes,—at least for Church purposes,—Raphael was justified; but had he painted so for family portraiture he would have been false. Had I written an epic about clergymen, I would have taken St. Paul for my model; but describing, as I have endeavoured to do, such clergymen as I see around me, I could not venture to be transcendental.[50]

Trollope was a great admirer of the early George Eliot; and he may well have been consciously recalling the seventeenth chapter of *Adam Bede* when he produced this variation on its argument. But more than the sanction of her authority accounts for the fact that he approaches the question far more comfortably—if less interestingly—than his predecessor; and the very absence of strain with which he chooses to "love" Raphael but imitate Rembrandt helps to clarify what was at stake for her. Despite his allusion to a hypothetical epic about clergymen, his *Autobiography* (1883) would later make quite clear that he had no epic ambitions; nor could he "venture to be transcendental," as the *Last Chronicle* puts it, in any case. By his own account, Trollope "never was a learned man nor even a philosopher"; and even allowing for his characteristic modesty, the disclaimer is telling. When he turned to the making of books, he seems to have had little trouble in following the advice he would later pass on to other aspiring writers: "let their work be to them as is his common work to the common labourer." He worked with words, needless to say, and not with things—or paint. But the novelist who notoriously insisted on churning out so many pages a week, viewed authorship as "a trade," and variously compared its products to those of a shoemaker, a tallow-chandler, and a dealer in broadcloth, was a novelist who seems to have had no need to school himself to identify with the art of the Dutch.[51]

In all this, of course, Trollope was very different from his formidably learned contemporary. As he himself characterized that difference in his *Autobiography*, "the nature of her intellect is very far removed indeed from that which is common to the tellers of stories." In fact it was precisely because he thought "the philosopher so greatly overtop[ped] the portrait-painter" in George Eliot's later novels that Trollope preferred her earlier fiction,[52] and many nineteenth-century readers apparently concurred in that judgment. But while they were not necessarily wrong to sense what one disappointed reviewer called a "transition from description to analysis" in the later novels, what needs explaining is not the analysis but the description.[53] For the George Eliot who ended her career as a philosopher also began it as one; and if she succeeded in persuading Trollope and others that she was a "portrait-painter" as well, she did so only by deliberately attending to the concrete and the commonplace. What she famously called, in a letter to Frederic Harrison, "the severe effort of trying to make certain ideas thoroughly incarnate, as if they had revealed themselves to me first in the flesh and not in the spirit" was just that, I think—a severe effort. Though the same letter goes on to deplore any "lapse" from "picture" to "diagram,"[54] its tell-tale hypothetical ("*as if* they had revealed themselves to me first in the flesh") implicitly confesses that for the writer herself "picture" inevitably came second.[55] The very fact that she set out to mount an explicit defense of Dutch painting marks her distance from Balzac, for whom pictures of all sorts were models for seeing rather than questions for theory. Henry James may have been unfair when he seized the occasion of Cross's *Life* to drive home the comparison, but he was nonetheless responding to a genuine difference between the two novelists. Pouncing upon a journal entry of 1859 in which she characterized *Père Goriot* simply as "a hateful book," James heard her silence about any other aspects of the novel as "eloquent": "It illuminates the author's general attitude with regard to the novel, which, for her, was not primarily a picture of life."[56]

In taking Dutch art as her model, then, the beginning novelist was partly training herself, as much as her reader, to look closely at what was around her. Not that seventeenth-century pictures were her only means to this end: the detailed descriptions of flora and fauna recorded in her "Recollections of Ilfracombe" (1856), for example—themselves repeatedly characterized as "pictures"—suggest that the future George Eliot learned from naturalists as well as painters, while exercising a skill that she would very soon adapt to the writing of fiction.[57] (She began "The Sad Fortunes of the Reverend Amos Barton," by her own account, within two months of concluding these "Recollections" of her seaside expedition with Lewes.)[58] Though the essay ends with "the sight of two 'Cockle women,' who would make a fine subject for a painter" (273), the writer's eye primarily concentrates on landscape rather than people, and the word-pictures that result are closer in spirit to Ruskin's Pre-Raphaelites than to the seventeenth-century Netherlands.[59] And though the same essay speaks of "the desire . . . to escape from all vagueness and inaccuracy into the daylight of distinct, vivid ideas," the "distinctive qualities" on which it focuses are almost all aspects of natural beauty or the picturesque, rather than the commonplace as such (272). Even the cockle women, significantly, hardly catch her eye by virtue of their ordinariness: "One of them was the grandest woman I ever saw—six feet high, carrying herself like a Greek Warrior, and treading the earth with unconscious majesty. . . . The other . . . was also a fine old woman, but less majestic in port than her companion" (273). There may be something of these grand cockle women in that "large, fair, gentle Madonna," Mrs. Amos Barton—"the flowing lines" of whose "tall figure made the limpest dress look graceful" (15)—but there is no sign of that "rustic stupidity" with which her husband struggles so haplessly (20), or of that "quintessential extract of mediocrity," the Reverend Amos himself (40). For George Eliot, Dutch painting almost always means genre painting; and it is with such subjects—what the seventeenth chapter of *Adam Bede* revealingly calls "these more or less ugly, stupid, inconsistent people" (17.176)—that she most insistently associates its example.

It was not just a need for "picture," in other words, that drew the beginning novelist to the model of the Dutch. By temperament, at least, she was a satirist as well as a philosopher; and even more than her liability to excessive abstraction, she continually struggled against her own impulse to judgment.[60] "Throughout her life," Rosemarie Bodenheimer has observed, "Marian Evans wrote elaborate notes of remorseful apology to people with whom she had allowed herself to speak harshly or critically of others"; and a similar rhythm, as Bodenheimer has shown, governs George Eliot's narratives as well, with their repeated impulse to "turn back" and "dissolve the satire in demands for sympathy."[61] But it is in the early fiction, I think, that this conflict manifests itself most acutely—not only because George Eliot was still training herself to produce imaginative narratives rather than theory or criticism, but because those narratives were so intimately connected to people with whom their author had decisively broken. As most students of the writer know, the scandal of the elopement with Lewes produced a radical divide in her history: though she began her career as a novelist by drawing liberally on the rural Warwickshire of her childhood, she did so as a cosmopolitan intellectual, living out of wedlock with a married man, and estranged from her family.[62] While she would later contend that "Adam is not my father, any more than Dinah is my aunt," one need not discount her claim that "there is not a single *portrait* in 'Adam Bede'" to recognize how deeply that novel is imbued with its author's conflicting responses to the world she had left behind.[63] And not least among those responses—though she struggled valiantly to conquer it—was her own sense of angry superiority to those who had judged and rejected her.[64] "It is these people—amongst whom your life is passed—that it is needful you should tolerate, pity, and love," says the narrator in the seventeenth chapter of the novel; but the very fact that the sentence immediately continues by invoking "these more or less ugly, stupid, inconsistent people" suggests how much contempt she struggles to counter with her strenuous injunctions to fellow-feeling (17.176).[65] Though one could argue that the contemptuous adjectives merely ventriloquize the views of the reader—"what clumsy, ugly people!" that same reader is quoted as saying of Dutch pictures a few paragraphs later (17.177)—it seems truer to say that George Eliot speaks for both parties here, and that her aggressive defense of Dutch painting testifies to a conflict that is first of all internal.

Indeed, she herself acknowledges as much in the rather tortured confession that concludes the chapter—a bit of rhetoric that simultaneously argues for the sincerity of simple feeling and testifies to the difficulty of disentangling it. Hitherto, the narrator tells us, she has "often smiled with hypocritical assent" when others spoke disparagingly of "their everyday fellow-men." But while she has cynically pretended otherwise, the truth, she now "confesses," is that she has in fact admired and loved the imperfect people around her—most prominent among them, a figure notably reminiscent of George Eliot's father: "I herewith discharge my conscience, and declare, that I have had quite enthusiastic movements of admiration towards old gentlemen who spoke the worst English, who were occasionally fretful in their temper, and who had never moved in a higher sphere of influence than that of parish overseer." All this talk of "conscience" and "confessing" is primarily meant to signify, of course, as ironic, since what the narrator purports to concede is the very love of the commonplace that she has been so strenuously urging. Yet even as she once more turns her irony against "that lofty order of minds who pant after the ideal," she also acknowledges that she has sometimes appeared to count herself among them. "I confess," she says—or rather, " I confess I have often meanly shrunk from confessing" (17.182–83). Blackwood's objections to her fallible clergymen may have provided the occasion for her manifesto, and a long tradition of aesthetic theorizing clearly contributed to its rhetoric; but the "lofty-minded people" (17.177) with whom George Eliot was quarreling clearly had their deepest origins in herself.[66]

"It is our habit to say that while the lower nature can never understand the higher, the higher nature commands a complete view of the lower," the narrator remarks a little earlier in *Adam Bede*. "But I think the higher nature has to learn this comprehension, as we learn the art of vision, by a good deal of hard experience" (15.160–61). The immediate reference is to Dinah's need to comprehend Hetty, but the remark has an obvious bearing on Hetty's creator as well; and the suggestion that vision itself is an "art" to be learned may help to explain why she might have associated such efforts with the need to look hard at some pictures. Though it is by no means self-evident that "delicious sympathy" was the primary response that Dutch painters intended to evoke in their viewers (17.177), George Eliot was hardly wrong, after all, to identify their work with a particular attentiveness to the dignity of common people. As Tzvetan Todorov has argued in his own homage to Dutch painting: "All pictorial representation of a being or object signifies . . . that it is worthy of being represented, that it deserves to retain the attention, to survive the moment of its appearance. Painting is, intrinsically, praise of that which is painted."[67] At the very least, by devoting entire canvases to anonymous figures and their activities, the Dutch had appeared to suggest that even the most ordinary of persons were worthy of sustained contemplation. That effect is particularly pronounced when a picture concentrates on a single figure, as in the Dou image of "an old woman . . . eating her solitary dinner" (17.177) that inspired the narrator's ekphrasis in *Adam Bede* (plate 10)—or still more visibly to a modern eye perhaps, in Vermeer's radically uncluttered canvases, with their enigmatic representations of solitary women absorbed in simple acts like pouring milk or mending lace (plates 11 and 12).[68] Other genre paintings present more ambiguous cases, especially when their representations of the lower orders verge on caricature. But even if some Dutch art was actually intended to "accentuate the distance between the viewer and the crude behavior of the figures depicted" rather than to elicit sympathy, as one modern scholar has contended,[69] the very capacity of pictures to outlast their interpretive context inevitably made them available for other uses.

And for the beginning novelist, her language suggests, one of the fundamental uses of Dutch pictures was their exhortation to memory. "It is so needful we should *remember* their existence," the narrator says of the "common, coarse people" whose painted likenesses she evokes in the seventeenth chapter of *Adam Bede*: "Therefore let Art always *remind* us of them" (17.178; emphasis mine). When that same narrator "turn[s] without shrinking" from angels and prophets to an old woman bending over her flower-pot, or "turn[s]" yet again to the village wedding, with its awkward bridegroom and broad-faced bride (17.177), she clearly speaks for the novelist as well, as George Eliot's imagination turns back to a world she has herself left behind. The "faithful representing of commonplace things" (17.178), one may speculate, is all the more imperative for a writer who fears she has already broken faith with them. Unlike the pictures of rusticity that she castigates in "The Natural History of German Life," pictures whose "idyllic" views depend on the artist's comfortable remove from his subjects,[70] the Dutch pictures of her manifesto presumably achieve their "truthfulness" from acts of looking closely (17.177), even as they provide a model for the narrator's own conjuring of the near and the immediate: "the few in the foreground . . . whose faces I know, whose hands I touch . . . the faulty people who sit at the same hearth with me, or . . . the clergyman of my own parish" (17.179).

Yet for all the novelist's efforts to bridge the distance between herself and her subjects, the fact remains that her own art of the everyday is highly mediated. The very turn to Dutch painting as a model already signals the remove at which she writes, as does the notebook she kept while working on the novel, with its testimony to how much research went into her representations of such commonplace things as country fashions, the look of cloud-formations, or the grazing behavior of sheep and cattle.[71] Her manifesto insists on the need for an art that truthfully records the coarse and the ugly; but recent scholars have emphasized the artifice that shaped even the most seemingly realistic of Dutch paintings, while readers long ago recognized how George Eliot's own pictures of rural life appear to be "gilded," in the words of Henry James, "by a sort of autumn haze . . . which mitigates the sharpness of portraiture."[72] Scenes in her early fiction do often recall Dutch art, but both the pictorial conventions of that art and the softening effects of nostalgia—what Marcel Proust would aptly term in another context the "genre paintings of memory"—necessarily intervene between the beginning novelist and the commonplace things she seeks to represent.[73]

"It is so needful we should remember" them, her narrator says of those things, "else we may happen to leave them quite out of our religion and philosophy" (17.178).

Though the fame of her manifesto has sometimes obscured the fact, the development of George Eliot's art increasingly inclined her toward the Italians. The obvious turn comes with *Romola* (1862–63), but the way was prepared well before that historical novel of fifteenth-century Florence. Indeed, there is an important sense in which she never altogether abandoned the traditional hierarchy that consigned Northern pictures, as she said of some Flemish works in 1854, "to a low development of art."[74] She was writing at the time from Berlin, on her first visit to Germany with Lewes; but even as she fed her "appetite" for Dutch and Flemish work at Dresden four years later,[75] she reserved her highest praise for the museum's celebrated Madonna by Raphael. Dresden was "a proper climax" to the journey, she reported, "for all other art seems only a preparation for feeling the superiority of the Madonna di San Sisto the more."[76] Lewes apparently shared her feeling for "Raphael's marvellous picture";[77] and in 1860 the couple set off on a much anticipated trip to Italy—the first of several such visits that effectively replaced their travels in Northern Europe of the decade before. Not surprisingly, perhaps, her record of that belated Grand Tour is a veritable catalogue of pictures seen and churches visited: so much did works of art appear to dominate the prospect that Lord Acton was later prompted to complain, "Italy was little more to her than a vast museum."[78] While her responses to individual artists and works were hardly uncritical—at Bologna, for example, she registered her "utter dislike of the Bolognese school" and "some disappointment in Raphael's St. Cecilia"—the predominant impression registered in her journal is of an overwhelming encounter with the great works of the past.[79] Apart from a passing mention of a Rembrandt self-portrait and an equivocal description of Tintoretto's *Cena* as "a bustling supper-party, with attendants and side-board accessories in thoroughly dutch fashion,"[80] the faithful representing of commonplace things has no place in this record.

This is not to contend that the familiar division between early and late George Eliot amounts to her discovery of Italian art, though she herself characterized her first visit as "one of those journeys that seem to divide one's life in two by the new ideas they suggest and the new veins of interest they open."[81] Nor is it simply to note that beginning with *Romola*—a novel perforce filled with Italian works, both real and invented—she was far more likely to look to the South rather than the North for her painterly references. *Middlemarch* (1871–72) opens by obliquely comparing Dorothea Brooke to "the Blessed Virgin" as she "appeared to Italian painters,"[82] and *Daniel Deronda* (1876), as Hugh Witemeyer has shown, turns especially to Venetian art for its representations of the Jews;[83] but the difference is less a matter of particular allusions than of George Eliot's greater willingness to acknowledge her own idealizing and abstracting impulses—impulses that had always tugged strongly at her version of realism. Even the narrator of *Adam Bede*, after all, had exhorted the artist to "paint us an angel, if you can"; and while she had begun her own artistic career by incarnating her ideals in humble form, the creator of Milly Barton and Dinah Morris—not to mention Romola de' Bardi and Dorothea Brooke—had obviously never been reluctant to "paint us yet oftener a Madonna" (17.178). In an essay written more or less concurrently with the second volume of *Adam Bede*, Lewes had already invoked the example of that "marvelous picture, the 'Madonna di San Sisto'" in order to demonstrate that "Realism" was not incompatible with "Idealism"; and his argument clearly resonated with the novelist as well. Though Lewes's observations about low genre have a more direct bearing on *Scenes of Clerical Life* and *Adam Bede*—especially his contention that the painter of a village group whose "sympathy" enabled him to express its emotional life would be "more *real* than a Teniers"—the piece as a whole presumes that the greatest art is "in the highest sense ideal" as well as "real"; and it automatically identifies such art with the religious history painting of the Italians. At the top of the hierarchy, together with the *Sistine Madonna*, is Titian's "unsurpassable head of Christ, in the famous 'Christo del Moneta'" (fig. 4-7),[84] a painting that George Eliot would explicitly invoke by its English name, *The Tribute Money*, as a model for a crucial meeting between her hero and Mordecai in *Daniel Deronda* (40.424).[85] Like their beloved Raphael, the Titian hangs in the gallery at Dresden, where she and Lewes had repeatedly gone to admire both works on their visit in 1858;[86] but there is no evidence that she had ever seen it again when she chose to evoke its precedent for her novel nearly two decades later. She may have begun her career as a novelist by deliberately turning away from such pictures, but she obviously did not share Thoré-Bürger's eagerness to consign them to the past.

Only with *Romola* did George Eliot try her hand at something like history painting; but by the time she was ready to embark on that novel, she seems to have been also ready, tellingly, to remove a bit of the excess defensiveness from her early defense of her art. In the eighth edition of *Adam Bede* (1861), the narrator no longer identifies herself, however ironically, with those "obliged to creep servilely after nature and fact," nor does she

Figure 4-7. Titian: *The Tribute Money*, 1516. Gemäldegalerie, Staatliche Kunstsammlungen, Dresden. Photo Credit: Erich Lessing/Art Resource, N.Y.

disclaim the "lofty vocation" of a "clever novelist." Gone, too, is the modest "no more" that originally limited her aspiration to give "no more than a faithful account of things as they have mirrored themselves in my mind." As a recent editor of the novel has observed, this is a newly confident narrator, whose greater assurance presumably reflects the consolidation of

George Eliot's own reputation since she had initially drafted her manifesto in Germany three years earlier.[87] The success of *Adam Bede* —"so triumphantly beyond anything I had dreamed of," as the author noted in her journal—had been quickly followed up by *The Mill on the Floss* (1860) and *Silas Marner* (1861);[88] and despite the controversy that greeted the final episodes of Maggie Tulliver's history, George Eliot was sufficiently assured of her achievement as a novelist that she need no longer struggle quite so hard against her own more idealizing impulses.

Yet the very success of the early novels, ironically, also meant that many nineteenth-century readers would long persist in measuring her art by her defense of the Dutch. "You seem to be wandering down a long gallery filled with the masterpieces of Dutch cabinet paintings," the critic for the *Westminster Review* observed of *The Mill on the Floss* in 1860, even as he also complained that George Eliot had "sacrificed too much to her beloved realism" in her portrait of its heroine. "When boors are to be painted"—by which the *Westminster* reviewer meant the Dodsons and the Tullivers—"we rejoice in Jan Steen," but the "poetical temperament" of Maggie herself apparently belonged in another picture.[89] Six years later, a youthful Henry James would begin an essay on the novelist by citing a passage from the seventeenth chapter of *Adam Bede* as the "key" to her "method" and go on to praise *Silas Marner* as the finest of her works to date—the one, that is, in which "she has come nearest the mildly rich tints of brown and gray, the mellow lights and the undreadful corner-shadows of the Dutch masters whom she emulates."[90] By then, George Eliot had also written *Romola* and *Felix Holt*; but "the popular notion about the excellence and brilliancy" of her style, as John Morley would observe that same year, "is that it is simply the excellence of a painter like Teniers."[91] Though Morley was partly concerned to dispel that notion, it clearly persisted. During her lifetime, at least, *Adam Bede* remained her most popular work;[92] and so persuasive had she been in identifying its reality effects with the art of the Dutch, that when her finest nineteenth-century critic came to the defense of a quite different George Eliot novel in 1877, he could only do it by paying tribute to the original power of her argument. In *Daniel Deronda*, Edward Dowden conceded, "the poetical or ideal element . . . decidedly preponderates," but there might be a kind of truth, he suggested, even without Dutch painting: "The Dresden Madonna, with awed rapture, a sacred joy and terror, in her eyes, bearing the divine Child, is not less true to the essential facts of womanhood than is a plain grandmother of Gerard Dow shredding carrots into her pot."[93]

five

Hardy's Rural Painting of the Dutch School

Thomas Hardy first published a sensation novel; then, by his own account, he published a painting. Though his works are famous for their visual effects, only *Under the Greenwood Tree* (1872)—subtitled "A Rural Painting of the Dutch School"—is explicitly characterized as a picture. By identifying his second published novel with the art of the Dutch, Hardy sought to capitalize on strengths that his earliest critics had identified in his work, even as he self-consciously called upon the well-established tradition of associating such art with the realist novel. George Eliot had done more than anyone to make that tradition respectable; and whether or not he modeled his early work on hers—he himself later disclaimed any influence—the very fact that he was now openly advertising it as Dutch depended greatly on her example.[1] There was apparently no more need for the defensiveness with which Balzac invoked Dutch art in his early preface to the *Scènes de la vie privée*, nor for directly coming to its defense, like the author of *Adam Bede.* At once bolder and more cryptic than his predecessors—neither of whom had ever labeled an entire novel a Dutch picture—Hardy simply took the identification for granted. Though he later claimed that *Under the Greenwood Tree* should really have been titled *The Mellstock Quire*, he never seems to have questioned his decision to call it "A Rural Painting of the Dutch School."

Hardy's Dutch painting was partly a creation of his readers. Like his first published novel—but more successfully—*Under the Greenwood Tree* reflected the beginning author's acute responsiveness to criticism. When George Meredith, acting as a reader for Chapman and Hall, advised him to withdraw the manuscript of his first novel and attempt something with "a more complicated 'plot,'" the result was the sensational narrative of *Desperate Remedies* (1871);[2] when critics faulted the latter while praising its pictures of rustic life, Hardy responded with his novelistic version of a Dutch painting. (The review that most seems to have wounded him specifically compared the "redeeming" bits to the paintings of Teniers.)[3] Yet matters were not quite this simple, if only because the evidence suggests that some of the scenes in *Under the Greenwood Tree* most reminiscent of Dutch painting were closely based on childhood memories, and that certain of these, at least, were already present in the unpublished manuscript of his first effort, *The Poor Man and the Lady*.[4] On the other hand, the fact that they, too, had been singled out by a reader who rejected the rest—*The Poor Man* having been shipped to Macmillan before being submitted to Chapman—confirms that Hardy was more than willing to let his artistic instincts be guided by the preference of his critics. When *Under the Greenwood Tree* appeared, the *Athenaeum* duly commended the still anonymous author for confining himself to the "graphic pictures of rustic life" it had praised in its earlier remarks on *Desperate Remedies*.[5] By the 1870s George Eliot's own novels may no longer have borne any obvious resemblance to Dutch pictures, but the more her contemporaries regretted the change the more they were inclined to welcome Hardy in her place. At a time when readers were increasingly nostalgic for her early fiction, it is not surprising that one reviewer should have fondly associated the anonymous serial of Hardy's *Far from the Madding Crowd* (1874) with her pen, or that another should have characterized *Under the Greenwood Tree* as "Dutch paintings of English country scenes after the manner of *Silas Marner*."[6]

Hardy's connection to pictures of all sorts was far more immediate than George Eliot's. He came to novel-writing from architecture, not reviewing and philosophy; and his repeated insistence that his novels were "impressions" rather than arguments could hardly be further from what she had memorably called "the severe effort of trying to make certain ideas thoroughly incarnate."[7] Like Trollope, in fact, he judged George Eliot a "great thinker" but "not a born storyteller by any means."[8] By his own account, Hardy's literary ideas often presented themselves to him first in the guise of pictures—a number of which he himself sketched and painted.[9] At one time he had thought of becoming an art critic, and he briefly kept to this end a "Schools of Painting" notebook (1863) that included entries for both the Flemish and the Dutch. In a rare characterization of a school as a whole, the notebook records that the Dutch School "owes none of its fame to dignity of subject."[10] But Hardy was more engaged in looking at pictures than in theorizing about them. While he was working for a London architect in the 1860s, according to the *Life*, he began the practice of devoting twenty minutes every day to the National Gallery, "confining his attention to a single master on each visit." "He went there from sheer liking, and not with any practical object; but he used to recommend the plan to young people, telling them that they would insensibly acquire a greater insight into schools and styles by this means than from any guide books to the painters' works and manners."[11] The Gallery already had substantial holdings in Dutch and Flemish art when Hardy visited it in the 1860s, but its strength in this area was vastly increased with the acquisition of Sir Robert Peel's celebrated collection in 1871—an event that coincided, as J. B. Bullen has noted, with the writing of *Under the Greenwood Tree*. Among the Peel Collection were a number of works by Teniers and Hobbema, both of whom were explicitly named by reviewers in connection with the rural scenes of *Desperate Remedies*.[12] Though Hardy appears to have been in the country when the Peel Collection was first put on display that June, one is tempted to imagine that he had it in mind when he completed his own "Dutch painting" later that summer.

But what did it mean for him to identify his novel with Dutch painting? Hardy's notebooks contain many comments on art, both literary and visual, but on this question, at least, the novel has had to speak for itself. For modern commentators who have considered the problem, that has primarily meant looking at how specific scenes in *Under the Greenwood Tree* appear to compose themselves like Dutch pictures.[13] And there is no doubt that the visual cues of many passages in this and other Hardy novels conjure up analogues from Dutch and Flemish art. Like Balzac and George Eliot before him, both of whom return repeatedly to the image of a woman posed in a doorway or window, Hardy adopts the Dutch practice of framing the female figure in the spaces of domestic architecture. Our first glimpse of the heroine, for example, is that of "a young girl framed as a picture by the window architrave"—a motif made familiar in numerous paintings by Gerrit Dou, among others.[14] Though Dou himself painted many candlelit scenes (fig. 5-1), the fact that Fancy Day is "unconsciously illuminating her countenance to a vivid brightness by a candle she held in her left hand, close to her face" (34) may also suggest the work of his pupil, Godfried Schalcken, who specialized in such scenes (fig. 5-2)—one of which later made its way into Hardy's own small collection.[15] A few chapters later, Fancy appears to her would-be lover, Dick Dewy, in another characteristic format: "the door opened and three-quarters of the blooming young schoolmistress's face and figure stood revealed before him—a slice on her left-hand side being cut off by the edge of the door" (64). As Bullen has observed, Hardy's pictorial

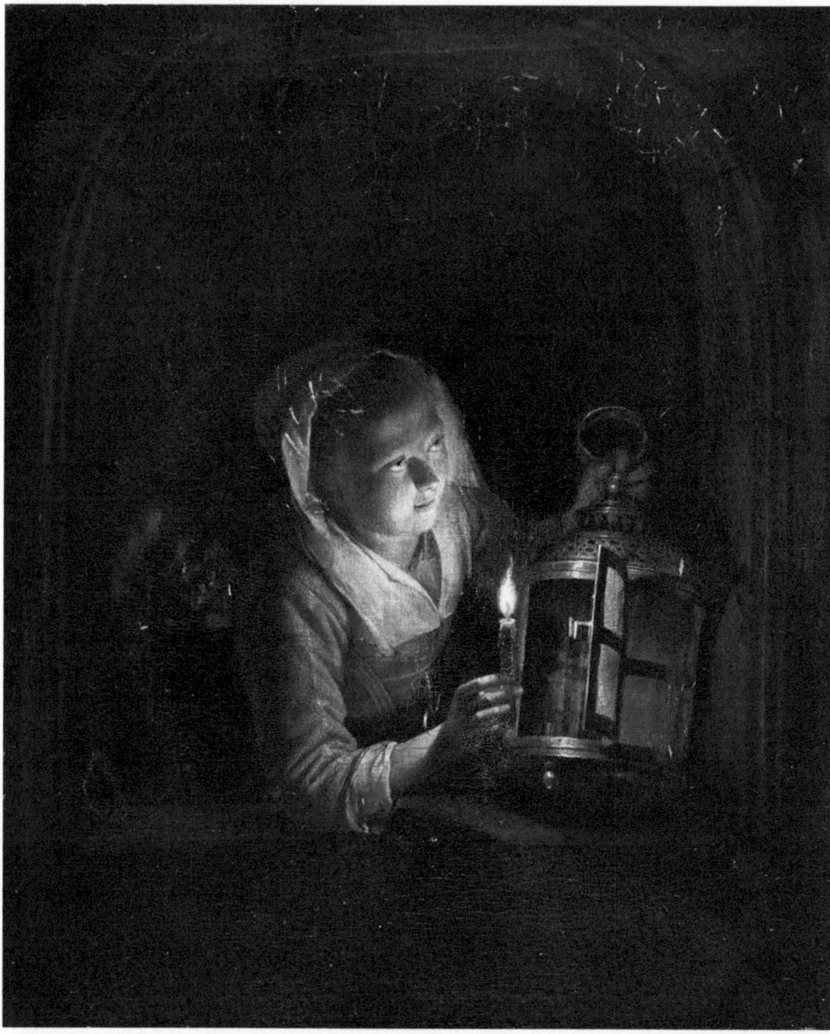

Figure 5-1. Gerrit Dou: *Girl at Window with Lantern*, c. 1660. Kunsthistorisches Museum, Vienna

vocabulary in such instances is more self-conscious than George Eliot's: when we first see the hero's mother in *Adam Bede*, for example, we are told that "the door of the house is open, and an elderly woman is looking out,"[16] but there is nothing like the allusion to Fancy "framed as a picture," or the effect of spatial relations on a flat surface conveyed by that truncated "slice" of her form.[17] Nor does George Eliot share Hardy's eye for dramatic effects

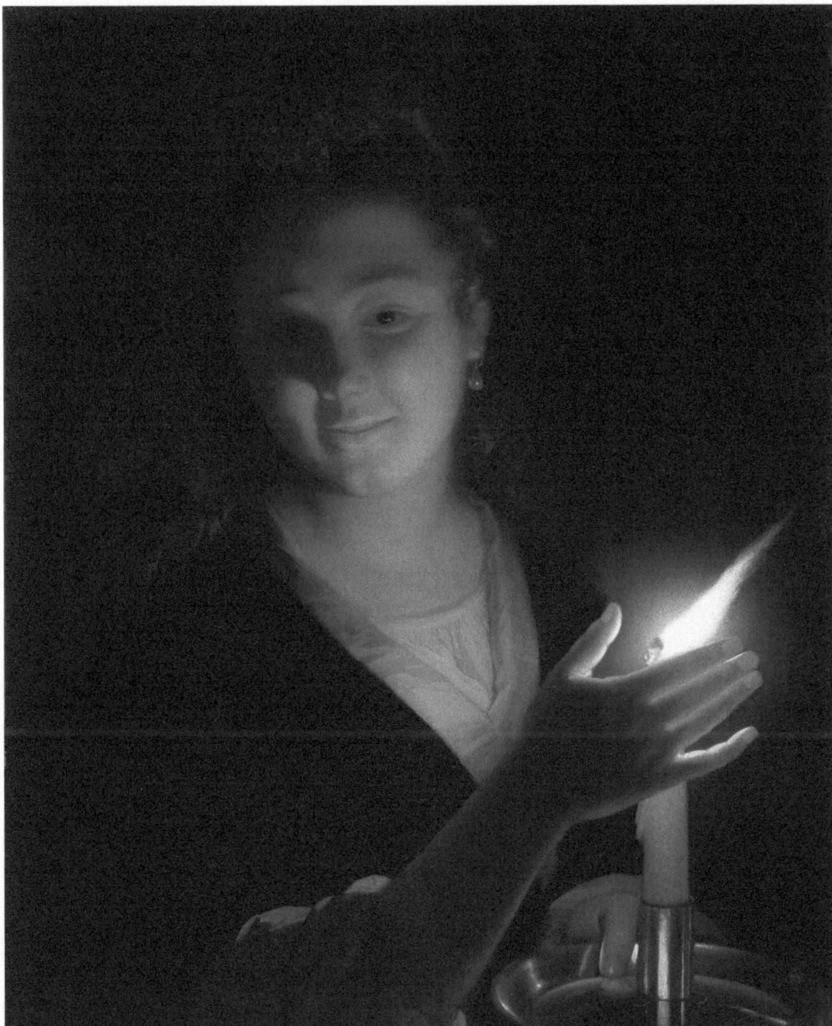

Figure 5-2. Godfried Schalcken: *Young Girl with a Candle*, late 1660s (?). Galleria Palatina, Palazzo Pitti, Florence. Photo Credit: Scala/Art Resource, N.Y.

of light: that Fancy should make her first appearance illuminated by a candle at once testifies to the painterly bias of her creator's imagination and to his habit of looking for the exceptional among even the most ordinary of images.

A similar self-consciousness about picture-making characterizes the group portrait of the choir on its visit to the vicar, when the accidental fall of his pen arouses the curiosity of those waiting in the hall to learn the outcome of the interview:

> Thus when Mr. Maybold raised his eyes after the stooping he beheld glaring through the door Mr. Penny in full-length portraiture, Mail's face and shoulders above Mr. Penny's head, Spinks's forehead and eyes over Mail's crown, and a fractional part of Bowman's countenance under Spinks's arm—crescent-shaped portions of other heads and faces being visible behind these—the whole dozen and odd eyes bristling with eager Enquiry. (87)

This passage has sometimes evoked comparisons to a nineteenth-century British picture, *A Village Choir* (1847) by Thomas Webster (fig. 5-3);[18] but the motif of the curious onlookers crowded in a doorway or window appears with some frequency in Dutch genre painting, while the comically reductive effect of the "fractional" body parts seems closer to the work of artists like Steen or Ostade than it does to Webster's more thoroughgoing illusionism. Note how the window post in Ostade's *Singers,* for example (fig. 5-4), divides the arm and head of one performer, or how the figure in

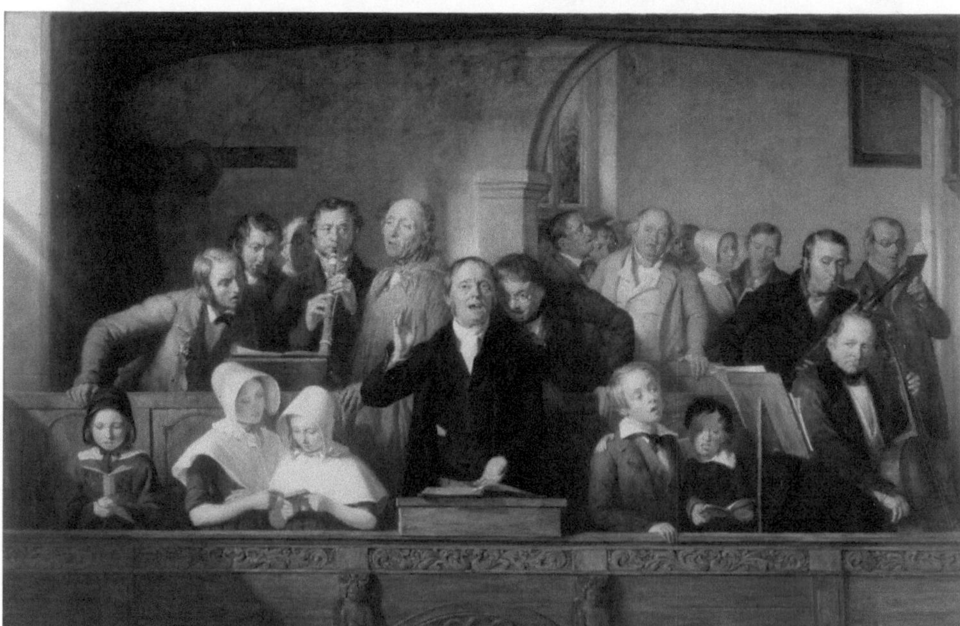

Figure 5-3. Thomas Webster: *A Village Choir*, 1847. Victoria and Albert Museum, London. Photo Credit: Victoria and Albert Museum, London/Art Resource, N.Y.

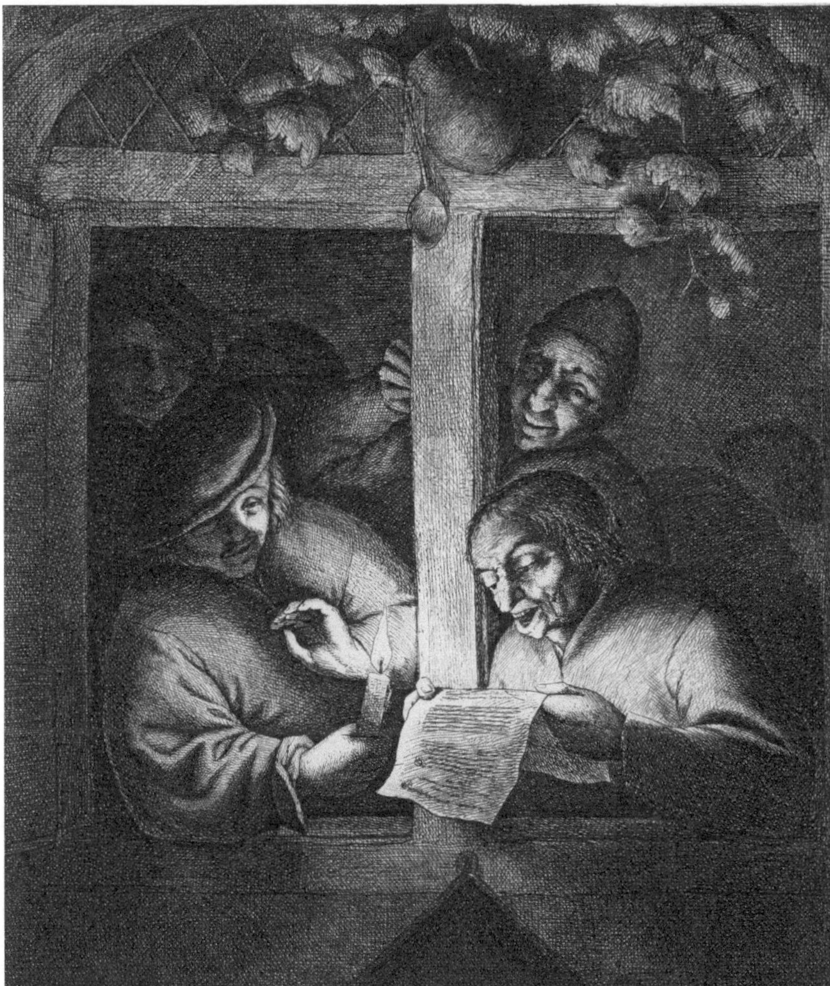

Figure 5-4. Adriaen van Ostade: *The Singers*, engraving and etching, c. 1667. Davis Museum and Cultural Center, Wellesley College. Photo: Davis Museum and Cultural Center, Wellesley College, Wellesley, Mass.

the left foreground—his own face half-obscured by the tilt of his hat and the shadow thrown by his candle—blocks all but a dimly observable portion of the fourth singer's head. By comparison to the members of Webster's choir, whose costumes and facial expressions are rendered with some meticulousness, Ostade's—like Hardy's—are radically simplified, the better to focus attention on a few prominent features.

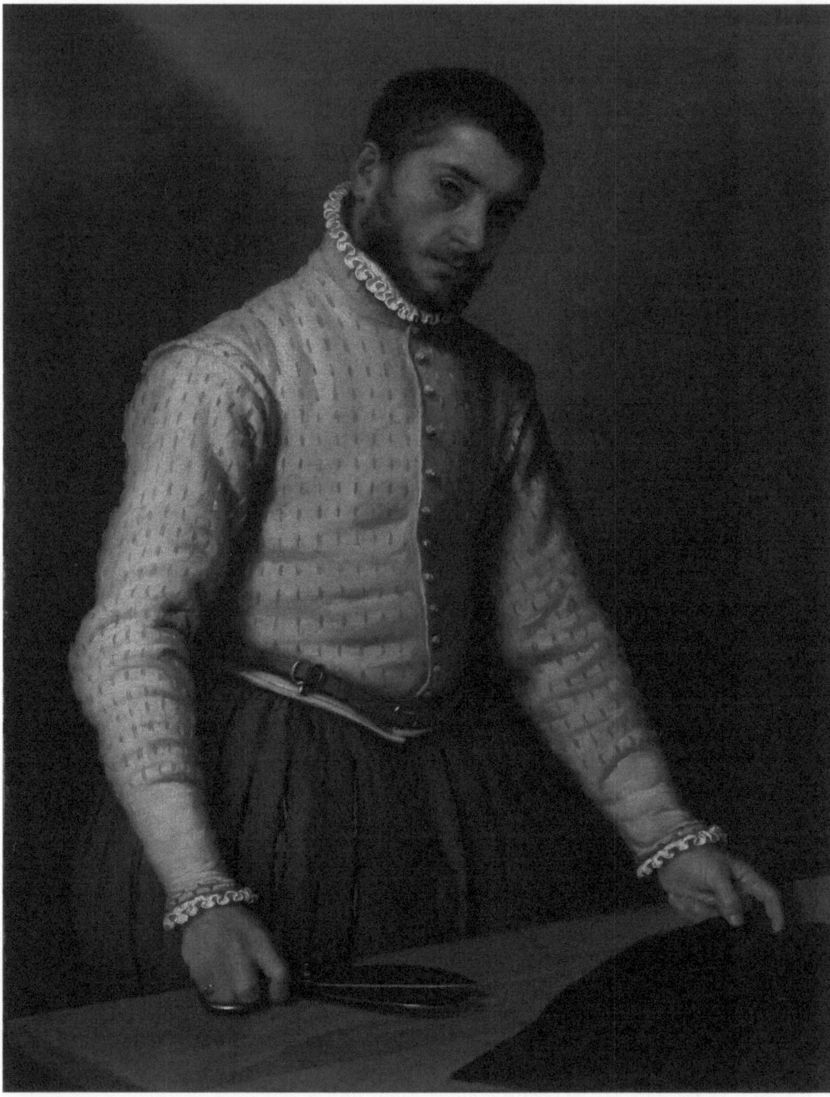

Figure 5-5. Giovanni Battista Moroni: *The Tailor*, c. 1565–70. National Gallery, London. © The National Gallery, London

In another often cited case, the depiction of the choir members grouped by the open window of Mr. Penny's workshop, Hardy combines a typical subject and format from Dutch genre with an explicit allusion to a sixteenth-century Italian painter—"Mr. Penny himself being invariably seen working inside like a framed portrait of a shoemaker by some modern Moroni" (70).

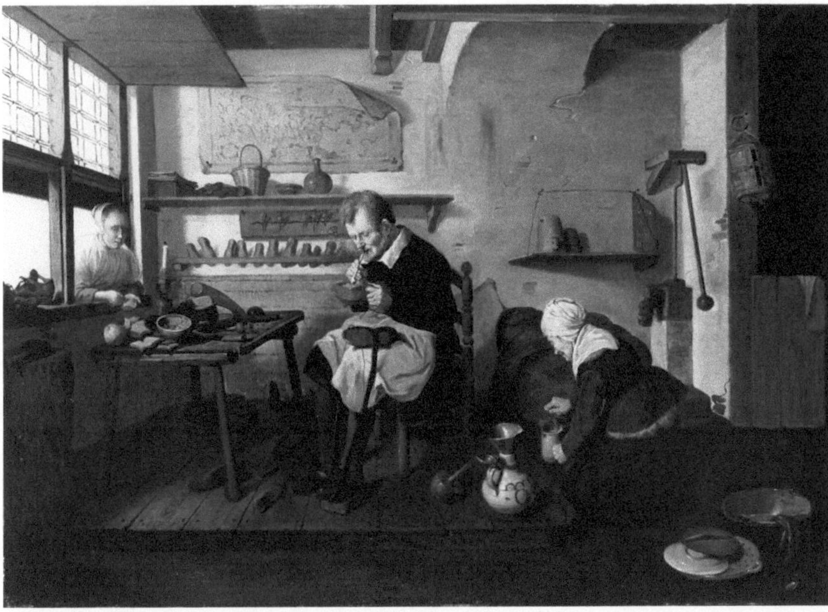

Figure 5-6. Quiringh Gerritsz. van Brekelenkam: *Shoemaker's Shop*, c. 1660. Norton Simon Art Foundation, Pasadena, Calif.

A belated addition to the manuscript, the reference was presumably inspired by Giovanni Battista Moroni's famous *Tailor* (c. 1565–70) in the National Gallery (fig. 5-5).[19] Yet apart from the fact that he, too, sports the tools of his trade, that distinguished-looking gentleman, standing erect in his elegant jacket, bears little resemblance to the rustic shoemaker seated near the window, "with a boot on his knees and the awl in his hand" (70). Hardy's genre picture is closer in conception to one of several studies of the subject by Quiringh Gerritsz. van Brekelenkam, for example (fig. 5-6), while the shoemaker himself, if not his setting, also bears comparison to a later acquisition by the National Gallery, Jan Victors's *Village Scene with a Cobbler* (fig. 5-7). Even when the author of *Under the Greenwood Tree* is invoking the Italian painter—or his modern equivalent—his own picture more nearly recalls the arrangements and subjects of the Dutch.

These are not the only moments in Hardy that resemble Dutch pictures. As Joan Grundy has remarked, "most of his later novels have passages in which he recognisably 'goes Dutch,'"[20] whether openly, as when he compares Liddy Smallbury's complexion in *Far From the Madding Crowd* to "the softened ruddiness on a surface of high rotundity that we meet with in a Terburg or a Gerard Douw,"[21] or more obliquely, as in the "dozen" such

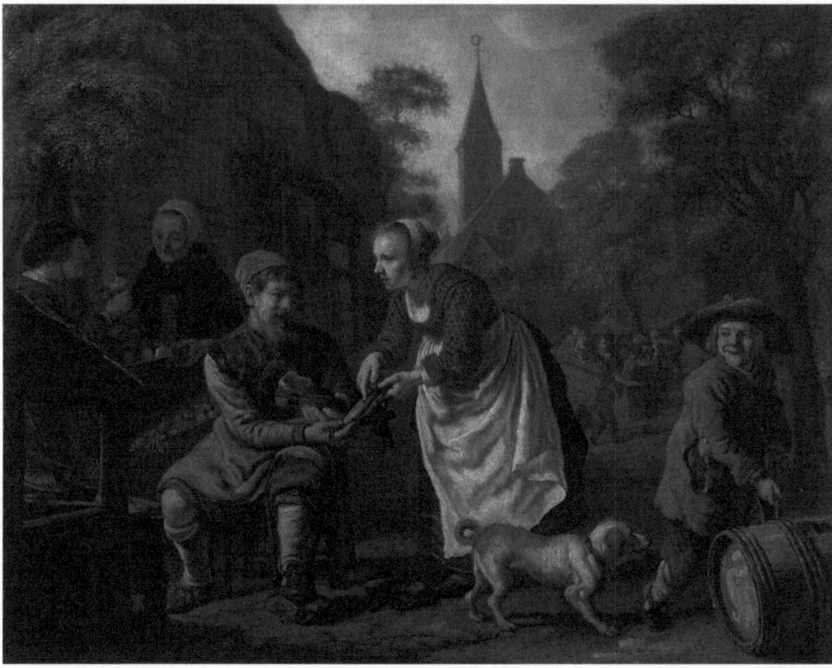

Figure 5-7. Jan Victors: *A Village Scene with a Cobbler*, c. 1650. National Gallery, London. © The National Gallery, London

pictures that the reviewer for the *Athenaeum* professed to find in *The Trumpet Major* (1880).[22] At memorable moments in both *Far from the Madding Crowd* and *The Return of the Native* (1878), Hardy's eye for dramatic lighting conjures up what he terms "Rembrandt effects," as he attends to "the few yellow sunbeams" that "spirted like jets of gold dust across the dusky blue atmosphere of haze" in the circus tent of the former novel, or looks for the first time with Eustacia Vye at the face of Clym Yeobright outlined against the dark wood of his mother's settle in the latter—the "spectacle constitut[ing] an area of two feet in Rembrandt's intensest manner."[23] But for the nineteenth century, "Dutch painting" was an idea (or set of ideas) as much as a model for local description; and rather than multiply such examples, I propose to take seriously Hardy's decision to identify his entire novel with a rural picture of the Dutch school. To do so may help to illuminate certain features of Dutch art itself, as well as the fiction that looked to it for a model.

Of course, Hardy knew that his subtitle was only a figure of speech. One need not adhere rigidly to Lessing's famous distinction between the temporal and spatial arts to recognize that a novel is not a painting, however vivid its visual imagination, and that even deliberately narrative paintings have at best a limited capacity for storytelling. As an artist who continued to sketch as well as write, Hardy had more reason than most to be conscious of the difference. But it was precisely his impulse to retreat from storytelling, I think, that inspired him to identify *Under the Greenwood Tree* with a painting of the Dutch school. The manuscript of Hardy's first novel, *The Poor Man and the Lady*, was originally subtitled, somewhat paradoxically, "A Story with no Plot";[24] and having perhaps taken too literally Meredith's advice that he attempt something more elaborately plotted in *Desperate Remedies*, he responded to the criticisms of that work by writing a novel with as little plot as possible. According to his own testimony, parts of *Under the Greenwood Tree* were directly lifted from the unpublished *Poor Man*,[25] among them, presumably, "the opening pictures of the Christmas Eve in the tranter's house" that John Morley had praised when he read the manuscript for Macmillan's. "What *Under the Greenwood Tree* owed to its unpublished predecessor," Michael Millgate has suggested, was "the evocation of a particular setting and a particular community, not a story." On the evidence of the manuscript, Millgate speculates that Hardy began writing the novel without having fully worked out its plot;[26] and the impulse to postpone narrative for picture-making is still apparent in the dilatory pace of the opening chapters. While *Under the Greenwood Tree* does finally have a plot of sorts, even two plots—that of the conflict over the choir and that of the courtship of Fancy Day—both of these are so managed, I shall argue, as to keep their disruptive effects at a minimum.

Because Victorian genre painters were more inclined to storytelling than their seventeenth-century predecessors, modern critics have sometimes suggested that Hardy's contemporaries offer the more relevant comparison;[27] but it is the very tendency to picture rather than story, I believe, that would have principally associated *Under the Greenwood Tree* with the Dutch. Unlike *Tess of the d'Urbervilles* (1891), whose "successive 'phases,'" as Millgate has noted, "are readily imaginable as the titles of Victorian paintings,"[28] the earlier fiction characteristically mutes the narrative implications of its parts. Rather than the moralized sequence of *Tess*—"Maiden No More," "The Consequence," "The Woman Pays"—*Under the Greenwood Tree* takes its part-titles from the seasons, while individual chapters more often identify places ("Mellstock-Lane," "The Tranter's," "Yalbury Wood and the Keeper's House"), groups ("The Assembled Quire," "The Listeners"), or recurrent acts ("Going the Rounds," "Passing by the School," "Going Nutting," "Honey-Taking, and Afterwards") than stages in a singular history. Though there are exceptions to this rule—"A Confession," for example, or "Into Temptation"—few of the titles in this hypothetical sketchbook would encourage the tendency to "read" pictures for cause-and-effect and thus to moralize them that Kate Flint has identified with Victorian genre painting.[29] Instead, they evoke an art of describing, of picture-making without narrative, that had long been associated with the work of the Dutch. We might recall in this connection how Scott had turned to "the Flemish school of painting" when he wished to characterize the merits of an Austen novel that had "even less story" than usual,[30] or how critics like Archibald Alison and R. H. Hutton had mapped the old opposition between the Dutch and the Italians onto the distinction between the descriptive and narrative aspects of fiction, in order to attack the contemporary vogue for realism. When Alison implied that "descriptions of still life—pictures of scenery, manners, buildings, and dresses" were the novelistic equivalent of works by Ostade and Teniers,[31] or Hutton associated the "statical" novel with Dutch painting, while arguing that the greatest fiction required the "rapid movement" of a plot,[32] they were drawing on generic hierarchies that had very little purchase for Hardy. But we need not assume that the author of *Under the Greenwood Tree* still adhered to the doctrines of classical art theory in order to understand why he would have identified his least plotted novel with a Dutch picture.

Under the Greenwood Tree happens also to be a scene of clerical life; but there is little evidence to suggest that Hardy was responding to the scriptural or moral implications of Dutch painting when he associated such a scene with the art of the Dutch. Though his 1896 preface notes with amusement how "sacred and secular met together in the middle" of the books in which the old church choirs recorded their tunes (4), the spirit of his own book is unmistakably secular. When he evokes the "quaint Christianity" of a hymn, its words "orally transmitted from father to son" (32), he approaches it—as he does all local ritual—from the perspective of an anthropologist. The novel begins with a round of Christmas caroling that the choristers take quite seriously; but the questions that animate them are aesthetic rather than doctrinal, and the "serpents" they condemn are wind instruments, not devils. "If you'd thrive in musical religion, stick to strings," says one (30). The arguments about Methodism and dissent that trouble the parishioners in *Scenes of Clerical Life* and *Adam Bede* have no place in Hardy's Mellstock. As for the new vicar of the parish, still more consistently than George Eliot, Hardy may be said to represent the clergy "solely in its *human* and *not at all* in its *theological* aspect," to quote again from Lewes's defense of "Amos Barton" in his letter to Blackwood.[33]

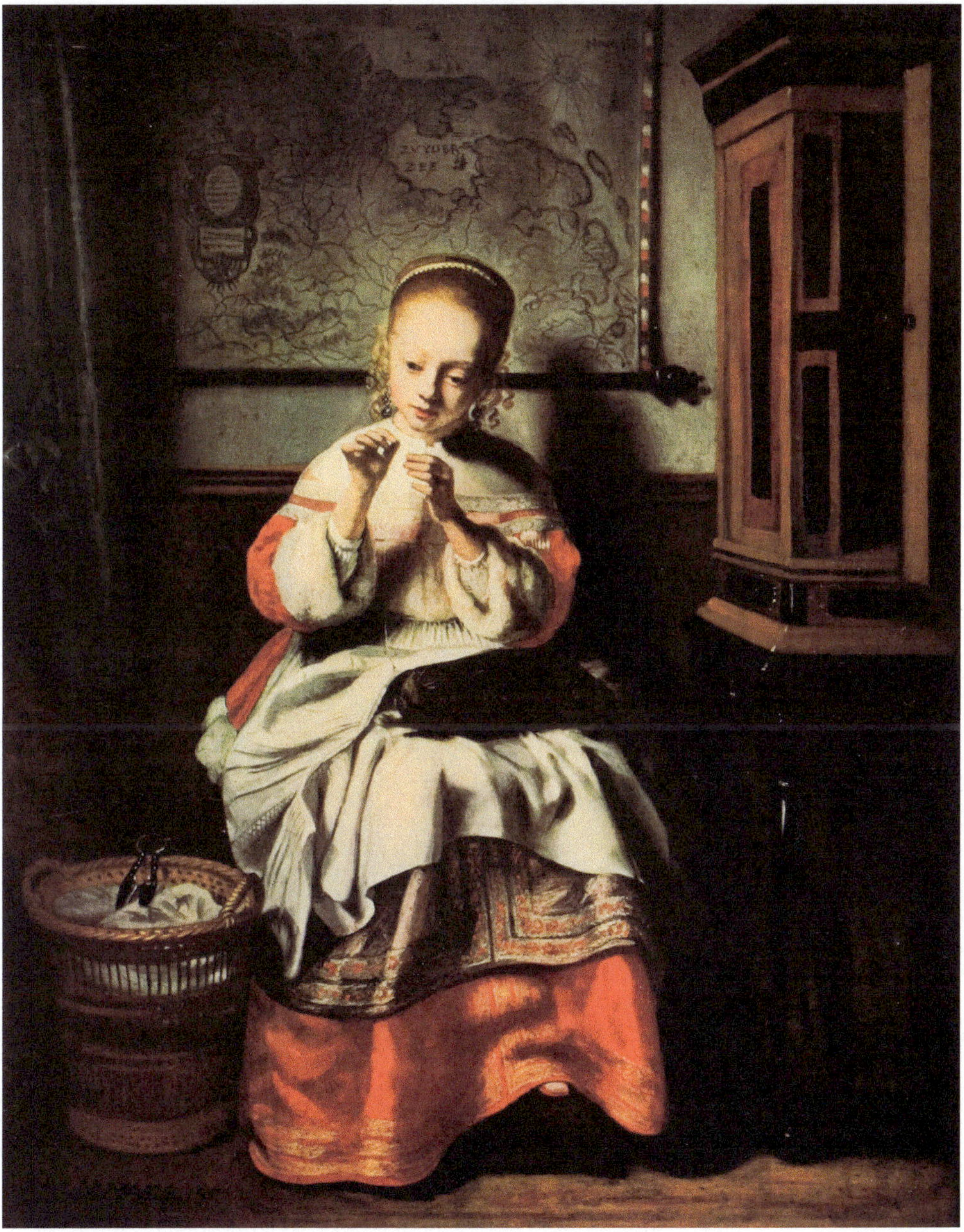

Plate 1. Nicolaes Maes: *Girl Sewing* (*Girl at Work*). Private collection

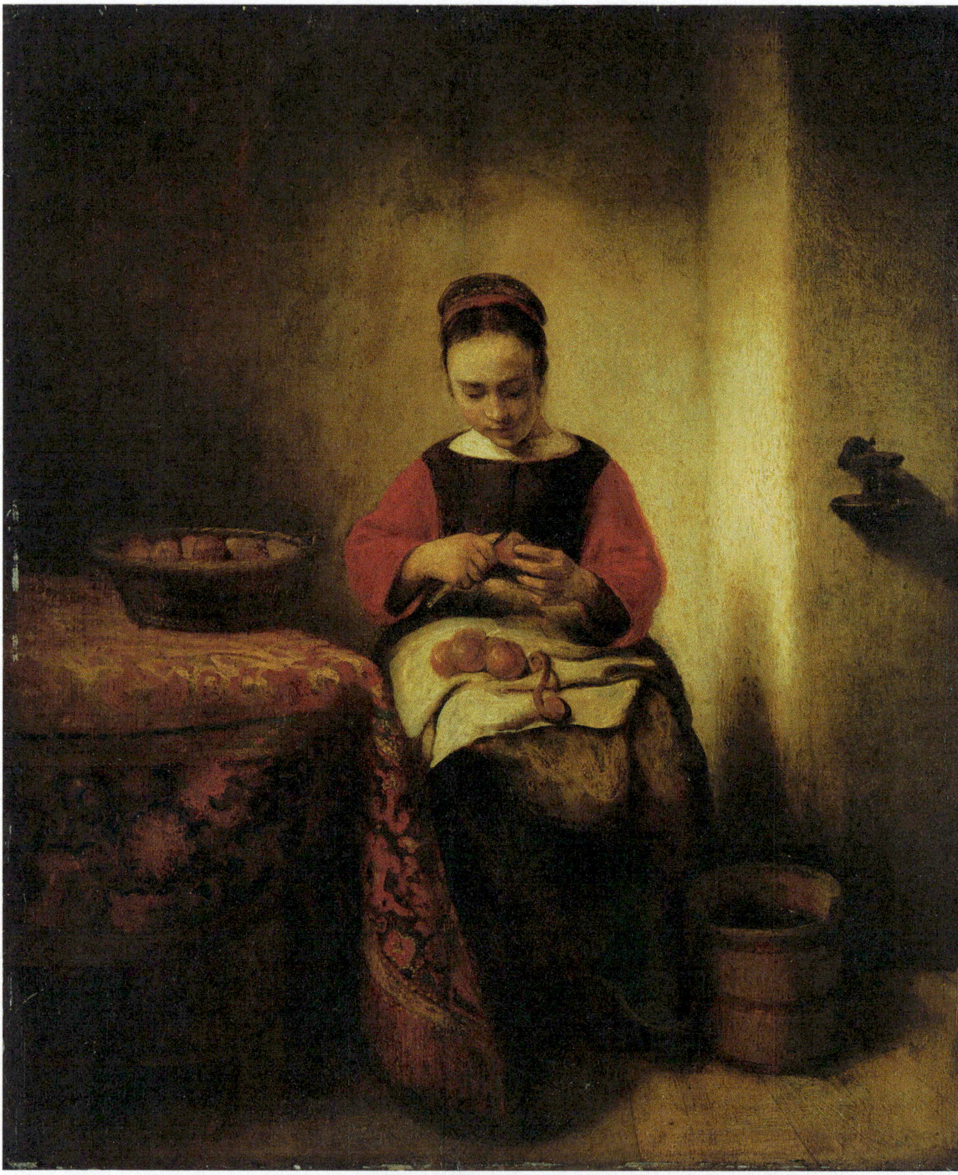

Plate 2. Nicolaes Maes: *Young Girl Peeling Apples*, c. 1655. The Metropolitan Museum of Art, New York. Bequest of Benjamin Altman, 1913 (14.40.612). Photograph © 1982 The Metropolitan Museum of Art

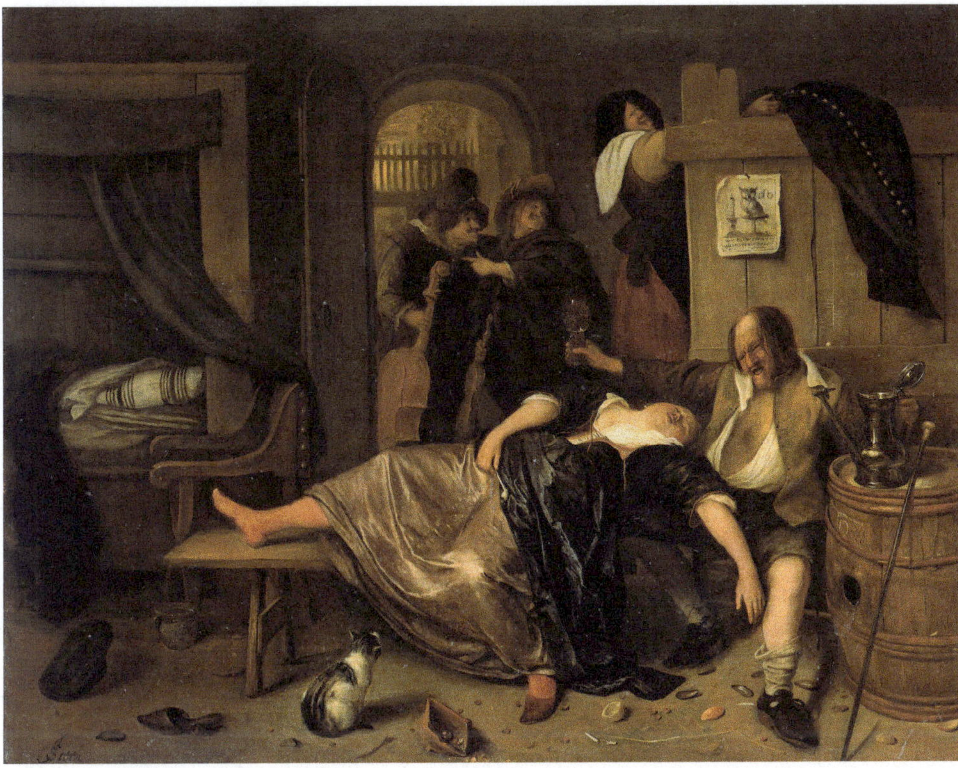

Plate 3. Jan Steen: *Drunken Couple*. Rijksmuseum, Amsterdam. © Rijksmuseum Amsterdam

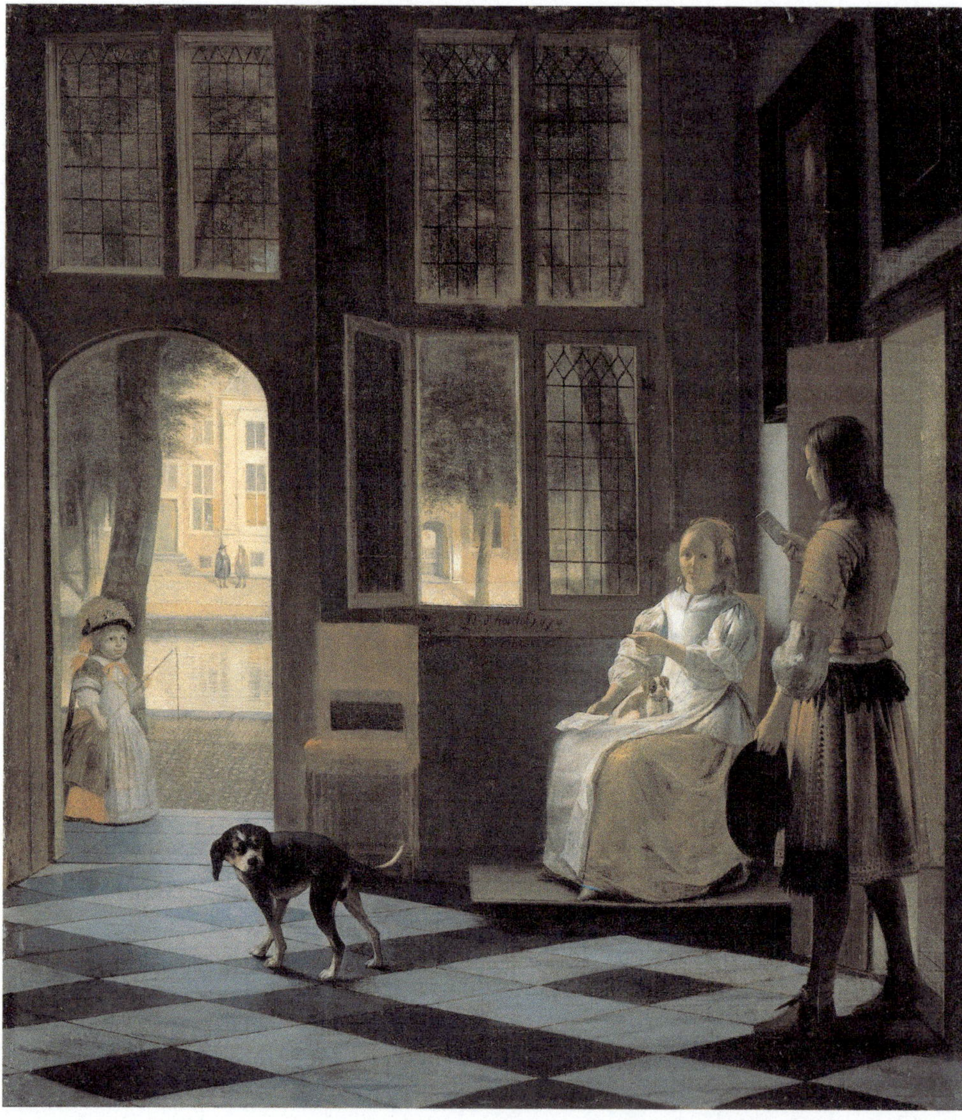

Plate 4. Pieter de Hooch: *Woman Directing a Young Man with a Letter*, c. 1670. Rijksmuseum, Amsterdam. © Rijksmuseum Amsterdam

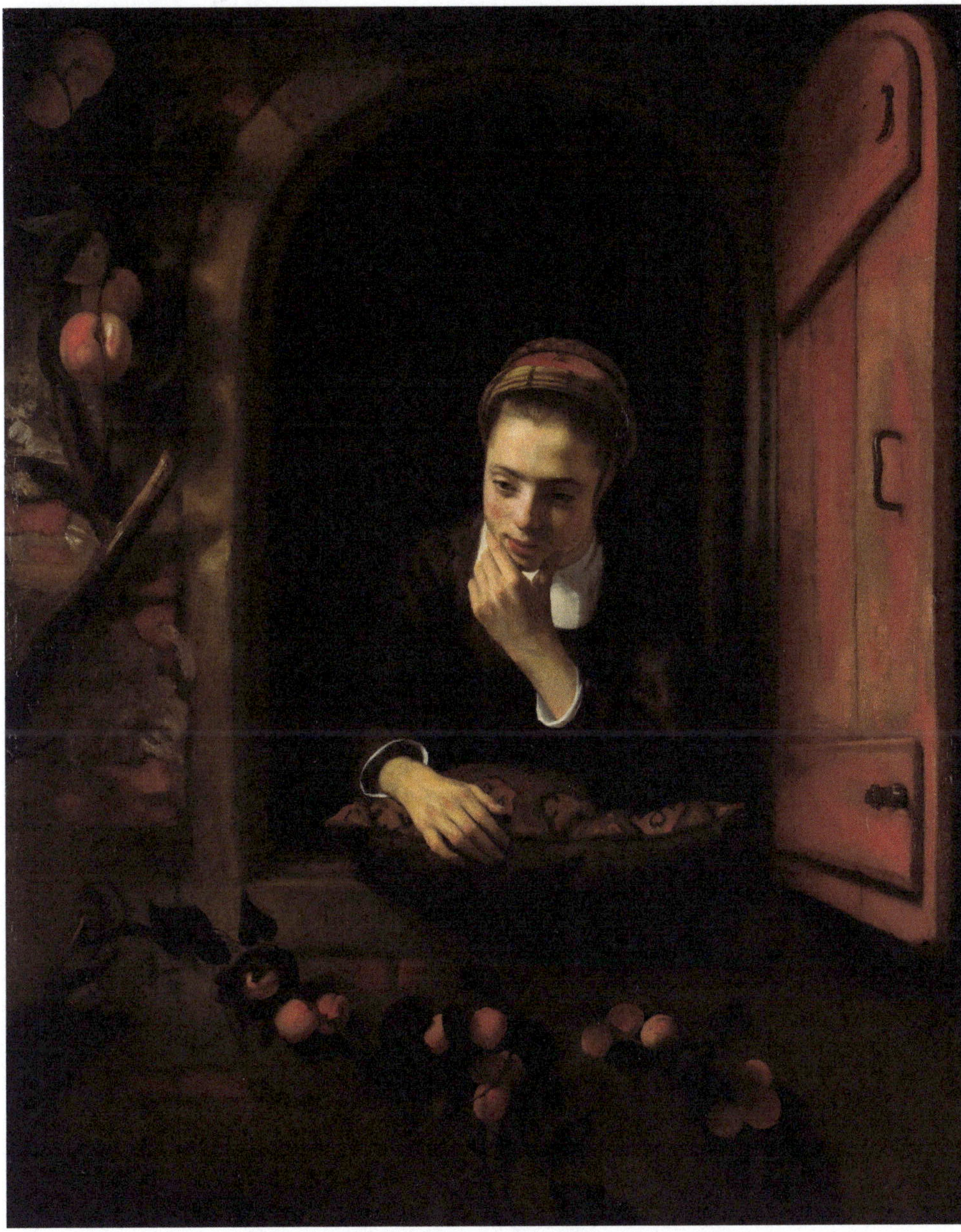

Plate 5. Nicolaes Maes: *Young Woman at a Window*, known as *The Daydreamer*, c. 1655. Rijksmuseum, Amsterdam. © Rijksmuseum Amsterdam

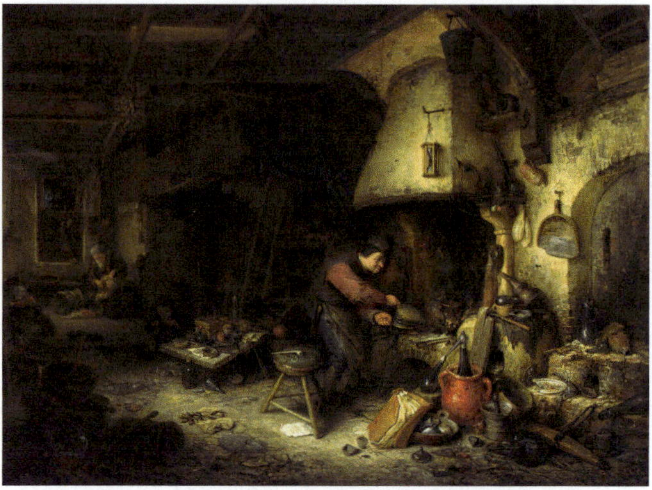

Plate 6. Adriaen van Ostade: *An Alchemist*, 1661. National Gallery, London. © The National Gallery, London

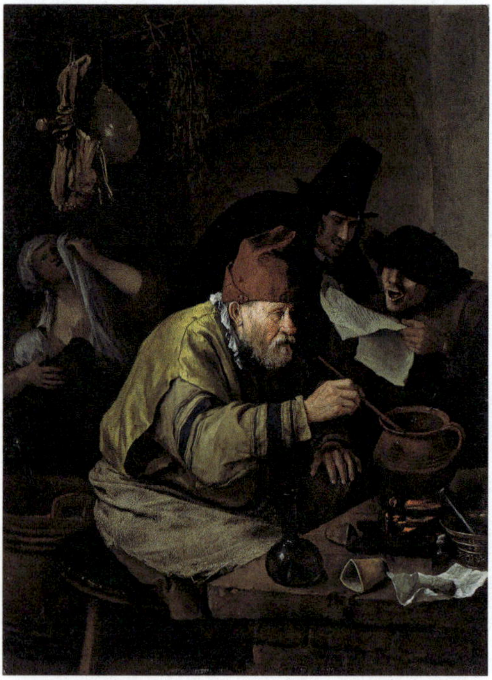

Plate 7. Jan Steen: *The Village Alchemist*. Wallace Collection, London. Reproduced by kind permission of the trustees of the Wallace Collection, London

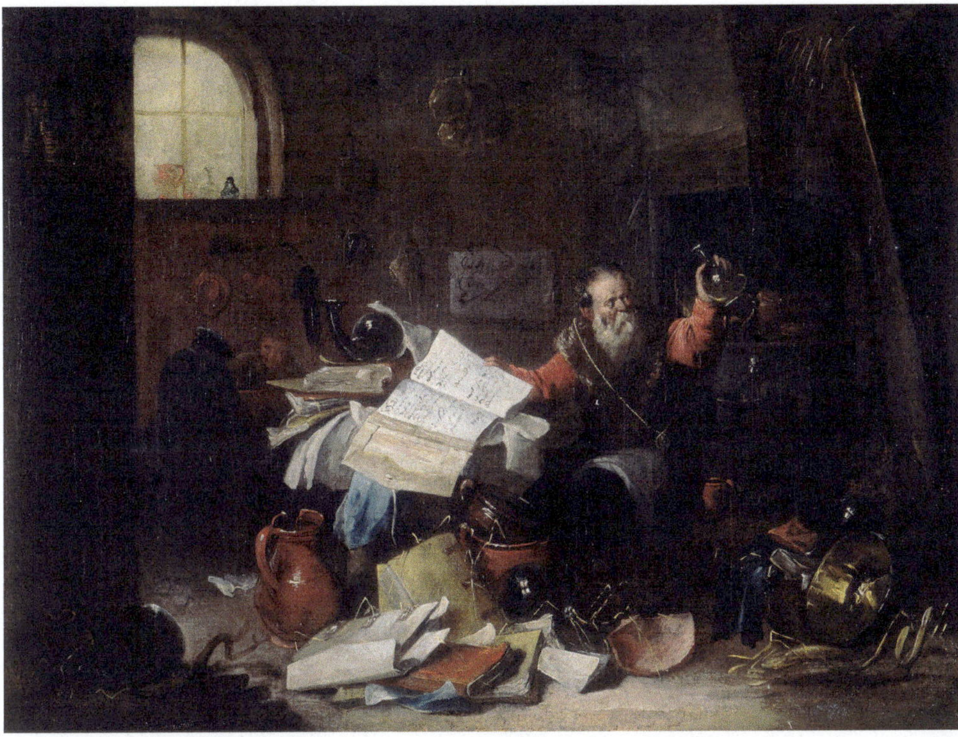

Plate 8. David Teniers the Younger: *The Alchemist.* Palazzo Pitti, Florence. Photo Credit: Alinari/Art Resource, N.Y.

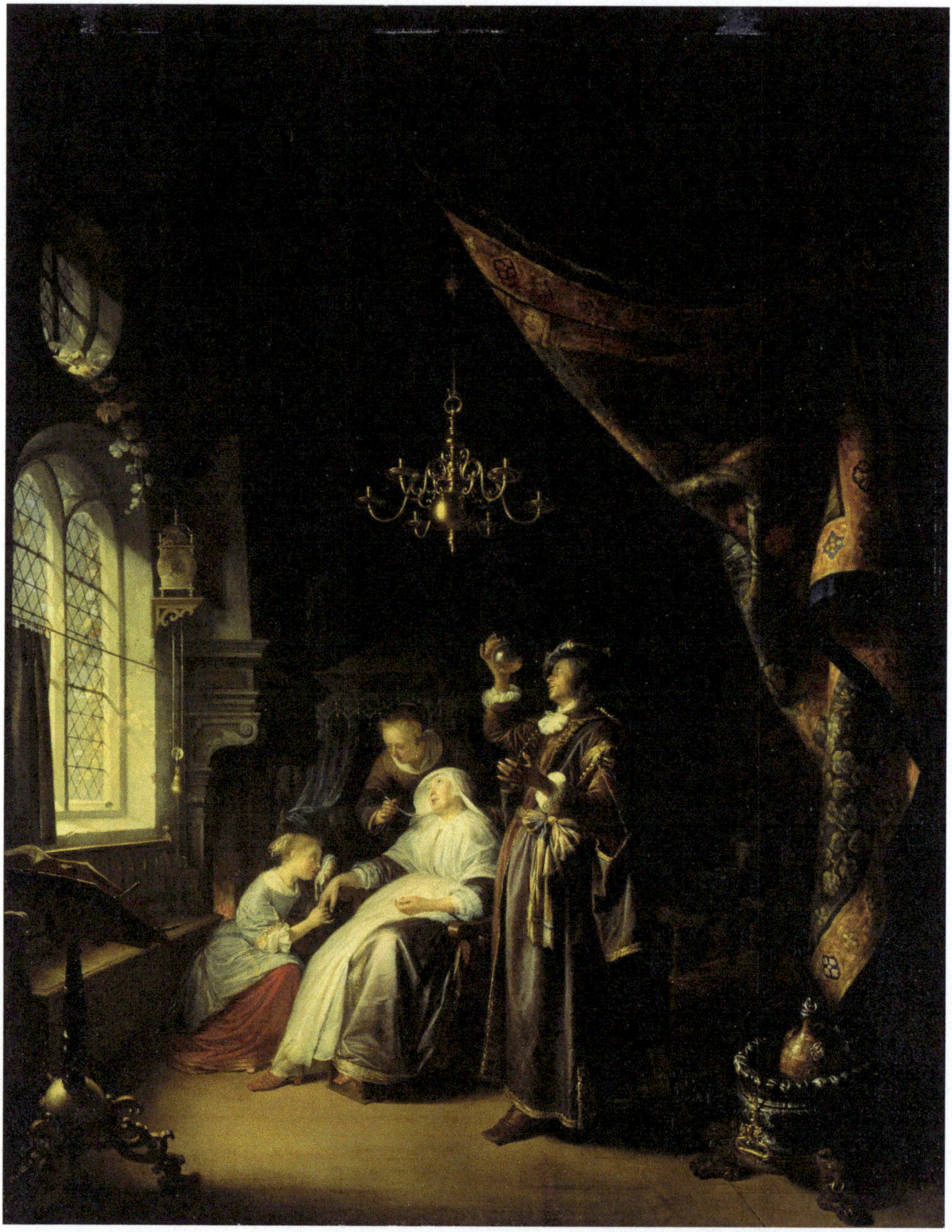

Plate 9. Gerrit Dou: *The Dropsical Woman*, 1663. Musée du Louvre, Paris. Photo Credit: Réunion des Musées Nationaux/Art Resource, N.Y.

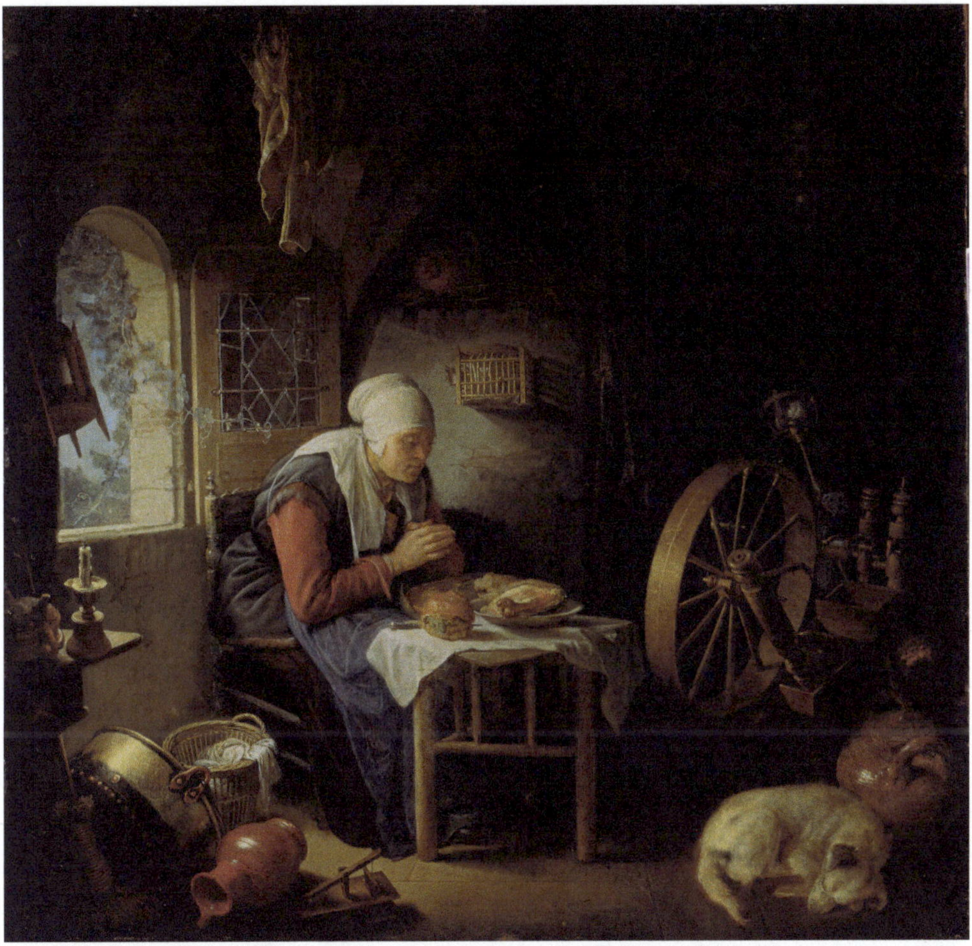

Plate 10. Gerrit Dou: *The Spinner's Grace*, c. 1645. Alte Pinakothek, Munich

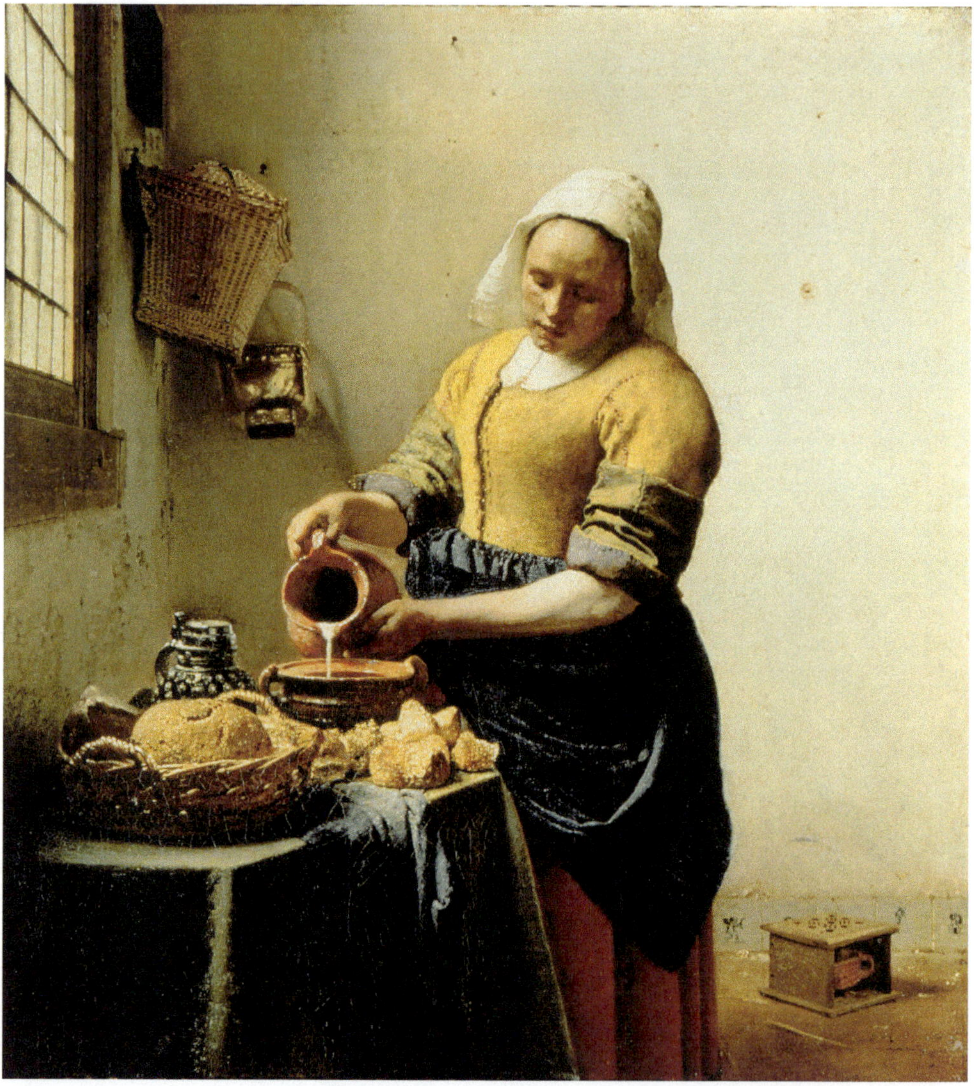

Plate 11. Johannes Vermeer: *The Milkmaid*, c. 1658–60. Rijksmuseum, Amsterdam. Photo Credit: Erich Lessing/Art Resource, N.Y.

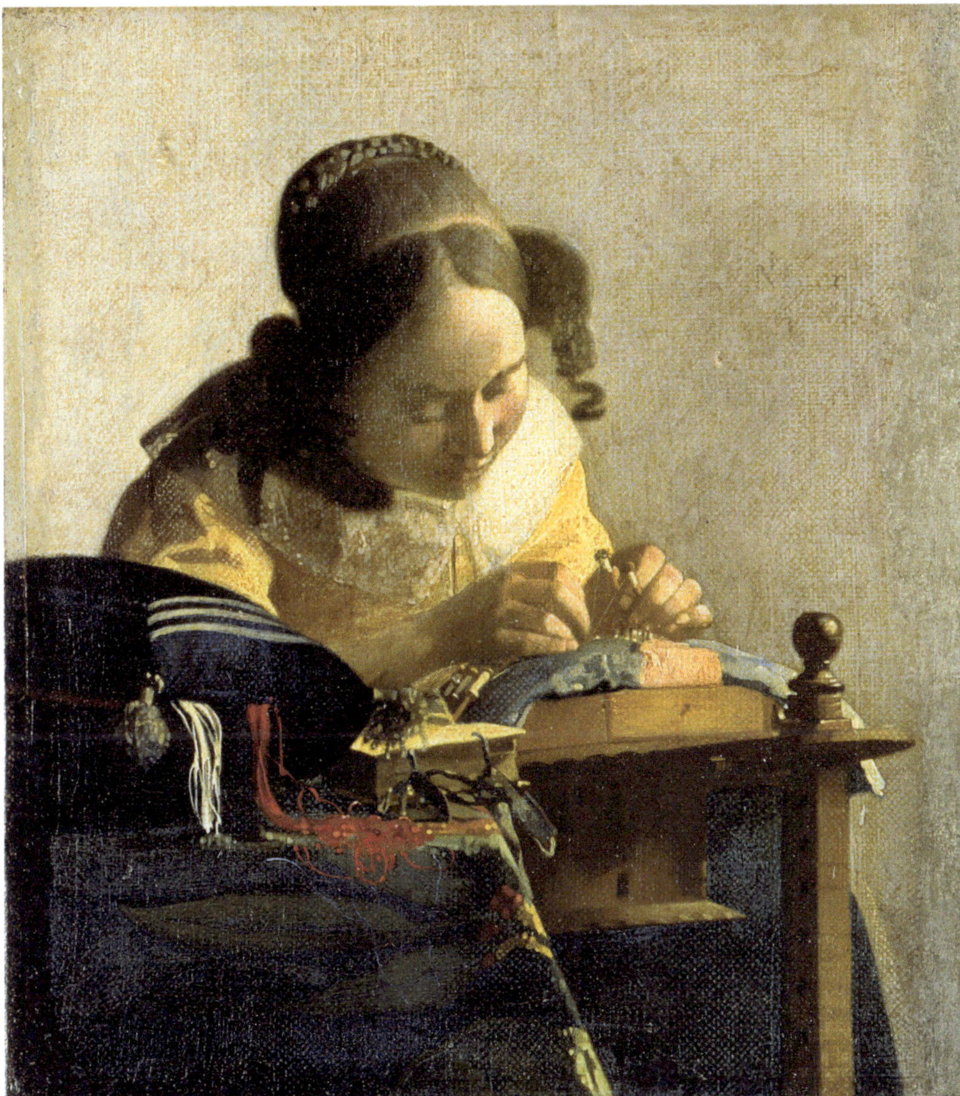

Plate 12. Johannes Vermeer: *The Lacemaker*, c. 1669–70. Musée du Louvre, Paris. Photo Credit: Réunion des Musées Nationaux/Art Resource, N.Y.

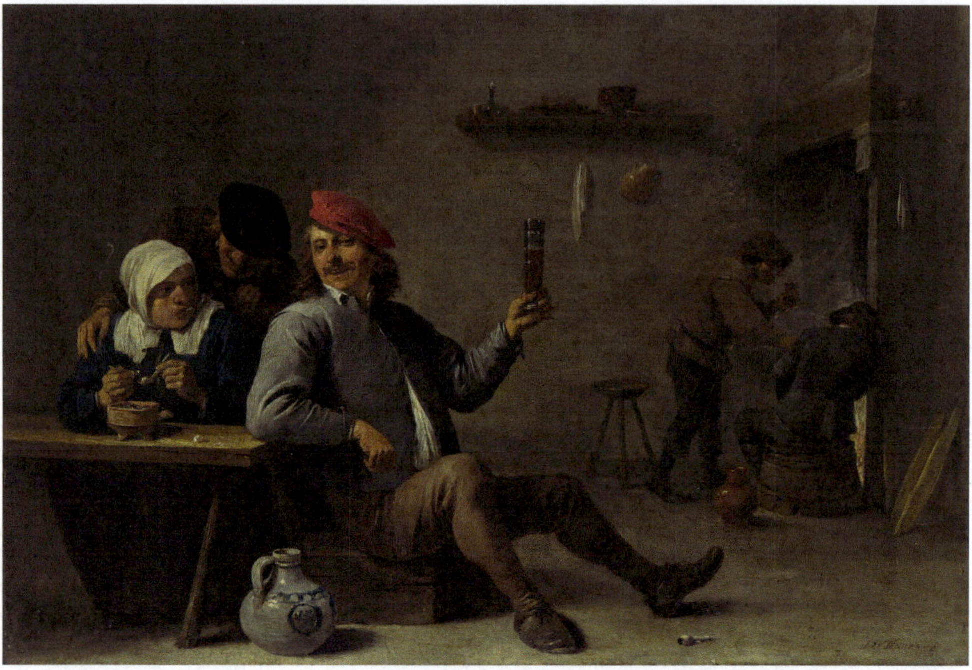

Plate 13. David Teniers the Younger: *A Man Holding a Glass and an Old Woman Lighting a Pipe*, c. 1645. National Gallery, London. © The National Gallery, London

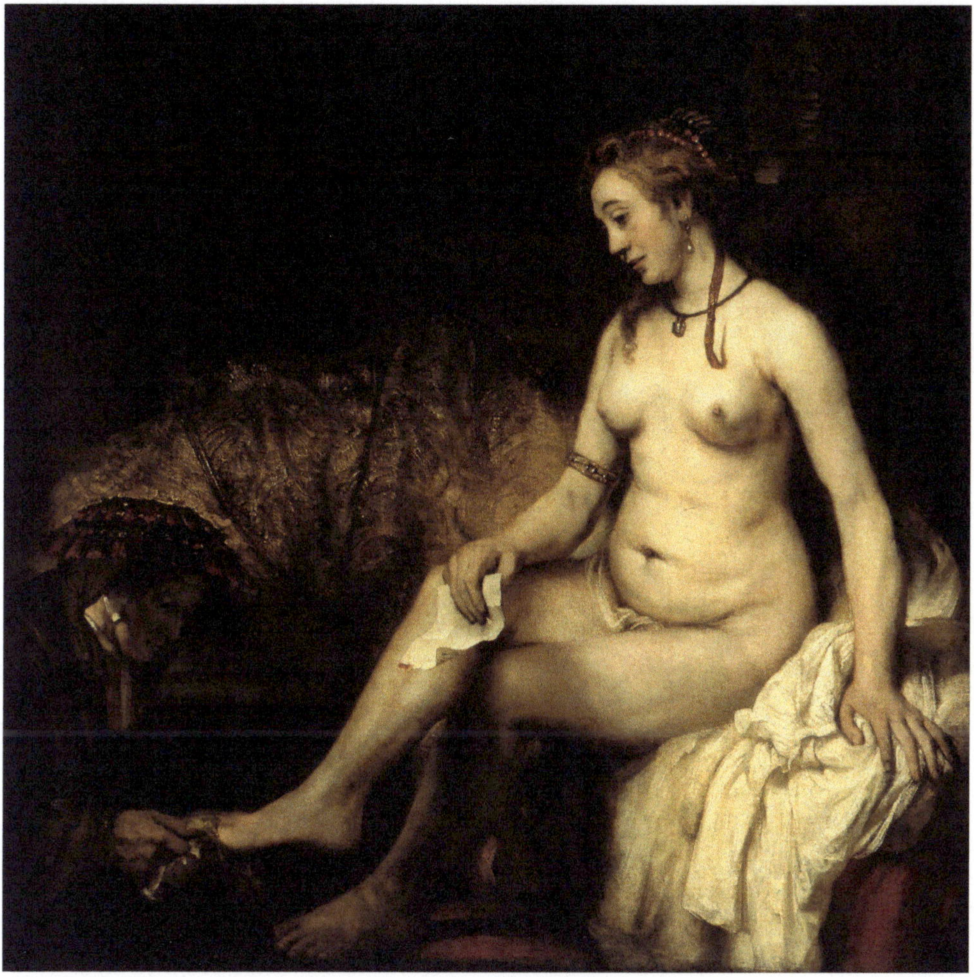

Plate 14. Rembrandt van Rijn: *Bathsheba at Her Bath*, 1654. Musée du Louvre, Paris. Photo Credit: Réunion des Musées Nationaux/Art Resource, N.Y.

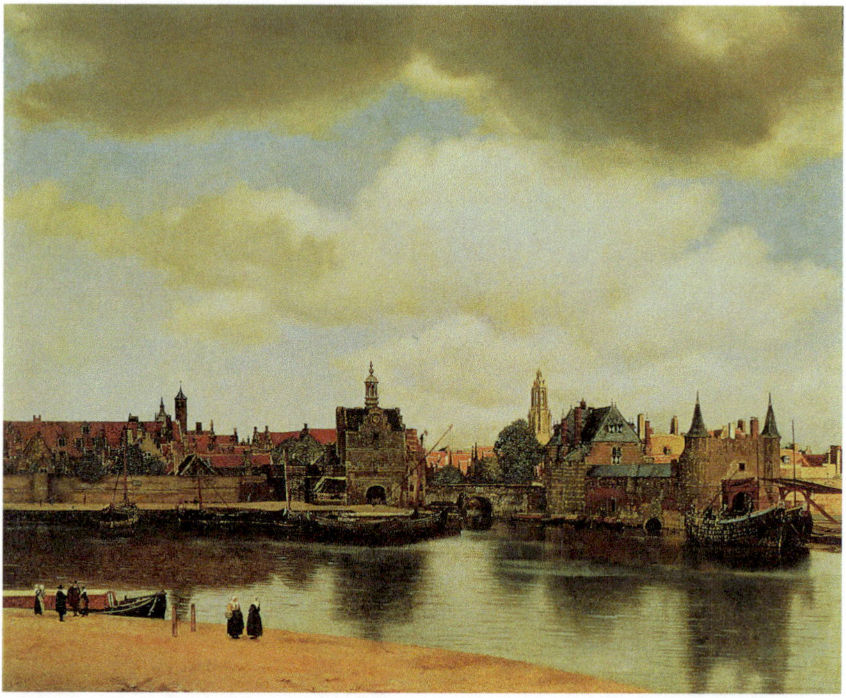

Plate 15. Johannes Vermeer: *View of Delft*, c. 1660–61. Mauritshuis, The Hague. Photo Credit: Scala/Art Resource, N.Y.

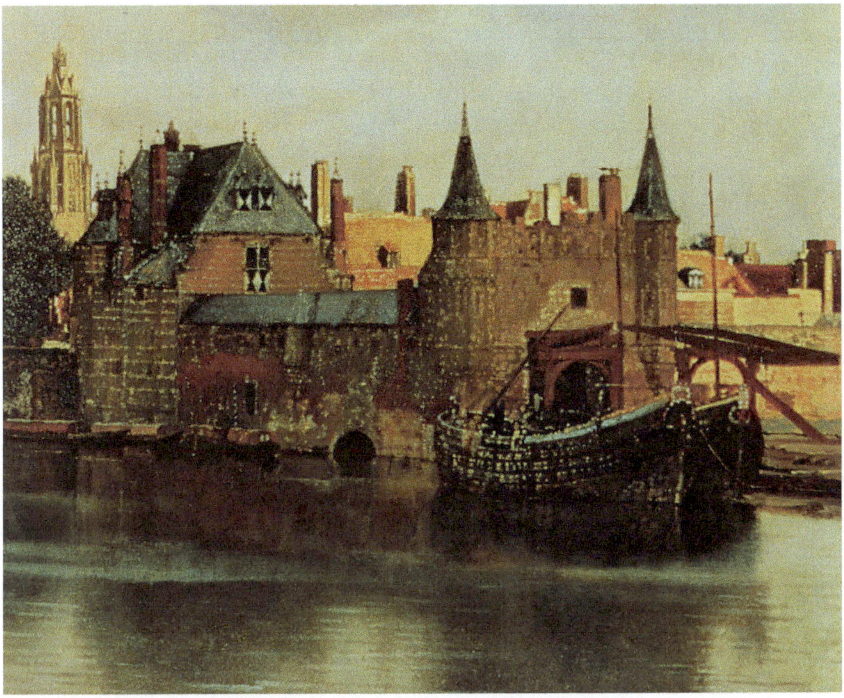

Plate 16. Johannes Vermeer: *View of Delft* (detail)

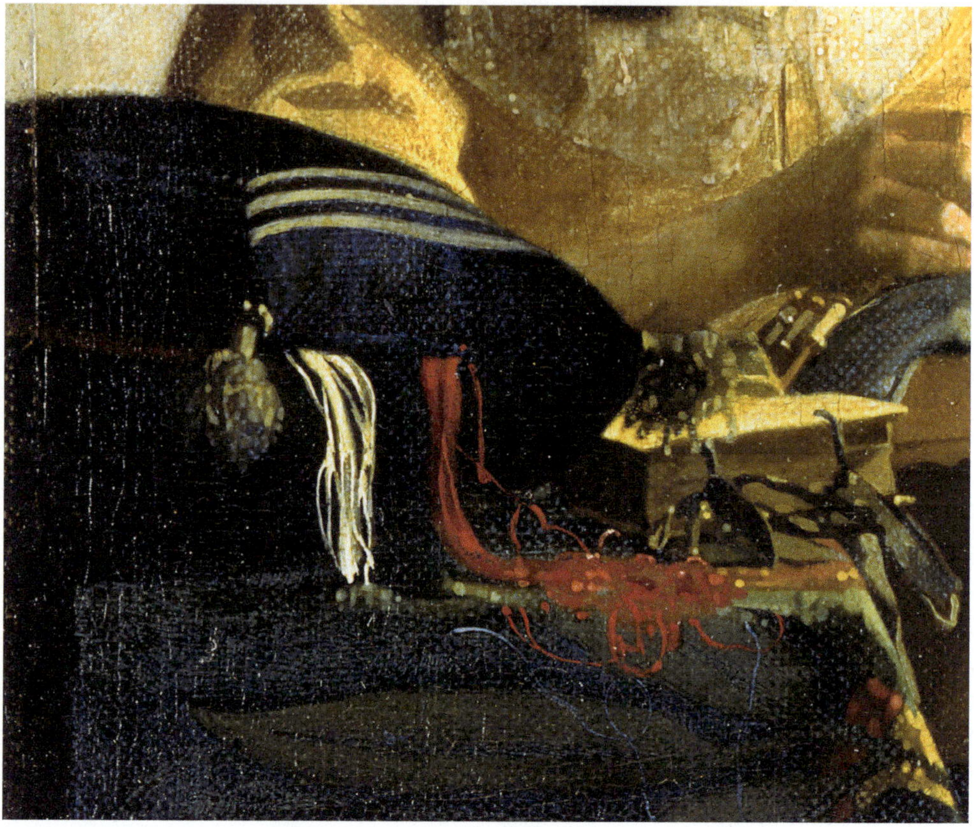

Plate 17. Johannes Vermeer: *The Lacemaker* (detail)

Though there is a faint suggestion that Mr. Maybold's preference for the organ over the choir corresponds to a difference between High Church and Low, it primarily testifies, of course, to his interest in the organist. The resulting triangle—in which the more refined suitor briefly replaces his humble rival—vaguely recalls that of *Adam Bede*, even to the scene in which the new lover belatedly discovers the prior claims of his inferior. In this case, the usurper is the clergyman himself rather than his old pupil, as in George Eliot's novel; but rather than exploit the potential conflict between the vicar's official morality and his temptation, *Under the Greenwood Tree* characteristically muffles it. The worst that threatens here is not seduction but jilting, and both lovers quickly withdraw from the brink. Fancy may be a "perfect woman" only "if you lay the stress," as she says, "on 'woman'" (135); but Hardy has no interest in moralizing her weakness. Unlike George Eliot's representation of Hetty Sorrel or even Janet Tryan, in other words, his picture of feminine frailty has little in common with the didacticism of the emblem books.

"If the story-tellers could ha' got decency and good morals from true stories," Reuben Dewy sensibly demands at one point, "who'd have troubled to invent parables?" The tranter's assumption that morality is necessarily a sign of the fictive might have troubled George Eliot; but his contention that "all true stories have a coarse touch or a bad moral" provides a working definition of realism that, in this novel at least, seems very close to Hardy's own.[34] Reuben has been prompted to articulate his theory by his wife's protest at a "coarse" story recounted by the old fiddler Michael Mail—a story whose lack of moralizing, and indeed of plot, is very much in the spirit of *Under the Greenwood Tree* as a whole. "Once," Mail says,

> I was a-setting in the little kitchen of the Dree Mariners at Casterbridge, having a bit of dinner, and a brass band struck up in the street. Such a beautiful band as that were! I was setting eating fried liver and lights I well can mind—ah, I was! And to save my life I couldn't help chawing to the tune. Band played six-eight time: six-eight chaws I, willynilly. Band plays common: common time went my teeth among the liver and lights as true as a hair. Beautiful 'twere!—Ah, I shall never forget that there band! (59)

Its coarseness from Mrs. Dewy's point of view presumably intensified by the organ meats Mail recalls consuming (the "lights" that accompany the liver are probably calf's lungs), this account of "chawing" in time to the band is not so much a story as a memory of rhythms, both instrumental and bodily.

And in this, too, I would argue, the old fiddler's fond reminiscence of "a beautiful band" may serve as something like an epitome of Hardy's novel.

That Hardy also associated such coarseness—and such truthfulness—with a certain kind of Dutch or Flemish picture is suggested by a brief entry in his "Schools of Painting" notebook of the decade before. "David Teniers," the note reads in full, "humour, drollery, vulgarity—truthful. d. 1694."[35] The National Gallery had not yet acquired the Peel Collection when Hardy recorded this note, but among the Teniers he could have seen on his visits there in the 1860s, the picture now labeled *A Man Holding a Glass and an Old Woman Lighting a Pipe* provides a good example of the kind of image he would have had in mind (plate 13).[36] I shall return to the effect of humor later; but for now it is simply worth noting that the "vulgarity" of such a picture is inseparable both from the status of the persons represented and from the basic activities in which they engage—those acts of drinking, smoking, sleeping, and possibly (in the case of the man touching the woman) preliminary love-making that make up the ongoing conduct of daily life. (The pissing figure who often appears in related images of course intensifies the vulgar effect [fig. 1-1].) Like Hardy's old fiddler, who "lifted the cup to his mouth and drank himself gradually backwards from a perpendicular position to a slanting one" before commencing his story (59), the principal figure in Teniers's picture slouches as he lifts his glass; but while there is some suggestion of speech in his neighbor's embrace of the woman, and perhaps in the gesture of the drinker by the fire, who tries to awake his sleeping companion, there is little implication of narrative in the scene they compose. Nor, as far as I can tell, is there any sign of moralizing.

Yet *Under the Greenwood Tree* does not only—or simply—resemble such a picture. Unlike George Eliot's representations of rural subjects, which almost always concentrate on the human figure, Hardy's "rural painting of the Dutch school" occupies a more ambiguous place between genre and landscape. Indeed, well into the nineteenth century, as we have seen, that distinction would itself have been an unsettled one. Originally used as a catchall for everything other than the pictures of historical or religious subjects traditionally classified as *peinture d'histoire*, the word *genre* did not finally settle into its present meaning until the 1860s and 70s—the very years that Hardy first began writing fiction.[37] Only gradually did the representation of anonymous persons engaged in everyday activities come to seem a separate category from pictures of the natural or man-made world; and even today, it is not always clear what distinguishes a landscape with human figures

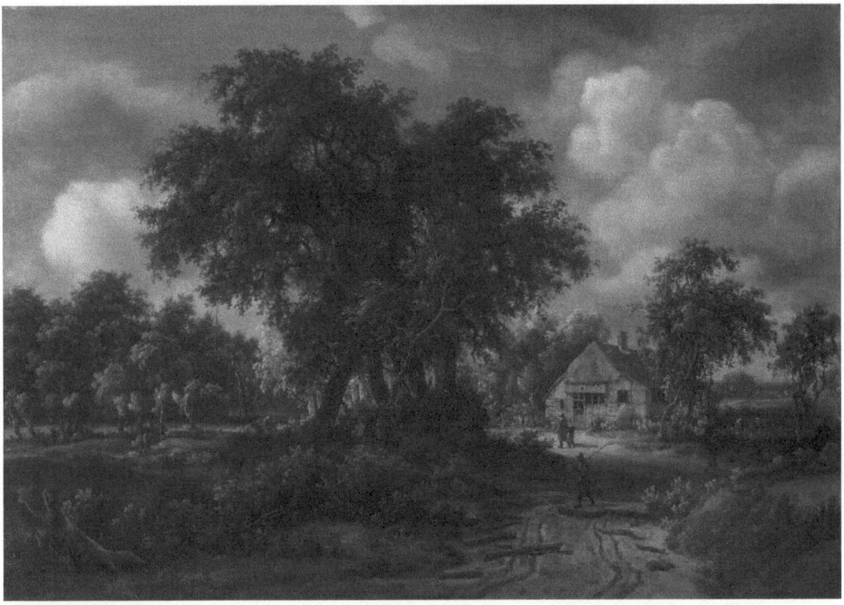

Figure 5-8. Meindert Hobbema: *A Woody Landscape*, c. 1665. National Gallery, London. © The National Gallery, London

from a genre painting set outdoors—except, presumably, the relative prominence of the people depicted. Doubtless Hobbema's *Woody Landscape* (fig. 5-8), another picture Hardy could have seen in the 1860s, justifies its present title, as does the same artist's *Stream by a Wood* (fig. 5-9), which arrived with the Peel Collection while *Under the Greenwood Tree* was being written. But what about Isack van Ostade's *Outskirts of a Village, with a Horseman* (fig. 5-10) or Teniers's *Cottage by a River with a Distant View of a Castle* (fig. 5-11), both of which were also acquired with the Peel Collection in 1871? In each of these cases, the National Gallery has presumably chosen to identify the image by its most prominent features; but the point is not to quibble over titles, or even to question the categories by which paintings are divided up and studied, so much as to register what genre and landscape have in common—and how one may be assimilated, both formally and thematically, to the other.

Like Hardy's novel, which subsumes the customary activities of its characters to the cycle of the seasons, each of these pictures subordinates the human figure to the landscape of which it is a part. (The very title of *Under the Greenwood Tree* has a related effect.) The Teniers is perhaps the closest to a genre painting of the four; but even as our eyes are drawn to the man

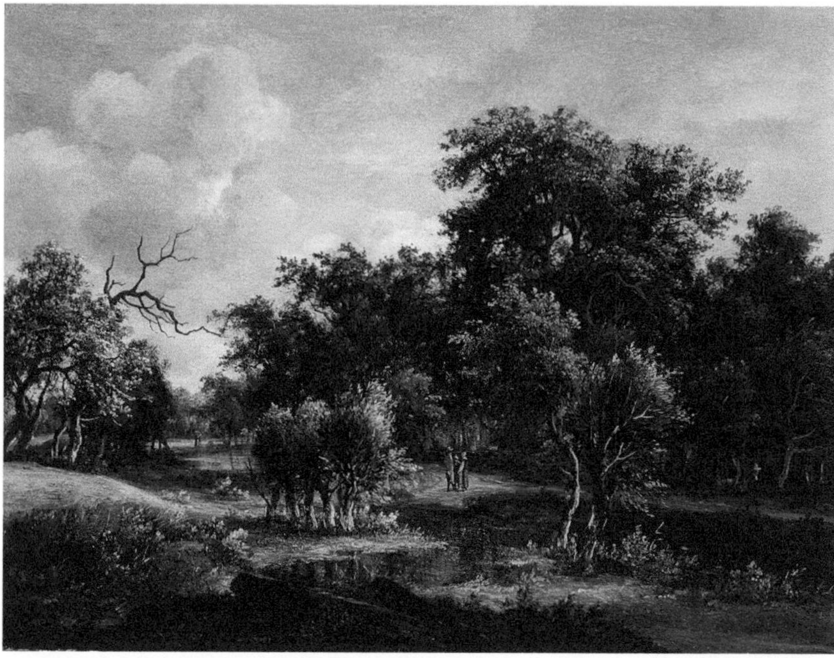

Figure 5-9. Meindert Hobbema: *A Stream by a Wood*, c. 1663. National Gallery, London. © The National Gallery, London

and woman in the foreground by their placement and lighting, their figures are more than offset by the prominent forms of the tree and the cottage itself, not to mention the bright expanse of the river and sky. While the distribution of attention in the Ostade is relatively even, Hobbema clearly devoted more care to particularizing his trees than he did to the people beneath them; yet details of both his pictures would constitute small genre paintings in their own right (figs. 5-12 and 5-13). Hardy himself would later adduce another Hobbema in the Peel Collection—the well-known *Avenue, Middelharnis* (fig. 5-14)—as evidence of how painters manage to "infuse . . . emotion into the baldest external objects either by the presence of a human figure among them, or by mark of some human connection with them."[38] But the association, of course, works in both directions; and in all these cases, the anonymity of the persons represented encourages their assimilation to the scene. Like the elements of the landscape itself, they acquire their reality effect by appearing at once individualized and typical. And as in more obvious genre paintings, any action in which they engage registers not as a unique event but as ongoing and repeatable.

Hardy's own rural picture creates its reality effects by analogous methods. "To dwellers in a wood," the novel begins, "almost every species of tree

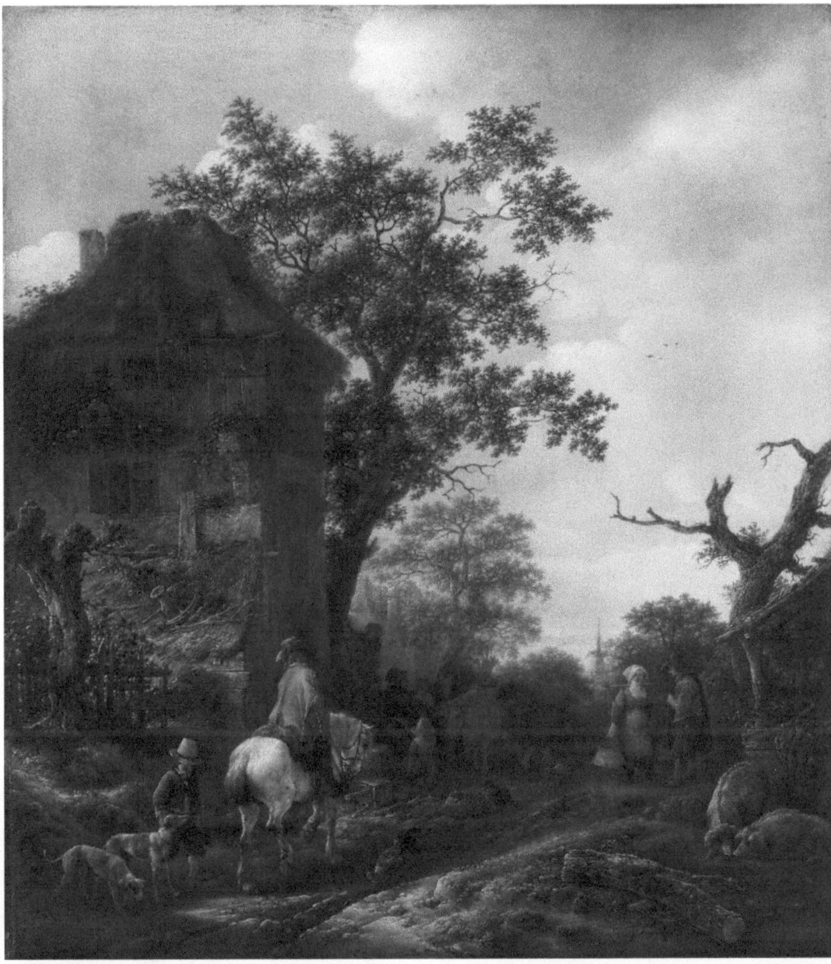

Figure 5-10. Isack van Ostade: *The Outskirts of a Village, with a Horseman*, 1640s. National Gallery, London. © The National Gallery, London

has its voice as well as its feature. At the passing of the breeze the fir-trees sob and moan no less distinctly than they rock: the holly whistles as it battles with itself: the ash hisses amid its quivering: the beech rustles while its flat boughs rise and fall. And winter, which modifies the note of such trees as shed their leaves, does not destroy its individuality" (11). Attention will soon shift from this chorus of trees to a chorus of people, but in both cases the narrative proceeds by simultaneously typing and individualizing. After a brief portrait of the novel's hero, whose only distinctiveness here is the utter ordinariness of his profile ("an ordinary-shaped nose, an ordinary chin,

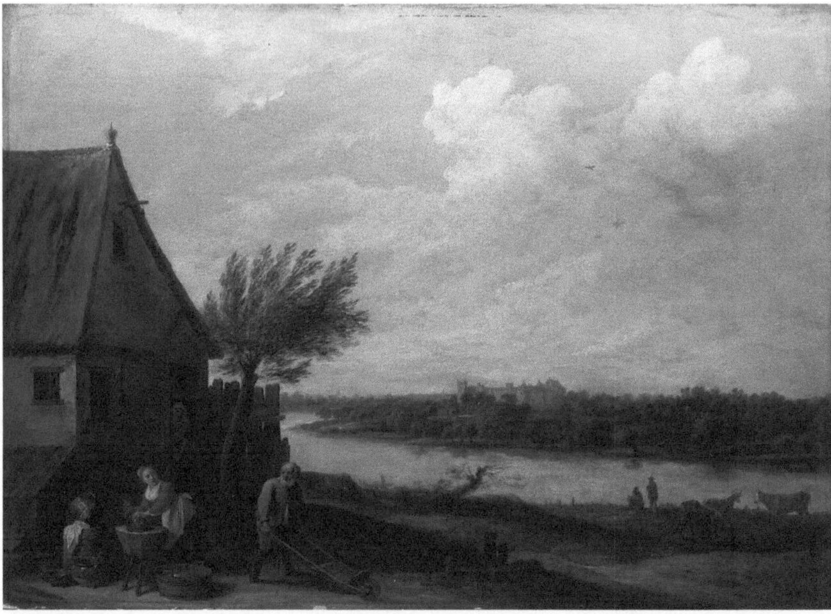

Figure 5-11. David Teniers the Younger: *A Cottage by a River with a Distant View of a Castle*, c. 1650. National Gallery, London. © The National Gallery, London

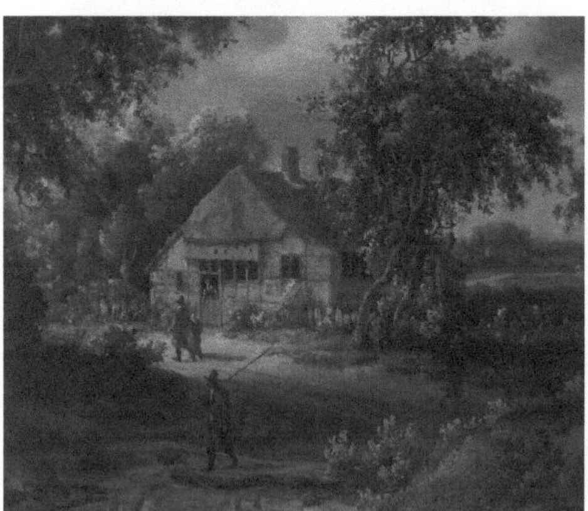

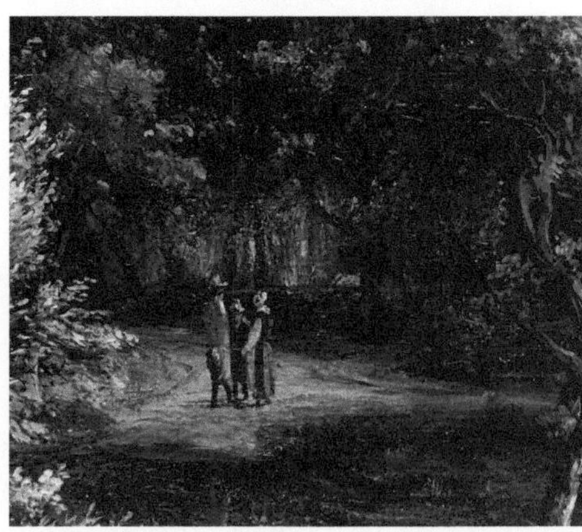

Left: Figure 5-12. Meindert Hobbema: *A Woody Landscape* (detail)
Right: Figure 5-13. Meindert Hobbema: *A Stream by a Wood* (detail)

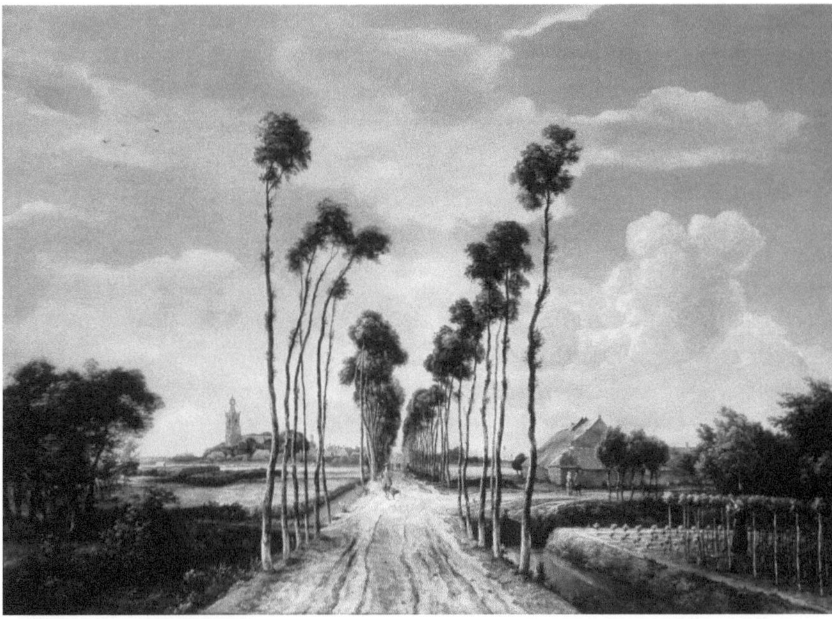

Figure 5-14. Meindert Hobbema: *The Avenue, Middleharnis*, 1689. National Gallery, London. Photo Credit: Art Resource, N.Y.

an ordinary neck and ordinary shoulders"), we are introduced to the other principal members of the choir:

> Scuffling halting irregular footsteps of various kinds were now heard coming up the hill, and presently there emerged from the shade severally five men of different ages and gaits—all of them working villagers of the parish of Mellstock. . . .
>
> The first was a bowed and bent man, who carried a fiddle under his arm, and walked as if engaged in studying some subject connected with the surface of the road. He was Michael Mail—the man who had hollaed to Dick.
>
> The next was Mr. Robert Penny, boot- and shoe-maker—a little man who, though rather round-shouldered, walked as if that fact had not come to his own knowledge, moving on with his back very hollow and his face fixed on the north-east quarter of the heavens before him, so that his lower waist-coat-buttons came first—and then the remainder of his figure. His features were invisible, yet when he occasionally looked round two faint moons of light gleamed for an instant from the precincts of his eyes, denoting that he wore spectacles of a circular form.

> The third was Elias Spinks who walked perpendicularly and dramatically. The fourth outline was Joseph Bowman's, who had now no distinctive appearance beyond that of a human being. Finally came a weak lath-like form trotting and stumbling along with one shoulder forward and his head inclined to the left, his arms dangling nervelessly in the wind as if they were empty sleeves. This was Thomas Leaf. (12–13)

Just as the trees have their characteristic notes, so the human beings have their characteristic gaits; yet even as Hardy takes care to distinguish one member of the group from another, he also continues to represent them as a collective. From the comparatively detailed sketch of Robert Penny to Joseph Bowman's wholly indistinctive outline is a difference of degree rather than of kind. What begins with a collective noun that is nonetheless said to be differentiated—those "shuffling halting irregular footsteps of various kinds"—ends with more collective nouns, as humans and trees alike are assimilated to the group: "they all advanced between the varying hedges and the trees dotting them here and there—kicking their toes occasionally among the crumpled leaves" (14).

Rather than a chorus in the Greek sense, which simply comments on the action, this chorus (or choir) nearly doubles as the protagonist. Though the courtship plot seems to have gained in prominence as Hardy revised,[39] almost half the published novel still concentrates on the musicians and their activities. Only in the ninth chapter do the two lovers first separate themselves from the others; and even after the courtship plot—such as it is—gets under way, the novel persists in its habit of identifying the individual with the group. "Ay, ay, my sonny: every lad has said that in his time," the tranter tells young Jimmy, when the latter protests that his brother said he would never marry (37); and something like this law of the typical and the repeatable governs the ordinary hero's surrender to love as well. As Dick's father sums up his condition:

> There's too many o' them looks out of the winder without noticing anything: too much shining of boots: too much peeping round corners—too much looking at the clock: telling about clever things She did till you be sick of it, and then upon a hint to that effect a horrible silence about her. I've walked the path once in my life and know the country, neighbours; and Dick's a lost man! (75)

Even without his final remark, the tranter's gerunds make clear that action in such a case is both generalizable and continuing.

As for the heroine of this story, the double set of furniture with which her father's house is stocked—the late Mrs. Day having provided for Fancy's eventual marriage by acquiring two of everything—clearly trumps her vague aspirations after "surroundings more elegant and pleasing than those which have been customary" (176). The "most noticeable instance" of this arrangement is "a pair of green-faced eight-day clocks ticking alternately" in the Day front room (93)—a detail that Hardy's friend and mentor Horace Moule particularly remarked when he cited the "picture" of this interior as "entirely justifying the author's mention of the Dutch school upon his title-page."[40] Like the Day boots, whose common last the shoemaker adapts, with small variations for bunions and such, from father to son, the two clocks offer inanimate versions of the individual as type: produced by rival clockmakers and marked with distinctive signatures, they keep slightly different times, while nonetheless signaling the fundamental repetition of history from mother to daughter. At the wedding itself, Fancy twice attempts to alter local custom in the direction of greater refinement, only to acquiesce and do just like her mother. "Why we did when we were married, didn't we Ann?" says the tranter of one such custom; "and so do everybody, my sonnies."

> "And so did we," said Fancy's father.
>
> "And so did Penny and I," said Mrs. Penny. "I wore my best Bath clogs I remember, and Penny was cross because it made me look so tall."
>
> "And so did father and mother," said Miss Mercy Onmey.
>
> "And I mean to, come next Christmas!" said Nat the groomsman, vigorously and looking towards the person of Miss Vashti Sniff.
>
> "Respectable people don't nowadays," said Fancy. "Still, since poor mother did, I will." (188–89)

From the dominance of the chorus—its individual voices at once mildly idiosyncratic and repetitive—to Fancy's brief protest and swift assimilation to the pattern, the sequence neatly sums up the action of the courtship plot as a whole.

When Hardy looked back on *Under the Greenwood Tree* more than a quarter century later, it was only the choir that he saw: the prefaces of 1896 and 1912 make no mention of the courtship plot at all. "This story of the Mellstock Quire and its old established west-gallery musicians," the 1896 preface begins, "is intended to be a fairly true picture . . . of the personages, ways, and customs which were common among such orchestral bodies in the villages of fifty or sixty years ago. One is inclined to regret the displacement of these ecclesiastical bandsmen by an isolated organist" (3). To the extent that the novel focuses on those "personages, ways, and customs"—rather than on that conflict with the "isolated organist"—it does in fact approximate to "picture." Though the story of the choir is finally one in which the group yields to the individual, *Under the Greenwood Tree* prefers to keep its eye on the group. "I never in my life seed a quire go into a study to have it out about the playing and singing! . . . And I should like to see it, just once," pleads the half-witted Leaf, when the musicians undertake their interview with the vicar in the hope of persuading him to postpone their displacement (81). The innocent Leaf speaks as if such a meeting were a customary practice, like caroling at Christmas or a wedding, rather than a singular episode in history; and despite the gentle joke at his expense, the novel almost manages to share his vision. The very ease with which the musicians give way to the vicar—not to mention the physical comedy of the scene—tends to mute any impression that something significant has occurred. And so, too, does the way the courtship plot reinstates the choir at the end, both by marrying the intrusive organist to one of their own and by bringing the musicians themselves back to perform at the ceremony.

By closing "Under the Greenwood Tree"—the title of the final chapter as well as of the work that contains it—the novel once more represents human custom as scarcely distinguishable from the rhythm of the natural world. The "ancient tree" beneath which the wedding festivities take place has apparently witnessed many mating rituals before this one:

> Many hundreds of birds had been born amidst the boughs of this single tree, tribes of rabbits and hares had nibbled at its bark from year to year, quaint tufts of fungi had sprung from the cavities of its forks, and countless families of moles and earthworms had crept about its roots. . . .
>
> . . . Whilst the dancing progressed, the older persons sat in a group under the trunk of the tree. . . . Here the gaffers and gammers whose dancing days were over told stories of great impressiveness, and at intervals surveyed the advancing and retiring couples from the same retreat. (193–94)

Whether "rabbits and hares" or "gaffers and gammers," the collective nouns reinforce the effect of ongoing life, in which generations succeed one another without any notable change. Such an effect may not quite be "still life"—a term that Hardy would sometimes use, suggestively, to characterize what we would ordinarily call landscape—but it nonetheless manages to produce a nearly static scene.[41]

Yet even in this most static of novels, picture inevitably gives way to history. Like George Eliot before him, Hardy associated Dutch painting with his own rural past; and however nostalgically he might view the image of reality it presented, he could hardly write fiction without plotting against it. Maybold himself is a recent arrival in Mellstock; and his decision to replace the choir with Fancy's organ-playing is not so different, after all, from the more momentous signs of historical change that Hardy would register in works like *The Mayor of Casterbridge* (1886) or *Tess of the d'Urbervilles* (1891). By the measure of such novels, Fancy's short-lived acceptance of the vicar's marriage proposal scarcely qualifies as an event, yet her momentary surrender to "ambition and vanity" (177) anticipates the restlessness that drives so many of Hardy's protagonists; while her decision to conceal her lapse hints, if ever so faintly, at betrayals to come. "It is only the old story that progress and picturesqueness do not harmonise," Hardy would later write in his essay on "The Dorsetshire Labourer" (1883); and though the novel concentrates more on what the essay calls "villagers immediately above the labouring class" than it does on the "workfolk" themselves, the picturesqueness of its representation clearly depends on the relative stasis of its figures. "The artistic merit of their old condition," Hardy would observe of the Dorset laborers, "is scarcely a reason why they should have continued in it when other communities were marching on so vigorously towards uniformity and mental equality." But when he writes of how "enlightenment" has enabled the worker to "rise above the condition of a serf who lived and died on a particular plot like a tree," his figure also implicitly acknowledges that it will no longer be so easy to picture such a person as part of the landscape.[42]

Behind both *Under the Greenwood Tree* and "The Dorsetshire Labourer," critics have sensed the presence of William Barnes (1801–1886), the regional poet and schoolmaster whom Hardy first met in the 1850s, and whose *Poems of Rural Life in the Dorset Dialect* (1879) the younger writer would review several years before publishing his essay. From the courtship of Dick and Fancy to episodes like the honey-taking and "going nutting," many scenes in the novel, William Rutland has argued, have their parallels in pieces from Barnes's first *Poems of Rural Life* (1844).[43] Even the subtitle of the novel, it has been speculated, may be traced back to Barnes, whose "Thoughts on Beauty and Art" (1861) had praised the "beauty and truth of colour and action in the Dutch school."[44] But whether or not Hardy was recalling such remarks when he composed his "Rural Painting of the Dutch School" seems less important, finally, than the associations that prompted him to identify his predecessor's own work with that of the Dutch. In the 1879 review Hardy invoked what he called Barnes's "whole poems of still life, brief and unaffected, but realistic as a Dutch picture";[45] and he was so taken with the formula that he repeated it, elegantly varied, in his obituary for the poet seven years later. Both versions suggest that Barnes had been moved to create such poems by "the pervading instinct of the nineteenth century," but the second makes clearer that the instinct in question is partly a function of memory:

> Moreover, when, moved by the pervading instinct of the nineteenth century, he gives us whole poems of still life, unaffected and realistic as a Dutch picture, the slow green river Stour of the same valley, with its deep pools, whence the trout leaps to the may-fly undisturbed by anglers, is found to be the stream dearest to his memory and the inspirer of some of his happiest effusions.[46]

By the time that Hardy wrote these words, his own art had moved significantly away from the model of the Dutch; and he had become increasingly resistant to the desire for "still life," in the sense of the impulse to arrest change in the motionless images of memory. Barnes's "rustics are, as a rule, happy people," he observed in the obituary, "and very seldom feel the sting of the rest of modern mankind—the disproportion between the desire for serenity and the power of obtaining it."[47] The poet died in the year that *The Mayor of Casterbridge* was published and *The Woodlanders* began its serial run; but not even the latter's Marty South—the principal figure in these works who remains closest to the rhythms of the landscape—bears much resemblance to Barnes's happy rustics. Only parts of *Far from the Madding Crowd* perhaps approach the spirit Hardy associated with his predecessor; and that novel retains its investment in the ordinary only by arranging for subordinate figures to act out the more restive impulses of its hero and heroine.[48] "And at home by the fire, whenever you look up there I shall be—and whenever I look up there will be you," Gabriel Oak proposes to Bathsheba at the novel's opening; but not until Boldwood is locked up and both Fanny and Troy are dead will the novel reward its "everyday sort of man" and settle into something like his picture of quotidian domesticity. Appropriately, a bit of Barnes's dialect poetry breaks into the fireside scene in which Oak and Bathsheba agree to marry:

> So down she sat, and down sat he, the fire dancing in their faces, and upon the old furniture,
>
> all a-sheenen
> Wi' long years o'handlen
>
> that formed Oak's array of household possessions, which sent back a dancing reflection in reply.

It is no accident that Oak's "special power, morally, physically, and mentally," as the narrator says in the second chapter, "was static."[49]

Another name for Hardy's "Rural Painting of the Dutch School," of course, is comedy. Looking back on *Under the Greenwood Tree* from the perspective of the *Life* more than fifty years later, the novelist himself would worry that he had "rather burlesqued" the choir;[50] but as his own note on Teniers might have reminded him, the humor and "drollery" of such art had long been loosely associated with its realism.[51] When Dryden drew his "Parallel betwixt Painting and Poetry" at the end of the seventeenth century, he took for granted that "the painting of Clowns" or "the representation of a *Dutch* Kermis" was to the visual hierarchy as comedy was to the literary—and that what they shared was a focus on "inferiour persons, and low Subjects."[52] Though Dryden's "Clowns" were probably rustics or boors rather than jesters, the very history of the word testifies to elite amusement at inferiors. Among the first Dutch images to circulate in England, as we have seen, were the inexpensive mezzotints known as "drolls" or "drolleries"—often coarse representations of peasants or servants, like the anonymous *Dutch Interior* (fig. 5-15), or the *Sleeping Woman* after Frans van Mieris (fig. 5-16), in which an apparently drunken stupor is about to be disturbed by a leering man with a chamber pot. While the nineteenth century was more inclined to prefer the comparatively sentimentalized images of the later Ostade—or his British descendents, such as Wilkie—to cruder images like these, *Under the Greenwood Tree* is still a remote heir of this tradition.[53] When the tranter's wife mildly laments her marriage into a family of "sich vulgar sweaters" as the Dewys (48), or Reuben concedes that his decision to strip in consequence is "rather pothousey" (54), their very attempts to distance themselves from such coarseness recall our amused attention to their bodily reality.

As in Balzac, Hardy's Dutch picture occasionally verges on caricature. Just as the exaggerated outlines of the miserly Grandet, for example, owe something to the comic distortions of contemporary printmakers like Gavarni or Monnier,[54] so Hardy's comic portraits—especially, Grundy has suggested, his portraits of rustics—may reflect the influence of a long line of British caricaturists, from Rowlandson and Gillray to Cruickshank and Phiz.[55] But there is no need to distinguish sharply between such effects and those inspired by the art of the Dutch: precisely because the figures in many seventeenth-century paintings of peasants and other low-life types were already subject to comic distortion, the novelists could readily assimilate these recent influences—all the more so, as Bonard has brilliantly argued in

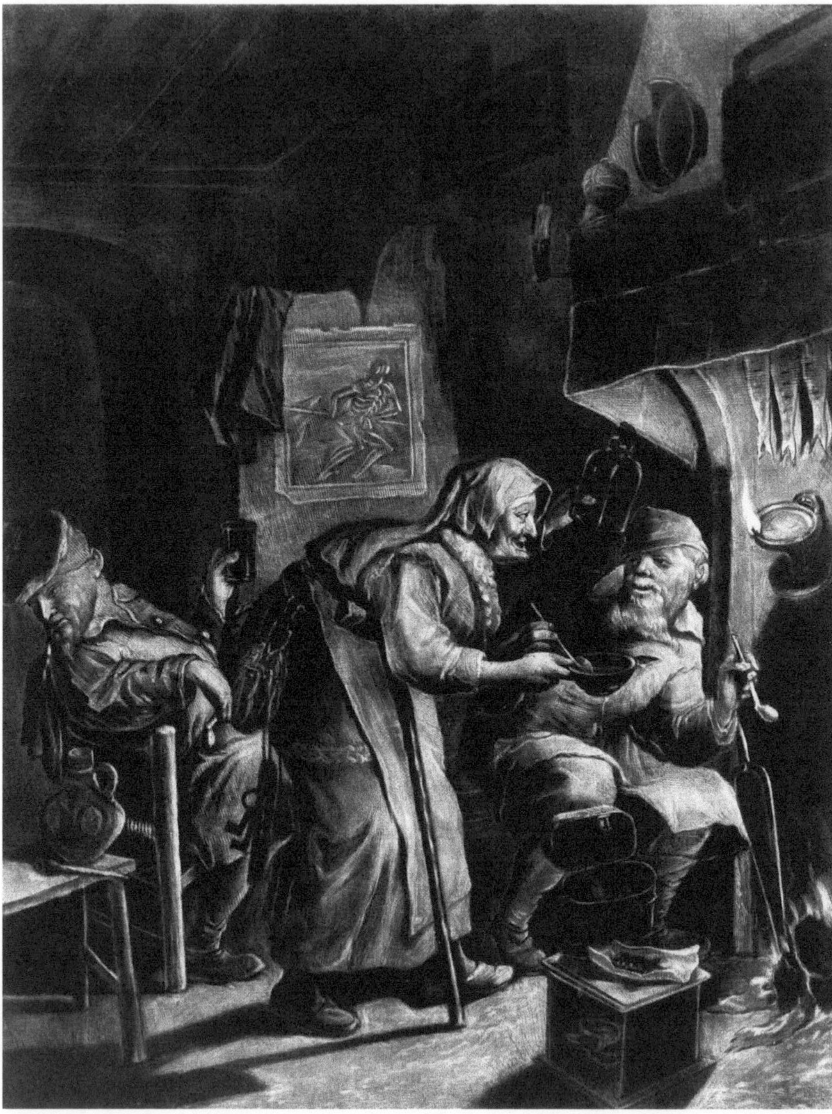

Figure 5-15. Anon.: *Dutch Interior* (?), mezzotint. Yale Center for British Art, Paul Mellon Fund

his study of Balzac, because they would have often encountered the Dutch pictures themselves in the form of black-and-white prints.[56] To look again at drolls like the *Dutch Interior* or the *Sleeping Woman* (figs. 5-15 and 5-16), or even at Ostade's *Singers* (fig. 5-4), is to see how easily nineteenth-century caricature might be mapped on these earlier images. In a somewhat related

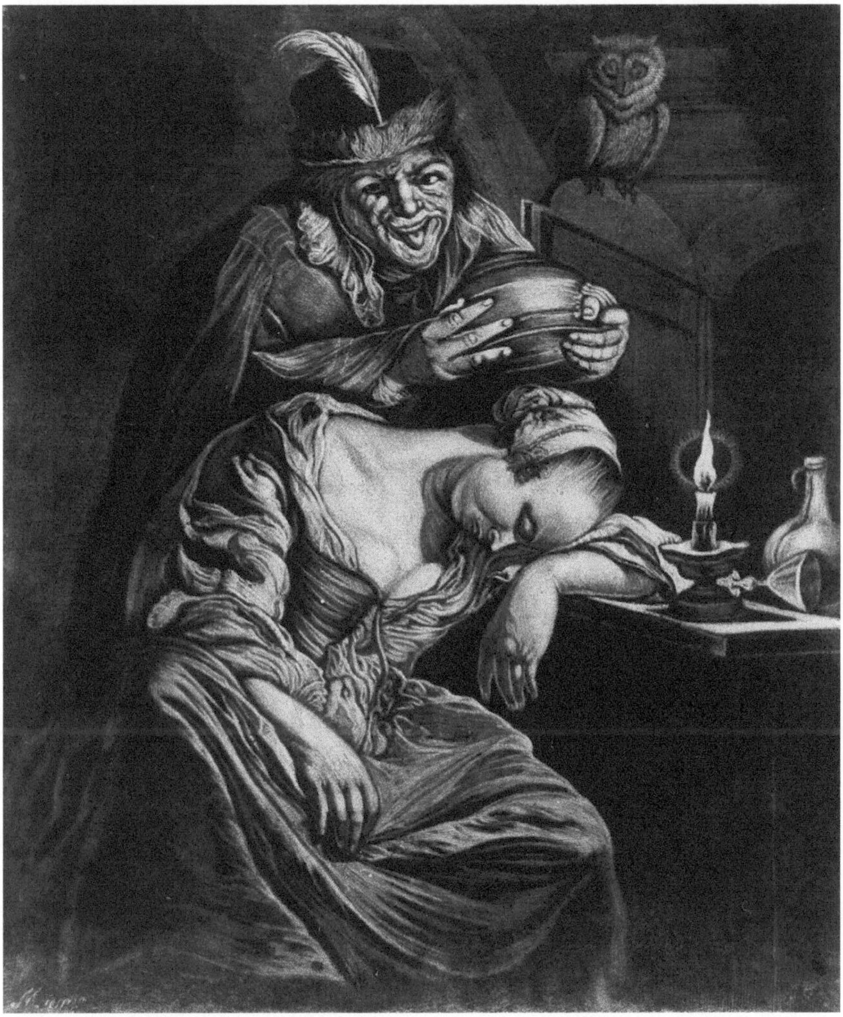

Figure 5-16. Anon. (after Frans van Mieris): *A Sleeping Woman*, mezzotint. Yale Center for British Art, Paul Mellon Fund

move, *Under the Greenwood Tree* also draws briefly, as Bullen has shown, on the comic potential of the silhouette—introducing its hero profiled against the sky "like the portrait of a gentleman in black cardboard," and following him with "the flat outlines" of the other choir members, even as it verbally intensifies this flattening by repeatedly characterizing the parts of Dick's profile as "ordinary" (12).[57] Like the "fractional" body parts of the choir framed in the vicar's doorway (87), such images achieve their comic effect by radically reducing the human form, as if the visual simplification were a matter of cutting people down to size.

The title of *Under the Greenwood Tree* comes from *As You Like It*, and the influence of Shakespearean pastoral, too, can be felt in Hardy's rural novel. The specific allusion is to Amiens' song in act two, scene five ("Under the greenwood tree / Who loves to lie with me . . .")—a song that echoes again when Fancy hears the nightingale sing its "come hither" refrain at the novel's close (198). Echoes of Shakespeare's play have also been heard in the repetitive chorus with which Hardy's characters, like Silvius, Phebe, and the rest, acknowledge their common surrender to the rituals of love, as well as in the novel's more general attentiveness to music and dance in a rural setting.[58] Hardy himself later contended that "it was Shakespeare's delineation of his Warwickshire clowns" that most influenced his own representation of the Wessex peasantry;[59] and as early as *Far from the Madding Crowd*, reviewers, too, took up the comparison.[60] Indeed, just as it would be futile to deny how much the dark comedy of *Eugénie Grandet*, for example, owes to Molière, or George Eliot's early pastoralism to Wordsworth, so it would be wrong not to recognize the presence of Shakespeare even in this most avowedly painting-like novel. To argue that novelists turned to Dutch art for a model is not to pretend that they took it for their only model, or that Hardy's rustics, in the present case, could not claim kinship with those in Shakespeare and in seventeenth-century painting simultaneously. That the boors and rustics of Golden Age art shared an historical moment with Shakespeare's clowns may well have facilitated the connection—encouraging Hardy to assimilate both to his representation of a fast-vanishing way of life in rural England more than two centuries later.[61]

But while Shakespeare would remain a continuing presence in Hardy's fiction, only in *Under the Greenwood Tree* does the entire form of a work bear any resemblance to a rural painting of the Dutch school. Though one might look for traces of such painting at many moments in the later novels, from the sheep-shearing in the great barn of *Far from the Madding Crowd* to the episodes at Talbothays dairy in *Tess of the d'Urbervilles*, never again would Hardy keep his eyes so consistently on the comic group; nor would he ever again attempt so static a picture. Rather than Dutch painting, he would return more consistently to the model of the dramatist, as he again relegated his low mimetic figures to their traditional choral function. The novel that immediately follows *Under the Greenwood Tree* has a grave-digging scene almost worthy of *Hamlet*—not to mention some lively talk of pig-killing—but like most of the later fiction, *A Pair of Blue Eyes* (1873) directs its principal attention to those who aspire to something more than the ordinary rhythms of life and death. The pig-killer may talk of animals he has "knowed" almost as if he were talking of his neighbors, but it is "the gentlemanly son of the house" who is one of the novel's protagonists; and "it must be owned," as the narrator says, that he "looked rather out of place in the course of [the] operations" by which "the firstfruits of the day's slaughter" are cut up, fried, and consumed.[62] Like that still more reluctant pig-killer Jude Fawley, in Hardy's last published novel, Stephen Smith no longer feels altogether comfortable in his animal skin. Not for such characters the appearance of easy subordination to the animal by which the two figures conversing in the middle distance of Isack van Ostade's *Outskirts of a Village* loosely echo the porcine pair nuzzling amiably in the foreground (fig. 5-10).

Nor are the later protagonists readily assimilated to the landscape, even if Hardy still chooses on occasion to conjure up such pictures. Silhouetted on top of the barrow in the opening pages of *The Return of the Native*, Eustacia Vye initially appears "an organic part of the entire motionless structure"; but the illusion is quickly dispelled when "the figure perceptibly [gives] up its fixity"—a vanishing act she longs to perform more substantively, of course, by escaping once and for all from Egdon Heath. Though Clym Yeobright, by contrast, temporarily finds peace as "a brown spot in the midst of an expanse of olive-green gorse, and nothing more," his time as a furze-cutter is only a brief interlude in the tragic narrative of the native's return.[63] Even Tess Durbeyfield cannot really settle into such a picture for very long: despite "the charm which is acquired by woman when she becomes part and parcel of outdoor nature," according to the narrator, both the historical changes Hardy had described in "The Dorsetshire Labourer" and her own "ache of modernism" keep his most bucolic heroine in restless motion until her death.[64] Only a figure like Amos Fry in *Two on a Tower* (1882) remains "as difficult to distinguish from the earth he trod as the caterpillar from its leaf"; but this "brown person" is, we are told, "one of a dying-out generation."[65] Amos—or "Haymoss," as he is generally known—also belongs to the local choir, whose rustic music-making vaguely recalls that of Mellstock. But *Two on a Tower* concentrates on the unhappy love affair between the abandoned wife of an aristocratic estate owner and an ambitious young astronomer; and this is the kind of choir that primarily serves to comment on the actions of its betters.

Both in fiction and in painting, Hardy himself would not long rest content with certain kinds of realism. Though he would never fully abandon the Dutch masters, his taste in pictures would increasingly incline toward

Turner and the impressionists, while his theoretical statements about art would repeatedly emphasize the subjective distortion of material appearances.[66] "The poetry of a scene varies with the minds of the perceivers," he had noted in his journal as early as 1865: "indeed, it does not lie in the scene at all."[67] This was recorded three years before he attempted to publish his first work of fiction; but the subjective bias it reflects would draw new strength from developments in visual art in the following decades. By the time he came to write *The Woodlanders* in 1886, the influence of contemporary painting would be explicitly registered in the narrative, as an early genre scene modulates from something like the Dutch manner to something much closer to these recent experiments.

Our first view of Marty South comes through the eyes of the barber, Mr. Percombe, as he watches her at work by the fire-lit window of her cottage:

> In the room from which this cheerful blaze proceeded he beheld a girl seated on a willow chair, and busily working by the light of the fire, which was ample, and of wood. With a bill-hook in one hand, and a leather glove much too large for her on the other, she was making spars—such as are used by thatchers—with great rapidity. She wore a leather apron for this purpose, which was also much too large for her figure. On her left hand lay a bundle of the straight smooth hazel rods called spar-gads—the raw material of her manufacture: on her right a heap of chips and ends—the refuse—with which the fire was maintained: in front a pile of the finished articles. . . .
>
> Beside her, in case she might require more light, a brass candlestick stood on a little round table, curiously formed of an old coffin-stool, with a deal top nailed on, the white surface of the latter contrasting oddly with the black carved oak of the substructure. The social position of the household in the past was almost as definitely shown by the presence of this article as that of an esquire or nobleman by his old helmets and shields.

At once detailing what the barber ostensibly sees and merging his viewpoint with that of the narrator, who expands on those details by interpreting their social and personal significance, the description continues in this quasi-Balzacian style for several paragraphs. Just as the unusual appearance of the coffin-stool provides the occasion for a brief account of local history, so the blistering of Marty's ungloved palm becomes a sign of the relative infrequency with which she works at her present task, or her facial expressiveness testifies to "a life of solitude."[68]

But unlike the reader, for whose benefit these details have presumably been elaborated, the barber is only interested in one thing—the beautiful mane of chestnut hair that he has been commissioned to purchase on behalf of a wealthy widow. What begins as a Dutch painting turns into a very different kind of picture, as Hardy recalls himself to the imagined subjectivity of the viewer:

> In her present beholder's mind the scene formed by the girlish spar-maker composed itself into an impression-picture of extremest type, wherein the girl's hair alone, as the focus of observation, was depicted with intensity and distinctness, and her face, shoulders, hands, and figure in general were a blurred mass of unimportant detail lost in haze and obscurity.[69]

In this version of the scene, nothing remains of the material facts that the narrator has just been recording but "a blurred mass of unimportant detail"—detail presumably still available to the barber's eye, but beneath the threshold of his attention, which is focused only on the hair he covets. Point of view, Hardy seems to remind himself, is not just a question of physical position but of desire and interest.

Though the novelist had already imagined this subjective revision of the scene before he visited an exhibit at the Society of British Artists that winter, the pictures he saw there apparently drove home the lesson. "The impressionist school is strong," he wrote in his notebook after the visit. But "it is even more suggestive in the direction of literature than in that of art. . . . [T]heir principle is, as I understand it, that what you carry away with you from a scene is the true feature to grasp; or in other words, *what appeals to your own individual eye and heart in particular* amid much that does not so appeal, and which you therefore omit to record." Apart from a subsequent allusion to "Whistler's study in red that I had seen in the morning at the Gallery"—presumably the *Harmony in Red, Lamplight* (fig. 5-17), which was conjured up that evening by the vision of a friend seated at her fireside in a "rich pinky-red gown"—the notebook does not identify which paintings Hardy had in mind.[70] Yet if his viewing of the exhibit probably inspired a change of label—the serial version of *The Woodlanders* alludes to a "post-Raffaelite" rather than an "impression-picture"—Hardy was already seeing such images even before he had a name for them.[71] Framed in the window as she works at her humble task, Marty South more nearly resembles the absorbed subjects of Whistler's *Pink Note: Shelling Peas*, or even his *Pink Note: The Novelette* (figs. 5-18 and 5-19), than she does the figure who poses theatrically for her portrait in the *Harmony in Red*; but the deliberate sketchiness of all three paintings would have helped to confirm the novelist's

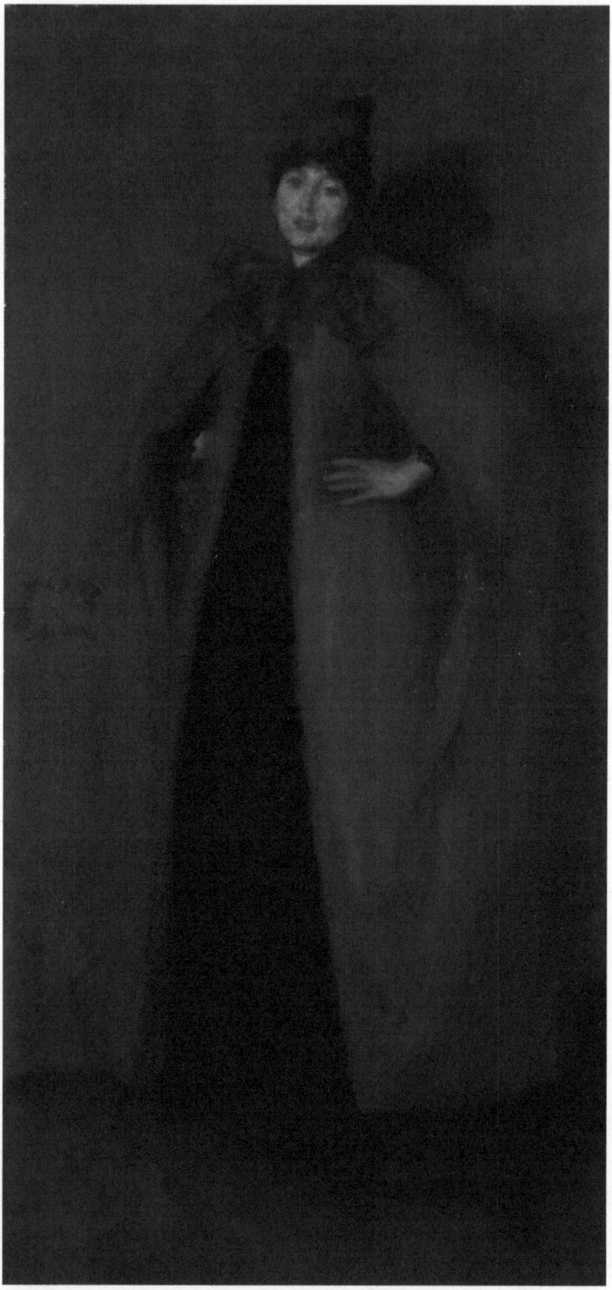

Figure 5-17. James McNeill Whistler: *Harmony in Red, Lamplight*, c. 1884–86. © Hunterian Museum and Art Gallery, University of Glasgow

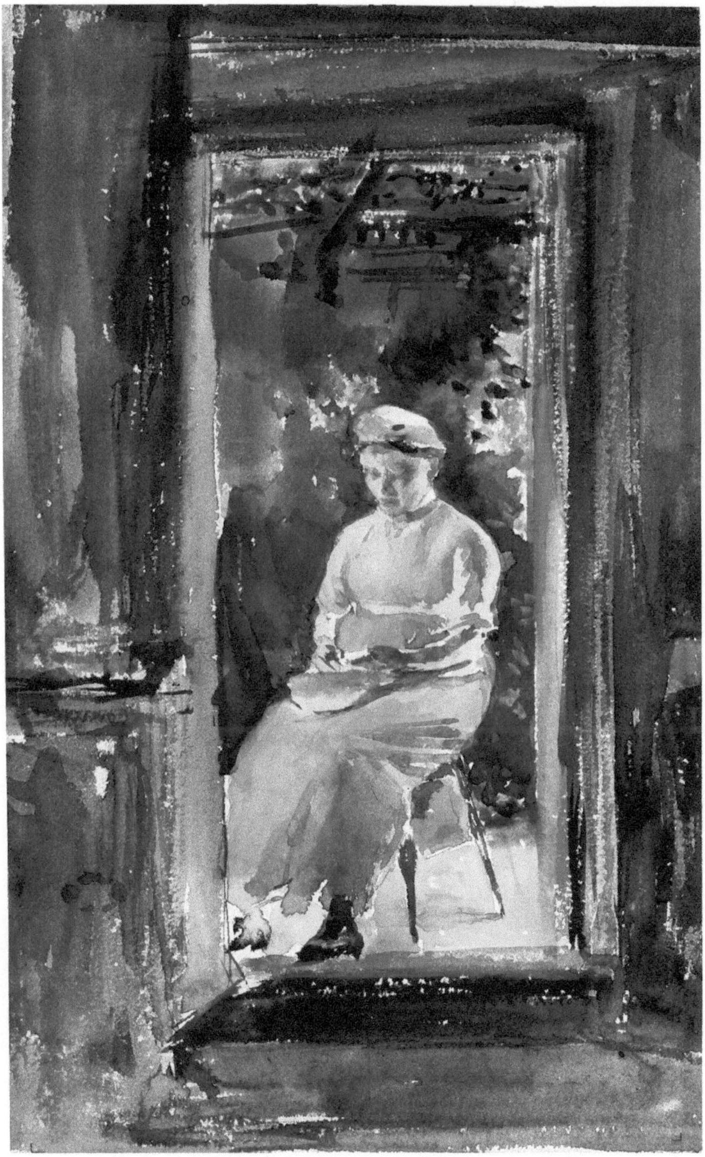

Figure 5-18. James McNeill Whistler: *Pink Note: Shelling Peas*, watercolor on paper, 1883 or 1884. Freer Gallery of Art, Smithsonian Institution, Washington, D.C., Gift of Charles Lang Freer, F1902.166a–c

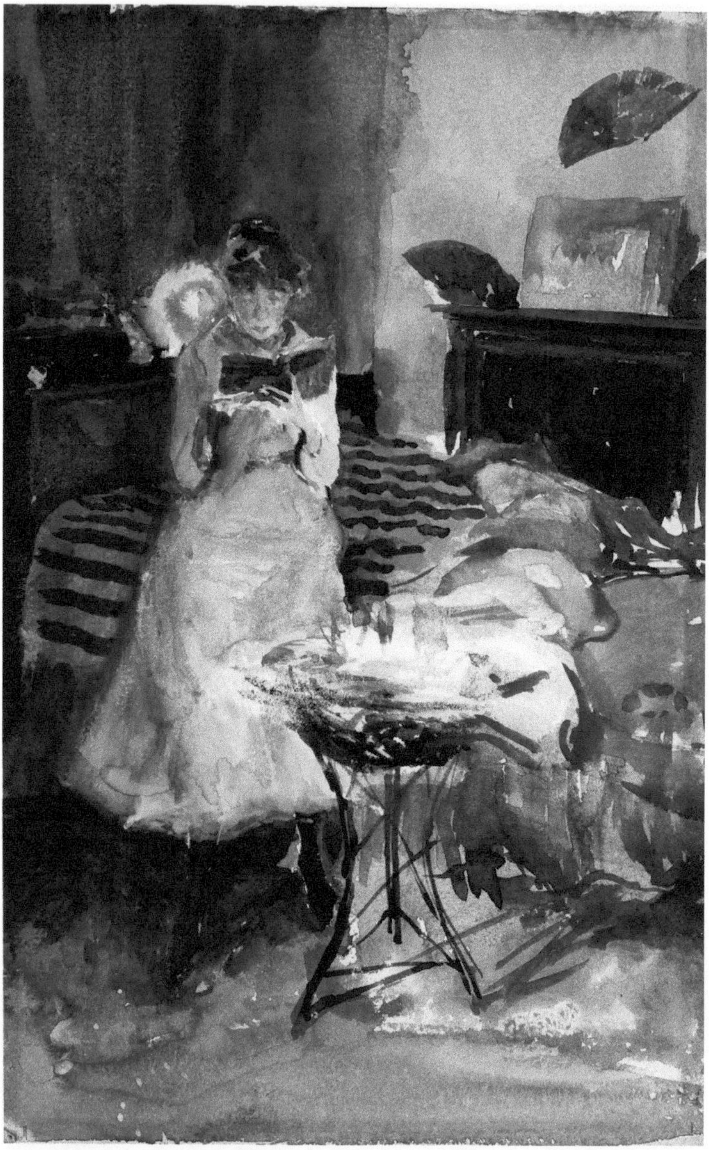

Figure 5-19. James McNeill Whistler: *Pink Note: The Novelette*, watercolor on paper, early 1880s. Freer Gallery of Art, Smithsonian Institution, Washington, D.C., Gift of Charles Lang Freer, F1902.158a–c

growing resistance to "unimportant" detail. Even as they look back, which they often do, to the subjects and arrangements of the Dutch, such "impression-pictures" give precedence to the viewer rather than the material fullness of the world before him.

A later image in the same novel testifies to a more radical impatience with daily appearances. The heroine's father is only taking tea at the family table while he awaits news of his daughter's engagement; but "could the real have been beheld instead of the corporeal merely," the narrator informs us, the corner of the room where the father sits "would have been filled with a form typical of anxious suspense, large-eyed, tight-lipped, awaiting the issue." If the subjectivity of the perceiver turned our first view of Marty South into an impressionist picture, the subjectivity of the perceived turns this into something more like an expressionist one—a painting by the young Edvard Munch, perhaps, in which "paternal hopes and fears" were rendered visible by the deliberate distortion of the "corporeal merely."[72] Could we truly see what most signifies at this moment in the narrative, in other words, we would not be viewing a genre scene of a rural family at tea. A little more than a week after completing *The Woodlanders*, Hardy would similarly conclude in his notebook that "the material is not the real—only the visible, the real being invisible optically."[73] Even as he aggressively maintained his allegiance to the "real," he made clear that his version of that protean idea is very far indeed from that long associated with Dutch painting.[74]

As early as *Far from the Madding Crowd*, one might argue, Hardy's eye had been as much drawn to the light of Dutch artists as to their rendering of concrete objects; and that novel's attentiveness to how the "transparent" air after a heavy rain suggests the "brightness of similar effects in the landscapes of Ruysdael and Hobbema," or how Rembrandt-like "jets of gold dust" penetrate the "dusky blue atmosphere" of the circus tent, anticipates the novelist's growing attraction to the dematerializing effects of light in the later Turner.[75] But by the time of *The Woodlanders*, he was increasingly prone to argue that only by dissolving and distorting visible surfaces could the artist capture what he termed "the true realities of life, hitherto called abstractions."[76] While he was hardly tempted to turn back, like Balzac and George Eliot, to the idealized forms of the Italian Renaissance, he had little more use for the materiality and dailiness of the Dutch. A notebook entry recorded a month after seeing the impressionists in London turns decisively away from "the exact truth as to material fact":

> After looking at the landscape by Bonington in our drawing-room I feel that Nature is played out as a Beauty, but not as a Mystery.

> I don't want to see landscapes, i.e., scenic paintings of them, because I don't want to see the original realities—as optical effects, that is. I want to see the deeper reality underlying the scenic, the expression of what are sometimes called abstract imaginings.
>
> The "simply natural" is interesting no longer. The much-decried, mad, late-Turner rendering is now necessary to create my interest. The exact truth as to material fact ceases to be of importance in art—it is a student's style—the style of a period when the mind is serene and unawakened to the tragical mysteries of life.[77]

Though the rejection of "optical effects" might seem to entail the dismissal of Turner as well as Bonington, the target here is "original realities." On Hardy, at least, Turner's light seems to have registered primarily as a means of penetrating such realities to arrive at the "deeper" one.[78] An essay published the following year would similarly strive to distinguish "the accidental from the essential" in fiction—citing in support the very passage in which Taine had disparagingly compared the painstaking detail of contemporary novels to the work of Dutch painters.[79] "Art is a disproportioning—(i.e., distorting, throwing out of proportion)—of realities, to show more clearly the features that matter in those realities," he announced in an oft-quoted notebook entry of 1890. "Hence 'realism' is not Art."[80]

When the art in question was that of the novelist, Hardy's rejection of realism was finally inseparable, I think, from his allegiance to plot. He immediately followed *Under the Greenwood Tree* with a novel whose "essence" was plot, as he told his publisher;[81] and plotting, as he conceived it, necessarily arose from resistance to the commonplace and the repetitive. The "purpose of fiction," he wrote in 1881, "is to give pleasure by gratifying the love of the uncommon in human experience. . . . The writer's problem is, how to strike the balance between the uncommon and the ordinary so as on the one hand to give interest, on the other to give reality." By 1893 he was even more emphatic: "A story must be exceptional enough to justify its telling. We tale-tellers are all Ancient Mariners, and none of us is warranted in stopping Wedding Guests (in other words, the hurrying public) unless he has something more unusual to relate than the ordinary experience of every average man and woman."[82] What warrants a story's telling, in other words, is precisely what distinguishes it from the familiar and repeatable acts depicted in genre painting; and after *Under the Greenwood Tree*, the plots of most Hardy novels would register the aspirations of characters to just such singularity. Dramatizing "the tragical mysteries of life" rather than their comic recurrences, the later fiction chafes against the vision of the real he had represented in his Dutch picture. Throughout Hardy's career, "ordinary experience" would continue to be the province of his rustics, but only his rural painting of the Dutch school would make such experience the principal subject of the work.

{ six }

Proust's Genre Painting and the Rediscovery of Vermeer

Dutch realism in the novel is a realism of the past. The art of the Golden Age was nearly two centuries old, after all, by the time that novelists took it as a model; and if such art could still figure the real for them, that was because they saw the everyday life they were depicting as itself a form of history. "Realism is nothing if not urban," Peter Brooks has recently contended;[1] but while French realism in particular has long been associated with the rise of the modern city, it is important to remember that each of the novelists we have thus far examined originally hailed from the provinces—and each of them partly looked to Dutch pictures as a way of looking backward. There is no doubt a realist tradition that descends from Balzac's *Illusions perdues* to the works of Zola and Gissing, as Brooks clearly demonstrates. But on both sides of the Channel, the novel's pictures of familiar objects and domestic routines were usually painted by memory.

For both George Eliot and Hardy, the representation of rural English life was at once a mode of fictional autobiography and a means of evoking the lives of the generation that had preceded them. From the *Scenes of Clerical Life* to the *Mill on the Floss*, the early fiction of George Eliot is famously suffused with recollections of her childhood. If "Amos Barton" was by her own account a Dutch painting, the original who had posed for it was sufficiently familiar to her Warwickshire neighbors to present the first threat to the secret of her pseudonym.[2] The hero of *Adam Bede* might not have been the writer's father, any more than Dinah Morris was her aunt; but her journal candidly acknowledged that they owed their fictional existence to an anecdote told by that aunt "from her own experience."[3] Recalling the origins of *Under the Greenwood Tree*, Hardy likewise claimed to have invented many of its people and incidents—"the choir as such" having "end[ed] their office when he was about a year old"—but he also made clear that the novel was inspired by the music-making of his father and grandfather, and that "Thomas Hardy the Third" was thus paying tribute to the "time-honoured observances" of Thomas Hardy the First and the Second.[4] Subsequent commentators have confirmed that the tranter's house strongly resembles the cottage in which Hardy was born, and that even Mellstock's topography closely conforms to the village landscape of his childhood.[5]

Balzac's case is more complicated—his most autobiographical fiction, *Louis Lambert*, is nearer to mystical treatise than to realism—but whether he actually sets his bourgeois interiors in provincial towns, like Saumur or Douai, or encloses them in the decaying old buildings that once lingered in the corners of Paris, virtually all his Dutch pictures in the *Comédie humaine* are strongly associated with the customs and objects of the past. The quest for the Absolute, we might recall, takes place in "a house whose physiognomy, interior arrangements and details have, more than those of any other building, preserved the character of those old Flemish structures, so naively appropriate to the patriarchal customs of that good country"—a house itself partly modeled on the Flemish buildings that the author had known in his native Tours.[6] As for the Dutch picture that opens the *Comédie humaine*: on his mother's side, Balzac was descended from a family of haberdashers who plied their trade on the very street in the Marais where he locates *La maison du chat-qui-pelote*; and his great-uncle was a draper whose commercial history evidently suggested the time-honored practices of its fictional shopkeepers.[7] Beginning the *Comédie humaine* with "one of those valuable houses that enable historians to reconstruct old Paris by analogy" (*CH* 1:39), Balzac thus also begins by imaginatively reconstructing some history of his own. And even in the course of the tale itself, its Dutch painting recedes further into the past, as Sommervieux's famous picture metamorphoses from an image of daily reality to a catalyst of memory. Having turned over their business to the next generation, the Guillaumes retire to another house, where the artist's interior scene holds the "place of honor" and affords them their chief "consolation" by recalling their former way of life. While Monsieur Guillaume had once been baffled by the appeal of a painting that simply appeared to duplicate "what one encounters every day in our street," he and his wife now turn their eyes "twenty times a day . . . toward this image of their former existence, for them so active and amusing" (*CH* 1:57, 80–81).

By the 1840s, something like this backward look would in turn be replicated by Balzac's critics, as they wistfully recalled his Dutch pictures in order to attack the recent development of his fiction. Nostalgically evoking the scenes of private life—which they routinely identified with the scenes of provincial life—such reviewers typically deplored Balzac's penchant for melodrama and mysticism, even as they contended that his true gift was for genre painting. "It is still the *Scenes of Provincial Life* that form the most beautiful flower in M. de Balzac's crown," as one put it in 1841: "there above all one finds those pictures of interiors in the Flemish style that he excels in painting."[8] Another suggested that Balzac's mistaken ambition for history painting had betrayed the spirit—and even, by implication, the chastity—of Eugénie Grandet, while depriving his readers of "those moments of oblivion and sweet repose" they had all enjoyed "in examining those charming interior scenes . . . of the Flemish school."[9] Like those who would wishfully recall George Eliot's own pictures of provincial life a few decades later, such readers compounded a response already built into the novels, as they looked with nostalgia toward an art that was itself grounded in the past.

In a brief meditation entitled "Tableaux de genre du souvenir" ("Genre Paintings of Memory"), the young Marcel Proust hinted at yet another explanation for the nostalgia his predecessors so often associated with Dutch art. Collected under the rubric of "Regrets, rêveries couleur de temps" and appearing in his first published book, *Les plaisirs et les jours* (1896), the piece is only two paragraphs long; but as so often with Proust, this early fragment adumbrates concerns to which he would return again and again over the following decades. The first paragraph reads in full:

> We have certain recollections that resemble the Dutch painting of our memory, genre pictures in which the figures are often in an ordinary [médiocre] condition, caught at a very simple moment of their existence, without solemn events, sometimes without events at all, in a setting without grandeur and in no way extraordinary. The nature of the characters and the innocence of the scene make for its charm; its distance from us interposes a soft light that bathes it in beauty.[10]

If Balzac's tale implies that art resembles memory by capturing images of our past lives in paint, Proust's essay reverses the direction of the comparison and suggests that memory itself sometimes works like a Dutch painter. And what we remember at such times are not distinctive scenes but typical ones: while the decisive moments in our histories are presumably memorable by virtue of their difference from our customary routines, we can only preserve the dailiness of the past, the essay implies, by both selecting and generalizing—fusing a number of similar scenes or acts in the representative images that constitute "the Dutch painting of our memory." These are the genre paintings in the mind's picture gallery because they are "without solemn events, sometimes without events at all"—representations of ordinary people in ordinary settings, whose temporal distance from us nonetheless bathes them in the beautifying light of nostalgia.[11] Had Proust not gone on to indicate otherwise, in fact, we might well imagine that he was thinking here quite directly of a longing for home—especially for those familiar scenes that in nineteenth-century France, as in seventeenth-century Holland, were associated with the daily rituals of the bourgeois household. Recall the remarkably similar language with which Thoré-Bürger had compared Balzac's domestic interiors to the paintings of Pieter de Hooch, as he evoked a scene where "the people . . . are inseparable from the place," everything is "created for them, especially the light that animates and enlivens them," and peace is constituted by an analogous *diminuendo* of significant action: "It's all a harmonious milieu, in which one goes to live as if at home—a place to do something, nothing much, perhaps nothing at all."[12]

As it happens, the *tableaux de genre* of Proust's own memory here are not domestic but vaguely military in character: scenes based, presumably, on his year of service in the army—he had volunteered at eighteen—and later recreated, also with allusions to Dutch painting, in the Doncières episodes of *Le côté de Guermantes* (1920). We know relatively little about Proust's experience in the army,[13] but 1889–90 was clearly not a time for actual combat duty; and the very routine of garrison life—what the essay calls "the calm of a life in which occupations are more regulated and the imagination less enslaved than in any other"—apparently encouraged the association with genre painting. Perhaps we are to think of these "little pictures full of happy truth and charm" as resembling all those Dutch paintings of soldiers whiling away their time in barracks or inns, engaged in peaceable activities like drinking, gambling, letter-writing, or flirting. No doubt an element of selectiveness has entered into the arrangement: the essay concedes that the series of little pictures is "broken by gaps, it is true";[14] and though Proust was later to recall his year in the army as a "paradise,"[15] his biographer confirms that both the softening effect of time and a measure of forgetfulness were required in order to stock this particular wing of the novelist's mental picture gallery with nothing but happy images.[16] But from the perspective of the present study, what is most striking is not so much the inevitable distortions of Proust's memory as his assimilation of Dutch painting to a mental activity. Indeed, memory's powers of selecting and generalizing are very much to the point: "la peinture hollandaise de notre mémoire" may only be a metaphor, but it is one far removed from the slavish copying of material appearances.

Whether it is far removed from the novelists we have been examining is another question, however. Theirs was always an art of words, after all; and insofar as they chose to reflect on it, the old division between the work of the hands and that of the mind, between the mere craft of the low genres and the literary "ideas" of the high, could never have had much bearing on their kind of Dutch picture. The most theoretically self-conscious of the three may have chosen to begin her career by paying tribute to manual craft, but even as she spoke of being "obliged to creep servilely after nature and fact," George Eliot knew full well that the mirror with which she worked was a mental instrument. "I aspire to give no more than a faithful account of men and things as they have mirrored themselves in my mind," says the narrator in the seventeenth chapter of *Adam Bede*.[17] In a formula that Proust would adapt more than once to uses of his own, Leonardo had famously contended that all painting is *cosa mentale*; and despite the tendency of classical theorists to question whether Dutch art really met that standard, "Tableaux de genre du souvenir" drives home the fact that the novelists' Dutch pictures had always been constructs of the mind.

Though it is a long way from *Adam Bede*'s ekphrasis of a little-known painting by Gerrit Dou to the climactic encounter with Vermeer's *View of Delft* that constitutes one the most celebrated episodes of *À la recherche du temps perdu* (1913–27), the modernity of Proust's masterwork—and of his taste in Dutch art—should not obscure the continuities that he himself repeatedly acknowledges. Only the shallowly up-to-date Madame de Cambremer imagines that admiring Monet's water-lilies means jettisoning that "old hack" Poussin.[18] "There are bits of Turner in the work of Poussin, phrases of Flaubert in Montesquieu," as the narrator observes in correcting her (3:211; 4:248), and more than a little Proust—as he makes us recognize—in Balzac, George Eliot, and Hardy as well. In relation to Dutch painting as to so much else, I shall argue, this last of the realists does not so much break with his precursors as help us to see them anew.

To begin with, of course, there was also more than a little Balzac, George Eliot, and Hardy in Proust—not to mention, for the moment, the crucial presence of Ruskin, whose profound influence on the novelist did not preclude the latter's strong attraction to the very painting his English mentor anathematized. Whether or not Proust was thinking of Balzac's *Recherche de l'absolu* when he chose the title of his own multivolume work in 1913, as Jean-Yves Tadié has speculated,[19] it is clear that the author of *À la recherche du temps perdu* had thoroughly assimilated the work of his predecessor. "To read Balzac was to speak the family language," Tadié observes;[20] and Proust continued to speak that language when he composed a pastiche of the novelist, among other writers, in the first decade of the twentieth century. Indeed, well before Baron de Charlus was to hold forth on the subject in *Sodome et Gomorrhe* 2 (1922), his creator had drafted a more extended tribute to Balzac's achievement in the abandoned work now known as *Contre Saint-Beuve.* Like Charlus, who irritably counters an attack on the novelist's style by praising his knowledge of "life" (3:438; 4:520), Proust invokes the "lifelike reality of Balzac's novels," even as he characteristically suggests that it is "the life of his novels" rather than "real life" that is the "only true one for the writer."[21] (Hence to find something in one's experience "very Balzacian"—as characters repeatedly do in *À la recherche*—is to feel an essentially aesthetic pleasure.) Though *Contre Saint-Beuve* wryly concedes both the earlier novelist's vulgarity and the faults of his prose, the intensity with which it defends "the very vastness" of his design anticipates the imaginative excitement with which the narrator of *À la recherche* reconstructs Balzac's exhilarated discovery of the fundamental coherence of the *Comédie humaine.*[22] "Casting over his books the eye at once of a stranger and of a father," and belatedly registering their "ulterior unity," Balzac "touch[es] up his work with a swift brush-stroke, the last and most sublime"—his "retrospective illumination" clearly serving as a model for the analogous vision with which Proust's own multivolume novel will end (3:666–67; 5:176–77).[23] Yet when Charlus declares himself equally fond of Balzac's "tiny miniatures" and his "large frescos" (3:437; 4:520), he also appears to speak for his creator, who more than once divided up the oeuvre in similar terms.[24] Though there is no evidence that Proust consciously identified those "miniatures" with Dutch painting, a similar resistance to aesthetic hierarchy, as we shall see, repeatedly drew him to the work of the Dutch.

The English writers appear to have affected Proust most deeply.[25] George Eliot, he told one correspondent, was the "cult of my adolescence";[26] while Ruskin, to whom he devoted more than half a decade at the turn of the century, was pronounced "one of the greatest writers of all times and of all countries."[27] Though Proust's encounter with Hardy was later and less consequential, he was still declaring himself both "Eliotiste" and "Hardyste" two years before his death.[28] Indeed, "it is strange," as he himself declared in 1910,

> that among all the most different genres, from George Eliot to Hardy, from Stevenson to Emerson, there is no literature that has on me a power comparable to that of English and American literature.

> Germany, Italy, very often France leave me indifferent. But two pages of *The Mill on the Floss* make me cry.

"I know that Ruskin execrated that novel," he immediately added, "but I reconcile these hostile gods in the Pantheon of my admiration."[29] The remark testifies not only to Proust's impressive knowledge of Ruskin, but to a capacity for imaginative reconciliation that would govern his approach to Dutch painting as well.

An analogous impulse had already prompted a long note to his translation of Ruskin's *Bible of Amiens* (1904), in which he compared the latter's portrait of a cheerful and kindly Saint Martin—"companionable even to the loving-cup"[30]—with the novelist's affectionate representations of her more secular clerisy: "M. Irwine dans *Adam Bede,* M. Gilfil dans les *Scènes de la vie du Clergé,* M. Farebrother dans *Middlemarch,* etc."[31] Quoting at length from the *Scenes of Clerical Life* and *Adam Bede,* including chapter 17, the note emphasizes the ordinary humanity of figures like the pipe-smoking and gin-drinking Gilfil, whose evident kinship with Ruskin's "patron of honest drinking" might tempt us to wonder yet again why the author of *Modern Painters* could not also share George Eliot's sympathy for a Dutch tavern scene.[32] Though Proust himself never directly associates her interest in Dutch painting with his own, an undated notebook entry that constitutes his fullest statement on the novelist makes the connection all but explicit.[33] "What strikes me in *Adam Bede,*" the entry begins, "is the attentive painting, detailed, respectful, poetic and sympathetic, of the most hardworking and the most humble life. To keep one's kitchen thoroughly clean is an essential duty, nearly a religious duty and a duty full of charm." From this brief evocation of Mrs. Poyser's housekeeping, the entry moves on to the moral resonance of the early fiction, repeatedly comparing *Adam Bede* to *Silas Marner* ("a sincere feeling for the concerns of a carpenter, of a weaver, etc.") and identifying both with the author's capacity to make humble things the signs of hitherto unobserved feeling: "Novelty of images coming from a tender and new view of things, which discovers in them unnoticed feelings and can then paint them as symbols of analogous sentiments."[34]

Even more than George Eliot, it was Ruskin, ironically, whom Proust chose to identify with his own love of the Dutch. In 1898, a year or more after he had first discovered the English critic,[35] Proust traveled to Holland in order to view the great Rembrandt exhibition then mounted in Amsterdam. Though the essay that resulted never appeared in his lifetime, its fantasy of an aging Ruskin who ventures from his deathbed to pay tribute to the painter is both an early attempt to reconcile "hostile gods" in the "Pantheon" of his admiration and a forerunner of one of the most celebrated episodes in *À la recherche du temps perdu*, the death of Bergotte.[36] More than two decades before that novel would send another dying writer for a last look at Vermeer, Proust was already associating Dutch art with the only form of immortality he ever chose to contemplate.

The 1898 trip was hardly Proust's first encounter with Rembrandt, whose work he had admired on frequent expeditions to the Louvre ever since his late adolescence.[37] Nor was this his first attempt to write on the subject. Three years earlier, he had composed a "short essay on the philosophy of art," as he tentatively characterized it, in which observations on Rembrandt supplemented and partly transformed an argument originally dedicated to the work of Chardin.[38] In that piece, he had imagined how a young man of "humble means and artistic tastes" might be awakened to the beauty of everyday scenes and objects by seeing their equivalents sumptuously rendered in genre painting and still life. In terms that Thoré-Bürger would have appreciated, the essay describes a Chardin who initiates us into "the unknown life of *nature morte*"—teaching us that "a pear is as alive as a woman, that a vulgar piece of pottery is as beautiful as a precious stone."[39] Though this essay, too, remained unpublished, Proust would later incorporate something very like its tribute to still life into his novel, when the narrator learns his own lesson about the beauty of ordinary things and "la vie profonde des 'natures mortes'" from another admirer of Chardin, the fictive painter, Elstir (2:224; 2:519).[40] But while Chardin "makes us leave behind a false ideal" and "opens the real world to us," with Rembrandt, as the essay puts it, "even reality itself is to be outdone." With him we see, paradoxically, that "beauty does not lie in objects, since then it would certainly not be so profound and so mysterious." The great Dutch painter reveals "that objects are nothing in themselves" and that it is rather light that constitutes "the principle" of their existence—that light "which we will never know and which we know so well, which is the beauty of everything we have ever seen, and which is also its mystery and unknowability."[41]

Something like this dialectic between objects and light, between material reality and the ineffable medium of perception, will repeat itself throughout Proust's work, as beauty alternately inheres or can be discovered in the most ordinary of things. In the Rembrandt essay, he imagines the painter's development as itself following a similar trajectory: beginning by representing things that appeal to him, this Rembrandt ends by representing "the very light [jour] of his thought"—"the kind of individual light in which we see things when we are thinking in an original way." While Rembrandt's early pictures "may bear more resemblance to nature than to himself," his later work, by this account, resembles nothing so much as his own way of seeing—a power of vision somehow conveyed by the golden light that has now become "the whole of reality for him." The essay opens by announcing boldly that "museums are dwellings that house only thoughts"; and by the time it turns to Ruskin, it has imagined a Rembrandt who triumphantly succeeded in capturing his "thought" on canvas. Not fame, but this, the essay declares, is the end for which artists are made.[42]

In 1895, Proust had pronounced Rembrandt and Leonardo his favorite painters;[43] and in thus emphasizing that Rembrandt's work was also *cosa mentale*, he was implicitly assimilating the Northern artist to a standard that had long been identified with the achievement of the South. Yet for all its stress on the mental character of Rembrandt's art, the essay nonetheless approaches him more like a painter of genre or still life than as a history painter or even a portraitist—which is to say that it associates his "thoughts" not with the titular subjects of individual works but with the familiar scenes and objects that he painted over and over again. "When one looks at a picture by Rembrandt," according to Proust,

> one sees an old woman cutting a young woman's nails, a string of pearls gleaming obscurely on some fur, red carpets or some reddish Indian fabrics, a fire that is being kindled and lights up the back of a dark room, while the evening light entering by the window lights up the doorway, a young woman's long silky hair that an old woman combs out, a burst of sunlight on the lock of a river on whose bank some horsemen are passing, while some windmills turn in the background; and one thinks that all these things are a part of nature and that Rembrandt painted them as he would have painted any others. But if you look at Rembrandt's pictures one after the other, near one young woman you will again find another old one who is getting ready to cut the other's nails, on another piece of fur you will again see the same somber glow of pearls. Now it is no longer Rembrandt's wife, it is *The Woman Taken in Adultery*, it is *Esther*; but she, too, has the submissive and sad face, she, too, has the golden brocades or the red cashmere under the pearls. It is no longer the house of a philosopher, it is a carpenter's workshop, it is the room of a young man who is reading, but in the depths that are scarcely illuminated except in places by the daylight still remaining outside, a kindling fire throws a livelier reflection. Here is a bullock in a butcher's shop; it is no longer the one where a kneeling woman on the left washes the floor, but the one where a woman on the right is looking back as she leaves;

> so that these old nail-cutters, combers of fine hair, the sad and modest woman under her furs and her pearls, the house where the fire kindles in the shadow of the dark rooms, these are not things that Rembrandt has painted, they are the tastes of Rembrandt, those ideas that for each great man are himself [ces ideés qui pour chaque grand homme sont lui-même].[44]

Though some of these things gradually take on a specifiable identity—Rembrandt's wife, say, or the biblical Esther—for Proust they are first and foremost the sort of things this artist sees, their repetitiveness inhering not so much in the generic character of what is represented as in the singular character of the painter's vision. As Marcel will later lecture Albertine about his beloved Vermeers, "they are fragments of an identical world": "it's always, however great the genius with which they have been re-created, the same table, the same carpet, the same woman, the same novel and unique beauty" (3:879; 5:430).

If this is not quite to praise either artist for his skill as a genre painter—let alone as a realist—it is nonetheless to insist that the artist's "ideas" cannot be separated from the material that he represents and to associate that material with the typical scenes and subjects of genre painting. Apart from the belated allusion to Esther, Proust scarcely acknowledges that Rembrandt's "old nail-cutters" and "combers of fine hair" almost invariably figure in history paintings, like the *Toilet of Bathsheba* (fig. 6-1) that he would have seen in Amsterdam, or the variation on the subject that he surely knew at the Louvre (plate 14).[45] The only exception of which I am aware is an image of a solitary woman cutting her nails that was in fact among the well-known paintings exhibited at Amsterdam but that is now generally attributed to one of Rembrandt's followers (fig. 6-2). While a contemporary review of the exhibit that specifically singles out this picture may have contributed to Proust's mental collection of the artist's "old nail-cutters," he himself never directly refers to it.[46] Indeed, he hardly needed this nineteenth-century addition to the small number of Rembrandt's genre paintings in order to subordinate the biblical subject of a picture to "the observed thing," in his phrase. So he evokes another picture by writing only of "the bucket, that descends in the silence of the evening, in the last scattered gleams of a sun long set, in front of the house where the Good Samaritan's life of service ended" (fig. 6-3).[47] Even as he hints at a figurative relation between the descent of the bucket and the death of the Samaritan, Proust refuses to detach any such tenor from his vehicle. Unlike Ruskin, whom he would later criticize for declaring a painting beautiful "in so far as the ideas

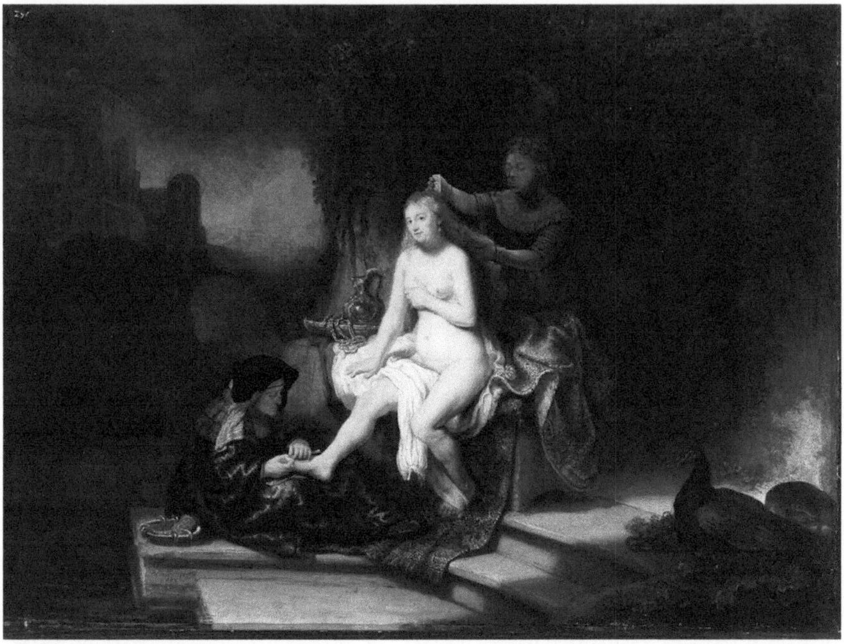

Figure 6-1. Rembrandt van Rijn: *The Toilet of Bathsheba*, 1643. The Metropolitan Museum of Art, New York, Bequest of Benjamin Altman, 1913 (14.40.651). Image © The Metropolitan Museum of Art

which it translated into images were independent of the language of images," Proust insisted that "painting could attain the very reality of things, and thus rival literature, only on the condition of not being literary."[48]

The audacious fiction with which the essay concludes sounds a related note. By imagining that the dying Ruskin has journeyed to Amsterdam to pay his final respects to the painter, Proust simultaneously pays his own tribute to both artist and critic and manages to identify the mind's continuing life with its persistent attachment to beloved images. For rather than suppose that the English critic has belatedly come to recognize Rembrandt's greatness, Proust chooses to pretend, still more wishfully, that Ruskin has loved the Dutch painter all along. "He was in his last days and yet he had come from England to see these Rembrandts, which at twenty had already seemed something essential to him and which were no less a reality for him now, in these last days."[49]

Conjuring up a doddering old man with wrinkled face and broken legs—a figure who anticipates, as Jean-Yves Tadié has noted, the tottering forms who gather in the last pages of *Le temps retrouvé* (1927)[50]—Proust hints at a

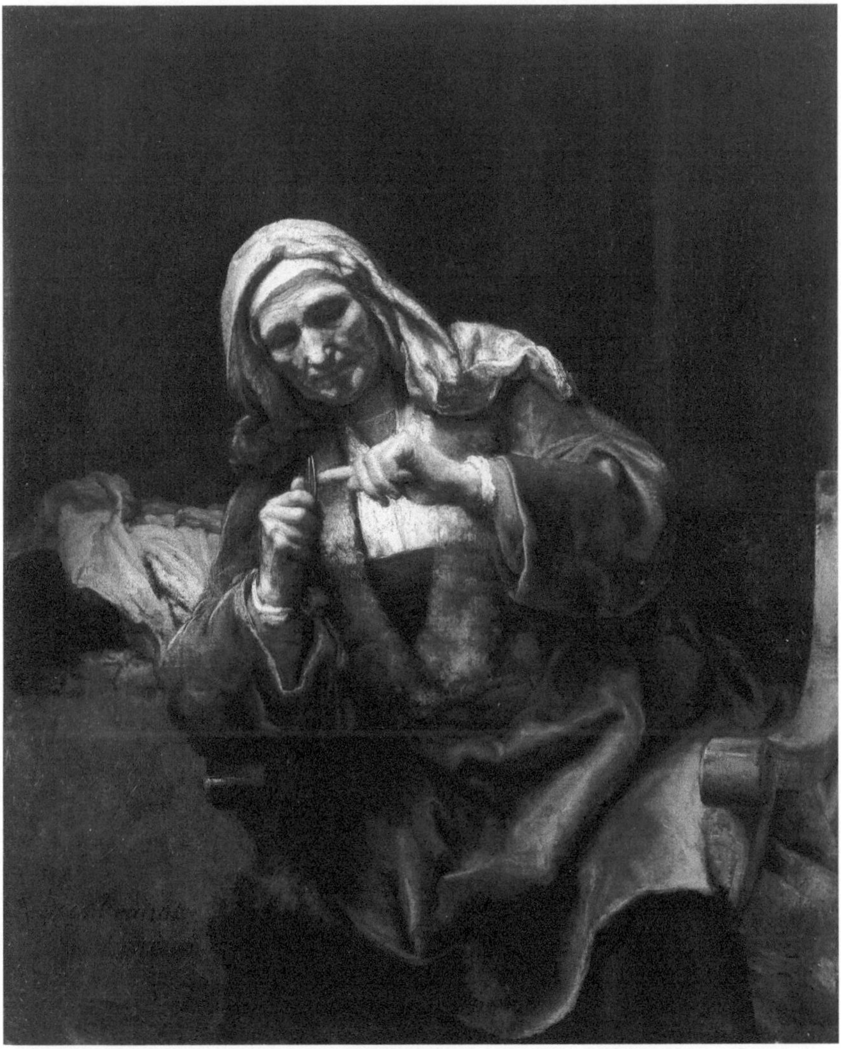

Figure 6-2. Style of Rembrandt: *Old Woman Cutting Her Nails*, 1655–60. The Metropolitan Museum of Art, New York, Bequest of Benjamin Altman, 1913 (14.40.609). Image © The Metropolitan Museum of Art

final divorce between spirit and body, mind and matter, even as he characteristically identifies the mind's survival with its recovery of the past. Despite the near-impossibility of reconciling this "groping" old man with his "idea" of Ruskin, "that immaterial thing," the narrator concludes that they are one and the same—their continuity guaranteed precisely by the elderly critic's return to the pictures about which he had written so ardently in his youth.

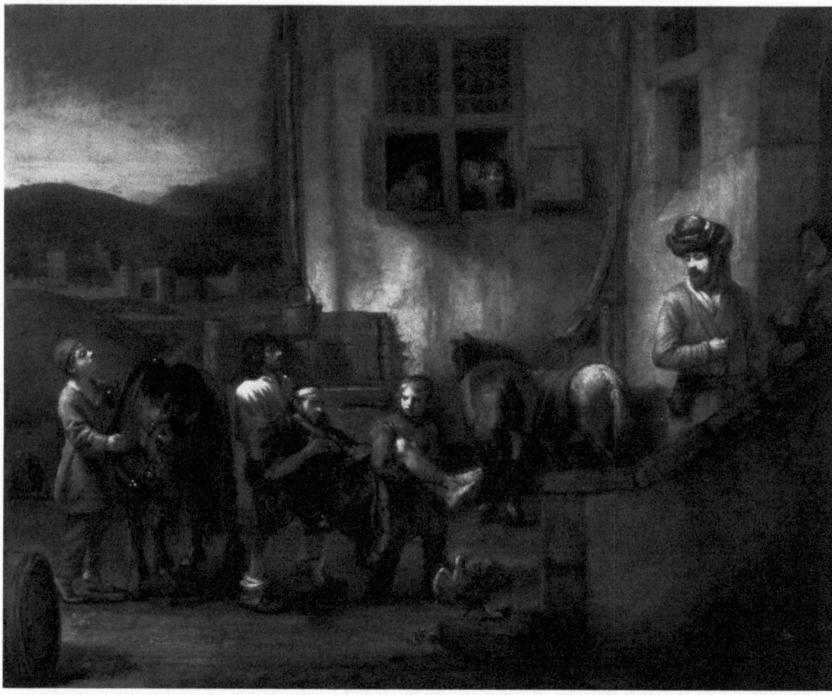

Figure 6-3. Constantijn Daniel van Renesse (pupil of Rembrandt): *The Good Samaritan*, c. 1650. Musée du Louvre, Paris. Photo Credit: Réunion des Musées Nationaux/Art Resource, N.Y.

As Proust stages it, Ruskin's final encounter with these pictures is a kind of recognition scene, in which the critic, himself "blackened like a Rembrandt by the shade of twilight, the patina of time, the effacement of the years," at once mirrors and confirms the artist's achievement:

> It suddenly seemed as if Rembrandt's canvases had become something worthier of being visited, since Ruskin, come from so far, had entered the room; it seemed also as if it was for Rembrandt like a reward that could have been sweet for him, and that, if Rembrandt's gaze, which seemed to consider us from the depths of his completed canvases, had been able to see Ruskin, the master would have approached him like a king who recognizes a king in the crowd. Yes, the canvases of Rembrandt seemed to us more worthy of admiration since Ruskin had entered, or rather painting itself, in that which it had the power to do best, seemed to us something more essential, since we had seen such an exalted spirit, so near death, considering it again.[51]

The essay no sooner reaches this apparent climax than it abruptly descends to humbler analogies, as the meeting of kings dissolves into scenes of daily life, and the apotheosis of art gives way to the operations of habit and "the attachment of our senses" to accustomed objects. Rather than contemplate the verdict of a great critic, we are invited to consider how Ruskin's love of Rembrandt resembles anyone's affection for "old notions, familiar likings, and habitual pleasures"—a grandfather's delight in the sight of his little granddaughter, for example, or a regular card-player's fondness for a game of bezique: "perhaps his housekeeper led him to the Rembrandts as she would have led another old man to watch a game of cards or brought him a bunch of grapes."[52] Though the real Ruskin would no more have acknowledged his affinity to an old card-player than he would have recognized himself in the long-time admirer of Rembrandt, Proust's fiction has other ends in view. What looks like the triumph of painting quietly dissolves into something more like the genre painting of memory.

In 1902, some four years after the Rembrandt exhibit, Proust returned to the Netherlands for another look at Dutch painting—the last artistic expedition abroad, as it happens, that he would make in his lifetime. Armed with copies of Fromentin's *Maîtres d'autrefois* and Taine's *Philosophie de l'art dans les Pays-Bas*, as well as a Baedeker that quoted generously from Thoré-Bürger, Proust and a friend spent several weeks wandering through the art capitals of Belgium and Holland.[53] Though he would later declare that Vermeer had been his "favorite painter" since the age of twenty, it was on this trip that he saw a number of the pictures themselves for the first time, including the *View of Delft* that he would call "the most beautiful painting in the world."[54] By the time he wrote those words, Vermeer had become for him the very epitome of artistic originality: the painter whose name, together with Rembrandt's, would serve to designate the distinctiveness of vision that he identified as the fundamental contribution of art. That the Delft painter could figure in that role suggests how much had changed since Thoré-Bürger set out to distinguish one "Van der Meer" from another; and I shall shortly return to the implications of that change for Proust's own art as well as that of the Dutch.

But Proust was also drawn, as we have seen, to what might be called the generic idea of Dutch painting; and like his predecessors, he sometimes chose to imagine Dutch pictures less as a collection of individual works than as a category. "The Dutch painting of our memory" is one such instance; and so is the repeated sequence in which the protagonist of *À la recherche* compares the ongoing life of those around him to a display of Dutch pictures. The sequence appears, with variations, three times in the novel: at Doncières, the garrison town where he has gone to visit his friend Saint-Loup; in the Hôtel de Guermantes, where his parents have recently moved into a new apartment; and at Venice, where he wanders through the streets as a tourist. On each occasion, the protagonist is himself an outsider, who often looks through windows and doorways at scenes into which, as he says of Doncières, "I might not penetrate." In the garrison town, he walks through the streets at night, pausing before windows that reveal to him now a "crimson tableau" of some card-playing officers, now a little curio shop, where a half-spent candle and a large lamp "made in fact of the whole hovel, in which there was nothing but pinchbeck rubbish, a marvellous composition by Rembrandt" (2:395; 3:104). From Dutch genre, the protagonist's mental images imperceptibly give way to Flemish history painting, as the reddened countenances of the soldiers he glimpses in the wintry streets recall "the rubicund faces which Breughel gives to his merry, junketing, frostbound peasants," and the crowds who gather at the hotel for the season's festivities suggest "some *Numbering of the People at Bethlehem* such as the Old Flemish masters used to paint" (2:397; 3:105, 106)—presumably the well-known version, also by Breughel, in which the biblical town figures as a snowy Flemish village (fig. 6-4).[55] As if prompted by the way Breughel's image hovers between the mundane and the sacred, genre painting and history, Proust's own evocation of the scene wittily plays on an analogous border—turning the very abundance of the feast being piled up in the hotel dining room into a sign of more than bodily appetites:

> And similarly, in the big dining-room which I passed through on the first day before coming to the little room where my friend was waiting for me, it was of some Biblical repast portrayed with old-fashioned naïvety and Flemish exaggeration that one was reminded by the quantity of fish, chickens, grouse, woodcock, pigeons, brought in dressed and garnished and piping hot by breathless waiters who slid along the polished floor for greater speed and set them down on the huge sideboard where they were carved at once, but where—for many diners were finishing when I arrived—they piled up untouched, as though their profusion and the haste of those who brought them were inspired far less by a desire to meet the requirements of the diners than by respect for the sacred text, scrupulously followed in the letter but naïvely illustrated with real details borrowed from local custom, and by an aesthetic and religious anxiety to make evident to the

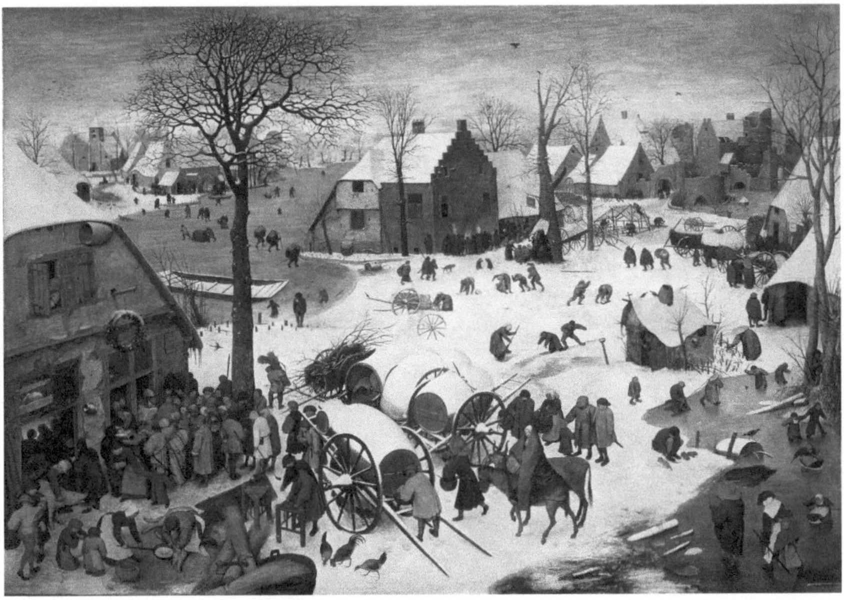

Figure 6-4. Pieter Breughel the Elder: *The Numbering of the People at Bethlehem*, 1566. Musée d'Art Ancien, Musées Royaux des Beaux-Arts, Brussels. Photo Credit: Scala/Art Resource, N.Y.

> eye the splendour of the feast by the profusion of the victuals and the assiduity of the servers. (2:397; 3:106)

Having momentarily substituted the agency of an imaginary artist for that of the waiters, Proust continues to make sophisticated comedy from the confusion, as others rush about dangling their napkins like wings and the protagonist flees to the room Saint-Loup has reserved for his dinner.

The evocations of Dutch painting in Paris and Venice are at once briefer and more generic—so generic, in fact, that the passages in question are virtually identical. In the first of these, the protagonist vainly watches for the return of the Duke and Duchess de Guermantes from a look-out post in his parents' apartment:

> As a matter of fact I had made a singularly bad choice of observatory, for I could scarcely see into our courtyard, but I caught a glimpse of several others, and this, though of no practical use to me, diverted me for a time. It is not only in Venice that one has these views on to several houses at once which have proved so tempting to painters; it is just the same in Paris. Nor do I cite Venice at random.

> It is of its poorer quarters that certain poor quarters of Paris remind one, in the morning, with their tall, splayed chimneys to which the sun imparts the most vivid pinks, the brightest reds—like a garden flowering above the houses, and flowering in such a variety of tints as to suggest the garden of a tulip-fancier of Delft or Haarlem planted above the town. And then the extreme proximity of the houses, with their windows looking across at one another over a common courtyard, makes of each casement the frame in which a cook sits dreamily gazing down at the ground, or, further off, a girl is having her hair combed by an old woman with a witchlike face, barely distinguishable in the shadow: thus each courtyard provides the neighbours in the adjoining house, suppressing sound by its width and framing silent gestures in a series of rectangles placed under glass by the closing of the windows, with an exhibition of a hundred Dutch paintings juxtaposed. (2:860; 3:661–62)

At Venice—which the language above obviously anticipates—the protagonist wanders through alleyways instead of looking down from a window, it is the light of evening rather than morning that turns the pinks and reds of the chimneys into a garden of tulips, and the pervading silence is no longer attributed to the breadth of courtyards or the presence of glass; but the pictures themselves have scarcely altered. Perhaps because she, too, is now at ground level, the dreamy cook no longer looks down; and even slighter verbal changes characterize the description of the figures in the hair-combing scene—itself so reminiscent of the images once attributed to Rembrandt. But if these are not the "same" pictures—what would that mean?—they unmistakably represent the same kind of vision. "Nor do I cite Venice at random," the narrator says of the view from the Hôtel de Guermantes; yet even as he gestures at specificity, the very recurrence of the scenes—not to mention their shared resemblance to the tulip gardens of Delft and Haarlem—tends to generalize them. So, too, does the temporal ambiguity, whereby the poor quarters of Paris in the earlier episode are said to "remind" one of Venetian scenes that the protagonist himself has yet to visit. (The much-anticipated trip to Italy does not take place until *Albertine disparue* [1925].) Just particularized enough to conjure an effect of the real—the cook is dreamy, the old hair-comber witchlike—"a hundred Dutch paintings juxtaposed" is less an account of actual scenes glimpsed in Paris or Venice than a representation of ongoing life, external to the viewer.

It is also, according to Georges Poulet, a vital clue to the novelist's method. For Poulet, who sought to counter the received idea of *À la recherche* by highlighting Proustian space rather than time, those "juxtaposed" paintings summed up Proust's habit of "eliminating duration" and "suppressing distance," so that successive moments in the protagonist's history, each identified with a distinct image, are simultaneously available to our view. Nothing could be further from Bergsonian duration, he argues, than the novelist's practice of localizing time in particular places and of triumphing over its passage by eliding the gaps between them. "The hundred Dutch pictures perceived in the framework that gives out upon the House of Guermantes are a figuration of the hundred other pictures juxtaposed, which, when the reader comes, he also, to hoist himself up to a certain point of view, are disclosed to him there, not less simultaneously disposed, in the whole of the Proustian novel."[56] Poulet says nothing about the Dutchness of these paintings, but the long association of such art with picture rather than narrative would only serve to drive home the argument.

And so, too, as I have already intimated, would Proust's affinity for the habitual and the recurrent. Though Proust's is an art of landscape and still life as well as of genre, what Gérard Genette has called his "*intoxication with the iterative*" (the emphasis is Genette's) is fundamental to the design of his novel. Unlike earlier fiction, in which "the iterative sections provide a sort of informative frame or background" for the narrative—Genette aptly instances the daily life of the miser's household in the opening pages of *Eugénie Grandet*—*À la recherche* refuses to subordinate the recurrent event to the singular.[57] Even when Proust chooses to forgo the imperfect tense, as in the line that famously opens his novel—"Longtemps, je me suis couché de bonne heure" ("For a long time I went to bed early")—he characteristically turns his text into a representation of what used to happen or what happened typically rather than a record of what happened once.[58] A singular event or scene may be precipitated out of recurrent ones, as a particular dinner in the hotel at Doncières gradually emerges out of scenes the protagonist "often" witnessed in the lighted windows of the town (2:395; 3:103), or a specific Breughel out of the anonymous genre paintings that preceded it; but Proust so manages these transitions as to blur rather than emphasize the difference. (Note that he merely invokes "some" *Numbering of the People at Bethlehem* such as the old Flemish masters "used to paint" [2:397; 3:106]: even the identification of a particular image is only an inference from the earlier allusion to Breughel.) In perhaps the most determinative of the novel's episodes, the protagonist's mother acquiesces in a bedtime kiss; yet it is not this singular act—memorable precisely because it violates all custom—that is recalled by the taste of a madeleine, but something more like the fullness of daily life: those details and impressions, otherwise evanescent, whose return to consciousness enables him to reconstitute the world he has lost. "Many years had elapsed during which nothing of Combray, except what lay in the theatre and the drama of my going to bed there, had any existence for me," the narrator reports, when his mother unwittingly offers him the cup of tea that conjures up the scenes and rhythms of his childhood (1:44; 1:51). Though Genette rightly observes that Proust's iterative style is not always based, as it is in "Combray," on the "actually repetitive and routine aspect" of provincial life,[59] the combined effects of that style and the rituals of village domesticity—not to mention the simple fact of coming first—give the opening chapters a particular weight for the novel that follows. The household order at Combray, in Germaine Brée's words, has "the reassuring stability of enduring reality."[60]

Like other novelists drawn to Dutch painting, Proust could be said to ground his narrative in such provincial reality—a figure of speech that he makes quite explicit. "It is pre-eminently as the deepest layers of my mental soil [comme à des gisements profonds de mon sol mental], as the firm ground on which I still stand [comme aux terrains résistants sur lesquels je m'appuie encore], that I regard the Méséglise and Guermantes ways," the narrator says toward the close of "Combray" (1:182; 1:220–21). So persuasive is that grounding, in fact, that we tend to forget that Combray is not the protagonist's native town but only the place where his maternal relatives live and where his family arrives each Easter for an extended holiday. Proust himself was actually born in the Parisian suburb of Auteuil, though he, too, spent his holidays with his mother's relatives in the country; and if it is true, as Tadié suggests, that Auteuil in those days still resembled a rural village, its fusion with the provincial Illiers in the making of "Combray" was still an act of the fictive imagination. (According to Tadié, "the whole drama of the bedtime scene," for example, almost certainly took place at Auteuil, rather than the country town that the novel encourages us to imagine.)[61] As if acknowledging that novels begin in the provinces even if writers do not, Proust subtly alters the facts to suit his fiction. Beginning with Combray, in other words, may be as much a way of looking back at his predecessors as it is a retrospect on the self.

In opening his novel with a rural childhood—or rather, more strictly speaking, with the narrator's memories of such a childhood—Proust was influenced especially by George Eliot, to whose *Mill on the Floss* in particular the opening pages of *À la recherche* are indebted.[62] Yet for all their shared emphasis on the power of recollection, the writer who suggests that "reality takes shape in the memory alone" (1:182; 1:221) can seem very far removed from the one who dedicated herself to the sort of realism she identified with Dutch painting. Proust's narrator says many things, not all of them consistent with one another; but it is hard to imagine his ever declaring himself "obliged to creep servilely after nature and fact," even in the ironic spirit with which the narrator of *Adam Bede* issues that challenge.[63] In the extended meditation that is triggered by the uneven paving-stones in the Guermantes courtyard, the narrator of *Le temps retrouvé* explicitly repudiates "so-called realist art [l'art prétendu réaliste]"—an art that is later identified with "the kind of literature which contents itself with 'describing things.'" Yet the fact that such art only "pretends" to realism while being "the furthest removed from reality" suggests that matters are still more complicated (4:460, 463; 6:235, 241). For even as Proust locates everything in the mind, down to the very "soil" on which he grounds himself (1:182; 1:221), his doctrine of involuntary memory accords to some mental experiences an epistemological privilege over others. Unlike memories that can be deliberately summoned to consciousness, the reminiscences that come flooding back with the bite of a madeleine or a stumble on a paving-stone prove their truthfulness, according to the narrator of *Le temps retrouvé*, precisely because he is not free to choose them. "Such as they were," in his words, "they were given to me":

> And I realised that this must be the mark of their authenticity. I had not gone in search of the two uneven paving-stones of the courtyard upon which I had stumbled. But it was precisely the fortuitous and inevitable fashion in which this and the other sensations had been encountered that proved the trueness of the past which they brought back to life, of the images which they released, since we feel, with these sensations, the effort that they make to climb back towards the light, feel in ourselves the joy of the real rediscovered [la joie du réel retrouvé]. And here too was the proof of the trueness of the whole picture formed out of those contemporaneous impressions which the first sensation brings back in its train, with those unerring proportions of light and shade, emphasis and omission, memory and forgetfulness to which conscious recollection and conscious observation will never know how to attain. (4:457–58; 6:232–33)

At once thoroughly subjective and yet somehow independent of the self, what returns at such moments is not a singular act but a "whole picture": the Combray of the novel's opening, or the Venice that now resurfaces with a stumble in a Paris courtyard. Proust loved Dutch painting; but both the assimilation of such a picture to *cosa mentale* and its paradoxical identification with the real—not to mention the joy of rediscovery—begin to suggest why he was drawn above all to the art of Vermeer.

Long before he extravagantly pronounced Vermeer "the greatest painter in the world," Proust had already turned his name into a touchstone of aesthetic judgment.[64] As early as *Du côté de chez Swann* (1913), the Delft painter figures as the subject of a work-in-progress that testifies to the sensibility—as well as the ultimate failure—of one of the novelist's principal alter-egos, Charles Swann. Tadié has suggested that Proust projected onto his character not only his own dream of writing about Vermeer but his fear of never completing his masterwork;[65] and the very first allusion to Swann's essay—"in reality . . . abandoned years ago"—tends to confirm that hypothesis. At the moment in question, Swann has invoked his work as a pretext for declining an invitation from Odette; and Proust amuses himself with imagining how the former *demimondaine* misapprehends the painter she chooses to treat as a rival. "You're going to laugh at me," she says to Swann,

> "but this painter who stops you from seeing me" (she meant Vermeer), "I've never even heard of him; is he alive still? Can I see any of his things in Paris, so I can picture for myself what you love, understand a little what's going on behind that great brow which works so hard, in that head which one feels is always puzzling away about things; to be able to say 'There, that's what he's thinking about!' What a joy it would be to be able to help you with your work." (1:195; 1:237)

The joke will be repeated in the case of Albertine, who responds to a question about a trip to Holland by imagining that the Vermeers she is expected to "know" are people outside her social circle (3:209; 4:246), and, with a variation, in the Duke de Guermantes' complacent failure to recall whether he has admired the *View of Delft* on a visit to The Hague. "If it's to be seen, I saw it!" he says (2:813; 3:606). As for Odette, she will soon betray her aesthetic ignorance in another sense, by losing all interest in the painter when Swann tells her that we know nothing about his private life. (She has asked whether a woman inspired him.) For Proust, who had argued strenuously against Saint-Beuve's method of identifying a writer's work with the man who created it, the very lack of biographical information that disappoints Odette only clarifies what "Vermeer" really signifies. To know Vermeer is to know not his history but his visual signature, his characteristic way of representing the world. That Swann should be imagined as hoping to visit The Hague in order to verify his belief that "a *Toilette of Diana* which had been

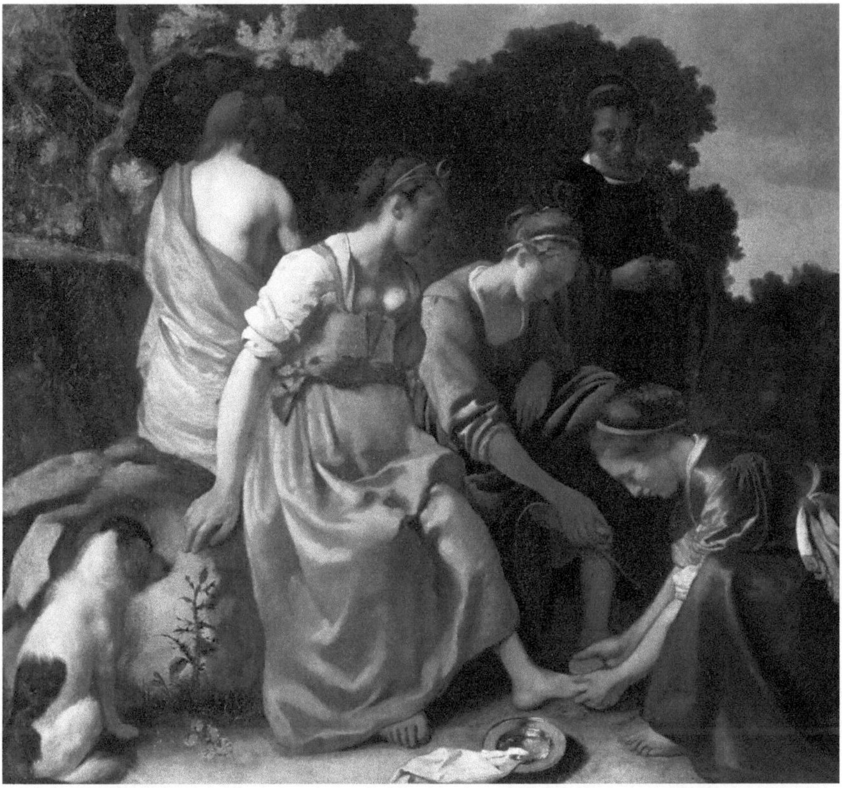

Figure 6-5. Johannes Vermeer: *Diana and Her Companions* (*Toilet of Diana*), c. 1653–56. Mauritshuis, The Hague. Photo Credit: Scala/Art Resource, N.Y.

acquired by the Mauritshuis at the Goldschmidt sale as a Nicolaes Maes was in reality a Vermeer" suggests just how closely Proust himself had tracked recent connoisseurship on the artist (1:347–48; 1:425). The picture, now known as *Diana and Her Companions* (fig. 6-5), was not securely attributed to the Delft painter until the beginning of the twentieth century.[66]

Proust's fictive art-lover, who never makes it to The Hague, can take no credit for that discovery. But Swann is not the only character in *À la recherche* whose unrealized ambition is identified with Vermeer. I am referring, of course, to the imaginary writer Bergotte, whose fatal encounter with "a little patch of wall" in the *View of Delft* (plate 15) was partly inspired by Proust's own view of the same picture at an exhibit of Dutch painting mounted by the Jeu de Paume in the spring of 1921 (3:692; 5:207).[67] In the novel as originally planned, Bergotte was to have survived through the war;

but while the evidence indicates that Proust had already intended to kill the character off before he himself visited the exhibit, the scene as published clearly drew on that experience.[68] The unnamed article that prompts Bergotte to leave his sickbed is one of a sequence by Jean-Louis Vaudoyer that had similarly inspired the ailing Proust; and phrases from the article—whose author was a friend of the novelist as well as a poet and art critic—are echoed, almost verbatim, in *La prisonnière* (1923).[69] Proust had written enthusiastically to Vaudoyer when the first installment appeared; and though he almost never attempted museums any longer—he made only three trips to the Louvre in his last quarter-century—he finally determined on the expedition.[70] "Corpse that I am," he wrote to Vaudoyer, "would you take me there?"[71] More than twenty years after he had imagined a dying Ruskin paying a similar tribute to Rembrandt, Proust thus set out for his own final encounter with Vermeer. The "corpse" would survive another year and a half; but the photographs taken on this occasion are the last we have of him alive.[72]

Recent attempts to dispel the myths that have surrounded this incident should not obscure how deeply Proust was engaged with Bergotte's final vision.[73] As Thierry Laget has shrewdly noted, the rare omniscience that the narrator permits himself in recording it—Bergotte having died in front of the picture, his final meditations are perforce unknowable—just drives home the fact that it is Proust who is thinking for him.[74] And what Bergotte is thinking, famously, is that nothing in his own work measures up to that "little patch of yellow wall" in Vermeer's painting:

> At last he came to the Vermeer which he remembered as more striking, more different from anything else he knew, but in which, thanks to the critic's article, he noticed for the first time some small figures in blue, that the sand was pink, and, finally, the precious substance of the tiny patch of yellow wall. His dizziness increased; he fixed his gaze, like a child upon a yellow butterfly that it wants to catch, on the precious little patch of wall. "That's how I ought to have written," he said. "My last books are too dry, I ought to have gone over them with a few layers of colour, made my language precious in itself, like this little patch of yellow wall."

Though Bergotte "adored" the *View of Delft* and "imagined that he knew [it] very well," he had not remembered this little patch of color until the critic called it to his attention; but it now becomes the standard by which his own achievement is judged. The last words he speaks before sinking down on the settee, ignominiously muttering about a touch of indigestion from undercooked potatoes, are: "Petit pan de mur jaune avec un auvent, petit pan de mur jaune"—"Little patch of yellow wall, with a sloping roof, little patch of yellow wall" (3:692; 5:207, 208).

To say that Proust thinks for his character here is not to say that he identifies with Bergotte's sense of failure. Like Swann (whose own death will be reported just ten pages later), the imaginary writer primarily serves as a model to be left behind, though like Swann, too, he may also carry with him anxieties not unfamiliar to his creator. On Bergotte, in any case, the narrator hedges his bets, by going on to hint at the possibility that the writer's works may not die with the writer: "They buried him, but all through that night of mourning, in the lighted shop-window, his books, arranged three by three, kept vigil like angels with outspread wings and seemed, for him who was no more, the symbol of his resurrection" (3:693; 5:209). But whatever the ambivalence with which the novelist represents his characters, on Vermeer himself Proust was unequivocal. More than a year later, he was still recalling "the luminous memory" of that morning when Vaudoyer guided his tottering steps "toward that Vermeer where the gables of the houses 'are like precious Chinese objects.'"[75] And when the narrator of *Le temps retrouvé* compares the work of "original artists" to worlds whose light still reaches us "centuries after the extinction of the fire from which their light first emanated," the names he gives those distant stars are Rembrandt and Vermeer (4:474; 6:254).

Though Proust told a friend beforehand that he knew the three Vermeers at the exhibit "by heart,"[76] the evidence suggests that the little patch of yellow came to him, too, as a revelation—or perhaps rather as a forgotten detail restored to consciousness. Just which detail he meant to conjure up with his incantatory phrase, however, has been far from clear to his commentators: though Bergotte speaks of a "petit pan de *mur* jaune," some critics have been persuaded that he could only mean the yellow roof that appears to the left of the Rotterdam gate in the painting, while others have pointed to one or more of the yellow walls on the right (plate 16).[77] But what seems most salient from our perspective is not so much the location of the detail as the kind of detail it is. Vaudoyer had written, tellingly, of "those brick houses, painted in a material so precious, so heavy, so full, that *if you isolate a small surface of it, forgetting the subject*, you believe you have ceramic before your eyes as much as paint" (emphasis mine); and Proust similarly focuses attention less on the wall itself than on the layers of paint that go to make up its surface.[78] That such a passage in the *View of Delft* would have been rendered newly visible by the eye-level hanging and uncluttered walls of the postwar museum is only one of the ways in which a modern aesthetic conspired with the revival of interest in the artist.[79] Not quite a piece of abstract art—it does, after all, still represent an object—Vermeer's yellow patch is nonetheless far removed from the sort of details with which Balzac, for example, ambivalently identified his work. What might be called the apotheosis of the Dutch detail paradoxically testifies to the modernity of novelist and painter alike.

There seems little question that Proust identified his own art with the ideal to which Bergotte belatedly aspires.[80] When the dying man concludes that he ought to have made his language "precious in itself, like this little patch of yellow wall" (3:692; 5:207), he draws an analogy between the writer's style and the painter's color on which the narrator too will rely in the extended revelation of *Le temps retrouvé.* "Style for the writer, no less than colour for the painter, is a question not of technique but of vision," he announces, before going on to invoke the light that still reaches us from the "special radiance" of Rembrandt and Vermeer (4:474; 6:254). Though the narrator of *À la recherche* may not always speak for the novelist, in this case he says very much what Proust had already said in his own voice on more than one occasion.[81] Vaudoyer, too, had identified the artist's color as a kind of language—"for Vermeer," he had written, "colors . . . are at once words of a physical vocabulary and words of an ideal vocabulary"—and his emphasis on how those colors transform "the most everyday and commonplace sights" was very much, I would argue, in the spirit of Proust's analogy.[82]

This is not the only reason why the novelist would have been moved to incorporate the *View of Delft* into his narrative. In evoking the picture, Vaudoyer had specifically emphasized its power to stamp itself on the memory—to make you "see again," in his repeated phrase, so that "the remembrance that you keep of it transfigures any reproduction":

> You see again that stretch of rose-gold sand, which makes up the foreground of the canvas and where there is a woman in a blue apron who creates around her, by this blue, a wonderful harmony; you see again the dark, moored barges; and those brick houses. . . . You see again, especially, that immense sky, which, from the town's roofs to the zenith, gives an impression of almost vertiginous infinity. Finally you savor that odor, that breath of the climate, exhaled toward you by the canvas, and which penetrates you like the unexpected perfume of water and the sudden sensation of air when, after you have spent a long time traveling in a closed compartment, you lower the

window and receive from nature, though invisible, the physical evidence of a change of scenery.[83]

If it is hard to believe that the *View of Delft* appeared in Paris because Proust wished to see it, as another friend claimed,[84] it is not at all hard to imagine that this account of the picture was written for the novelist. Even the allusion to a landscape unexpectedly sensed from a passing train—not to mention the reiterated "see again" and the synaesthesia of his metaphors—reveal a writer thoroughly familiar with the first volumes of *À la recherche*.[85]

While Proust himself gives the experience of seeing the picture again to Bergotte rather than the narrator, his writing of the episode characteristically summons up still further echoes. Christiane Hertel has suggested that the *petit pan de mur jaune* recalls the *pan lumineux* that for a long time figures the narrator's only memory of Combray—the scene of his mother's kiss standing out like a "sort of luminous panel, sharply defined against a vague and shadowy background" (1:43; 1:49).[86] Yet closer, perhaps, is the *pan de château* projected by the protagonist's magic lantern for the story of Geneviève de Brabant—a vivid patch of yellow in front of which stands Geneviève herself, dressed, like Vermeer's small figures, in blue (1:9; 1:9).[87] One might think also think of *le même pan de soleil plié à l'angle du mur extérieur* ("the same patch of sunlight folded in the corner of the outer wall") that the protagonist repeatedly sees from his window in the final paragraph of *À l'ombre des jeunes filles en fleurs* (1918)—although in this case its "immutable colour" appears "less moving as a sign of summer than dismal like that of an inert and artificial enamel" (2:306; 2:618). But more important than these distant echoes is how Vermeer's vividly recollected townscape conjures up the narrator's own representations of Combray—representations themselves often couched in the language of painting, as when the steeple of Saint-Hilaire appears "so slender, so pink, that it seemed to be only scratched on the sky by a finger-nail that would have liked to give to this landscape, this painting that is pure nature, that little mark of art" (1:62; 1:74). Though the protagonist's first piece of writing represents the steeples of Martinville in motion rather than as a static tableau, it too is partly inspired by a vision of sunlight on stone.

The same consciousness of the picture plane that invites us to see the steeple of Saint-Hilaire as a mark scratched by a finger-nail—or the representation of a wall in the *View of Delft* as a vivid patch of color—figures in another passage that may profitably be compared to these, a passage that more directly addresses the pictorial experiments of Proust's contemporaries.

The narrator is describing some Elstirs that he has asked to see on his first visit to the Guermantes—paintings, as the context makes clear, that represent the artist's latest and least "realistic" manner:

> Among these pictures, some of those that seemed most absurd to people in fashionable society interested me more than the rest because they re-created those optical illusions which prove to us that we should never succeed in identifying objects if we did not bring some process of reasoning to bear on them. How often, when driving, do we not come upon a bright street beginning a few feet away from us, when what we have actually before our eyes is merely a patch of wall glaringly lit [un pan de mur violemment éclairé] which has given us the mirage of depth! This being the case, isn't it logical, not from any artifice of symbolism but from a sincere desire to return to the very root of the impression, to represent one thing by that other for which, in the light of a first illusion, we mistook it? Surfaces and volumes are in reality independent of the names of objects which our memory imposes on them when we have recognised them. Elstir sought to extract what he already knew from what he had just felt; he had often been at pains to dissolve that compound of reasoning that we call vision. (2:712–13; 3:484)

Though this may appear the opposite of the effect created by Bergotte's view of Vermeer, where a piece of wall is identified with layers of paint rather than a mirage of depth, what they have in common is a peculiarly modern attentiveness to the artifice of pictorial illusion. With its account of how the painter defers our knowledge of what things are for a representation of our initial impression, it is also another analogue for Proust's own art of the novel.

Proust himself never associates his modern painter with the Delft artist, but his account of Elstir's practice notably anticipates some of the terms in which subsequent commentators would seek to characterize the modernity of Vermeer's art.[88] In his influential study of the painter, Lawrence Gowing, for example, suggests that "Vermeer seems almost not to care, or not even to know, what it is that he is painting. What do men call this wedge of light?"—he asks rhetorically—"A nose? A finger? What do we know of its shape? To Vermeer none of this matters, the conceptual world of names and knowledge is forgotten, nothing concerns him but what is visible, the tone, the wedge of light." Unlike the formal ordering of his pictures, Gowing contends, Vermeer's representational vocabulary "is the kind which abhors preconception and design and relies entirely on the retina as its guide, the kind which in contrast to conceptual representation we know as impressionism."[89] Daniel Arasse makes a related point, when he associates Vermeer's modernity with his apparent inversion of the classical doctrine according to which the painter's knowledge of an object took precedence over the seemingly unmediated perception of the eye.[90] At the same time, if paradoxically, Vermeer's optical effects do not always correspond to an observed reality. The best-known example of this is his so-called *pointillé*—those little drops of luminous color that suggest the play of light in an unfocused camera obscura but that increasingly appear at places where the represented materials should preclude them. Both *The Lacemaker* (a picture Proust thought "exquisite")[91] and the *View of Delft* are especially notable for these glowing drops: dotting the young woman's collar and the rug in the former picture (plate 12) and "coruscating like dewdrops," as Harry Berger has observed, over the latter (plate 15), they simultaneously evoke an impression of light and call attention to themselves as marks of the artist's brush.[92] But even when that brush seems merely to be rendering an observable effect—as in the blurred appearance of the threads that spill out of the cushion in the foreground of *The Lacemaker* (plate 17)—it also draws our eyes to the abstract patterns it has created. "The textures Vermeer creates with his painting techniques continually remind the viewer that he is viewing a painting of nature and not nature itself," Arthur Wheelock has written of the *View of Delft* in particular;[93] and a number of commentators have agreed—remarking, as Berger does, for example, how its monocular perspective subtly flattens the city's façades and renders them impalpable, so that "brickwork and patchwork metamorphose before the eyes into pure esthetic patterns."[94] There is no need to imagine that such metamorphoses directly influenced Elstir's experiments in order to see why Proust was so enthusiastic a participant in the continuing moment of Vermeer's recovery.

Strictly speaking, Vermeer had never been entirely lost. Much admired by discerning collectors in his own day, he still appeared from time to time in later catalogues of Dutch art, like the *Galerie des peintres flamands, hollandais et allemands* issued by Jean Baptiste Pierre Lebrun in the 1790s, or the *Catalogue Raisonnée of the Works of the Most Eminent Dutch, Flemish and French Painters* published by John Smith in the 1830s. But if it is something of a myth that Vermeer was altogether unknown before Thoré-Bürger rescued him from "oblivion" (the word is Thoré-Bürger's),[95] there is no question that the latter's pioneering work marked the decisive turning point in his reputation.[96] By the time Proust saw his paintings for the last time more than fifty years later, several important studies had followed in Thoré-Bürger's wake—one of which, a 1908 work by Gustave Vanzype, Proust himself acquired as a sort of *aide memoire* after his visit to the exhibit. (With its numerous reproductions, he told Vaudoyer, the book permitted him "to recognize in different paintings the identical accessories"—thus presumably confirming his protagonist's remarks to the same effect in his lecture to Albertine.)[97] Like others of his generation, including Proust himself, Vanzype eagerly welcomed Vermeer as a contemporary. "We go to him," he wrote, "because a sort of mysterious prescience made him see as we see, made him discern, divine, anticipate a sensibility that would not develop until two centuries after him."[98] Vaudoyer, too, spoke of Vermeer's "modern feeling"—his example, perhaps surprisingly, was the Italianate *Diana*—and made clear how much had changed in the half-century since Thoré-Bürger patiently strove to identify the painter's corpus. It was "beyond imagination," Vaudoyer declared, that anyone could have ever confused a Vermeer with the work of another artist.[99]

Yet the aura of the unknown that continued to surround Vermeer was as much a part of his appeal as the distinctiveness of his vision. Nearly fifty years after Thoré-Bürger had introduced his "sphinx,"[100] the Delft painter was still figuring as "un inconnu" (Vanzype) and "le mystérieux Vermeer" (Vaudoyer) in the sources Proust consulted;[101] and what had been forgotten or could never be recovered of the artist's history remained the constant ground against which his achievement was articulated. Indeed, despite the assiduous research of John Michael Montias and others, this is still to a great extent the idea of the artist we have inherited; and if there are good reasons for this—the very small output of completed work, the narrow circle of patrons among which it circulated, the relative provinciality of Delft, even perhaps the necessary reticence of a Catholic convert in Protestant Holland—the aura of mystery nonetheless remains.[102] In Proust's case, the effect of the unknown, or the partially known, was intensified by his inability to see a number of the paintings for himself, as his repeated allusions to those at Dresden and Vienna suggest. "And still I know almost nothing of Vermeer," he had written to Vaudoyer in the same letter that called the *View of Delft* "the most beautiful painting in the world"; and even as he yearned to know more, he continued to revel in the mystery.[103] He more than once attacked Fromentin for never having "even named" Vermeer, though this was not in fact true, as if the utter absence of the painter from *Les maîtres d'autrefois* would only heighten his allure.[104] To Vaudoyer, he wrote of "ce maître inouï," the adjective nicely hovering between what is unheard of in this master and what is extraordinary.[105] And in the meditation

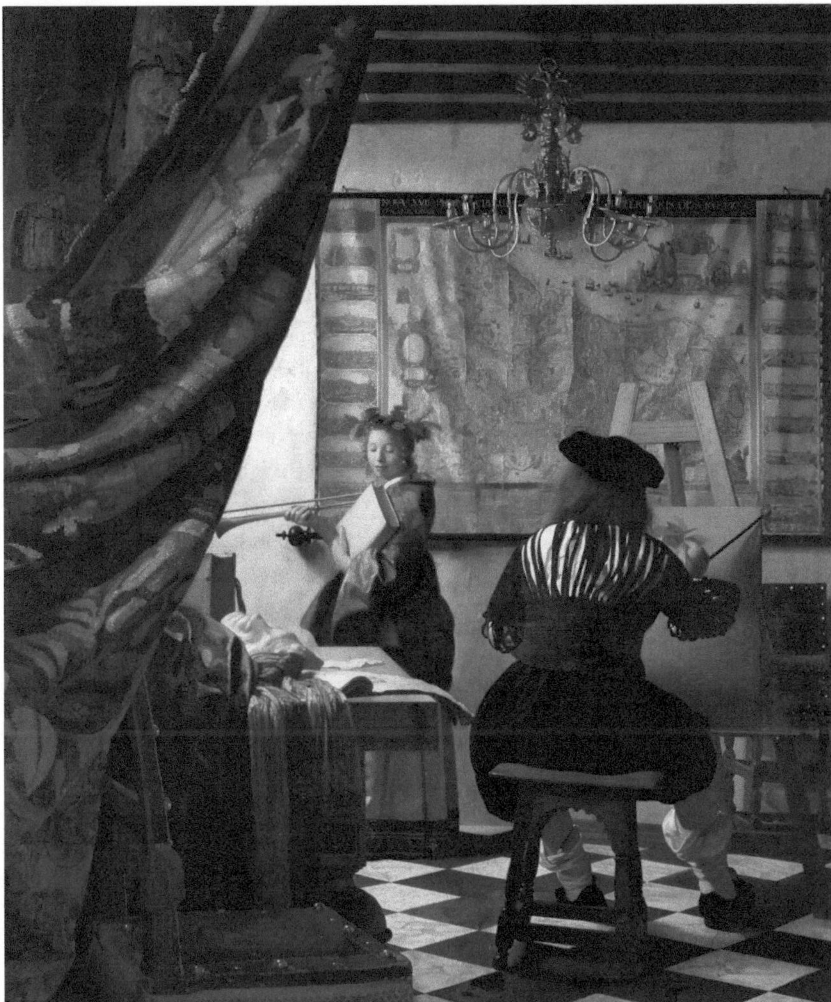

Figure 6-6. Johannes Vermeer: *The Art of Painting*, 1665–66. Kunsthistorisches Museum, Vienna. Photo Credit: Erich Lessing/Art Resource, N.Y.

that follows Bergotte's death, it is "an artist forever unknown [un artiste à jamais inconnu] and barely identified under the name of Vermeer" who ambiguously serves as the figure of artistic afterlife (3:693; 5:208).

"This painter turns his back on us," Vaudoyer had written in the evocative description of *The Art of Painting* (fig. 6-6) that closes his article; and Proust had responded by finding the idea both "admirable" and "poignant."[106] Though the painting was among those he only knew through reproductions, its image of the artist who refuses our gaze and turns instead to his work clearly spoke to the novelist who argued that the writer's true self "is manifested in his books alone."[107] Vaudoyer had also observed that most of Vermeer's figures, too, seem to be unaware of the viewer; and while he did not expand on this point, one might suggest that the oft-remarked elusiveness of the painter's human subjects would likewise have resonated with a novelist whose own art repeatedly demonstrates that the subjectivity of others remains unknowable. The protagonist of *À la recherche* may imagine that he will arrive at the truth about Albertine, but all he can know is a series of different aspects or impressions, none of which gives him the reality of the woman herself. The more obsessively he concentrates on her, the more elusive she becomes. Vermeer, too, simultaneously focuses our attention on his women and heightens their mystery: closing off the space of a painting (even as Proust's protagonist seeks to confine Albertine) and often eliminating all intruders, he tantalizes us with the nearness of figures who refuse to acknowledge our presence. The solitary subjects of pictures like *The Milkmaid* (plate 11) or *The Lacemaker* (plate 12), for example, are women wholly absorbed in their tasks, their expressions unreadable—women who retain their reserve even as they invite us to intimacy.[108] (The former was among those paintings Proust claimed to know "by heart" before he saw them again at the 1921 exhibit.)[109] But if we are denied access to the women themselves, what we can know, as the narrator of *À la recherche* implicitly argues, is how the artist saw them.[110] This is the burden of the passage from *Le temps retrouvé* that compares the writer's style to the painter's color—and identifies both with the "revelation" that alone enables us to escape our subjectivity. Only in art, the narrator argues, can we glimpse "the uniqueness of the fashion in which the world appears to each one of us, a difference which, if there were no art, would remain for ever the secret of every individual." Albertine retains her secret, but by the close of *À la recherche*, Proust—not the man, but the novelist—has allowed us to share his. "Thanks to art," the narrator goes on to declare, "we have at our disposal as many worlds as there are original artists" (4:474; 6:254). Though a number of these, from Giotto to Debussy, have been invoked in the course of the narrative, the only names who figure in this crucial passage are those exemplary originals, Rembrandt and Vermeer.

In one sense, the rediscovery of Vermeer did little to transform the idea of Dutch painting the nineteenth century had inherited. "Vermeer of Delft resembles no one," Vanzype had written in his study of the artist;[111] and there is some evidence that Proust, too, increasingly wished to mark the artist's difference from his compatriots. If he had his way, he wrote to Vaudoyer in 1920, he would demand that the Louvre not hang *The Lacemaker* with other pictures from the same country, but "as a masterpiece, apart."[112] (It was then the only Vermeer in the museum.) The following year, more Dutch pictures briefly appeared on view in Paris, but in Proust's fictional version of the exhibit, Bergotte has no use for anything but his beloved *View of Delft*. "He walked past several pictures and was struck by the aridity and pointlessness [inutilité] of such an artificial kind of art, which was not worth the air and sunlight of a Venetian palazzo, or of a simple house by the sea. At last he came to the Vermeer . . ." (3:692; 5:207). Though neither "an artificial kind of art"—Proust's adjective is "factice"—nor the comparison to a Venetian palazzo would ordinarily seem to point at Dutch painting, the context implies that here, too, Vermeer is being set apart from his countrymen. Indeed, even within the artist's very small oeuvre, Proust appears to single out a few works from the others. The only two Vermeers that figure by name in the course of *À la recherche* are not, after all, those "fragments of the same world" about which the narrator lectures Albertine (3:879; 5:430) but relative anomalies in the artist's career—the one a mythological subject, whose very difference from the domestic interiors had long rendered its attribution doubtful, and the other a rare townscape (fig. 6-5, plate 16). Neither the *View of Delft*—so remote and quiet that it has frequently been likened to still life—nor the classically elegant *Diana* is a genre painting. And neither bears much resemblance to those "faithful pictures of a monotonous homely existence" with which George Eliot had identified her art of the novel.[113]

I have been arguing that Proust responded to the protomodernity of Vermeer, yet the *Diana* reminds us that there is another, arguably less anachronistic, way of understanding the formal abstraction of his art, which is by looking to the Italians. Though there is no evidence that Vermeer ever traveled to Italy, scholars have often been tempted to speak of his "classicism" and to think of his bringing to bear on the typical subjects of the North the clarifying and idealizing impulses historically identified with the South.[114] Montias has suggested that in certain respects, Vermeer comes closer to Raphael than to any of his Northern contemporaries.[115] This is not the place to explore such connections; but to the extent that Vermeer is indeed "profoundly different from the Dutch art of his time," as Vanzype contended,[116] Proust's own affinity for the Delft painter might be understood as yet another turn away from the low materialism with which other Dutch artists had long been associated. It is that, of course—but only because Proust had always believed that "museums are buildings that house only thoughts," even if those thoughts take the guise of still life or genre.[117] "I didn't dare to hope that you would render such justice to this extraordinary master," he wrote to Vaudoyer after the first installment of "Le mystérieux Vermeer," "because I know your ideas (very true) on hierarchy in Art, and I feared him a little too Chardin for you."[118] As late as 1920, Vaudoyer was still prepared to assert that "the 'hierarchy' of subject," in his words, "implies the 'hierarchy' of genius";[119] but despite the polite concession of Proust's letter, nothing in *À la recherche* suggests that its author concurred. It is only the Duke of Guermantes, we might recall, who stubbornly "refuse[s] to swallow" Elstir's *Bundle of Asparagus* (2:791; 3:578)—a picture that owes its immediate inspiration to Manet, but traces its more distant lineage, by way of Chardin, to the humble still life of the Dutch. When Swann compares the sudden appearance of the "little phrase" in Vinteuil's sonata to the revelation of "a different colour, velvety with the radiance of some intervening light" in a distant doorway by Pieter de Hooch (1:215; 1:262), the connection, at once sensory and abstract, cuts across all hierarchies of subject and genre. And though Proust's novel never directly alludes to Vermeer's *Lacemaker*, it is easy to imagine that he would have sympathized with those who have sensed some covert identification between the painter and his subject, as she bends, utterly absorbed, to her work.[120] When the narrator of *À la recherche* finally gets down to his own work, it is not to Bergotte or even Elstir that he turns for a model, but to Françoise, his seamstress and cook: "I should construct my book, I dare not say ambitiously like a cathedral, but quite simply like a dress" (4:610; 6:432).

For all his affinities with seventeenth-century painting, Proust's very taste in Dutch art identifies him as a modern. Rather than Teniers or Gerrit Dou, he invokes de Hooch and Vermeer, even as his Anglo-Irish contemporary George Moore had called on the same painters two decades earlier in order to praise the artful selection of Flaubert. "Every detail contributes to enforce the unity of the picture," to quote Moore again: "For beauty of selection, for beauty of drawing, for beauty of colour, the Dutchmen have not done better."[121] Unlike Balzac, George Eliot, and Hardy, each of whom was a writer before turning to the Dutch for a model, Proust had no need to counter a tendency toward sensational plotting or philosophical abstraction by attending closely to pictures of daily life. Nor did he share their impulse to chafe at the model after they had adopted it. Alone among the novelists studied here, Proust began with an idea of Dutch painting that did not require him to choose between the everyday detail and the aspirations of high art.

notes

CHAPTER ONE
The Novel as Dutch Painting

Unless otherwise specified, all translations are my own, though I have taken the liberty of consulting English editions when available. Except where noted, all authors of anonymous articles in nineteenth-century periodicals are identified in the *Wellesley Index of Victorian Periodicals* (Cambridge: Chadwyck-Healey, 2005).

1. [Walter Scott], review of *Emma*, in *Quarterly Review* 14 (1815–16); rpt. in *Sir Walter Scott on Novelists and Fiction*, ed. Ioan Williams (London: Routledge and Kegan Paul, 1968), 230, 231, 235.
2. Ibid., 231.
3. *An Account of All the Pictures Exhibited in the Rooms of the British Institution from 1813 to 1823* . . . (London: Priestley and Weale, 1824), 200. It may be that Scott was thinking of the rather idealized images of rural life for which Teniers, as Vivian Atwater has recently shown, was chiefly popular in mid-eighteenth-century France: at one point he absent-mindedly refers to the "cornfields and cottages and meadows" that supposedly constitute Austen's world as opposed to the grounds of a "show mansion" or the "rugged sublimities" of a mountain landscape (Scott, review of *Emma,* 235). As we shall see, this would not be the only instance in which a nineteenth-century viewer approached Netherlandish painting both as a realistic representation of ordinary life and as a nostalgic image of a simpler past. But Austen's well-known tribute to "English verdure" in the "sweet view" of Abbey-Mill Farm notwithstanding, it remains difficult to identify her fiction with Teniers's pastoral images of the Flemish countryside. For Teniers in France, see Vivian Lee Atwater, "Les graveurs et la vogue néerlandaise dans le Paris du XVIIIe siècle," *Nouvelles de l'estampe*, nos. 142–43 (1995): 3–12.
4. Cf. Max J. Friedländer, *Landscape, Portrait, Still-Life: Their Origin and Development*, trans. R. F. C. Hull (New York: Schocken, 1963): "The pictorial idea, as an end, leads the genre-painter to the type, while observation, as the means, leads him to the individual" (191).
5. The very ubiquity of the allusion makes claims for priority hazardous. In his important article on the subject, Peter Demetz, for example, contends that Scott's

review marks the first use of "the Dutch (or rather Flemish) analogy" for fiction in English ("Defenses of Dutch Painting and the Theory of Realism," *Comparative Literature* 15 [1963]: 98). For a study that draws extensively on the analogy between the novel and Dutch art, see Mario Praz, *The Hero in Eclipse in Victorian Fiction*, trans. Angus Davidson (London: Oxford, 1956.) Despite its great suggestiveness, Praz's work does not so much analyze the analogy as indulge it: most of the comparisons between novels and paintings in the book are his own.

6. Mrs [Anna] Barbauld, "The Life of Mr. Richardson," in *Correspondence of Samuel Richardson*, 6 vols. (London: Richard Phillips, 1804), 1:cxxxvii; and [Leslie Stephen], "Richardson's Novels," *Cornhill Magazine* 17 (1868): 56. For Barbauld, it should be noted, Richardson is not only a "Dutch" painter, since he also has "the fine ideas of an Italian one" (1:cxxxvii). Ian Watt, *The Rise of the Novel: Studies in Defoe, Richardson and Fielding* (1957; rpt. Berkeley: University of California Press, 1967), 17, first directed me to Barbauld.

7. [Richard Whately], "Modern Novels," *Quarterly Review* 24 (1821): 362. I owe the identification of Whately's authorship to Brian Southam, ed., *Jane Austen: The Critical Heritage*, 2 vols. (London: Routledge, 1968).

8. [George Henry Lewes], "The Novels of Jane Austen," *Blackwood's Edinburgh Magazine* 86 (1859): 104.

9. [C. H. Pearson], "Chronicles of Carlingford," *National Review* 32 (1863): 361.

10. [H. F. Chorley], "*Martin Chuzzlewit*," *Athenaeum*, 20 July 1844, 666; Charles Kingsley, *Alton Locke: Tailor and Poet* (London: Dent, 1970), 73. I owe the identification of Chorley's authorship to John Charles Olmsted, ed., *A Victorian Art of Fiction: Essays on the Novel in British Periodicals,* 3 vols. (New York: Garland, 1979).

11. Walter Scott, "Daniel Defoe" (1827); rpt. Williams, *Sir Walter Scott on Novelists*, 179–80.

12. [Scott], review of *Emma*, 235, 231.

13. Walter Scott, *The Journal of Sir Walter Scott*, ed. W. E. K. Anderson (Oxford: Clarendon, 1972), 114. The entry is dated 14 March 1826.

14. H[ippolyte] Taine, *Histoire de la littérature anglaise*, 4 vols. (Paris: Hachette, 1863–64), 3: 492, 494–95.

15. Simon Schama, *The Embarrassment of Riches: An Interpretation of Dutch Culture in the Golden Age* (1987; rpt. New York: Vintage, 1997), 318.

16. Taine, *Histoire*, 3:495.

17. H[ippolyte] Taine, *Philosophie de l'art dans les Pays-Bas* (Paris: Germer Baillière, 1869), 162. For the prominence of the analogy in relation to Balzac, see Bernard Weinberg, *French Realism: The Critical Reaction, 1830–1870* (Chicago: Modern Language Association of America, 1937), 55, 65, 72. I am indebted to a number of Weinberg's leads in the French criticism.

18. F. Buloz, "Chronique de la quinzaine," *Revue des deux mondes*, 14 October 1833: 244. Théodore Muret, "'Le Père Goriot,'" *Quotidienne*, 11 April 1835, as

quoted in Weinberg, *French Realism*, 55; Philarète Chasles, "Histoire de la grandeur et de la décadence de César Birotteau," *Journal des debats politiques et littéraires*, 30 January 1838.

19. [John Wilson Croker], "French Novels," *Quarterly Review* 56 (April 1836): 91; "*Un ménage de Garçon en Province* (A Provincial Bachelor's Household)," *Foreign Quarterly Review* 30 (1843): 369; [George Henry Lewes], "Recent Novels: French and English," *Fraser's Magazine* 36 (1847): 695. On the English criticism, see Walter M. Kendrick, "Balzac and British Realism: Mid-Victorian Theories of the Novel," *Victorian Studies* 20 (1976): 5–24. As will become clear, however, I think much more was entailed in Victorian analogies to Dutch painting than the implication of a "purely decorative" artistry (12).

20. G. de Molènes, "Revue dramatique: 'Les ressources de Quinola,'" *Revue des deux mondes*, 1 April 1842, 147.

21. Gustave Merlet, *Le réalisme et la fantaisie dans la littérature* (Paris: Didier, 1861), 96. See Demetz, "Defenses of Dutch Painting," both for this reference (98) and for a brief survey of other writers who were compared—or compared themselves—to Netherlandish artists.

22. Henry James, "Honoré de Balzac" (1875), rpt. in *Henry James: Literary Criticism: French Writers, Other European Writers, The Prefaces to the New York Edition*, ed. Leon Edel and Mark Wilson (New York: Library of America, 1984), 50.

23. According to Bernard Weinberg, it was Arsène Houssaye's *Histoire de la peinture flamande et hollandaise* of 1846 that first gave the word "réalisme" in this sense "any real prominence," although he finds isolated uses of the term for art and literature in the previous decade. Among the earliest of the latter is an article by Gustave Planche in the *Revue des deux mondes* for 1835, where "réalisme" is used to characterize the "vérité humaine" (as opposed to "idéalité poétique") of Rembrandt. See *French Realism*, 118–19, 114n.

24. [Henry Sutherland Edwards], "Balzac and his Writings," *Westminster Review* 60 (1853): 208. For "realism," see 203, 212. This use of "realism" in an aesthetic sense antedates the first citation given in the *OED*, which is to the fourth volume of Ruskin's *Modern Painters* (1856). I owe its identification to Richard Stang, *The Theory of the Novel in England, 1850–1870* (New York: Columbia University Press, 1961), 148. Stang in turn credits Robert Gorham Davis, "The Sense of the Real in English Fiction," *Comparative Literature* 3 (1951): 214. A well-known piece on Dickens and Thackeray by David Masson in the *North British Review* for 1851 had already compared the styles of the two novelists by way of an extended analogy to the "Ideal" and the "Real" in painting.

25. Watt, *Rise of the Novel*, 34.

26. See, e.g., George J. Becker, preface, *Documents of Modern Literary Realism*, ed. Becker (Princeton: Princeton University Press, 1963), 4.

27. Marten Jan Bok, "The Painter and His World: The Socioeconomic Approach to Seventeenth-Century Dutch Art," in *The Golden Age of Dutch Painting in*

Historical Perspective, ed. Frans Grijzenhout and Henk van Veen, trans. Andrew McCormick (Cambridge: Cambridge University Press, 1999), 244.

28. On the French vogue for Netherlandish art, see F. J. B. Watson, *The Choiseul Box* (London: Oxford University Press, 1963); Anita Brookner, *Greuze: The Rise and Fall of an Eighteenth-Century Phenomenon* (Greenwich, Conn.: New York Graphic Society, 1972), 37–53; Petra ten Doesschate Chu, *French Realism and the Dutch Masters: The Influence of Dutch Seventeenth-Century Painting on the Development of French Painting between 1830 and 1870* (Utrecht: Haentjens Dekker and Gumbert, 1974); Oliver T. Banks, *Watteau and the North: Studies in the Dutch and Flemish Baroque Influence on French Rococo Painting* (New York: Garland, 1977); Thomas E. Crow, *Painters and Public Life in Eighteenth-Century Paris* (New Haven: Yale University Press, 1985), 45–74; Carol S. Elial, "Genre Painting During the Revolution and the *Goût Hollandais*," in *1789: French Art During the Revolution*, ed. Alan Wintermute (New York: Colnaghi, 1989), 47–61; and Atwater, "Les graveurs et la vogue néerlandaise," *Nouvelles de l'estampe*, no. 141 (1995): 3–10 and nos. 142–43 (1995): 3–12. For England and Scotland, see Harry Thomas Mount, *The Reception of Dutch Genre Painting in England, 1695–1829* (Ph. D. Diss.: University of Cambridge, 1991); Frank Herrmann, *The English as Collectors: A Documentary Sourcebook* (New Castle, Del.: Oak Knoll Press and London: John Murray, 1999), 13, 139, 142–43, 147–52; Oliver Millar, *Dutch Pictures from the Royal Collection* (London: Lund Humphries, 1971); Christopher White, *The Dutch Pictures in the Collection of Her Majesty the Queen* (Cambridge: Cambridge University Press, 1982); Andrew W. Moore, *Dutch and Flemish Painting in Norfolk: A History of Taste and Influence, Fashion and Collecting* (London: H. M. S. O., 1988); and Julia Lloyd Williams, *Dutch Art and Scotland: A Reflection of Taste* (Edinburgh: National Gallery of Scotland, 1992). See also Gerald Reitlinger, *The Economics of Taste: The Rise and Fall of Picture Prices, 1760–1960*, vol. 1 (London: Barrie and Rockliff), 11–25; and for stimulating if intermittent discussions of the subject, Francis Haskell, *Rediscoveries in Art: Some Aspects of Taste, Fashion and Collecting in England and France* (Ithaca: Cornell University Press, 1976).

29. I have borrowed the term "paradigm" from Mount, *Reception of Dutch Genre Painting*, where it functions somewhat more narrowly as the "negative presentation" of such painting in English art theory (3).

30. To Mary Russell Mitford, 30 June 1843, in *The Letters of Elizabeth Barrett Browning to Mary Russell Mitford, 1836–1854*, ed. Meredith B. Raymond and Mary Rose Sullivan, 3 vols. ([Waco, TX]: Armstrong Browning Library of Baylor University, 1983), 2:259, 260.

31. [Pearson], "Chronicles of Carlingford," 361, 360. The allusion is to Luke 10:38–42. A few years later, Taine would suggest that the Low Countries themselves had adopted the role of Martha, while they left to neighboring nations the "contemplative" role of Mary (*Philosophie*, 36).

32. For a simple but vivid demonstration of the small scale of genre paintings as compared to other pictures, especially of religious and mythological subjects, see the graph on p. 323 of Ad van der Woude, "The Volume and Value of Paintings in

Holland at the Time of the Dutch Republic," in *Art in History/History in Art: Studies in Seventeenth-Century Dutch Culture*, ed. David Freedberg and Jan de Vries (Santa Monica, Calif.: Getty Center, 1991). Van der Woude's graph, which represents the mean sizes of paintings in the Dutch collection of the Rijksmuseum, shows that even still life was typically larger than genre.

33. Henry James, "The Novels of George Eliot" (1866); rpt. in *Henry James: Literary Criticism: Essays on Literature, American Writers, English Writers*, ed. Leon Edel and Mark Wilson (New York: Library of America, 1984), 926, 917. For the general association of the detail and the feminine, see Naomi Schor, *Reading in Detail: Aesthetics and the Feminine* (New York: Methuen, 1987).

34. [Stephen], "Richardson's Novels," 55, 50, 56.

35. Roland Barthes, "The World as Object," in *Critical Essays*, trans. Richard Howard (Evanston, Ill.: Northwestern University Press, 1972), 7.

36. James, "Honoré de Balzac," 50.

37. Emmanuel Gonzalès, "M. de Balzac," *Art et progrès* 7 (1836): 244, as quoted in Weinberg, *French Realism*, 40.

38. James, "Honoré de Balzac," 48.

39. Honoré de Balzac, *Eugénie Grandet* (1833), ed. Nicole Mozet, in Balzac, *La comédie humaine*, ed. Pierre-Georges Castex, 12 vols., Bibliothèque de la Pléiade (Paris: Gallimard, 1976), 3:1039; Jane Austen, *Emma* (Oxford: Oxford University Press, 1995), 3, 5. Further references to these novels will appear parenthetically in the text, preceded by *CH* 3 and *E*, respectively.

40. [Whately], "Modern Novels," 363.

41. [Edward Bulwer-Lytton], "On Art in Fiction," *Monthly Chronicle* 1 (1838): 45.

42. [R. H. Hutton], "The Empire of Novels," *Spectator* 42 (1869): 43. I owe the identification of Hutton's authorship to Olmsted, *Victorian Art of Fiction*.

43. [Scott], review of *Emma*, 232.

44. For helpful critiques of this distinction, which persuasively argue that the difference between the spatial and the temporal arts is far from absolute, see Bernard Lamblin, *Peinture et temps* (Paris: Klincksieck, 1983), 1–125; and W. J. T. Mitchell, *Iconology: Image, Text, Ideology* (Chicago: University of Chicago Press, 1986), 95–115. The remainder of Lamblin's book provides a magisterial demonstration of the variety of ways in which time enters into our experience of painting.

45. Samuel Taylor Coleridge, *Lectures 1808–1819: On Literature*, ed. R. A. Foakes, 2 vols. (Princeton: Princeton University Press, 1987), 1:362.

46. [Archibald Alison], "The Historical Romance," *Blackwood's Edinburgh Magazine* 58 (1845): 354, 342.

47. [R. H. Hutton], "A Novel or Two," *National Review* 1 (1855): 337, 339–40. Among the novels addressed in Hutton's review was Gaskell's *North and South*.

48. Arthur Tilley, "The New School of Fiction," *National Review* 1 (1883): 265.

49. This was more than simply a visual convention. According to Jonathan Israel, foreign visitors frequently remarked what amounted to "a powerful repression of the erotic" in seventeenth-century Dutch culture. In 1690, one Italian observer noted that while women of the higher classes eagerly followed French fashion,

their style-consciousness did not extend to the décolleté popular in other European countries at the time. "In the Republic," says Israel, "high necklines were *de rigueur* for fine ladies and serving maids alike" (*The Dutch Republic: Its Rise, Greatness, and Fall, 1477–1806* [1995; rpt. Oxford: Clarendon, 1998], 682).

50. Taine, *Philosophie de l'art dans les Pays-Bas*, 16.

51. Martha Hollander, *An Entrance for the Eyes: Space and Meaning in Seventeenth-Century Dutch Art* (Berkeley: University of California Press, 2002), 198. For the comparatively fluid borders between house and world, see idem, 176; and especially Elizabeth Alice Honig, "The Space of Gender in Seventeenth-Century Dutch Painting," in *Looking at Seventeenth-Century Dutch Art: Realism Reconsidered*, ed. Wayne Franits (Cambridge: Cambridge University Press, 1997), 187–201. In *Home: A Short History of an Idea* (New York: Viking, 1986), Witold Rybczynski suggests that English domestic architecture itself was strongly influenced by the Dutch example (113).

52. See Svetlana Alpers, "Picturing Dutch Culture," in *Looking at Seventeenth-Century Dutch Art*, ed. Franits, 57–67.

53. Many recent art historians have argued for the strong influence of Jacob Cats's emblem books, including his 1625 *Houwelyck* (Marriage), on seventeenth-century Dutch art. But for the role of domestic conduct books more generally, including the "enormous influence" of works published in England (5–6), see Wayne E. Franits, *Paragons of Virtue: Women and Domesticity in Seventeenth-Century Dutch Art* (Cambridge: Cambridge University Press, 1993). On the conduct book and the English novel, see Nancy Armstrong, *Desire and Domestic Fiction: A Political History of the Novel* (New York: Oxford University Press, 1987), esp. 59–160; and Ruth Bernard Yeazell, *Fictions of Modesty: Women and Courtship in the English Novel* (Chicago: University of Chicago Press, 1991), esp. 3–80.

54. Mrs [Anna] Jameson, *Companion to the Most Celebrated Private Galleries of Art in London* (London: Saunders and Otley, 1844), 142.

55. As quoted in Mitchell, *Iconology*, 179–80.

56. Weinberg, *French Realism*, 73.

57. To G[eorge] H[enry] Lewes, 12 January 1848, *The Letters of Charlotte Brontë: With a Selection of Letters by Family and Friends*, ed. Margaret Smith, 3 vols. (Oxford: Clarendon Press, 1995–2004), 2:10.

58. For a useful discussion of how photographers in turn sought to distinguish their art from that of a copying-machine, see Jennifer Green-Lewis, *Framing the Victorians: Photography and the Culture of Realism* (Ithaca: Cornell University Press, 1996), esp. 37–64.

59. George Moore, "A Tragic Novel," *Cosmopolis* 7 (1897): 43.

60. For "conspicuous exclusion" in Vermeer, see Harry Berger, Jr., *Second World and Green World: Studies in Renaissance Fiction-Making* (Berkeley: University of California Press, 1988), 441–509. By calling attention to the *pentimenti* in several Vermeer paintings, Martha Hollander provides some specific examples of such omissions. See *An Entrance for the Eyes*, 97–101 and 215n72.

61. The classic critique of the idea of unmediated copying in the visual arts is E. H. Gombrich, *Art and Illusion: A Study in the Psychology of Pictorial Representation* (New York: Pantheon, 1961). For especially helpful further discussions, see Nelson Goodman, *Languages of Art: An Approach to a Theory of Symbols,* 2nd ed. (Indianapolis: Hackett, 1976), 3–43; and Norman Bryson, *Vision and Painting: The Logic of the Gaze* (New Haven: Yale University Press, 1983), 1–86. On Dutch art in particular, see Walter Liedtke, "Style in Dutch Art," and Lawrence O. Goedde, "Naturalism as Convention: Subject, Style, and Artistic Self-Consciousness in Dutch Landscape," in *Looking at Seventeenth-Century Dutch Art*, ed. Franits, 116–43.

62. How literally theorists and critics believed in that copying is a difficult question. As I shall suggest in the following chapter, it may be more useful to think of such talk as a sort of code for more general anxieties about art's relation to the material world—as if "mere" imitation were not so much a considered theory of how pictures were made as a way of dismissing images that appeared excessively particularized or too little governed by ideas, whether intellectual or spiritual.

63. Peter Sutton, *Masters of Seventeenth-Century Dutch Genre Painting* (Philadelphia: Philadelphia Museum of Art, 1984), lx, xxxvi. For the argument that the violence of war and its aftermath was also registered by Netherlandish pictures of soldierly plunder and banditry, see David Kunzle, *From Criminal to Courtier: The Soldier in Netherlandish Art, 1550–1672* (Leiden: Brill, 2002), esp. 282–392.

64. Goedde, "Naturalism as Convention," 131.

65. Honig, "The Space of Gender," 195. For some brilliant speculations on that absent householder and his replacement by the figure of the soldier in painting of the 1650s and 1660s, see Richard Helgerson, *Adulterous Alliances: Home, State, and History in Early Modern European Drama and Painting* (Chicago: University of Chicago Press, 2000), 79–119.

66. Franits, *Paragons of Virtue*, 71–73.

67. For a useful summary, see Eric J. Sluijter, "New Approaches in Art History and the Changing Image of Seventeenth-Century Dutch Art Between 1960 and 1990," in *Golden Age of Dutch Painting*, ed. Grijzenhout and van Veen, 247–76.

68. Denis Diderot, *Essai sur la peinture*, in *Oeuvres*, ed. André Billy, Bibliothèque de la Pléiade (Paris: Gallimard, 1951), 1189. Though the *Essai* was written in 1765, it was not published until 1795.

69. Wolfgang Stechow and Christopher Comer, "The History of the Term *Genre*," *Allen Memorial Art Museum Bulletin* 33 (1975–76): 91.

70. Sutton, *Masters of Seventeenth-Century Dutch Genre Painting*, xiv.

71. Mount, *Reception of Dutch Genre Painting*, 9; Stechow and Comer, "History of the Term *Genre*," 92–94. As Stechow and Comer point out, the first English edition of Kugler's *Handbook* appeared in 1846, but it was not until Gustav Waagen's expanded edition of 1860 that no definition of the term was thought to be necessary. Jacob Burckhardt's influential lectures "On Netherlandish Genre Painting" ("Über die niederländische Genre malerei") were delivered in 1874.

72. Albert Blankert, "What is Dutch Seventeenth Century Genre Painting? A Definition and its Limitations," in *Holländische Genremalerei im 17. Jahrhundert: Symposium Berlin 1984*, ed. Henning Bock and Thomas W. Gaehtgens (Berlin: Mann, 1987), 9–32. For another useful discussion of the term, which also briefly makes the argument about anonymity, see Friedländer, "The Nature and Origins of Genre as a Category," in *Landscape, Portrait, Still-Life*, 154–69.

73. Tzvetan Todorov, *Éloge du quotidien: Essai sur la peinture hollandaise du XVII*[e] *siècle* (Paris: Adam Biro, 1993), 14.

74. For a seminal formulation of the iconological approach, see Eddy de Jongh, "Realism and Seeming Realism in Seventeenth-Century Dutch Painting" (1971), rpt. in *Looking at Seventeenth-Century Dutch Art*, ed. Franits, 21–56. For a major anti-iconological argument, which emphasizes instead the visual and descriptive aspects of Dutch culture, see Svetlana Alpers, *The Art of Describing: Dutch Art in the Seventeenth Century* (Chicago: University of Chicago Press, 1983). Helpful attempts to stake out intermediate positions include Peter Hecht, "The Debate on Symbol and Meaning in Dutch Seventeenth-Century Art: An Appeal to Common Sense," *Simiolus* 16 (1986): 173–87; Eric J. Sluijter, "Didactic and Disguised Meanings? Several Seventeenth-Century Texts on Painting and the Iconological Approach to Dutch Paintings of This Period" (1988), and Hecht, "Dutch Seventeenth-Century Genre Painting: A Reassessment of Some Current Hypotheses" (1992), both rpt. in *Looking at Seventeenth-Century Dutch Art*, ed. Franits, 78–97; and Lyckle de Vries, "The Changing Face of Realism," in *Art in History/History in Art*, ed. Freedberg and de Vries, 209–44. Though it would be premature to declare this battle over, a tentative truce appears to have been negotiated over the last decade or so. Without denying the scriptural and emblematic origins of many of the motifs that Dutch genre painters adopted, recent scholarship has tended to stress the variety of viewers to whom such painters appealed and the multiplicity of interpretations to which their pictures would have been subject.

75. Roland Barthes, "The Reality Effect," in *French Literary Theory Today: A Reader*, ed. Tzvetan Todorov, trans. R. Carter (Cambridge: Cambridge University Press, 1982), 11–17.

76. Jameson, *Companion to the Most Celebrated Private Galleries*, 342.

77. For an argument that sternly seeks to counter such readings, see Hessel Miedema, "Realism and Comic Mode: The Peasant," *Simiolus* 9 (1977): 205–19.

78. Catherine Gallagher, *Nobody's Story: The Vanishing Acts of Women Writers in the Marketplace, 1670–1820* (Berkeley: University of California Press, 1994), 174, 172.

79. George Eliot, *Adam Bede*, ed. Valentine Cunningham (Oxford: Oxford University Press, 1996), 177.

CHAPTER TWO
Low Genre and High Theory

1. John Ruskin, *Modern Painters I*, in *The Works of John Ruskin*, ed. E. T. Cook and Alexander Wedderburn, 39 vols. (London: George Allen, 1903–12), 3:85, 188–89.

Further references to this edition of Ruskin's works will be given by volume and page number parenthetically in the text.

2. Introduction, *Works of John Ruskin*, 1:xxxi.

3. Mrs [Anna] Jameson, *A Handbook to the Public Galleries of Art in and near London*, 2 vols. (London: John Murray, 1842), 2:442, 440.

4. Letter to [Clarkson] Stanfield, 22 August [1859], *Works*, 7:liii.

5. Harry Mount concludes his valuable study of English responses to Dutch painting before Ruskin, on the grounds that the old paradigm had substantially broken down by the 1830s. See Harry Thomas Mount, *The Reception of Dutch Genre Painting in England, 1695–1829* (Ph. D. Diss.: University of Cambridge, 1991). For Ruskin's reversal of Reynolds on landscape, see Tim Barringer, *Reading the Pre-Raphaelites* (New Haven: Yale University Press, 1998), 59–60.

6. [George Eliot], "John Ruskin's *Modern Painters*, Vol. III" (1856), in *George Eliot: Selected Critical Writings*, ed. Rosemary Ashton (Oxford: Oxford University Press, 1992), 248.

7. For a helpful account of Ruskin's shifting religious positions, see George P. Landow, *The Aesthetic and Critical Theories of John Ruskin* (Princeton: Princeton University Press, 1971), 243–317.

8. *Hogan-Moganides: or, the Dutch Hudibras* (London: 1674), 82; as quoted in Mount, *Reception of Dutch Genre Painting*, 29.

9. Gerard de Lairesse, *The Art of Painting in All its Branches . . .* , trans. John Frederick Fritsch (London: J. Brotherton, 1738), 129.

10. Roger de Piles' commentary appears in his *L'art de peinture* (1668), an anonymous prose translation of Charles Alphonse Dufresnoy's Latin poem, *De Arte Graphica*. I quote from John Dryden's translation of the composite work, which was first published in London in 1695. *The Works of John Dryden*, ed. Edward Niles Hooker, H. T. Swedenberg, Jr., et al., 20 vols. (Berkeley: University of California Press, 1956–2000), 20:116.

11. Horace Walpole, *Aedes Walpolianae: Or, A Description of the Collection of Pictures at Houghton-Hall in Norfolk . . .* , 3rd ed. (London, 1767), xi; W. Wilkie Collins, *Memoirs of the Life of William Collins, Esq., R. A.: With Selections from his Journals and Correspondence*, 2 vols. (1848; rpt. London: EP Publishing, 1978), 1:112.

12. Humphrey Repton, "Observations, &c. on the Pictures of Adrian van Ostade . . ." (1808), 144; as quoted in Mount, *Reception of Dutch Painting*, 179.

13. William Hazlitt, *Complete Works*, ed. P. P. Howe, 21 vols. (New York: AMS, 1967), 11:166; 18:123. The first quotation is from an essay of 1825 on "Mr. Campbell and Mr. Crabbe," the second from an entry on "Fine Arts" for the *Encyclopedia Britannica* of 1817. The poetry of Crabbe is a notable exception to the general tendency to associate Dutch painting with the novel, and Hazlitt was not alone in making the comparison.

14. Mount, *Reception of Dutch Genre Painting*, 178–226.

15. *Mercure de France*, November 1753, 161. Though the translation is my own, I owe the discovery of this passage and the identification of its author to

Thomas E. Crow, *Painters and Public Life in Eighteenth-Century Paris* (New Haven: Yale University Press, 1985), 137.

16. Ronald Paulson, *Hogarth's Graphic Works*, 3rd rev. ed. (London: The Print Room, 1989), 152. The print in question is Hogarth's *Paul Before Felix Burlesqued* (1751).

17. Horace Walpole, *Anecdotes of Painting in England*, 4 vols. (New York: Arno, 1969), 3:2n. The four volumes of Walpole's *Anecdotes* originally appeared from 1762 to 1780.

18. Richard Redgrave and Samuel Redgrave, *A Century of Painters of the English School; with Critical Notices of Their Works, and An Account of the Progress of Art in England*, 2 vols. (London: Smith, Elder and Co., 1866), 1:55–56.

19. The first example is from Andrew Marvell's *Character of Holland* of 1665 and the second from the anonymous *Dutch Boare Dissected* of the same year. I owe these references to Mount, *Reception of Dutch Genre Painting*, 31, and Simon Schama, *The Embarrassment of Riches: An Interpretation of Dutch Culture in the Golden Age* (1987; rpt. New York: Vintage, 1997), 263, respectively.

20. David H. Solkin, *Painting for Money: The Visual Arts and the Public Sphere in Eighteenth-Century England* (New Haven: Yale University Press, 1992), 51; Frans Grijzenhout, "Between Reason and Sensitivity: Foreign Views of Dutch Painting, 1660–1800," in *The Golden Age of Dutch Painting in Historical Perspective*, ed. Grijzenhout and Henk van Veen (Cambridge: Cambridge University Press, 1999), 15–16.

21. H[ippolyte] Taine, *Histoire de la littérature anglaise*, 4 vols. (Paris: Hachette, 1863–64), 3:492, 495; Benjamin Haydon, *The Diary of Benjamin Robert Haydon*, ed. Willard Bissell Pope, 5 vols. (Cambridge, Mass.: Harvard University Press, 1960–63), 1:7, 5–6. The entry is dated 23 July 1808. I am indebted to Harry Mount for alerting me to this passage.

22. Mount, *Reception of Dutch Painting*, 24–68.

23. Dryden, "A Parallel betwixt Painting and Poetry," in *Works* 20:55. Though the analogy between the literary hierarchy and the visual one was common on both sides of the Channel, Mount argues that the more vigorous development of literary theory in England meant that the English were more prone than Continental writers to associate Dutch genre with comedy (*Reception of Dutch Painting*, 43–53).

24. Martin Archer Shee, R. A., *Elements of Art, A Poem; in Six Cantos; with Notes and a Preface; Including Strictures on the State of the Arts, Criticism, Patronage, and Public Taste* (London: William Miller, 1809), 216–17.

25. According to Wolfgang Stechow and Christopher Comer, the distinction between high (höheren) and low (niedern) genre first appears in the 1842 edition of Franz Kugler's *Handbuch*; the earlier attempt to distinguish between the coarsely comic and the well-to-do comes from Karl Schnaase's *Niederländische Briefe* of 1830, a work with which Kugler was evidently familiar. See Stechow and Comer, "The History of the Term *Genre*," *Allen Memorial Art Museum Bulletin* 33 (1975–76): 93–94. As Mount notes, the distinction is also partly anticipated by Gerard de Lairesse, who cautiously allows for modern paintings of "City-life . . . with its daily

Occurrences of Assemblies, Pastimes, Family-affairs, and other Particulars" but contemptuously dismisses "low and unbecoming Subjects," such as "*Cottages, Brandy-shops, Ale-houses, Bawdy-houses, Corps-de-gard*, and the like" (*Art of Painting*, 138, 129, 139). Mount credits Shaftesbury (in an unfinished essay on "Plastics") as the first theorist in England to formulate the distinction, but Shaftesbury is attempting a tripartite division among types of painting, and he does not use the terms "high" and "low genre" as such (*Reception of Dutch Painting*, 48–50).

26. Mrs [Anna] Jameson, *Companion to the Most Celebrated Private Galleries of Art in London* (London: Saunders and Otley, 1844), xxxviii–xxxix.

27. [Archibald Alison], "The Historical Romance," *Blackwood's Edinburgh Magazine* 58 (1845): 342–43.

28. Ibid.

29. Compare the terms in which Alison, by contrast, praises Manzoni: "though he paints them [his peasants] with the fidelity of an artist, it is yet with the feelings of a gentleman" ("The Historical Romance," 356).

30. For his useful summary of this history, I am particularly indebted to David Irwin, "Art, Theory and Morality," in *Winckelmann: Writings on Art*, ed. Irwin (New York: Phaidon, 1972), 30–47. On the Neoplatonic and Aristotelian aspects of Bellori's argument, see Rensselaer W. Lee, "*Ut Pictura Poesis*: The Humanistic Theory of Painting," *Art Bulletin* 22 (1940): 207–10; and the editors' "Commentary" to Dryden's *De Arte Graphica*, in *Works* 20:350. Erwin Panofsky's *Idea: A Concept in Art Theory* (1924), trans. Joseph J. S. Peake (New York: Harper and Row, 1968) traces the concept from antiquity to the seventeenth century.

31. Dryden, "Parallel betwixt Painting and Poetry," in *Works* 20:40.

32. Mr [Jonathan] Richardson, *An Essay on the Theory of Painting* (London: 1715), 162, 160–62.

33. Dryden, *De Arte Graphica*, in *Works* 20:126. For Roger de Piles, see note 10, above.

34. Quoted in Anita Brookner, *Greuze: The Rise and Fall of an Eighteenth-Century Phenomenon* (Greenwich, Conn.: New York Graphic Society, 1972), 39.

35. Henry James "The Metropolitan Museum's '1871 Purchase'" (1872), rpt. in *The Painter's Eye: Notes and Essays on the Pictorial Arts*, ed. John L. Sweeney (Madison: University of Wisconsin Press, 1989), 61.

36. Richardson, *Essay on the Theory of Painting*, 19.

37. Iain Pears, *The Discovery of Painting: The Growth of Interest in the Arts in England, 1680–1768* (New Haven: Yale University Press, 1988), 118–19.

38. John Brewer, *The Pleasures of the Imagination: English Culture in the Eighteenth Century* (Chicago: University of Chicago Press, 1997), 219.

39. Pears, *Discovery of Painting*, 123.

40. John Barrell distinguishes between Reynolds and Barry, for example, on the grounds that the latter was more ready to welcome artisans and tradesmen into the political commonwealth—and thus more sympathetic to the "mechanical" aspects of painting—than was Reynolds. On this, as well as the subtle changes in

Reynolds's own position over the course of his career, see *The Political Theory of Painting from Reynolds to Hazlitt* (New Haven: Yale University Press, 1986), 163–221; 136–62. On Reynolds's shift toward a somewhat more tolerant view of Dutch painting—an accommodation that nonetheless had its limits—see Harry Mount's introduction to his edition of Reynolds's *Journey to Flanders and Holland* (Cambridge: Cambridge University Press, 1996), xxix–lxx.

41. Richardson, *Essay on the Theory of Painting*, 5, 30. For the political resonance of "mechanical" and "servile" in eighteenth-century writing on art, see Barrell, *Political Theory of Painting*, 13–18.

42. In fairness to Ruskin, he had earlier complained that the dog itself was brutalized by Dutch painting: "The dog is used by Teniers, and many other Hollanders, merely to obtain unclean jest, while by the more powerful men, Rubens, Snyders, Rembrandt, it is painted only in savage chase, or butchered agony." Though his alertness to what he here terms the "slightest taint of obscenity" in Dutch art makes Ruskin a partial exception to the rule that the nineteenth century did not usually associate that art with sexuality as such, the passage as a whole renders the butchering as obscene as the joking—indeed makes it impossible to distinguish between them: "the occupation of magnificent art-power in giving semblance of perpetuity to those bodily pangs which Nature has mercifully ordained to be transient, and in forcing us, by the fascination of its stormy skill, to dwell on that from which eyes of merciful men should instinctively turn away, and eyes of high-minded men scornfully, is dishonourable, alike in the power which it degrades, and the joy to [*sic*] which it betrays" (7:337). Only the context suggests that this probably refers to the hunt rather than sex.

43. Joshua Reynolds, Discourse 12 (10 December 1784), in *Discourses on Art*, ed. Robert R. Wark (New Haven: Yale University Press, 1997), 210.

44. Joshua Reynolds, *Idler* no. 79 (20 October 1759), in *Works of Sir Joshua Reynolds*, ed. Edmond Malone (London: 1798), 2:231.

45. Reynolds, Discourse 3 (14 December 1770), in *Discourses*, 41, 50; Discourse 13 (11 December 1786), in *Discourses*, 232, 235.

46. Reynolds, Discourse 3 (14 December 1770), in *Discourses*, 50; Discourse 1 (2 January 1769), in *Discourses*, 19.

47. Dryden, "Parallel betwixt Poetry and Painting," in *Works* 20:71–72. On color, see Mount, *Reception of Dutch Painting*, 93–97.

48. I wish to thank my colleague Tim Barringer for calling this point to my attention.

49. Reynolds, Discourse 4 (10 December 1771), in *Discourses*, 69.

50. Winckelmann, "On the Greeks" (1755), in *Writings on Art*, 65; Reynolds, Discourse 13 (11 December 1786), in *Discourses*, 244.

51. By showing how Shaftesbury and others associated minuteness in painting with the atheism supposedly fostered by the microscopic vision of seventeenth-century science, Harry Mount has suggested another way in which high theory could identify Dutch painting with godlessness. See his "Morality, Microscopy and

the Moderns: The Meaning of Minuteness in Shaftesbury's Theory of Painting," *British Journal for Eighteenth-Century Studies* 21 (1998): 125–41.

52. Jameson, *Companion to the Most Celebrated Private Galleries*, 3.

53. For more on this history, see Mount, *Reception of Dutch Genre Painting*, 113–28. According to Frank Herrmann, Dutch pictures had been collected in England "to some extent" before 1750, but they became "extremely popular afterwards." See Hermann, *The English as Collectors: A Documentary Sourcebook* (New Castle, Del.: Oak Knoll / London: John Murray, 1999), 13.

54. I am grateful to Pears, *Discovery of Painting*, 97–99, for first directing me to these images.

55. John Smith, *A Catalogue Raisonné of the Works of the Most Eminent Dutch, Flemish, and French Painters*, 9 vols. (London: Smith and Son, 1829–42), 1:xix.

56. "One would imagine that the great and exalted in station would like lofty subjects in works of art," he remarks ironically, "whereas they seem to have an exclusive predilection for the mean and the mechanical. . . . Even arts with them must be servile to be tolerated" (Hazlitt, *Complete Works*, 20:130). The inevitable comparison, of course, is with the works of the Italian school, which "baffle and confound their self-will, and make them feel that there is something in the mind of man which they can neither give nor take away" (131). These remarks originally appeared as "Common Places" in the *Literary Examiner* of 25 October 1823.

57. Mount, introduction to Reynolds, *Journey to Flanders and Holland*, lxvi.

58. Peter Demetz implies that because the English lacked a strong classical tradition, they worried the Dutch question less than their counterparts on the Continent. But I would argue, to the contrary, that their very closeness to the Dutch meant that they were all the more concerned to distinguish themselves: precisely because England was "the home of Hogarth, Lillo, and Wordsworth," in Demetz's phrase, many arbiters of taste—not to mention Hogarth himself—struggled to keep Dutch realism at a distance. See Demetz, "Defenses of Dutch Painting and the Theory of Realism," *Comparative Literature* 15 (1963): 115. Of course, as in most matters of intellectual and cultural history, attitudes did not develop uniformly or monolithically. In *Painting for Money*, David Solkin has argued that mid-eighteenth-century England briefly witnessed an emerging consensus more sympathetic to the imitation of nature (and by extension to Netherlandish painting) that was then disrupted by the founding of the Royal Academy and the increasing influence of Reynolds's *Discourses*.

59. Oliver T. Banks, *Watteau and the North: Studies in the Dutch and Flemish Baroque Influence on French Rococo Painting* (New York: Garland, 1977), 15–59. Calling attention to the neoclassical theorizing of Gerard de Lairesse in particular, Banks emphasizes the ironic inversion by which the Dutch began to embrace academic dogma at the very moment that the French themselves were beginning to abandon it.

60. Vivian Lee Atwater, "Les graveurs et la vogue néerlandaise dans le Paris du XVIIIe siècle," *Nouvelles de l'estampe*, no. 141 (1995): 3–10.

61. F. J. B. Watson, *The Choiseul Box* (London: Oxford University Press, 1963), 6–8; and Banks, *Watteau and the North*, 84. Watson quotes the art dealer E. F. Gersaint's introduction to a 1744 sale catalogue: "l'école flamande . . . est ici fort à la mode et plaît universellement" (7). Cf. also Francis Haskell: "In mid-eighteenth-century France almost everyone admitted, usually with some dismay, that Dutch and Flemish cabinet pictures were more popular with most collectors than large-scale Italian paintings of the Renaissance or Baroque periods; but no one ever wrote (as Théophile Thoré was to do a hundred years later) that they were of higher moral—and hence aesthetic—quality." See Haskell, *Rediscoveries in Art: Some Aspects of Taste, Fashion and Collecting in England and France* (Ithaca: Cornell University Press, 1976), 6. For Thoré, see below.

62. Gerald Reitlinger, *The Economics of Taste: The Rise and Fall of Picture Prices, 1760–1960*, vol. 1 (London: Barrie and Rockcliff, 1961), 11, 302, 458.

63. Carol S. Eliel, "Genre Painting During the Revolution and the *Goût Hollandais*," in *1789: French Art During the Revolution*, ed. Alan Wintermute (New York: Colnaghi, 1989), 48.

64. Denis Diderot, *Pensées détachées*, in *Oeuvres complètes*, ed. J. Assézat, 20 vols. (Paris: Garnier Frères, 1875–77), 12:75.

65. For Raynal on Chardin, see note 15, above. On the general indebtedness of eighteenth-century French painters to the North, see Brookner, *Greuze*; Banks, *Watteau and the North*; and Crow, *Painters and Public Life in Eighteenth-Century Paris*, esp. 45–74 and 134–74.

66. Brookner includes Watteau, Chardin, Greuze, and Lépicié among those known as "the French Teniers" (*Greuze*, 42), while Elial reports that Louis-Léopold Boilly was hypothetically accorded "le surnom du Teniers moderne" ("Genre Painting during the Revolution," 51).

67. For the most part, this holds true in the Netherlands as well as outside it, though the work of Celeste Brusati suggests that a partial exception should be made for Samuel van Hoogstraten's 1678 treatise, *Inleyding tot de hooge schoole der schilderkonst* (*Introduction to the Advanced School of Painting*). As modern commentators on seventeenth-century Dutch painting frequently observe, the Dutch themselves left very little by way of theoretical writing on their art; and the principal works that do exist—the others are Karel van Mander's *Schilder-boeck* (1604) and Gerard de Lairesse's *Groot schilderboek* (1707)—largely adapt neoclassical standards. While Brusati concedes what she terms the "classicizing veneer" of van Hoogstraten's treatise (222), she contends that he appropriates humanist rhetoric "to legitimize painting as he and his compatriots understood it" (227). In her persuasive reading, van Hoogstraten associates painting with craft rather than a theory based on literary models, praises the imitation of likenesses rather than the creation of ideal forms, and significantly modifies the generic hierarchy. See Celeste Brusati, *Artifice and Illusion: The Art and Writing of Samuel van Hoogstraten* (Chicago: University of Chicago Press, 1995), 218–56.

68. Walpole, *Aedes Walpolianae*, xi.

69. Mount, introduction to Reynolds, *Journey to Flanders and Holland*, lviii.

70. Reynolds, *A Journey to Flanders and Holland*, 107, 110. Cf. his related remarks in a letter written to Edmund Burke on the same journey: "Dutch Pictures are a representation of nature, just as it is seen in a Camera Obscura. . . . They are certainly to be admired, but do not shine much in description, a figure asleep with another figure tickling his or her nose, which is a common subject with the Painters of this School, however admirable would have no effect in writing" (To Edmund Burke [14, 24, 20 August 1781], in *The Letters of Sir Joshua Reynolds*, ed. John Ingamells and John Edgcumbe [New Haven: Yale University Press, 2000], 100).

71. Reynolds, *Journey*, 107.

72. Collins, *Memoirs of the Life of William Collins*, 1:113.

73. Jameson, *Companion to the Most Celebrated Private Galleries*, 7–8, 48, 207.

74. Richard Payne Knight, *An Analytical Inquiry into the Principles of Taste*, 4th ed. (1808; rpt. Westmead: Gregg International, 1972), 70, 71. The first edition of Knight's *Inquiry* appeared in 1805.

75. For the persistence of narrative language in Victorian criticism of the visual arts, see Kate Flint, *The Victorians and the Visual Imagination* (Cambridge: Cambridge University Press, 2000), 197–235.

76. G. W. F. Hegel, *Aesthetics: Lectures on Fine Art*, trans. T. M. Knox, 2 vols. (Oxford: Clarendon, 1975), 1:169, 598. Originally delivered in the 1820s, Hegel's lectures were edited from manuscript notes and first published posthumously by H. G. Hotho in 1835. A five-volume French translation appeared from 1840 to 1852. For the influence of Hegel's defense of Dutch art on subsequent writers, particularly in Germany, see Demetz, "Defenses of Dutch Painting," 104–15. For a critique of that influence, especially as it contributes to persistent ideas of Dutch "realism," see Gary Schwartz, "Art in History," in *Art in History/History in Art: Studies in Seventeenth-Century Dutch Culture*, ed. David Freedberg and Jan de Vries (Santa Monica, Calif.: Getty Center, 1991), 7–16.

77. Eugène Fromentin, *Oeuvres complètes,* ed. Guy Sagnes, Bibliothèque de la Pléiade (Paris: Gallimard, 1984), 669.

78. See, e.g., the article by Gary Schwartz cited in note 76, above, or Walter Liedtke's testy response to the work of Svetlana Alpers and others: "Their [Dutch artists'] eyes may have been comparable to the camera obscura, but their heads were filled with ideas" ("Style in Dutch Art," in *Looking at Seventeenth-Century Dutch Art: Realism Reconsidered*, ed. Wayne E. Franits [Cambridge: Cambridge University Press, 1997], 125).

79. Hegel, *Aesthetics*, 1:598, 171.

80. Fromentin, *Oeuvres complètes*, 676.

81. W. Bürger [Théophile Thoré], *Musées de la Hollande*, 2 vols. (Paris: Jules Renouard, 1858–60), 1:326. Further references to this edition are given by volume and page number in the text.

82. For a useful account of his career, see Frances Suzman Jowell, *Thoré-Bürger and the Art of the Past* (New York: Garland, 1977). As is customary, I will henceforth refer to him by the compound name.

83. W. Bürger [Théophile Thoré], *Trésors d'art en Angleterre*, 3rd ed. (Paris: Jules Renouard, 1865), 407. The first edition of this work, an account of the Manchester Exhibition of 1857, appeared in that year. Jowell speculates that Thoré adopted his English first name as a tribute to Shakespeare (*Thoré-Bürger and the Art of the Past*, 180).

84. Peter C. Sutton, *Masters of Seventeenth-Century Dutch Genre Painting* (Philadelphia: Philadelphia Museum of Art, 1984), xlvi.

85. Thoré-Bürger sometimes does make an exception for Rembrandt, who is "without equal in his country—and in the world" (1:79).

86. W. Bürger [Théophile Thoré], "Van der Meer de Delft," *Gazette des beaux-arts* 21 (1866): 458–59.

87. Bürger, "Van der Meer de Delft," 307.

88. Hegel, *Aesthetics*, 1:170.

89. Jowell, *Thoré-Bürger and the Art of the Past*, 252. For Hegel's influence on this line of argument, see also Demetz, "Defenses of Dutch Painting," 112–13.

90. Demetz, "Defenses of Dutch Painting," 112.

91. H[ippolyte] Taine, *Philosophie de l'art dans les Pays-Bas* (Paris: Germer Baillière: 1869), 118.

92. For an account of Thoré-Bürger's practical involvement with the contemporary art market, see Frances Suzman Jowell, "Thoré-Bürger and Vermeer: Critical and Commercial Fortunes," in *Shop Talk: Studies in Honor of Seymour Slive*, ed. Cynthia P. Schneider et al. (Cambridge, Mass.: Harvard University Press, 1995), 124–27; and Jowell, "Thoré-Bürger—A Critical Rôle in the Art Market," *Burlington Magazine* 138 (1996): 115–29. Jowell is surely right to suggest that Thoré-Bürger's various interventions in the market, including purchases of his own as well as advice to collectors, were not wholly disinterested; but this useful reminder of mixed motives should not obscure the fact that the potential conflicts of interest she identifies appear in no way exceptional for art scholarship well into the twentieth century.

93. In the chapter on the "English school" in *Trésors d'art*, Thoré-Bürger writes with some irony, but not unsympathetically, of Ruskin's almost "delirious" enthusiasm for Turner (420). Ruskin himself he calls "altogether independent of any prejudices whatever—except English prejudices" (421n). It is amusing to speculate on what Ruskin would have said of Thoré-Bürger's judgment that the best Turners on display at Manchester "come close to" the work of the Dutch or of Claude (422).

94. Bürger, *Trésors d'art*, 185; Ruskin, *Works*, 22:42. Ruskin's response was elicited by a London exhibition of the painting in 1871; there is no evidence that he knew of Thoré-Bürger's remarks of thirteen years earlier.

95. According to Seymour Slive, the Dutch only began to use this term around 1650. Before then, they either called such pictures "still standing objects" (*stilstaende dingen*), or classified them by subject—"banquet" (*bancquet*), "fruit piece" (*fruytagie*),

"flower pot" (*blompot*), and so forth. See Slive, *Dutch Painting: 1600–1800* (New Haven: Yale University Press, 1995), 277.

96. Bürger, *Trésors d'art*, 314.

97. Cf. Ovid, *Metamorphoses*, 15:165—*omnia mutantur, nihil interit*. Thoré-Bürger is presumably quoting from memory.

98. Only in defense of Dutch painting, in fact, was Thoré-Bürger prepared to endorse such a radical equivalence of persons and things. Writing on Manet in a *Salon* of 1868, he would explicitly criticize the "sort of pantheism which thinks no more of a head than a slipper, [and] which sometimes bestows even more importance on a basket of flowers than on a woman's face" (*Salon de 1868*, 2:531–33; as translated and quoted by Francis Haskell, *Rediscoveries*, 89–90). It is possible, of course, that Thoré-Bürger's sense of priorities had actually shifted in the eight years that had intervened since the appearance of *Musées de la Hollande*; but it seems more likely that his enthusiasm for the "ART OF MAN" was so powerful that it drove him, paradoxically, thus to override his fundamental humanism.

CHAPTER THREE
Balzac's Bourgeois Interiors and the Quest for the Absolute

1. W. Bürger [Théophile Thoré], *Musées de la Hollande*, 2 vols. (Paris: Jules Renouard, 1858–60), 2:58–59.

2. For this shift in de Hooch's style, which follows his move from Delft to Amsterdam, see Wayne Franits, *Dutch Seventeenth-Century Genre Painting: Its Stylistic and Thematic Evolution* (New Haven: Yale University Press, 2004), 185–87. As Franits makes clear, however, the spacious rooms and marble floors of such paintings should be viewed more as tokens of luxury aimed at upper-class patrons than as faithful representations of the houses in which those patrons actually lived. For commentary on this image in particular, including its appeal to Thoré-Bürger, see Peter C. Sutton's entry in the catalogue of Sutton et al., *Love Letters: Dutch Genre Paintings in the Age of Vermeer* (Greenwich, Conn. and Dublin, Ireland: Bruce Museum of Arts and Science and National Gallery of Ireland, 2003), 176.

3. Honoré de Balzac, *Eugénie Grandet* (1833), ed. Nicole Mozet, in Balzac, *La comédie humaine*, ed. Pierre-Georges Castex, 12 vols., Bibliothèque de la Pléiade (Paris: Gallimard, 1976), 3:1027. Further citations to this edition, preceded by *CH*, will be given parenthetically in the text. Balzac's habit of endlessly revising and reassembling his work often makes the textual history of individual novels quite complicated: for simplicity's sake, the dates given throughout this chapter are those of initial book publication.

4. Sutton, *Love Letters*, 176.

5. Armand Baschet, *Honoré de Balzac: Essai sur l'homme et sur l'oeuvre, avec notes historiques par Champfleury* (Paris: D. Giraud et Dagneau, 1852), 209.

6. This was not the only time Thoré-Bürger had associated Balzac with a particularly English idea of home. Observing that David Wilkie's *Letter of Introduction*

(1814) in the Manchester Art Exhibition of 1857 could have been "taken from a novel by Balzac," Thoré-Bürger simultaneously paid tribute to the English gift for rendering private life—what he called, in a characteristic mix of French and English, "les drames et les mystères de la vie intérieure, du chez soi, *the home*, la citadelle de la famille et des serviteurs, *servants and attendants*, de tous les degrés"—and declared that the novelist, on this side of him, had "un peu du génie britannique." See W. Bürger [Théophile Thoré], *Trésors d'art en Angleterre*, 3rd ed. (Paris: Jules Renouard, 1865), 407. (The first edition of *Trésors* appeared in 1857.) As Thoré-Bürger clearly knew, "home" is not a word that can be directly translated into French, though it has good cognates in Dutch and German. (See John Hollander, "What You Mean by Home," in *The Work of Poetry* [New York: Columbia University Press, 1997], 70.) As he also surely knew, the particular English artist with whom he associated Balzac here was himself heavily indebted to the art of the Netherlands.

7. In his role as a dealer, Thoré (as he then was) had apparently offered to purchase two paintings in the novelist's collection—a head by Greuze and a work described only as the "groupe de la grosse flamande et de son enfant"—but Balzac declined to part with them. See his letter to Thoré of 13 December 1846 (number 2458), in Honoré de Balzac, *Correspondance*, ed. Roger Pierrot, 5 vols. (Paris: Garnier, 1960–69), 5:169.

8. See, e.g., the oft-quoted assertion of the "Avant-propos" (1842) to the *Comédie humaine* that identifies "the Family and not the Individual as the true social element" (*CH* 1:13).

9. To Madame Hanska, 14 December 1846, in Honoré de Balzac, *Lettres à Madame Hanska*, ed. Roger Pierrot, 2 vols. (Paris: Robert Laffont, 1990), 2:466.

10. The phrase is George Henry Lewes's. See "Recent Novels—French and English," *Fraser's* 36 (1847): 695.

11. Cf. Margaret Cohen, who approaches these lines from a somewhat different perspective in *The Sentimental Education of the Novel* (Princeton: Princeton University Press, 1999), 115–16. Seeking to understand how Balzac and Stendhal managed to wrest the novel away from their female contemporaries, Cohen argues that here and elsewhere Balzac aggressively deployed his realist details, implicitly coded as masculine, against the deliberate generalizing of the female sentimental tradition. I find her argument as a whole compelling; but rather than presume, as she appears to do, that the realist detail arrived on the scene securely gendered from the start, I would suggest that it was only when Balzac managed to identify it primarily with science rather than Dutch painting that it lost the vaguely feminine aura with which it had long been associated. Balzac's early defensiveness about Dutch painting (which Cohen does not mention) is very far from his bold comparisons of his work to that of the naturalists in his "Avant-propos" to the *Comédie humaine* twelve years later. For the feminine associations of the detail and its role in Dutch art, see Naomi Schor, *Reading in Detail: Aesthetics and the Feminine* (New York: Methuen, 1987), esp. 11–41.

12. The advertisement of 1828 attributed these words to one "Victor Morillon," the ostensible author of a forthcoming novel then to be called *Gars*; but by the

time the work was published as *Le dernier Chouan*, Balzac had evidently decided to issue it under his own name (*CH* 8:1669n).

13. Review of *Scènes de la vie privée*, *Le globe*, 25 June 1830, 518.

14. S[amuel] Henry Berthoud, "Études littéraires: M. Honoré de Balzac," *Musée des familles* 9 (October 1841): 31–32. For Berthoud's relations with Balzac and his possible influence on the Flemish setting of *La recherche de l'absolu*, see Madeleine Ambrière, *Balzac et "La recherche de l'absolu"* (1968; rpt. Paris: Quadrigue, 1999), 257–67. (The first edition of 1968 appeared under the name of Madeleine Fargeaud.)

15. In 1830 the tale now called *La maison du chat-qui-pelote* had introduced the second volume of the *Scènes de la vie privée*, under the title *Gloire et malheur*.

16. As one critic sums up the critical consensus on this opening: "c'est un peu *la Comédie humaine* tout entière qui s'ouvre sur ce tableau." See Oliver Bonard, *La peinture dans la création Balzacienne: Invention et vision picturales de "La maison du chat-qui-pelote" au "Père Goriot"* (Geneva: Librairie Droz, 1969), 18.

17. One of the most popular Dutch painters in the first half of the nineteenth century, Dou virtually invented the so-called niche format in the 1640s. See Martha Hollander, *An Entrance for the Eyes: Space and Meaning in Seventeenth-Century Dutch Art* (Berkeley: University of California Press 2002), 48.

18. The phrase "qui se souvient du ciel," probably inspired by a poem of Lamartine, was added in 1835; the text published in 1830 simply compared Augustine to "un ange exilé." (See Anne-Marie Meininger's note to the Pléiade text—*CH* 1:1194.)

19. The ms. originally set the tale in 1808 (*CH* 1:1184).

20. Cf. Bonard, who argues that the entire tale should be read from the painter's point of view, "as if Balzac had found in this character . . . not only a poetic figure in himself, but above all a means of seeing and apprehending reality, a view of the world that at the same time creates and justifies the pictorial technique of the narrative." Bonard ingeniously suggests that what we are given in the opening pages is not so much "reality as such" as the "literary transcription" of the two pictures that the artist later exhibits at the Salon (*Peinture dans la création Balzacienne*, 18, 22).

21. For brief accounts of Balzac's fondness for this feminine type, see Bonard, *Peinture dans la création Balzacienne,* 96, and Philippe Le Leyzour, "Liminaires," in *Balzac et la peinture*, ed. Jean-Pierre Boyer and Élisabeth Boyer-Peigné (Tours: Musée des Beaux-Arts de Tours, 1999), 18. On Balzac's lifelong admiration of Raphael—who remained for him, as for most of his contemporaries, the supreme artist in paint—see Pierre Laubriet, *L'intelligence de l'art chez Balzac: D'une esthétique Balzacienne* (Paris: Didier, 1961), 399–400.

22. To Mme Hanska, 4 February 1844, in Balzac, *Lettres à Madame Hanska*, 1:801.

23. See *CH* 3:1718. The Pléiade text of *Eugénie Grandet*, edited by Nicole Mozet, follows the Furne edition of 1843, as subsequently corrected by the novelist.

24. For the speculation that the "sketchily indicated map on the wall" in Metsu's painting alludes to the author of the woman's letter, see Jennifer Kilian's catalogue entry in *Love Letters*, 122.

25. [John Wilson Croker], "French Novels," *Quarterly Review* 56 (April 1836): 91.

26. Reprinted in 1839, the preface to *Eugénie Grandet* was cut, like other prefaces to individual novels, from the Furne edition of the *Comédie humaine* in 1843.

27. Cf. Bonard, *Peinture dans la création Balzacienne,* 138–54. Bonard, who likewise takes for granted that the author of *Eugénie Grandet* had Dutch painting in mind, notes that this dark palette was further emphasized for the novelist by the fact that much of his acquaintance with that painting came through black-and-white engravings. Here and elsewhere in his book, Bonard also shrewdly suggests that Balzac's imagination was often stimulated by this fact to produce work that fused the influences of Dutch painting and contemporary caricature.

28. Other instances of this formula and its variant, "jamais" (i.e., never before), can be found at *CH* 3:1059, 1096, 1097, 1100. For a feminist and psychoanalytic reading of the novel that also calls attention to this pattern, see Naomi Schor, *Breaking the Chain: Women, Theory, and French Realist Fiction* (New York: Columbia University Press, 1985), 97–98.

29. F. W. J. Hemmings, *Balzac: An Interpretation of "La Comédie Humaine"* (New York: Random House, 1967), 19.

30. On the looseness of Balzac's classificatory system, see Herbert J. Hunt, *Balzac's "Comédie Humaine"* (London: Athlone, 1959), 125–34. For a reading of *La recherche de l'absolu* that consigns it firmly to the class of *Études philosophiques* and dismisses any connection with realism, see Maurice Bardèche, *Une lecture de Balzac* (Paris: Les Sept Couleurs, 1964), 80–85.

31. Ambrière, *Balzac et "La recherche de l'absolu,"* 24–33. As will become evident, my account of this novel is much indebted to Ambrière's patient detective work, both in this book and in her editing of the text for volume 10 of the Pléiade *Comédie humaine*, where she appears as Madeleine Fargeaud.

32. For some related observations on the confluence in the novel of the realist and the visionary, see Albert Béguin, *Balzac lu et relu* (Paris: Éditions du Seuil, 1965), 234–38. Cf. also Ambrière, who argues that by finding his "balance" between *Étude des moeurs* and *Étude philosophique* in the writing of *La recherche*, Balzac discovered, in effect, "his formula for the novel" (*Balzac et "La recherche de l'absolu,"* 455).

33. Ambrière, *Balzac et "La recherche de l'absolu,"* 331. The most famous of such collections appears in the late novel, *Cousin Pons* (1848).

34. For the modern reader, perhaps the most familiar version of this law is the oft-quoted line about the relation between the Maison Vauquer and its proprietor in *Père Goriot* (1835)—"her whole person, in short, explains the boarding-house, just as the boarding-house implies her person" (*CH* 3:54).

35. Cf. Taine, who manages to tease the slightest of narratives out of a remarkably similar vision: "A peaceful and happy harmony emanates from all these pictures; one rests oneself in looking at them; the spirit of the artist like that of his figures is in equilibrium; one would feel very much at ease in his picture. One sees that he imagines nothing beyond that; it seems as if he is, like his figures, content to live;

nature seems to him good; all that he thinks of adding to it is an arrangement, a shade near a shade, an effect of light, a choice of attitudes; before it, he is like a happily married Hollander before his wife; he doesn't wish her at all different: he loves by a habit of heart and intimate compatibility; all the same, some holiday, he asks her to put on her red dress instead of her blue dress" (H[ippolyte] Taine, *Philosophie de l'art dans les Pays-Bas* [Paris: Germer Baillière, 1869], 161).

36. Michael Fried, *Absorption and Theatricality: Painting and Beholder in the Age of Diderot* (Berkeley: University of California Press, 1980).

37. See Ambrière, *Balzac et "La recherche de l'absolu,"* 293–320.

38. Norman Bryson, *Looking at the Overlooked: Four Essays on Still Life Painting* (Cambridge, Mass.: Harvard University Press, 1990), 135. (The definition of *rhopos* appears on 61.) Bryson in turn borrows these terms from Charles Sterling, *Still Life Painting: From Antiquity to the Twentieth Century* (New York: Harper and Row, 1981).

39. The pleasure with which Madame Claës awaits her husband once lights up her face "like that of a beautiful Italian Madonna"; and Marguerite's lover briefly compares her to an angel by Guido (*CH* 10:670, 741).

40. Cf. Ambrière, who adopts the idiom of *Eugénie Grandet* (where the daughter finally proves "plus Grandet" than her father) to observe that "Marguerite se révèle 'plus Claës' que Balthazar" (*Balzac et "La recherche de l'absolu,"* 431).

41. As one of the novelist's finest critics has written, "I defy a reader of good faith to say where Balzac's sympathies lie this time" (Béguin, *Balzac lu et relu*, 235). Though Béguin immediately goes on to invoke a "loi romanesque" by which Balthazar's folly, rather than his family's suffering, inevitably dominates the reader's memory (236), the memory of at least one celebrated reader would appear to call that law into question: for Marcel Proust, the novel is "far more concerned with the havoc that the egoism of a ruling passion spreads in the loving family that suffers it, whatever the object of that passion may be," than it is with Balthazar's quest. See Marcel Proust, *Contre Saint-Beuve, précédé de Pastiches et mélanges et suivi de Essais et articles*, ed. Pierre Clarac and Yves Sandre, Bibliothèque de la Pléiade (Paris: Gallimard, 1971), 269n. For other accounts of Balzac's divided sympathies in this novel, see Hemmings, *Balzac*, 24, and Ambrière's remarks on its "balance" cited in note 32, above.

42. To Mme Hanska, 26 August 1834, in *Lettres à Madame Hanska* 1:188.

43. Josué Harari, "The Pleasures of Science and the Pains of Philosophy: Balzac's *Quest for the Absolute*," *Yale French Studies* 67 (1984): 144n.

44. See, e.g., Hemmings, *Balzac*, 20; or Nicole Mozet, *La ville de province dans l'oeuvre de Balzac: L'espace romanesque: fantasmes et idéologie* (Paris: Société d'édition d'enseignement supérieur, 1982), 156. Hemmings gives **BAL**tha**ZA**r **C**laës, while Mozet simply notes the echo of Bal(tha)zar and Balzac. Ambrière's demonstration that both the chemist's first and last names have good Flemish precedents does not, of course, preclude this sort of word play, of which the novelist was quite fond (*Balzac et "La recherche de l'absolu,"* 427–28). For the argument that Balzac's project

as a whole shares Balthazar's impulse to reduce all of creation to a "unique principle," see André Allemand, *Unité et structure de l'univers Balzacien* (Paris: Plon, 1965), 49–51.

45. A loose translation in the first complete English edition of the *Comédie humaine* ironically perpetuates this confusion: by gliding over the implications of the "disait-on" that immediately precedes one of Balzac's allusions to "la pierre philosophale" (*CH* 10:688), the English version has Mme Claës simply "learn[ing]" from "officious" friends that her husband "was bent on discovering the Philosopher's Stone." See volume 21 of *Honoré de Balzac in Twenty-Five Volumes: The First Complete Translation into English* (New York: Peter Fenelon Collier and Son, 1900): 329. The translation in question, by Ellen Marriage, first appeared as a separate volume in 1896, and remains to the best of my knowledge the only one widely available in English.

46. Cf. Pierre Laubriet, who groups Balthazar with Frenhofer (*Chef d'oeuvre inconnu*) and Gambara, on the grounds that all three can be seen as ahead of their time—sublime madmen who are also "precursors" of modernity (*Intelligence de l'art chez Balzac*, 221).

47. See Franits, *Dutch Seventeenth-Century Genre Painting*, 140–42.

48. Christopher Brown, *Images of a Golden Past: Dutch Genre Painting of the Seventeenth Century* (New York: Abbeville, 1984), 100.

49. For Ostade's echo of Breughel, see Brown, *Images,* 100. For the costume of Steen's alchemist, see H. Perry Chapman, "The Merry Threesome," in Chapman et al., *Jan Steen: Painter and Storyteller*, ed. Guido M. C. Jansen (New Haven: Yale University Press, 1996), 237n1.

50. This suggestion is partly inspired by Nanette Salomon's recent observation that Dutch genre painting after 1650 helped to create a feeling of nostalgia for the "domestic" by defining it "as a sort of representational opposite, a countersign, as it were, of the tropes of public interior spaces such as guesthouses, taverns, and bordellos." An alchemist's study is not, of course, a public space in this sense; but its messy interior can similarly work, I believe, to conjure up what it violates, especially when the objects strewn about closely resemble the housekeeper's pots and pans. See Nanette Salomon, *Shifting Priorities: Gender and Genre in Seventeenth-Century Dutch Painting* (Stanford: Stanford University Press, 2004), 52.

51. For the manuscript reading, see Ambrière, *Balzac et "La recherche de l'absolu,"* 382–83, and the note to the Pléiade edition (*CH* 10:1592).

52. Ambrière, *Balzac et "La recherche de l'absolu,"* 78–84, 233–34, 285–93, 329–34.

53. Cf. Hemmings, who calls it "a book for the *balzacien* rather than for the general reader" and concludes that "it does not reflect life so much as demonstrate a theorem" (*Balzac*, 29).

54. As it happens, the first two full-length novels that appeared in English (both in 1859) were *Eugénie Grandet* and *Balthazar; or, Science and Love*. See Walter M. Kendrick, "Balzac and British Realism: Mid-Victorian Theories of the Novel," *Victorian Studies* 20 (1976): 6.

55. To Mary Russell Mitford, 20 May 1844, in *The Letters of Elizabeth Barrett Browning to Mary Russell Mitford*, ed. Meredith B. Raymond and Mary Rose Sullivan, 3 vols. ([Waco, Tex.]: Armstrong Browning Library of Baylor University, 1983), 2:414. The ellipses are Barrett Browning's.

56. Cf. Peter Brooks, who argues that "the whole of Balzac's work strives toward . . . the question of what is by its nature not directly representable, yet also the most significant" and who briefly identifies this striving with the quest for the Absolute. In Balthazar Claës, Brooks aptly remarks, the novelist "elaborates most fully the figure who neglects the vehicles of representation in the search for an ineffable tenor" (*The Melodramatic Imagination: Balzac, Henry James, Melodrama, and the Mode of Excess* [New Haven: Yale University Press, 1976], 115, 116).

57. Henry James, "Honoré de Balzac" (1902), rpt. in *Henry James: Literary Criticism: French Writers, Other European Writers, The Prefaces to the New York Edition*, ed. Leon Edel and Mark Wilson (New York: Library of America, 1984), 95. Another equivocal admirer is Albert Béguin, who claims to have long thought it Balzac's "masterpiece, or at least . . . the best of his non-'Balzacien' novels"—though subsequent rereading of other parts of the *Comédie humaine* apparently moderated that preference (*Balzac lu et relu*, 195).

58. Maurice Bardèche calls it "the story of a soul" (*Une lecture de Balzac*, 375).

59. André Lorant, the editor of the Pléiade text, identifies a precedent as far back as one of the pseudonymous fictions of 1824, *Annette et le criminel ou suite du Vicaire des Ardennes*. Lorant also notes strong affinities between *Le curé de village* and *Le lys dans la vallée* of 1836 (*CH* 9:616–19)—the novel that Barrett Browning seems to have had most immediately in mind when she alluded to Balzac's "Italian soul" (To Mary Russell Mitford, 20 May 1844, *Letters of Elizabeth Barrett Browning to Mary Russell Mitford*, 2:414).

60. Schor, *Breaking the Chain*, 106–7.

61. The words I quote refer immediately to the novel's shrewd bishop, but similar insights are attributed to the titular curé as well as to a doctor who attends the dying woman. Though the doctor's agnosticism might seem to exclude him from this visionary company, he is miraculously converted to Catholicism by the spectacle of Véronique's deathbed repentance.

62. Brooks, *Melodramatic Imagination*, 142.

63. To Mme Hanska, 10 May 1841, Balzac, *Lettres à Madame Hanska*, 1:510.

64. That a critic otherwise sympathetic to Catholic fiction finds the whole spectacle of the deathbed ritual in *Le curé de village* lacking in "verisimilitude" may only confirm how little the novel is concerned with any form of realism. See Philippe Bertault, *Balzac and the Human Comedy*, trans. Richard Monges (New York: Gotham Library, 1963), 111.

65. Bürger, *Musées de la Hollande*, 1:326.

66. W. Bürger [Théophile Thoré], "Van der Meer de Delft," *Gazette des beaux-arts* 21 (1866): 458.

67. See the note to the Pléiade text, edited by Anne-Marie Meininger (*CH* 6:1565). Though Meininger finds this account of the dealer's origins "surprising," Magus is not the only character in the *Comédie humaine* to undergo such metamorphoses; and his multiply Netherlandish identity in this tale is, of course, very much to the point.

68. Arthur K. Wheelock, Jr., "Dou's Reputation," in *Gerrit Dou 1613–1675: Master Painter in the Age of Rembrandt*, ed. Wheelock (New Haven: Yale University Press, 2000), 13.

69. Whether deliberately or not, *La rabouilleuse* alters this history: with the help of Gros and Gérard, according to the later fiction, Joseph won the Legion of Honor at the Salon of 1827.

70. Martin Kanes, *Balzac's Comedy of Words* (Princeton: Princeton University Press, 1975), 208.

71. Bürger, *Musées de la Hollande*, 1:80.

CHAPTER FOUR
George Eliot's Defense of Dutch Painting

1. George Eliot, *Adam Bede*, ed. Valentine Cunningham (Oxford: Oxford University Press, 1996), 17.175. Unless otherwise specified, all further references to the novel are to this edition (which is based on the first edition of 1859) and are given parenthetically by chapter and page number in the text. I cite this Oxford edition rather than the Clarendon (2001), since the latter follows the corrected (1861) eighth edition, which introduces several significant changes to chapter 17 in particular. (See notes 3 and 87, below.)

2. Though the novelist implicitly genders the narrators of her early fiction as masculine, "George Eliot" clearly names a woman author, whose identity became widely known after the publication of *Adam Bede*; and this chapter has so often been taken—rightly, in my view—as a defense of her own art as to warrant the feminine pronoun for its speaker. For particularly helpful discussions of the early masculine persona and the lifting of the pseudonym, see Gillian Beer, "Putting on Man's Apparel: The Early Fiction," in *George Eliot* (Brighton: Harvester, 1986), 52–81; and Rosemarie Bodenheimer, "The Outing of George Eliot," in *The Real Life of Mary Ann Evans: George Eliot, Her Letters and Fiction* (Ithaca: Cornell University Press, 1994), 119–60.

3. According to the editor of the Clarendon *Adam Bede*, the manuscript records that the "Dutch" paintings in this famous passage were originally "Flemish": at some point, George Eliot crossed out the latter word and substituted the former. Though the novelist presumably thought her final choice more accurate, the ease with which she made the correction is yet one more sign of how relatively interchangeable these national designations often were for nineteenth-century commentators. See Carol A. Martin, introduction, *Adam Bede* (Oxford: Clarendon, 2001), xxxvi.

4. George Eliot arrived in Munich on April 14, 1858; by her own account, she began the second volume of the novel in the second week of her stay. See her

"History of 'Adam Bede,'" in *The George Eliot Letters*, ed. Gordon S. Haight, 9 vols. (New Haven: Yale University Press, 1954–78), 2:504. On April 16, she noted in her journal, "We have been taking sips of the Glypothek, and the two Pinacotheks, in the mornings, not having settled to work yet." A month later, she was still apparently looking at Netherlandish painting, but she had finished both the seventeenth and eighteenth chapters of her novel. The entry for May 14 notes: "After writing we went for an hour to the Pinacothek and looked at some of the Flemish pictures." The following day's entry begins, "Read the 18th chapter of Adam Bede to G." See *The Journals of George Eliot*, ed. Margaret Harris and Judith Johnston (Cambridge: Cambridge University Press, 1998), 310, 316.

5. Hugh Witemeyer, *George Eliot and the Visual Arts* (New Haven: Yale University Press, 1979), 108. Witemeyer in turn credits two unpublished dissertations: Norma Jean Davis, "Pictorialism in George Eliot's Art" (Ph. D. Diss., Northwestern University, 1972), 71; and Bernard A. Richards, "The Use of the Visual Arts in the Nineteenth-Century Novel" (Ph. D. Diss., Oxford University, 1972), 152.

6. Cf. J. Hillis Miller's subtle account of this chapter in *The Ethics of Reading: Kant, de Man, Eliot, Trollope, James, and Benjamin* (New York: Columbia University Press, 1987), 61–80. Though I agree with Miller that this famous appeal to Dutch genre painting may encourage us to forget the "problem of the medium in literary realism" (67), his argument for the necessary figurativeness of language takes for granted that pictures, by contrast, are somehow unproblematic. "An exact copy" is not possible in painting either (77); nor does George Eliot really suggest that it is.

7. Joshua Reynolds, Discourse 12 (10 December 1784), in *Discourses on Art*, ed. Robert R. Wark (New Haven: Yale University Press, 1997), 210. According to Witemeyer, George Eliot's library included an 1825 edition of the *Discourses*, though she never explicitly referred to it in writing (*George Eliot and the Visual Arts*, 18).

8. John Ruskin, *Modern Painters III*, in *The Works of John Ruskin*, ed. E. T. Cook and Alexander Wedderburn, 39 vols. (London: George Allen, 1903–12), 5:141. Further references to this edition of Ruskin's works will be given by volume and page number parenthetically in the text.

9. [George Eliot], "John Ruskin's *Modern Painters*, Vol. III," in *George Eliot: Selected Critical Writings*, ed. Rosemary Ashton (Oxford: Oxford University Press, 1992), 248. The *Oxford English Dictionary* dates the first use of "realism" in this aesthetic sense to the fourth volume of *Modern Painters*, also published in 1856; but as I have noted above, the English word had already been given this meaning in an essay on Balzac published by the *Westminster Review* three years earlier. See chapter 1, note 23, above.

10. Cf. Darrel Mansell, Jr., "Ruskin and George Eliot's 'Realism,'" *Criticism* 7 (1965): 203–16. Though Mansell is surely right to note the affinities between the two writers, he works so hard to argue for their shared emphasis on "subjective truth" that he ends up identifying the "mirror of the author's mind" with George Eliot's most famous metaphor for the power of egoistic distortion—the image of the candle organizing the scratches of the pier-glass in *Middlemarch* (207, 215).

Witemeyer, who cites Mansell approvingly, is more nuanced; but his understandable impatience with Mario Praz's "crude and unilluminating characterization of Eliot's art as 'Biedermeier'" leads him to minimize her early defense of Dutch genre and to gloss over her differences with Ruskin in this regard. It is hard to know what to make of his claim that chapter 17 of *Adam Bede* "echo[es] Ruskin's defense of Dutch painting against the categorical strictures of Reynolds" (*George Eliot and the Visual Arts*, 106–7). For Praz, see *The Hero in Eclipse in Victorian Fiction* (London: Oxford, 1956), 319–83. See also G. Wittig Davis, "Ruskin's *Modern Painters* and George Eliot's Concept of Realism," *English Language Notes* 18 (1981): 194–201.

11. For an exemplary discussion of the ways in which the imaginative landscape of realistic English fiction, George Eliot's included, differs from Ruskin's, see George Levine, *The Realistic Imagination: English Fiction from Frankenstein to Lady Chatterley* (Chicago: University of Chicago Press, 1981), 204–26.

12. Cf. Gillian Beer's astute characterization of George Eliot's intent in this novel: "The writing should *work*, through description, through analysis, through rumination. It should be a part of the working world it describes" (*George Eliot*, 60).

13. "Gerard Douw," *The Illustrated Magazine of Art* 3, no. 14 (1854): 127, as quoted in Arthur K. Wheelock, Jr., "Dou's Reputation," in *Gerrit Dou 1613–1675: Master Painter in the Age of Rembrandt*, ed. Wheelock (New Haven: Yale University Press, 2000), 13.

14. Seymour Slive, *Dutch Painting: 1600–1800* (New Haven: Yale University Press, 1995), 103.

15. To Sara Sophia Hennell, 10–13 May 1858, *Letters*, 2:454.

16. George Eliot and Lewes had traveled from Munich to Dresden by way of Vienna, where they might well have seen Dou's *Old Woman at the Window, Watering Her Flowers* (fig. 4-1). See Witemeyer, *George Eliot and the Visual Arts*, 217n14.

17. As Witemeyer has remarked, the specificity of these details "show[s] how attentively Eliot could look at a picture that interested her" (*George Eliot and the Visual Arts*, 108).

18. Ian Watt, *The Rise of the Novel: Studies in Defoe, Richardson and Fielding* (Berkeley: University of California Press, 1967), 18–21. As Watt conceded, however, even the most realistic of novelists often flirt with names that carry symbolic or other significance: witness the double suggestion of an idealized past, both biblical and Anglo-Saxon, in George Eliot's naming of her carpenter-hero.

19. "Recollections of Our Journey from Munich to Dresden" (1858), in *Journals*, 326.

20. For identifications of some of these, see Praz, *The Hero in Eclipse*, 359–62; Witemeyer, *George Eliot and the Visual Arts*, 108–10; and Martin Meisel, *Realizations: Narrative, Pictorial, and Theatrical Arts in Nineteenth-Century England* (Princeton: Princeton University Press, 1983), 59–60.

21. Mrs [Anna] Jameson, *Companion to the Most Celebrated Private Galleries of Art in London* (London: Saunders and Otley, 1844), 142.

22. As Hugh Witemeyer has shrewdly remarked, nineteenth-century photographs of the Warwickshire countryside "suggest how readily the scenes and customs Eliot knew as a girl could be perceived in terms of genre painting" (*George Eliot and the Visual Arts*, 106).

23. Levine, *Realistic Imagination*, 204–26.

24. For some related observations on this tendency to picture-making in the early parts of the novel, see John Goode, "'Adam Bede,'" in *Critical Essays on George Eliot*, ed. Barbara Hardy (New York: Barnes and Noble, 1970), 22; Ian Adam, "The Structure of Realisms in *Adam Bede*," *Nineteenth-Century Fiction* 30 (1975): 131–33; and Meisel, *Realizations*, 59–60.

25. Cf. Gillian Beer's characteristically acute, if unelaborated, observation on the novel's close: "So at the end of the book we are left with genre-painting and the frame restored" (*George Eliot*, 73).

26. For illuminating observations on the stasis of *Adam Bede* from the perspective of natural history, see Sally Shuttleworth, *George Eliot and Nineteenth-Century Science: The Make-Believe of a Beginning* (Cambridge: Cambridge University Press, 1984), 24–50.

27. George Henry Lewes to John Blackwood, 6 November [1856], *George Eliot Letters*, 2:269.

28. The first to argue this connection was Roland F. Anderson, "George Eliot Provoked: John Blackwood and Chapter Seventeen of *Adam Bede*," *Modern Philology* 71 (1973): 39–47.

29. John Blackwood to George Henry Lewes, 12 November 1856, *George Eliot Letters*, 2:272.

30. George Eliot to William Blackwood, 4 February 1857, ibid., 291–92.

31. John Blackwood to George Eliot, 8 June 1857, and 7 July 1857, ibid., 345, 360.

32. "Art must be either real and concrete, or ideal and eclectic," the letter also observes. "Both are good and true in their way, but my stories are of the former kind" (George Eliot to John Blackwood, 12 [July] 1857, ibid., 362).

33. See "How I Came to Write Fiction," in *Journals*, 291; and Martin, introduction, *Adam Bede* (Clarendon, 2001), xiv–xv, xxii–xxiii.

34. John Blackwood to George Eliot, 31 March 1858, *George Eliot Letters*, 2:445.

35. Anderson, "George Eliot Provoked," 46–47. As Anderson notes, the second volume of the original three-volume edition opened with chapter 17.

36. George Eliot, *Scenes of Clerical Life*, ed. Thomas A. Noble (Oxford: Oxford University Press, 1988), 37. Future page references to this edition will be given parenthetically in the text.

37. More precisely, "he preached Low-Church doctrine—as evangelical as anything to be heard in the Independent Chapel; and he made a High-Church assertion of ecclesiastical powers and functions" (ibid., 14–15).

38. David Carroll, *George Eliot and the Conflict of Interpretations: A Reading of the Novels* (Cambridge: Cambridge University Press, 1992), 71. Carroll, too, instances this passage.

39. George Eliot, *Daniel Deronda*, ed. Graham Handley (Oxford: Oxford University Press, 1988), 56.591, 595, 597. "There were no words of comfort," Deronda thinks after hearing her out, "that did not carry some sacrilege" (597). Future references to this edition will be given parenthetically by chapter and page number in the text.

40. "Worldliness and Other-Worldliness: The Poet Young" (1857), in *Essays of George Eliot*, ed. Thomas Pinney (New York: Columbia University Press, 1963), 336. Future references to this essay will be given parenthetically by page numbers in the text.

41. For some principal contributions to the debate, see chap. 1, note 74, above.

42. Barry Qualls, "George Eliot and Religion," in *The Cambridge Companion to George Eliot*, ed. George Levine (Cambridge: Cambridge University Press, 2001), 119–37.

43. Ludwig Feuerbach, *The Essence of Christianity*, trans. George Eliot (New York: Harper and Row, 1957), 247. George Eliot translated the second edition (1843) of Feuerbach's *Das Wesen des Christentums*; the first appeared in 1841.

44. U. C. Knoepflmacher, *Religious Humanism and the Victorian Novel: George Eliot, Walter Pater, and Samuel Butler* (Princeton: Princeton University Press, 1965), 51–59. Cf. also George R. Creeger, "An Interpretation of *Adam Bede*" (1956), rpt. in *George Eliot: A Collection of Critical Essays*, ed. Creeger (Englewood Cliffs, N. J.: Prentice-Hall, 1970), 102–3; and Valentine Cunningham, introduction, *Adam Bede* (Oxford, 1996), xxxi–xxxii.

45. Feuerbach, *Essence of Christianity*, 278.

46. See David Leon Higdon, "The Iconographic Backgrounds of *Adam Bede*, Chapter 15," *Nineteenth-Century Fiction* 27 (1972): 155–70. Higdon associates the juxtaposition of Dinah and Hetty in chapter 15 with the paired female figures of Flesh and Spirit as they are represented in Emblem III, 14, of Francis Quarles's influential *Emblems* (1635). The parallels are not exact—in the engraving, the naked Flesh peers into a prism rather than a mirror, while the clothed Spirit looks through a telescope rather than a window—but Higdon makes a persuasive case for a shared iconographic "vocabulary" (162). See also Qualls, "George Eliot and Religion," 125.

47. See Wayne E. Franits, *Paragons of Virtue: Women and Domesticity in Seventeenth-Century Dutch Art* (Cambridge: Cambridge University Press, 1993), esp. 71–73. Among his many examples, interestingly, is the Dou painting of the *Spinner's Grace* that George Eliot recalls in chapter 17 of *Adam Bede* (*Paragons of Virtue*, 171–72).

48. Though Witemeyer acknowledges that the "painstaking realism" with which George Eliot represents the two women "emulates the spirit of Dutch painting," his apparent rejection of the analogy on the ground that "these concrete descriptive details compose themselves into coherent symbolic patterns as well" has been called into question by much recent work on the iconology of Dutch genre painting. He is probably right, however, to suggest that such painting rarely offers

the "sort of stark moral contrast" evident in the fifteenth chapter of *Adam Bede* (*George Eliot and the Visual Arts*, 90, 91).

49. For the argument that the female mirror-gazers in figs. 4-5 and 4–6 exemplify "an imitation of reality which is at the same time a realized abstraction," see Eddy de Jongh, "Realism and Seeming Realism in Seventeenth-Century Dutch Painting" (1971), rpt. in *Looking at Seventeenth-Century Dutch Art: Realism Reconsidered*, ed. Wayne Franits (Cambridge: Cambridge University Press, 1997), 51.

50. Anthony Trollope, *The Last Chronicle of Barset* (Oxford: Oxford University Press, 1967), 451–52.

51. Anthony Trollope, *An Autobiography* (Berkeley: University of California Press, 1947), 37, 303, 64, 181. For the comparisons of writing to specific trades, see 102, 268, 91. Though it was written in 1875–76, the *Autobiography* was only published posthumously in 1883.

52. Ibid., 205–6.

53. [A. V. Dicey], review of *Daniel Deronda*, *Nation* 23 (19 October 1876): 245. I owe the identification of Dicey's authorship to David Carroll, ed., *George Eliot: The Critical Heritage* (New York: Barnes and Noble, 1971), 399.

54. To Frederic Harrison, 15 August [1866], *Letters*, 4:300.

55. Cf. John Kucich, "George Eliot and Objects: Meaning as Matter in *The Mill on the Floss*," *Dickens Studies Annual* 12 (1983): 323.

56. Henry James, "The Life of George Eliot" (1885), rpt. in *Henry James: Literary Criticism . . . English Writers*, ed. Leon Edel and Mark Wilson (New York: Library of America, 1984), 1002.

57. "Recollections of Ilfracombe" (1856), in *Journals*, 264, 267, 268, 272. Future references to this essay will be given parenthetically by page numbers in the text.

58. "How I Came to Write Fiction," in *Journals*, 289.

59. See the editors' headnote to the "Recollections," in *Journals*, 259; and Witemeyer, *George Eliot and the Visual Arts*, 134–35.

60. Several of the essays that immediately preceded her turn to fiction, especially "Silly Novels by Lady Novelists" and the attack on Young, make clear how vehement her satire could be when largely unchecked by such compensatory impulses. The closest she comes to checking herself in the essay on Young is when she ironically enjoins us to "hope" that "he was not so bad as he pretended to be! The tides of the divine life in man move under the thickest ice of theory" ("Worldliness and Other-Worldliness," in *Essays*, 378).

61. Bodenheimer, *Real Life*, 119, 83.

62. For a particularly illuminating account of how this rupture in her identity shaped George Eliot's fiction, see Alexander Welsh, *George Eliot and Blackmail* (Cambridge, Mass.: Harvard University Press, 1985).

63. "History of 'Adam Bede'" (30 November 1858), in *Journals*, 297.

64. Noting the frequent use of words like "bovine" and "bucolic" to describe the peasantry in this novel, Ian Adam sharply remarks, "George Eliot's attitude

towards her past is sometimes very close to Pip's attitude towards Joe" ("Structure of Realisms," 149).

65. In an important essay on the novelist, George Levine suggests that the word "common" begins to take on negative overtones in her later fiction, as it comes to imply "not a democratic approval but a contemptible coarseness"; and he associates the turning point with Lydgate's "spots of commonness" in *Middlemarch* ("George Eliot's Hypothesis of Reality," *Nineteenth-Century Fiction* 35 [1980]: 16). But while there is no question about the dismissive resonance of that "common"—as opposed, say, to *Adam Bede*'s "faithful representing of commonplace things" (17.178)—George Eliot's unguarded use of the term in the later novel has as much to do with Lydgate's otherwise distinguished status, I think, as with any newfound distaste for the stupid and the vulgar. When the commonness in question attaches to those who are more obviously the novelist's moral and intellectual inferiors—*Deronda*'s "common Jews," for example—her last novel, like her first, struggles to conquer its squeamishness: "The fact was, notwithstanding all his sense of poetry in common things, Deronda, where a keen personal interest was aroused, could not, more than the rest of us, continuously escape suffering from the pressure of that hard unaccommodating Actual, which has never consulted our taste and is entirely unselect. Enthusiasm, we know, dwells at ease among ideas, tolerates garlic breathed in the middle ages, and sees no shabbiness in the official trappings of classic processions: it gets squeamish when ideals press upon it as something warmly incarnate, and can hardly face them without fainting" (33.321).

66. Cf. Bodenheimer, who notes how the early George Eliot characteristically invents "oppositional" readers in order to argue with herself (*Real Life*, 51–56). Though Bodenheimer does not mention the running argument with Blackwood, there is a deeper sense in which she is still right to include the resisting reader of *Adam Bede* in this invented company. Of the novelist's deployment of such rhetorical quarrels, she astutely observes: "the reading audience is not so much addressed as called to witness a confrontation between the writer and an audience located in some fearful and scornful part of her consciousness" (51–52).

67. Todorov, *Éloge du quotidien: Essai sur la peinture hollandaise du XVII*[e] *siècle* (Paris: Adam Biro, 1993), 74.

68. That Dou's spinner is actually saying grace for her meal rather than consuming it may further dignify her, but George Eliot says—or recalls—nothing of the fact, her imagination preferring to assimilate the sacral implications of the original to the simple act of eating itself.

69. Hessel Miedema, "Realism and Comic Mode: The Peasant," *Simiolus* 9 (1977): 210. Miedema has in mind primarily representations of peasants "gorging and swilling, capering and gambling, embracing and fighting." Cf. Wayne Franits, who attributes the greater decorum of peasants in Dutch art after 1650 to patrons' increasing preference for more dignified images and resists the idea that they responded with what modern viewers would identify as "sympathy" (*Dutch Seventeenth-Century Genre Painting: Its Stylistic and Thematic Evolution* [New Haven: Yale University Press, 2004], 138).

70. "The Natural History of German Life" (1856), in *Essays*, 269. The essay opposes such idyllic images to the "truthfulness" of genre paintings by Teniers and Murillo. "Rather than such cockney sentimentality as this," she remarks at one point, "we prefer the most crapulous group of boors that Teniers ever painted" (268).

71. See Joseph Weisenfarth, "George Eliot's Notes for *Adam Bede*," *Nineteenth-Century Fiction* 32 (1977): 127–65.

72. James, "Life of George Eliot," in *Literary Criticism . . . English Writers*, 1004. For some representative discussions of *Adam Bede* and the other early novels as pastoral, see R. A. Foakes, "*Adam Bede* Reconsidered," *English* 12 (1959): 173–76; U. C. Knoepflmacher, *George Eliot's Early Novels: The Limits of Realism* (Berkeley: University of California Press, 1968), 89–127; Michael Squires, *The Pastoral Novel: Studies in George Eliot, Thomas Hardy, and D. H. Lawrence* (Charlottesville: University of Virginia Press, 1974), 53–105; Kenny Marotta, "*Adam Bede* as a Pastoral," *Genre* 9 (1976): 59–72; and Welsh, *George Eliot and Blackmail*, 132–56. Cf. also Raymond Williams's oft-quoted complaint that "George Eliot restores the real inhabitants of rural England to their places" but "does not get much further than restoring them *as a landscape*" (*The Country and the City* [New York: Oxford University Press, 1973], 168).

73. Marcel Proust, "Tableaux de genre du souvenir," in *Les Plaisirs et les jours* (1896). I quote from Proust, *Jean Santeuil précédé de Les plaisirs et les jours*, ed. Pierre Clarac and Yves Sandre (Paris: Gallimard, 1971), 130.

74. *Journals* (17 November 1854), 34. That she could simultaneously find "the beauty of detail" and "marvellous painting of still life" in such pictures "very remarkable" hardly distinguishes her position, after all, from Reynolds's. Cf. Darrel Mansell, Jr., who draws on such passages in order to argue that George Eliot therefore shared Ruskin's views on Dutch art ("Ruskin and George Eliot's 'Realism,'" 208–9).

75. "Recollections of our Journey from Munich to Dresden," in *Journals*, 326.

76. To Sara Sophia Hennell, 28 July 1858, *Letters*, 2:471. Cf. the "Recollections" quoted above, which record her "awe" before "this sublimest picture" (*Journals*, 325).

77. [George Henry Lewes], "Realism in Art: Recent German Fiction," *Westminster Review* 70 (1858): 493.

78. Lord Acton, *Nineteenth Century* 17 (March 1885), as quoted in *Journals of George Eliot*, 328. Acton was reviewing Cross's *Life* of the novelist, which included a virtually complete version of the journal she kept on the first trip to Italy.

79. "Recollections of Italy 1860," in *Journals*, 360.

80. Ibid., 364.

81. To Sara Sophia Hennell, 2 July 1860, *Letters*, 3:311.

82. George Eliot, *Middlemarch*, ed. David Carroll (Oxford: Oxford University Press, 1998), 1.7. Later Dorothea is compared to "a picture of Santa Barbara looking out from her tower into the clear air" (10.81)—a picture that Praz identifies as a work by Palma Vecchio that George Eliot recorded having seen at Santa Maria Formosa in Venice (*Hero in Eclipse*, 358)—and, more equivocally, to a Saint Catherine (54.503) that Witemeyer associates with Raphael (*George Eliot and the Visual Arts*, 88).

83. Witemeyer, *George Eliot and the Visual Arts*, 97–104. Witemeyer also notes that there is some evidence of what Lewes called "a Rembrandtish background" to George Eliot's representation of the Jews in *Daniel Deronda* (96), though the only explicit reference is Hans Meyrick's praise of Mordecai as "a better model than Rembrandt had for his Rabbi" (*Deronda*, 52.549). As Witemeyer observes, she used Dutch models very sparingly in this novel "because she shared with a substantial part of her audience the venerable prejudice that Dutch painting rarely achieves the sublime" (97).

84. [Lewes], "Realism in Art," 493–94.

85. For further remarks about *Deronda*'s use of the Titian, including the connection to Lewes's essay, see Witemeyer, *George Eliot and the Visual Arts*, 101–4.

86. "We go three days a week to the gallery," she wrote from Dresden in August, "and every day after looking at other pictures, we go to take a parting draught of delight at Titian's Zinngroschen and the *Einzige* Madonna" (To Sara Sophia Hennell, 28 July 1858, *Letters* 2:471–72).

87. See Martin, introduction, *Adam Bede* (Clarendon, 2001), cxxii–iv, as well as page 164 of the text, where the relevant changes are indicated in the notes. George Eliot worked on the corrections for the eighth edition in the autumn of 1861, while continuing the research for *Romola* that she had begun in Italy; she formally embarked on the writing of her Italian novel on New Year's Day 1862. Among the other changes she made to the seventeenth chapter of *Adam Bede*, the most significant is probably her decision to de-sex the protesting reader. Martin suggests that "Eliot no longer needed to dress her reader in female clothes to disguise the male publisher underneath" (cxxii), but it seems more likely that the lifting of the pseudonym meant that the novelist no longer needed to disguise her own sex by correcting the taste of a "lady."

88. "History of 'Adam Bede,'" in *Journals*, 300.

89. [John Chapman?], review of *The Mill on the Floss*, *Westminster Review* 74 (1860): 29, 28–29.

90. Henry James, "The Novels of George Eliot" (1866), rpt. in *Henry James: Literary Criticism . . . English Writers*, 912, 917.

91. [John Morley], review of *Felix Holt*, *Saturday Review* 21 (1866): 723. I owe the identification of Morley's authorship to Carroll, *George Eliot: The Critical Heritage*, 251.

92. For the sales figures, see Martin, introduction, *Adam Bede* (Clarendon, 2001), liv–lviii.

93. Edward Dowden, "'Middlemarch' and 'Daniel Deronda,'" *Contemporary Review* 29 (1877): 351, 355.

CHAPTER FIVE
Hardy's Rural Painting of the Dutch School

1. See his protest to Samuel Chew, who had posited such influence in his *Thomas Hardy: Poet and Novelist* (1921): "It was Shakespeare's delineation of his

Warwickshire clowns (who much resemble the Wessex peasantry) that influenced Hardy most. He found no clowns i.e. farm-labourers or rustics, anywhere in G. Eliot's books, and considered her country characters more like small townspeople than peasantry" (To Samuel Chew, 17 September 1922, *The Collected Letters of Thomas Hardy*, ed. Richard Little Purdy and Michael Millgate, 7 vols. [Oxford: Clarendon, 1978–88], 6:155). For related evidence, see also *The Literary Notebooks of Thomas Hardy*, ed. Lennart A. Björk, 2 vols. (London: Macmillan, 1985), 1:381.

2. See Thomas Hardy, *The Life and Work of Thomas Hardy*, ed. Michael Millgate (Athens: University of Georgia Press, 1985), 64. This is a modern edition of the autobiographical volumes *The Early Life of Thomas Hardy* (1928) and *The Later Years of Thomas Hardy* (1930), both published over the name of Florence Emily Hardy.

3. *Spectator* 44 (1871): 482.

4. See Michael Millgate, *Thomas Hardy: His Career as a Novelist* (New York: Random House, 1971), 57–61, 19. Cf. also Millgate, *Thomas Hardy: A Biography* (New York: Random House, 1982), 137–38.

5. *Athenaeum*, 15 June 1872, 748.

6. *Spectator* 47 (1874): 22; *Saturday Review* 39 (1875): 57.

7. For Hardy, see, e.g., his 1892 preface to *Tess of the d'Urbervilles* and his 1895 preface to *Jude the Obscure* in the Wessex Edition. The quotation from George Eliot is from a letter to Frederic Harrison, 15 August [1866], in *The George Eliot Letters*, ed. Gordon S. Haight, 9 vols. (New Haven: Yale University Press, 1954–78), 4:300.

8. Hardy, *Life*, 100.

9. J. B. Bullen, *The Expressive Eye: Fiction and Perception in the Work of Thomas Hardy* (Oxford: Clarendon, 1986), 2, 15–19.

10. *The Personal Notebooks of Thomas Hardy*, ed. Richard H. Taylor (New York: Columbia University Press, 1979), 112.

11. Hardy, *Life*, 53.

12. Bullen, *Expressive Eye*, 43–44. According to Bullen, the *Catalogue of Furniture and Paintings . . . from Max Gate* (1938) suggests that Hardy's "most prized possessions . . . were several pictures of the Dutch school," including a wooded landscape with a holy family and figures engaged in an archery contest, two merrymaking scenes, and a candlelit interior attributed to Godfried Schalcken (28). Though it is not clear when Hardy acquired these, it seems highly unlikely that any of them belonged to the struggling author of *Under the Greenwood Tree*.

13. See especially Norman Page, *Thomas Hardy* (London: Routledge and Kegan Paul, 1977), 68–69; Joan Grundy, *Hardy and the Sister Arts* (London: Macmillan, 1979), 26–31; and Bullen, *Expressive Eye*, 42–53.

14. Thomas Hardy, *Under the Greenwood Tree*, ed. Simon Gatrell (Oxford: Oxford University Press, 1999), 34. All further references to this edition are given parenthetically by page number in the text.

15. See note 12, above.

16. George Eliot, *Adam Bede*, ed. Valentine Cunningham (Oxford: Oxford University Press, 1996), 39.

17. Bullen, *Expressive Eye*, 46–47.

18. Page, *Thomas Hardy*, 68; Bullen, *Expressive Eye*, 46.

19. For the ms. information, see Gatrell's note to the Oxford edition, 210. Cf. also Norman Page's brief remarks on this allusion in "Art and Aesthetics," in *The Cambridge Companion to Thomas Hardy*, ed. Dale Kramer (Cambridge: Cambridge University Press, 1999), 42–43. For an elaboration of the Moroni comparison, see Bullen, *Expressive Eye*, 49.

20. Grundy, *Hardy and the Sister Arts*, 29.

21. Thomas Hardy, *Far from the Madding Crowd*, ed. Suzanne B. Falck-Yi (Oxford: Oxford University Press, 2002), 74.

22. *Athenaeum*, 20 November 1880, 672.

23. Hardy, *Far from the Madding Crowd*, 333; Thomas Hardy, *The Return of the Native*, ed. Simon Gatrell (Oxford: Oxford University Press, 2005), 134.

24. Hardy, *Life*, 58.

25. See *Thomas Hardy's Public Voice: The Essays, Speeches, and Miscellaneous Prose*, ed. Michael Millgate (Oxford: Clarendon, 2001), where these are characterized (in an article published by Florence Dugdale but "edited" by Hardy) as "delightful pictures of rural life" (314).

26. Millgate, *Thomas Hardy: His Career*, 43.

27. See esp. Page, *Thomas Hardy*, 70–78; and Grundy, *Hardy and the Sister Arts*, 30–40.

28. Millgate, *Thomas Hardy: A Biography*, 285.

29. Kate Flint, *The Victorians and the Visual Imagination* (Cambridge: Cambridge University Press, 2000), 198.

30. [Walter Scott], review of *Emma*, in *Quarterly Review* 14 (1815–16), rpt. in *Sir Walter Scott on Novelists and Fiction*, ed. Ioan Williams (London: Routledge and Kegan Paul, 1968), 235, 232.

31. [Archibald Alison], "The Historical Romance," *Blackwood's Edinburgh Magazine* 58 (1845): 354.

32. [R. H. Hutton], "A Novel or Two," *National Review* 1 (1855): 337, 339–40.

33. George Henry Lewes to John Blackwood, 6 November [1856], *George Eliot Letters*, 2:269.

34. For a somewhat different approach to these lines, which emphasizes their relevance for the later Hardy, see George Levine, *The Realistic Imagination: English Fiction from Frankenstein to Lady Chatterley* (Chicago: University of Chicago Press, 1981), 229.

35. Hardy, *Personal Notebooks*, 112.

36. According to the National Gallery's website (http://www.nationalgallery.org.uk), the Teniers in question was bequeathed by Lord Farnborough in 1838.

37. Wolfgang Stechow and Christopher Comer, "The History of the Term Genre," *Allen Memorial Art Museum Bulletin* 33 (1975–6): 89–94.

38. Notebook entry of 22 April 1878, in Hardy, *Life*, 124. When the same entry continues by declaring "the beauty of association . . . entirely superior to the beauty

of aspect . . . and a beloved relative's old battered tankard to the finest Greek vase," it appears to offer one rationale, at least, for what I shall be calling the genre painting of memory.

39. See Simon Gatrell's introduction to his Oxford edition, xi–xiii.

40. [Horace Moule], review of *Under the Greenwood Tree*, in *Saturday Review* 34 (1872): 418. I owe the identification of Moule's authorship to *Thomas Hardy: The Critical Heritage*, ed. R. G. Cox (London: Routledge and Kegan Paul, 1970).

41. For Hardy's use of "still life" to characterize a landscape, see the notebook entry cited in Millgate, *Thomas Hardy: A Biography*, 247, and the two pieces on William Barnes reprinted in *Thomas Hardy's Public Voice*, 18, 70. I will return to the latter examples below.

42. Hardy, "The Dorsetshire Labourer" (1883), rpt. in *Thomas Hardy's Public Voice*, 49, 50.

43. For Barnes and "The Dorsetshire Labourer," see Millgate's note to the essay in *Thomas Hardy's Public Voice*, 40; for his influence on the novel, see especially William R. Rutland, *Thomas Hardy: A Study of his Writings and their Background* (New York: Russell and Russell, 1962), 8–10.

44. Evelyn Hardy, *Thomas Hardy: A Critical Biography* (London: Hogarth, 1954), 124–25. Barnes's essay appeared in *Macmillan's Magazine* (May–October, 1861).

45. Hardy, [review of William Barnes's Poems, 1879], in *Thomas Hardy's Public Voice*, 18. Millgate's edition publishes this review as originally set in galley proofs rather than the cut version that actually appeared in the *New Quarterly Magazine*.

46. Hardy, "The Rev. William Barnes, B. D." (1886), rpt. in *Thomas Hardy's Public Voice*, 70.

47. Ibid.

48. For evidence that Boldwood partly took over Oak's original role in the novel, especially by acting out what was once the latter's violence against Troy, see Millgate, *Thomas Hardy: His Career*, 84–85.

49. Hardy, *Far from the Madding Crowd*, 34, 32, 381, 16. The quotation is from Barnes's "Woak Hill."

50. Hardy, *Life*, 17. Cf. his preface for the Wessex edition of 1912, where he half-regrets having treated the musicians "so lightly, even so farcically and flippantly at times" (*Under the Greenwood Tree*, 5).

51. Hardy, *Personal Notebooks*, 112.

52. John Dryden, "A Parallel betwixt Painting and Poetry," in *The Works of John Dryden*, ed. Edward Niles Hooker, H. T. Swedenberg, Jr., et al., 20 vols. (Berkeley: University of California Press, 1956–2000), 20:55.

53. On this evolution in British taste, see Harry Thomas Mount, *The Reception of Dutch Genre Painting in England, 1695–1829* (Ph. D. Diss., University of Cambridge, 1991), 24–68, 178–226. For the increasing decorum of low genre in Holland itself during the latter half of the seventeenth century, see Wayne Franits, *Dutch Seventeenth-Century Genre Painting: Its Stylistic and Thematic Evolution* (New Haven: Yale University Press, 2004), 135–39.

54. Oliver Bonard, *La peinture dans la création Balzacienne: Invention et vision picturales de "La maison du chat-qui-pelote" au "Père Goriot"* (Geneva: Librairie Droz, 1969), 144–54. Ever since Balzac's time, critics have understandably been tempted to invoke the name of Daumier as well; but Bonard contends that very little is known of Daumier's influence on the novelist and argues instead for a convergence of styles between them (125–27).

55. Grundy, *Hardy and the Sister Arts*, 48–50.

56. Bonard, *Peinture dans la création Balzacienne*, 123–54, 165–78.

57. Bullen, *Expressive Eye*, 50–52.

58. See Michael Squires, *The Pastoral Novel: Studies in George Eliot, Thomas Hardy, and D. H. Lawrence* (Charlottesville: University of Virginia Press, 1974), 114; and Millgate, *Thomas Hardy: His Career*, 44–49. It is Squires who notes the echoes of "And so am I for Phebe," etc. (*As You Like It*, 5.2), in the sequence that begins with the tranter's "and so do everybody, my sonnies" (*Under the Greenwood Tree*, 188–89).

59. To Samuel Chew, 17 September 1922, *Letters of Thomas Hardy*, 6:155.

60. The comparison was not always in Hardy's favor. "Shakespeare also has his metaphysical clowns," an anonymous review of *Far from the Madding Crowd* conceded, "but neither his clowns, nor George Eliot's rustics, nor Scott's peasants, rise to anything like the flights of abstract reasoning with which Mr. Hardy credits his cider-drinking boors" (*Saturday Review*, 39 [1875]: 57).

61. For general observations about the echoes of Shakespearean low-life in novelistic realism, see Alexander Welsh, "Contrast of Styles in the Waverley Novels" (1973), rpt. in *The Hero of the Waverley Novels: With New Essays on Scott* (Princeton: Princeton University Press, 1992), esp. 180–81, 190.

62. Thomas Hardy, *A Pair of Blue Eyes*, ed. Alan Manford (Oxford: Oxford University Press, 1998), 225, 228.

63. Hardy, *Return of the Native*, 17, 244.

64. Thomas Hardy, *Tess of the d'Urbervilles*, ed. Juliet Grindle and Simon Gatrell (Oxford: Oxford University Press, 2005), 100, 140. Compare the novel's description of the "fever of mobility" that afflicts the work-folk on Old Lady-Day with the related account in "The Dorsetshire Labourer." Like the essay—and in virtually the same words—the novel argues that the increasing depopulation of the villages is compelled as much as willed: "the process, humorously designated by statisticians as 'the tendency of the rural population towards the large towns,' being really the tendency of water to flow uphill when forced by machinery" (*Tess of the d'Urbervilles*, 372–73). Cf. "The Dorsetshire Labourer," in *Thomas Hardy's Public Voice*, 56.

65. Thomas Hardy, *Two on a Tower*, ed. Suleiman M. Ahmad (Oxford: Oxford University Press, 1998), 13.

66. See Grundy, *Hardy and the Sister Arts*, 50–64; Shelagh Hunter, *Victorian Idyllic Fiction: Pastoral Strategies* (Atlantic Highlands, N.J.: Humanities Press, 1984), 186–94; and Bullen, *Expressive Eye*, esp. 169–222.

67. Hardy, *Life*, 52.

68. Thomas Hardy, *The Woodlanders*, ed. Dale Kramer (Oxford: Oxford University Press, 2000), 9–10, 11. A coffin-stool is a stand or support for a coffin.

69. Ibid., 11. For related observations on this scene, see Bullen, *Expressive Eye*, 180–82.

70. Hardy, *Life*, 191. The emphasis is Hardy's.

71. See Kramer's note to this passage in *The Woodlanders*, 368. By "post-Raffaelite," Hardy presumably means a style of painting that came after the Pre-Raphaelites.

72. Hardy, *The Woodlanders*, 162.

73. Notebook entry of 13 February 1887 (Hardy, *Life*, 192).

74. Cf. George Levine's fine discussion of *The Mayor of Casterbridge*, significantly subtitled "Reversing the Real," in *The Realistic Imagination*, 229–51. If the author of *The Mayor* is still a realist, in Levine's capacious understanding of the term, he nonetheless abandons or reverses many of the assumptions on which English realists before him had proceeded—not least, as Levine notes, those of the early George Eliot.

75. Hardy, *Far from the Madding Crowd*, 308, 333.

76. Hardy, *Life*, 183. The phrase comes from a notebook entry of 4 March 1886.

77. Ibid., 192.

78. "Turner's water-colours," he recorded in his notebook after a visit to the Royal Academy in January of 1889: "each is a landscape *plus* a man's soul. . . . What he paints chiefly is *light as modified by objects*" (Hardy, *Life*, 225; the ellipses as well as both emphases are the novelist's). For the argument that *Tess of the d'Urbervilles* in particular is much influenced by the late Turner, see Bullen, *Expressive Eye*, 191–222.

79. Hardy, "The Profitable Reading of Fiction" (1888), rpt. in *Thomas Hardy's Public Voice*, 82. See also "The Science of Fiction" (1891), which adduces the case of "an accomplished lady," who "once confessed to the writer that she could never be in a room two minutes without knowing every article of furniture it contained and every detail in the attire of the inmates, and, when she left, remembering every remark" in order to argue that such a person was not in fact "a born novelist." Rather than Dutch painting, however, the paradigm for such "complete copyism" has now become photography (*Thomas Hardy's Public Voice*, 109).

80. Hardy, *Life*, 239.

81. Millgate, *Thomas Hardy: His Career*, 66.

82. Hardy, *Life*, 154, 268. Cf. another variant on these remarks, which dates from 1891: "Howells and those of his school forget that a story *must* be striking enough to be worth telling. Therein lies the problem—to reconcile the average with that uncommonness which alone makes it natural that a tale or experience would dwell in the memory and induce repetition" (251; emphasis Hardy's).

CHAPTER SIX

Proust's Genre Painting and the Rediscovery of Vermeer

1. Peter Brooks, *Realist Vision* (New Haven: Yale University Press, 2005), 131.

2. For excellent accounts of this complicated history and its implications for the novelist's career, see especially Alexander Welsh, *George Eliot and Blackmail*

(Cambridge, Mass.: Harvard University Press, 1985), 113–31; and Rosemarie Bodenheimer, *The Real Life of Mary Ann Evans: George Eliot, Her Letters and Her Fiction* (Ithaca: Cornell University Press, 1994), 119–60.

3. See "History of 'Adam Bede'" (30 November 1858), in *The Journals of George Eliot*, ed. Margaret Harris and Judith Johnston (Cambridge: Cambridge University Press, 1998), 296.

4. Thomas Hardy, *The Life and Works of Thomas Hardy*, ed. Michael Millgate (Athens: University of Georgia Press, 1985), 17.

5. See Michael Millgate, *Thomas Hardy: His Career as a Novelist* (New York: Random House, 1971), 57. Simon Gatrell observes that the resemblance between the tranter's cottage and Hardy's childhood home was not really noticeable until the novel was revised for the Wessex edition of 1912. Gatrell, "Wessex," in *The Cambridge Companion to Thomas Hardy*, ed. Dale Kramer (Cambridge: Cambridge University Press, 1999), 31.

6. Honoré de Balzac, *La recherche de l'absolu*, in Balzac, *La comédie humaine*, ed. Pierre-Georges Castex, 12 vols., Bibliothèque de la Pléiade (Paris: Gallimard, 1976), 10:657. Subsequent references to the *Comédie humaine* are given by volume and page number, preceded by *CH*, in the text.

7. For these and other links between Balzac's family history and *La maison du chat-qui-pelote* (including the argument that its unhappy marriage was inspired by that of the novelist's sister Laurence), see Anne-Marie Meininger's introduction to her edition of the tale (*CH* 1:25–38).

8. [Louis de Loménie], "M. de Balzac," in *Galerie des contemporains illustres, par un homme de rien*, vol. 3 (Paris: René et Cie, 1841): 33.

9. Hippolyte Babou, review of *La muse du département*, in *Revue de Paris* 22 (1843): 53. (On *Eugénie Grandet* and female chastity, see esp. 55, 58.)

10. Marcel Proust, "Tableaux de genre du souvenir," in *Les plaisirs et les jours* (1896). I quote from Proust, *Jean Santeuil précédé de Les plaisirs et les jours*, ed. Pierre Clarac and Yves Sandre, Bibliothèque de la Pléiade (Paris: Gallimard, 1971), 130.

11. Cf. Christiane Hertel, *Vermeer: Reception and Interpretation* (Cambridge: Cambridge University Press, 1996): "Pictorial remembrance pertains here only to a certain part of the faculty of memory, that part which deals with regularity, the everyday, the only slightly varied or plainly repetitive aspects of life." While I agree with Hertel that the passage relies on "commonplaces about Dutch art" (122), I am less prepared to take for granted its governing comparison of the memory to a genre painter.

12. W. Bürger [Théophile Thoré], *Musées de la Hollande*, 2 vols. (Paris: Jules Renouard, 1858–60), 2:58–59.

13. Jean-Yves Tadié, *Marcel Proust: A Life*, trans. Euan Cameron (New York: Penguin, 2001), 94–95.

14. Proust, "Tableaux de genre du souvenir," 130–31.

15. To Maurice Duplay [toward the end of May 1905], Marcel Proust, *Correspondance*, ed. Philip Kolb, 21 vols. (Paris: Plon, 1970–93), 5:183.

16. Tadié, *Marcel Proust*, 95–97. Cf. Hertel, who rightly calls attention to the self-consciousness of Proust's sentimentality in the essay, even as she somewhat exaggerates his irony at his own expense by tendentiously translating "coupée de lacunes" as "with many blanks" (*Vermeer*, 123).

17. George Eliot, *Adam Bede*, ed. Valentine Cunningham (Oxford: Oxford University Press, 1996), 175.

18. Marcel Proust, *À la recherche du temps perdu*, ed. Jean-Yves Tadié, 4 vols., Bibliothèque de la Pléiade (Paris: Gallimard, 1987–89), 3:206. I generally adopt the English translation of C. K. Scott Moncrieff and Terence Kilmartin, as revised by D. J. Enright, *In Search of Lost Time*, 6 vols. (London: Chatto and Windus, 1992), though I have made some silent alterations from time to time. For the convenience of the reader, volume and page references to this edition appear parenthetically after those to the Pléiade edition in the text. (The reference here is to 4:243.)

19. Tadié, *Marcel Proust*, 292, 591.

20. Ibid., 291.

21. Marcel Proust, *Contre Saint-Beuve, précédé de Pastiches et mélanges et suivi de Essais et articles*, ed. Pierre Clarac and Yves Sandre, Bibliothèque de la Pléiade (Paris: Gallimard, 1971), 276, 266. Translations from this volume are my own, though I have gratefully consulted Sylvia Townsend Warner's English versions in *Marcel Proust: On Art and Literature, 1896–1919* (New York: Caroll and Graf, 1997).

22. Ibid., 275.

23. The Pléiade editors suggest that in comparing his future work to the *Thousand and One Nights* at the close of *Le temps retrouvé*, the narrator may also be thinking of Balzac, who "prided himself on being the author of the 'Thousand and One Nights of the West'" (4:1316).

24. See the letters to Mme Carman-Chimay [20 July 1907 or a little after] and René Boylesve [a little before 25 October 1917] in *Correspondance*, 7:226 and 16:266, respectively.

25. With the partial exception of Ruskin, whom he translated with considerable assistance from his mother and Marie Nordlinger, Proust appears to have depended on French editions for his acquaintance with the English. Though he clearly knew both *Scenes of Clerical Life* and *Adam Bede* (in addition to *The Mill on the Floss*, *Silas Marner*, and *Middlemarch*), there is no evidence that he ever read *Under the Greenwood Tree*, which did not appear in French until the year after his death. Robert Fraser's helpful *Proust and the Victorians: The Lamp of Memory* (New York: St. Martin's, 1994) includes a list of the relevant French editions (293–99). For other accounts of Proust's relation to English writers, see P.-E. Robert, *Marcel Proust: Lecteur des Anglo-Saxons* (Paris: A.-G. Nizet, 1976); and Emily Eells, *Proust's Cup of Tea: Homoeroticism and Victorian Culture* (Aldershot, Hant's: Ashgate, 2002).

26. To Jacques Rivière [18 February 1920], *Correspondance*, 19:124.

27. Marcel Proust, "Préface du traducteur," in John Ruskin, *La Bible d'Amiens*, trans. Proust (Paris: Mercure de France, 1926), 85. *La Bible d'Amiens* was first published in 1904. Cf. also the Pléiade *Contre Saint-Beuve*, 134, which reproduces

Proust's preface and notes as he later revised them for inclusion in his 1919 *Pastiches et mélanges*.

28. To Jacques Rivière [18 February 1920], *Correspondance*, 19:124.

29. To Robert de Billy [March 1910], *Correspondance*, 10:55. Cf. an earlier letter to another friend, which follows up an admonitory quotation from Ruskin by observing: "That doesn't prevent the works of Ruskin from often being stupid, fanatical, irritating, false, ridiculous; but they are always laudable and always great. He was, you know, very admired by George Eliot" (To Georges de Lauris [8 November 1908], *Correspondance*, 8:286–87).

30. John Ruskin, *The Bible of Amiens*, in *The Works of John Ruskin*, ed. E. T. Cook and Alexander Wedderburn, 39 vols. (London: George Allen, 1903–12), 33:44.

31. Proust, note to *La Bible d'Amiens*, 132. The note also includes "les prophètes de Carlyle" in this comparison (131). Cf. Proust, "Mélanges," in *Contre Saint-Beuve*, 73n.

32. Ruskin, *The Bible of Amiens*, in *Works*, 33:44.

33. Cf. both Fraser, *Proust and the Victorians*, 96–97, and Eells, *Proust's Cup of Tea*, 82, who likewise assume that Proust is thinking of Dutch painting in these notes on George Eliot.

34. Proust, [Sur George Eliot], *Contre Saint-Beuve*, 656–57.

35. Just when Proust first encountered Ruskin remains unclear. Tadié attributes the future novelist's discovery of the English critic to an article by Robert de La Sizeranne on "Ruskin et la religion de la beauté" in the *Revue des deux mondes* of 1 March 1897 (*Marcel Proust*, 279). But according to Diane R. Leonard, Marie Nordlinger recalled that when she first met Proust in the winter of 1896, he had already read everything by Ruskin then translated into French. Leonard herself notes that brief extracts from Ruskin's work had been appearing in the *Bulletin de l'union pour action morale* since 1893. See Leonard, "Ruskin and the Cathedral of Lost Souls," in *The Cambridge Companion to Proust*, ed. Richard Bales (Cambridge: Cambridge University Press, 2001), 43.

36. For passing comments on how the Rembrandt essay anticipates the death of Bergotte, see Helen Borowitz, "The Rembrandt and Monet of Marcel Proust," *Bulletin of the Cleveland Museum of Art* 70 (1983): 73, 77; Fraser, *Proust and the Victorians*, 83–85; Tadié, *Marcel Proust*, 312; Hertel, *Vermeer*, 117–18; and Eells, *Proust's Cup of Tea*, 177. Only Fraser and Eells (157–58) remark the wishful character of Proust's fiction about Ruskin. In addition to this undated and unpublished essay, Proust also wrote a brief official obituary of Ruskin that appeared in January 1900 (*Contre Saint-Beuve*, 439–41).

37. On Proust and the Louvre, see Antoine Compagnon, "Proust au musée," in *Marcel Proust: L'écriture et les arts*, ed. Jean-Yves Tadié and Florence Callu (Paris: Gallimard, 1999), 67–79. According to Compagnon, from the late 1880s to the early 1890s "Proust a vécu au musée" (68).

38. To Pierre Mainguet [toward the end of November 1895], *Correspondance*, 1:444. The editors of the Pléiade *Contre Saint-Beuve* speculate that the pages on Rembrandt may have been added to the essay after its initial composition (885).

39. Proust, [Chardin et Rembrandt], *Contre Saint-Beuve*, 372, 380.

40. On the echo of the essay in the novel, see the editors' note to the Pléiade edition, 2:1451.

41. Proust, [Chardin et Rembrandt], *Contre Saint-Beuve*, 380, 381.

42. Proust, [Rembrandt], *Contre Saint-Beuve*, 660, 659, 662.

43. Tadié, *Marcel Proust*, 205.

44. Proust, [Rembrandt], *Contre Saint-Beuve*, 659–60. The ms. originally read, "ces idées qui pour chaque grand homme est lui-même"; but the Pléiade editors have replaced Proust's singular verb with a plural (967).

45. Though the essay refers explicitly to the Amsterdam exhibit, the evidence makes clear that Proust was drawing on his memories of the Louvre as well: the *Good Samaritan* to which he alludes, for example, did not apparently travel from Paris, nor did the museum's version of *The Slaughtered Ox*—"the one," as Proust says, "where a woman on the right is looking back as she leaves" (*Contre Saint-Beuve*, 660). For the nineteenth-century exhibition history of these pictures—including works no longer securely attributed to Rembrandt—see C. P. Hofstede de Groot, *Catalogue Raisonné of the Works of the Most Eminent Dutch Painters of the Seventeenth Century . . .*, trans. and ed. Edward G. Hawke, vol. 6 (London: Macmillan, 1916).

46. For the history of this painting, see Walter Liedtke et al., *Rembrandt/Not Rembrandt in the Metropolitan Museum of Art: Aspects of Connoisseurship*, 2 vols. (New York: Abrams, 1995), 2:125–28. For the suggestion that Proust's essay was inspired by Émile Michel's review of the Amsterdam exhibit in the *Gazette des beaux-arts* (November and December 1898), which specifically remarked how Rembrandt "transforms" and "poetizes" common types like *The Old Woman Cutting Her Nails*, see Borowitz, "The Rembrandt and Monet of Marcel Proust," 74.

47. Proust, [Rembrandt], *Contre Saint-Beuve*, 661. As it happens, this image, too, has now been demoted to a school piece. For a helpful account of the nineteenth century's radical expansion of the Rembrandt corpus, see Catherine B. Scallen, *Rembrandt, Reputation, and the Practice of Connoisseurship* (Amsterdam: Amsterdam University Press, 2004).

48. Proust, "Préface," *Bible d'Amiens*, 57. Cf. Proust, "Mélanges," *Contre-Saint Beuve*, 112.

49. Proust, [Rembrandt], *Contre Saint-Beuve*, 663.

50. Tadié, *Marcel Proust*, 312.

51. Proust, [Rembrandt], *Contre Saint-Beuve*, 663–64.

52. Ibid., 664.

53. Tadié, *Marcel Proust*, 392–93, 859.

54. To Jean-Louis Vaudoyer [14 May 1921]; To Jean-Louis Vaudoyer [1 May 1921], *Correspondance*, 20:263, 226.

55. For the identification of this picture, see the editors' note to the Pléiade edition (2:1569).

56. Georges Poulet, *Proustian Space*, trans. Elliott Coleman (Baltimore: The Johns Hopkins University Press, 1977), 99, 100. *L'espace proustien* was first published in 1963.

57. Gérard Genette, *Narrative Discourse: An Essay in Method*, trans. Jane E. Lewin (Ithaca: Cornell University Press, 1980), 123, 117. The French text originally appeared as part of Genette's *Figures III* in 1972.

58. For the "paradoxical presence of an iterative" in Proust's *passé simple* or *passé composé*, see ibid., 132. According to the notes to the Pléiade edition, earlier drafts of the novel's opening did resort to the imperfect (1:1085–86).

59. Genette, *Narrative Discourse*, 123.

60. Germaine Brée, *The World of Marcel Proust* (Boston: Houghton Mifflin, 1966), 152.

61. Tadié, *Marcel Proust*, 6. On Auteuil and Illiers more generally, see 1–12.

62. One line in an early notebook for *À la recherche* reads simply, "1re page du *Moulin sur la Floss*." See Marcel Proust, *Le carnet de 1908*, ed. Philip Kolb (Paris: Gallimard, 1976), 94. For commentary on the connection, see L. A. Bisson, "Proust, Bergson, and George Eliot," *Modern Language Review* 40 (1945): 104–14; Robert, *Marcel Proust*, 62–65; and Fraser, *Proust and the Victorians*, 107–11.

63. George Eliot, *Adam Bede*, 175.

64. To Walter Berry [10 July 1919], *Correspondance*, 18:321. For virtually the same formula, see his letter to Fernand Vandérem [4 or 5 May 1921], ibid., 20:245. Proust was not always quite so extravagant. In 1895, as we have seen, he still counted Leonardo and Rembrandt as his favorite painters; while a letter of 1907 pronounces the *View of Delft* "the painting that I most admired [j'ai le plus aimé] in Holland" before going on to declare, somewhat bafflingly, "Obviously, there are at Amsterdam three or four Rembrandts that I admire still more. But this *View of Delft* seems to me one of the five or six most beautiful paintings that I know in the whole world, likewise a woman by the same Vermeer at The Hague, and (less beautiful but charming) a street in Delft by the same hand, at the Maison Six in Amsterdam" (To the Princess Alexandre de Caraman-Chimay [a little before June 28 1907], *Correspondance*, 21:615). If pictures could serve as war reparations, he wrote in 1920, he would prefer the Vermeers at Dresden and Vienna to additional Watteaus—only to add, "All this doesn't mean that I prefer Vermeer to Watteau" (To Jean-Louis Vaudoyer [first days of February 1920], *Correspondance*, 19:108). Cf. also To Walter Berry [10 July 1919], *Correspondance*, 18:321.

65. Tadié, *Marcel Proust*, 323.

66. Originally identified as the work of Maes when it entered the Mauritshuis in 1876, the *Diana* was tentatively assigned to Vermeer in 1885, only to be reattributed to Jan Vermeer van Utrecht in the 1890s. It was not until the identification of another early history painting by the Delft artist, the *Christ in the House of Martha and Mary* now in Edinburgh, that the *Diana*'s attribution was securely settled. For the history of the painting, see the catalogue entry by Arthur K. Wheelock, Jr., and Ben Broos in *Johannes Vermeer*, ed. Frederick J. Duparc and Wheelock (Washington, D.C.: National Gallery of Art, 1995), 100. For Proust's knowledge of the disputed attribution, see the note to the Pléiade edition (1:1243–44).

67. This scene may have inspired almost as much commentary as the mother's kiss or the tasting of the madeleine. For some relevant discussions, see René Huyghe, "Affinités électives: Vermeer et Proust," *L'amour de l'art*, January 1936, 7–15; Hélène Adhémar, "La vision de Vermeer par Proust, à travers Vaudoyer," *Gazette des beaux-arts* 68 (1966): 291–302; Giovanni Macchia, *L'ange de la nuit: Sur Proust*, trans. Marie-France Merger, Paul Bédarida, and Mario Fusco (Paris: Gallimard, 1993), 185–96; and Hertel, *Vermeer*, 116–36.

68. For the history of this episode and its composition, see Pierre-Edmond Robert's "Notice" to *La prisonnière* (3:1683–84); and Tadié, *Marcel Proust*, 756–57. This history also explains the oft-remarked fact that Bergotte still appears to be alive in some later, and presumably unrevised, passages of *La prisonnière* and *Le temps retrouvé.*

69. For some relevant excerpts, see the editor's note to the Pléiade edition, 3: 1740. Vaudoyer's article originally appeared in *L'opinion* of 30 April, 7 and 14 May 1921: 487–89, 514–16, 542–44. An English translation, on which I have partly relied, is given as an appendix to Daniel Arasse, *Vermeer: Faith in Painting*, trans. Terry Grabar (Princeton: Princeton University Press, 1994), 87–97.

70. Compagnon, "Proust au musée," 67. On the afternoon of his visit to the Jeu de Paume, Proust did, however, also take in an Ingres exhibit—the last paintings he apparently ever went to see (Tadié, *Marcel Proust*, 745–56).

71. To Jean-Louis Vaudoyer [between 18 and 24 May 1921], Proust, *Correspondance*, 20:289.

72. William C. Carter, *Marcel Proust: A Life* (New Haven: Yale University Press, 2000), 753.

73. Following Philip Kolb's argument in his introduction to vol. 20 of the Proust *Correspondance* (x–xii), both Tadié (*Marcel Proust*, 745) and Carter (*Marcel Proust*, 753) are concerned to correct the story circulated by the novelist's brother, according to which Proust was inspired to kill off Bergotte when he himself was taken ill at the exhibition.

74. Thierry Laget, "Le vernis d'un autre maître: Proust et la peinture ancienne," in *Marcel Proust: L'écriture et les arts*, 27. The effect is perhaps closest to the *style indirect libre* by which Proust records the thoughts of "Swann in Love," but in that case, at least, there is always the possibility that the narrator has somehow learned these from Swann after the fact. That Proust was still dictating fragments about Bergotte's death on his own deathbed only confirms the intensity with which he had imagined the episode (Tadié, *Marcel Proust*, 776).

75. To Jean-Louis Vaudoyer [a little after 17 June 1922], *Correspondance*, 21:291–92.

76. To Fernand Vandérem [4 or 5 May 1921], *Correspondance*, 20:245.

77. Proponents of the roof include Huyghe, "Affinités électives," 14; Adhémar, "La vision de Vermeer," 291; Jeffrey Meyers, "Proust and Vermeer," *Art International* 17, no. 5 (1973): 69; and Arthur K. Wheelock, Jr., *Vermeer and the Art of Painting*

(New Haven: Yale University Press, 1995), 76. Those who argue for the wall (or walls) to the right include Jean Pavans, *Petit pan de mur jaune* (Paris: Éditions de la Différance, 1986), 41–45, and the editors of the Pléiade edition (3:1740). In a recent study of the question, *Proust e Vermeer: Apologia dell' imprecisione* (Bologna: Il Mulino, 1999), Lorenzo Renzi contends that Proust deliberately kept the allusion vague.

78. Jean-Louis Vaudoyer, "Le mystérieux Vermeer II," *L'opinion,* 7 May 1921, 515.

79. Compagnon, "Proust au Musée," 77.

80. Given Proust's own letter to Vaudoyer about the gables "like precious Chinese objects" (see note 75, above), I am not persuaded by the argument that the novelist implicitly criticizes Bergotte here for detaching a part of the work from its context: the yellow patch seems to me rather to operate as a synecdoche for the whole. For the critique of Bergotte, see Alexander Nehamas, *Nietzsche, Life as Literature* (Cambridge, Mass.: Harvard University Press, 1985), 229; and Joshua Landy, *Philosophy as Fiction: Self, Deception, and Knowledge in Proust* (Oxford: Oxford University Press, 2004), 82, 220. Cf. also Vincent Descombes, *Proust: Philosophy of the Novel* (Stanford: Stanford University Press, 1992), who argues, to the contrary, that at every stage of Marcel's aesthetic education, he learns to accentuate "a *part* at the expense of the *whole*" (108; emphasis in original). Among other cases in point, Descombes cites both the Bergotte episode and the famous "little phrase" from the sonata of Vinteuil.

81. "Style is in no way an embellishment, as certain people think, it is not even a question of technique; it is—like color with certain painters—a quality of vision, a revelation of a private universe which each of us sees and which others do not see. The pleasure an artist gives us is to make us know an additional universe" (To Antoine Bibesco [November 1912], in *Lettres de Marcel Proust à Bibesco*, ed. Thierry Maulnier [Lausanne: Guild du Livre, 1949], 177; and [*Swann* expliqué par Proust], *Contre Saint-Beuve*, 559). (The latter is an interview which essentially recycles the language of the letter.) I am indebted to Landy, *Philosophy as Fiction*, 36, for alerting me to these lines.

82. Vaudoyer, "Le mystérieux Vermeer III," *L'opinion*, 14 May 1921, 543, 542.

83. Vaudoyer, "Le mystérieux Vermeer II," 515.

84. Paul Morand to Marcel Proust, 1 May 1921, *Correspondance*, 20:222–23.

85. Adhémar, "La vision de Vermeer," 294. Vaudoyer had been reading Proust at least since 1910, when the future novelist sent him a copy of *Les plaisirs et les jours* (Carter, *Marcel Proust*, 493).

86. Hertel, *Vermeer*, 123. For Hertel, this belongs to a series of metaphorical panels, gates, and thresholds that are both summoned up and obscurely criticized by the novel's representation of the *View of Delft*.

87. By translating *pan de château* as "the wing of a castle" (rather than a wall), Moncrieff et al. muffle this echo (1:9).

88. Though the novel never directly names Vermeer in this connection, it does tell us that Elstir recognizes in Chardin, among others, "attempts of the same kind, anticipatory fragments, so to speak, of works of his own" (2:713; 3:484–85).

89. Lawrence Gowing, *Vermeer* (1952; rpt. Berkeley: University of California Press, 1997), 19.

90. Arasse, *Vermeer*, 53–54.

91. "Exquisite," Proust wrote, "but not enough," since *The Lacemaker* was, he complained, the only Vermeer in the Louvre (To Walter Berry [10 July 1919], *Correspondance*, 18:321).

92. Harry Berger, Jr., *Second World and Green World: Studies in Renaissance Fiction-Making* (Berkeley: University of California Press, 1990), 484. On the general subject of Vermeer's *pointillé*, I am especially indebted to Arasse, *Vermeer*, 69–75.

93. Arthur K. Wheelock, Jr., review of Albert Blankert, *Johannes Vermeer van Delft 1632–1675*, in *The Art Bulletin* 59 (1977): 440. In a subsequent study, Wheelock and C. J. Kaldenbach have shown through x-rays and infrared reflectography how Vermeer altered the picture to reinforce its two-dimensional effect. See their "Vermeer's *View of Delft* and his Vision of Reality," *Artibus et Historiae* 3, no. 6 (1982): 9–35.

94. Berger, *Second World and Green World*, 484.

95. W. Bürger [Théophile Thoré], "Van der Meer de Delft," *Gazette des beaux-arts* 21 (1866): 297.

96. For summaries of the relevant evidence, see Albert Blankert et al., *Vermeer of Delft: Complete Edition of the Paintings* (Oxford: Phaidon, 1978), 61–69; and Ben Broos, "Un celebre Peijntre nommé Verme[e]r," in *Johannes Vermeer*, ed. Duparc and Wheelock, 47–65. For a cogent response to Broos, which argues that he tends unduly to minimize Thoré-Bürger's contribution, see Frances Suzman Jowell, "Vermeer and Thoré-Bürger: Recoveries of Reputation," in *Vermeer Studies*, ed. Ivan Gaskell and Michiel Jonker (Washington, D. C.: National Gallery of Art, 1998), 35–57.

97. To Jean-Louis Vaudoyer [a little after 17 June 1922], *Correspondance*, 21:292.

98. Gustave Vanzype, *Vermeer de Delft* (Brussels: G. Van Oest, 1908), 65. Proust apparently read a revised and augmented edition of 1921; see *Correspondance*, 21:293n9.

99. Vaudoyer, "Le mystérieux Vermeer II," 515; "Le mystérieux Vermeer I," *L'opinion*, 30 April 1921, 488.

100. Bürger, "Van der Meer de Delft," 299.

101. Vanzype's phrase is the title of his first chapter (*Vermeer de Delft*, 3).

102. See John Michael Montias, *Vermeer and His Milieu: A Web of Social History* (Princeton: Princeton University Press, 1989). To emphasize what we do not know is not in any way to diminish Montias's achievement: it is thanks to his work in the archives that we have a much clearer picture both of the world from which Vermeer came and of the reasons why other kinds of information appear to be unrecoverable.

103. To Jean-Louis Vaudoyer [1 May 1921], *Correspondance*, 20:226.

104. Proust, [Préface], *Contre-Saint Beuve*, 580. This is a preface to Jacques-Émile Blanche, *Propos de peintre* (1919); see also the letter to Blanche [toward the middle of October 1918], *Correspondance*, 17:390. Despite this insistence that Vermeer was never even mentioned in *Les maîtres d'autrefois,* Fromentin had in fact

suggested that a wish to be well informed about "this singular presence [particularité] in Dutch art" might be one reason for visiting Holland, since the painter was almost unrepresented in France (Eugène Fromentin, *Oeuvres complètes*, ed. Guy Sagnes, Bibliothèque de la Pléiade [Paris: Gallimard, 1984], 685). Presumably it was after reading the first installment of Vaudoyer's article, which quotes these lines, that Proust realized his mistake: a subsequent letter chides Fromentin for "citing the name scarcely and without praise" (To Fernand Vandérem [4 or 5 May 1921], *Correspondance*, 20:245). One wonders whether the novelist also knew that in some notes on Dutch and Flemish art published posthumously in the *Revue de Paris* (1911–12), Fromentin had called the *View of Delft* "very charming" and "altogether modern" (*Oeuvres complètes*, 1140).

105. To Jean-Louis Vaudoyer [1 May 1921], *Correspondance*, 20:226.

106. Vaudoyer, "Le mystérieux Vermeer III," 544; To Jean-Louis Vaudoyer [14 May 1921], *Correspondance*, 20:263.

107. Proust, "La méthode de Saint-Beuve," *Contre Saint-Beuve*, 225.

108. My reading of these paintings is particularly indebted to Arasse, *Vermeer*, 63–69. Like Gowing before him (*Vermeer*, 34), Arasse also draws attention to Vermeer's practice of placing a barrier or barriers between such women and the viewer, as if to collude with their privacy: note how the still life partly bars our way to the milkmaid, for example, or the cushions and work table obtrude between us and the lacemaker.

109. To Fernand Vandérem [4 or 5 May 1921], *Correspondance*, 20:245.

110. Joshua Landy has observed how "the human adventure" in Proust "is a matter of repeatedly bumping up, in increasing frustration, against the variably colored, translucent 'barrier' between mind and world . . . only to realize that the glass itself—our individual perspective—is far more interesting than any aspect of external reality, however accurately grasped, could be." Though he is not writing of the novelist's relation to Vermeer, that "variably colored, translucent 'barrier,'" more interesting than reality itself, comes very close to Proust's view of the artist (Landy, *Philosophy as Fiction*, 51).

111. Vanzype, *Vermeer de Delft*, 23.

112. To Jean-Louis Vaudoyer [first days of February 1920], *Correspondance*, 19:108. Cf. Giovanni Macchia, who reads these lines as affirming Proust's fundamental agreement with Ruskin's view of Dutch painting (*L'ange de nuit*, 192).

113. George Eliot, *Adam Bede*, 177.

114. See, e.g., Gowing, *Vermeer*, 62–64; Montias, *Vermeer and His Milieu*, 106; and Arthur K. Wheelock, Jr., "Vermeer of Delft: His Life and His Artistry," in *Johannes Vermeer*, ed. Duparc and Wheelock, 27. For a subtle reading of the *Art of Painting* that shows how Vermeer lays claim to the realm of *cosa mentale* even as he criticizes the classical conception of such mental work, see Arasse, *Vermeer*, 40–58.

115. Montias, *Vermeer and His Milieu*, 197.

116. Vanzype, *Vermeer de Delft*, 23. A few pages later, it should be noted, Vanzype radically modifies this claim, by declaring that it is Vermeer's very resemblance to

other Dutch painters that demonstrates his difference—a position that seems to me much closer in spirit to Proust's. In this paradoxical formula, Vermeer "is superior to the painters of his time in resembling them; he is superior to his country in completely belonging to that country. . . . He paints the most ordinary things, the same things as Pieter de Hooch, ter Borch, Nicolaes Maes or Metsu. . . . [H]e looks only at everyday life, like Ostade, Brouwer or Jan Steen. And he does not resemble one of them" (28–29).

117. Proust, [Rembrandt], *Contre Saint-Beuve*, 659.

118. To Jean-Louis Vaudoyer [1 May 1921], *Correspondance*, 20:226.

119. For the article by Vaudoyer to which Proust was alluding, see the editor's note, *Correspondance*, 20:227–28.

120. See, e.g., Berger, *Second World and Green World*, 473–75; and Svetlana Alpers, "Picturing Dutch Culture," in *Looking at Seventeenth-Century Dutch Art: Realism Reconsidered*, ed. Wayne Franits (Cambridge: Cambridge University Press, 1997), 67.

121. George Moore, "A Tragic Novel," *Cosmopolis* 7 (1897): 43.

{ index }

All works of literature and art are indexed under their creators. Locations of images are given in boldface. For the reader's convenience, first notes to all works cited are included in the index.